ANCIENT INDIAN TRADITION & MYTHOLOGY

Translated by
A BOARD OF SCHOLARS

Edited by
Dr. G.P. BHATT

VOLUME 36

ANCIENT INDIAN TRADITION AND MYTHOLOGY SERIES

[PURĀṆAS IN TRANSLATION]

Volumes Released

ŚIVA 1-4
LIṄGA 5-6
BHĀGAVATA 7-11
GARUḌA 12-14
NĀRADA 15-19
KŪRMA 20-21
BRAHMĀṆḌA 22-26
AGNI 27-30
VARĀHA 31-32
BRAHMA 33-36
VĀYU 37-38
PADMA 39-48
SKANDA, PARTS I-XX, 49-68

Volumes Under Preparation

SKANDA, PARTS XXI-XXIV
BHAVIṢYA
BRAHMAVAIVARTA
DEVĪBHĀGAVATA
KĀLIKĀ
MĀRKAṆḌEYA
MATSYA
VĀMANA
VIṢṆU
VIṢṆUDHARMOTTARA

BRAHMA PURĀṆA

GAUTAMĪ-MĀHĀTMYA

Translated and Annotated by
A BOARD OF SCHOLARS

PART IV

MOTILAL BANARSIDASS PUBLISHERS
PRIVATE LIMITED • DELHI

First Edition: Delhi, 1986
Reprint: Delhi, 2004

ISBN: 81-208-0271-3

MOTILAL BANARSIDASS
41 U.A. Bungalow Road, Jawahar Nagar, Delhi 110 007
8 Mahalaxmi Chamber, 22 Bhulabhai Desai Road, Mumbai 400 026
236, 9th Main III Block, Jayanagar, Bangalore 560 011
120 Royapettah High Road, Mylapore, Chennai 600 004
Sanas Plaza, 1302 Baji Rao Road, Pune 411 002
8 Camac Street, Kolkata 700 017
Ashok Rajpath, Patna 800 004
Chowk, Varanasi 221 001

UNESCO COLLECTION OF REPRESENTATIVE WORKS—Indian Series
This book has been accepted in the Indian Translation Series of the UNESCO Collection of Representative Works, jointly sponsored by the United Nations Educational, Scientific and Cultural Organization (UNESCO) and the Government of India.

Printed in India
BY JAINENDRA PRAKASH JAIN AT SHRI JAINENDRA PRESS,
A-45 NARAINA, PHASE-I, NEW DELHI 110 028
AND PUBLISHED BY NARENDRA PRAKASH JAIN FOR
MOTILAL BANARSIDASS PUBLISHERS PRIVATE LIMITED,
BUNGALOW ROAD, DELHI 110 007

PUBLISHER'S NOTE

The purest gems lie hidden in the bottom of the ocean or in the depth of rocks. One has to dive into the ocean or delve into the rocks to find them out. Similarly, truth lies concealed in the language which with the passage of time has become obsolete. Man has to learn that language before he discovers that truth.

But he has neither the means nor the leisure to embark on that course. We have, therefore, planned to help him acquire knowledge by an easier course. We have started the series of Ancient Indian Tradition and Mythology in English Translation. Our goal is to universalize knowledge through the most popular international medium of expression. The publication of the Purāṇas in English Translation is a step towards that goal.

PREFACE

This thirty-sixth volume in the series on *Ancient Indian Tradition and Mythology* forms the fourth and last part of the *Brahma Purāṇa*. It contains the entire *Gautami-Māhātmya* consisting of 105 chapters which eulogize a number of sacred places situated on the banks of the river Godāvarī flowing south of the Vindhya mountain through the well-known forest named Daṇḍakāraṇya.

This part of the *Brahma Purāṇa* is an independent work, since it has no organic relationship with this Purāṇa and the only affinity that it shows to the latter is a minor one, namely, that the main speaker here also happens to be Brahmā. A very relevant thing to be noticed here is that it differs in style from the *Brahma Purāṇa*. In each of its chapters it describes one *Tirtha* with the legends and anecdotes associated with it, how it got its name, what is its importance, what merits accrue from visiting it and offering worship etc. By all internal and external evidence the *Gautami-Māhātmya* appears to have been added to the *Brahma Purāṇa* at some late stage.

In the first chapter of the work some general features of the Tīrthas, their varieties, nature etc. are described. The second one relates the story of the demon Tāraka, atrocities inflicted by him on the Devas, their prayer to Viṣṇu for protection, the latter's advice to them to persuade Lord Śiva to marry the daughter of Himālaya with the aim of giving birth to a valiant son who would kill the demon, the burning of the God of Love by the fire emanating from Śiva's third eye and the ultimate winning of his consent by the Devas to marry Pārvatī. The third chapter describes the marriage of Śiva with Pārvatī and the birth of Kārttikeya. In the fourth chapter the story of Viṣṇu's incarnation as Vāmana is narrated and also the origination of the waters of Gaṅgā from the foot of Viṣṇu washed by Brahmā with the water of Kamaṇḍalu, and the bearing of the waters of Gaṅgā by Śiva in his matted hair. The fifth and next two chapters describe how Pārvatī gets jealous of Gaṅgā due to her closer association with Śiva, how a plot is hatched up so that Śiva abandons her, how the sage Gautama gets falsely implicated and ultimately succeeds in bringing Gaṅgā from Śiva's matted hair to Brahmagiri and from there down to the earth in the form of Godāvarī. The eighth chapter narrates the story of Sagara, the burning of his sons by the infuriated sage Kapila and the taking of Gaṅgā to the Nether World by Bhagīratha to redeem the ancestors burnt by the curse of Kapila. After this chapters 9-104 take up a detailed description of a large number of sacred places with associated stories. The last chapter repeats the story of Gaṅgā brought down to the earth by the sage Gautama with the difference that he is not here falsely accused of cow-slaughter, and also the benefits of perusing and hearing the *Gautamī-Māhātmya*.

Acknowledgement of obligations

It is our pleasant duty to put on record our sincere thanks to Dr. R.N. Dandekar and the UNESCO authorities for their kind encouragement and valuable help which render this work more useful than it would otherwise have been. We are extremely grateful to Shri T.V. Parameshwar Iyer for his valuable assistance in the preparation of this work. We also thank all those who have been helpful in our project.

And, lastly, we should not forget our pious duty to remember and pay homage to the late Lala Sundar Lal ji of Messrs. Motilal Banarsidass, the wise and far-sighted author of the project of *Ancient Indian Tradition and Mythology* under which this volume has appeared.

—*Editor*

CONTENTS

GAUTAMĪ-MĀHĀTMYA
[THE GLORIFICATION OF GAUTAMĪ]

ABBREVIATIONS

Common and self-evident abbreviations such as Ch(s)—Chapter(s), p—page, pp—pages, V—Verse, VV—Verses, Ftn—footnote, Hist. Ind. Philo.—History of Indian Philosophy are not included in this list.

ABORI	*Annals of the Bhandarkar Oriental Research Institute*, Poona
AGP	S. M. Ali's *The Geography of Purāṇas*, PPH, New Delhi, 1973
AIHT	*Ancient Indian Historical Tradition*, F. E. Pargiter, Motilal Banarsidass (MLBD), Delhi
AITM	*Ancient Indian Tradition and Mythology* Series, MLBD, Delhi
AP	*Agni Purāṇa*, Guru Mandal Edition (GM), Calcutta, 1957
Arch.S.Rep.	Archaeological Survey Report
AV	*Atharva Veda*, Svādhyāya Mandal, Aundh
Bd. P.	*Brahmāṇḍa Purāṇa*, MLBD, Delhi 1973
BG	*Bhagavadgītā*
Bh. P.	*Bhāgavata Purāṇa*, Bhagavat Vidyapeeth, Ahmedabad
Br.	*Brāhmaṇa* (preceded by name such as Śatapatha)
BS. P.	*Bhaviṣya Purāṇa*, Vishnu Shastri Bapat, Wai
BV. P.	*Brahma Vaivarta Purāṇa*, GM, 1955-57
CC	*Caturvarga Cintāmaṇi* by Hemādri
CVS	*Caraṇa Vyūha Sūtra* by Śaunaka; Com. by Mahidāsa
DB	*Devī Bhāgavata*, GM, 1960-61
De or GDAMI	*The Geographical Dictionary of Ancient and Mediaeval India*, N. L. De, Oriental Reprint, Delhi, 1971
Dh. S.	*Dharma Sūtra* (preceded by the author's name such as Gautama)
ERE	*Encyclopaedia of Religion and Ethics* by Hastings
GP	*Garuḍa Purāṇa*, ed. R. S. Bhattacharya, Chowkhamba, Varanasi, 1964

GS	*Gṛhya Sūtra* (preceded by the name of the author such as Āpastamba)
HD	*History of Dharma Śāstra*, P. V. Kane, G. O. S.
IA	*The Indian Antiquary*
IHQ	*The Indian Historical Quarterly*
JP	*Purāṇa* (Journal of the Kashiraj Trust), Varanasi
KA	*Kauṭilya Arthaśāstra*
KP	*Kūrma Purāṇa*, Veṅkaṭeśvara Press Edn., Bombay; also Kashiraj Trust Edn., Varanasi, 1971
LP	*Liṅga Purāṇa*, GM, 1960; also MLBD, Delhi, 1981
Manu.	*Manusmṛti*
Mbh.	*Mahābhārata*, Gītā Press, Gorakhpur, VS 2014
MkP	*Mārkaṇḍeya Purāṇa*
MN	*Mahābhārata Nāmānukramaṇi*, Gītā Press, Gorakhpur, VS 2016
MtP	*Matsya Purāṇa*, GM, 1954
MW	Monier Williams' *Sanskrit-English Dictionary*, MLBD, Delhi, 1976
NP	*Nāradiya* or *Nārada Purāṇa*, Veṅkaṭeśvara Press, Bombay
PCK	*Bhāratavarṣiya Prācina Caritrakośa*, Siddheshwar Shastri, Poona, 1968
Pd.P.	*Padma Purāṇa*, GM, 1957-59
PE	*Purāṇic Encyclopaedia*, V. Mani, English version, MLBD, Delhi, 1975
PR or PRHRC	*Puranic Records on Hindu Rites and Customs*, R. C. Hazra, Calcutta, 1948
ṚV	*Ṛg-Veda*, Svādhyāya Mandal, Aundh
Śat.Br.	*Śatapatha Brāhmaṇa*
SC or SMC	*Smṛti Candrikā* by Devanna Bhaṭṭa
SEP	*Studies in Epics and Purāṇas*, A.D. Pusalkar, Bharatiya Vidya Bhavan (BVB), Bombay

GAUTAMĪ-MĀHĀTMYA
[THE GLORIFICATION OF GAUTAMĪ]

CHAPTER ONE
Holy Centres

The sages said :

1. Listening to the description of holy centres in detail, we never feel satiated. We ask you to narrate the great secret once again, the great grandeur of the holy centre, the most excellent of all excellent holy centres.

Brahmā said :

2. Formerly, O excellent brahmins, I was asked this very same question by Nārada. Then I told him that with great effort.

Nārada said :

3. This has been heard by me from you, O lord of the universe, O source of origin of the Universe, viz. that the resorting to the holy centres is better than austerities, sacrifices and charitable gifts.

4. O lord of the Devas, how many varieties of holy centres are there? What are their benefits? Which is more excellent than all the other holy centres for ever?

Brahmā said :

5-7. There are four varieties of holy centres, O most venerable sage, viz. Daiva, Āsura, Ārṣa and Mānuṣa. They are well-known in heaven, on Earth, nether regions—nay, in all the three worlds and resorted to by gods etc. The holy centre Ārṣa is more desirable than the holy centres pertaining to human beings. The holy centre belonging to Asuras bestows more benefit than the holy centres belonging to sages. O son, the holy centre belonging to gods is more desirable than the holy centres belonging to Asuras.

8. The holy centre created by Brahmā, Viṣṇu, Maheśa and others is called Daiva (Divine). They do not know anything greater than this because one is produced from the three.

9. The holy centre of the three worlds is cited as human. There also, the holy centre in the Jambū island is highly excellent with many qualities.

10. Among the holy centres of Jambū[1] island Bhārata Varṣa is the holy centre well known in the Vedas. Among the holy centres of Bhārata Daṇḍaka[2] forest is the most excellent of all holy centres. O son, it is called a holy centre because it is a sphere of holy rites.

11. The holy centres mentioned by me to you are there itself. Listen to their names mentioned by me briefly.

12-13. The different types of holy centres are Daiva, Āsura, Ārṣa and Mānuṣa i.e. divine, demoniac, saintly and human.

Between Himavān and Vindhya there are six rivers of divine origin. Similarly, O brahmin, there are six rivers of divine origin between Vindhya and the Southern Sea. These twelve rivers are glorified as the most important of all.

14. Since Bhārata bestows much merit it is highly honoured. Hence that sub-continent is called the sphere of holy rites by Devas.

15-19. In some places the holy centres of mountains are Divine ones.

That which is surrounded by demons is called Āsura.

In the divine regions great sages perform penances and create holy centres due to the divine power or the power of their penance. They create these centres for their own welfare, prosperity, worship and salvation. They are called Ārṣa (Saintly holy centres).

O Nārada, they call the holy centres created by men as the human holy centres. These centres are created by men for their own benefit and prosperity or for the acquisition of fame.

1. One of the seven continents of the earth having nine divisions or *varṣas* including Bhārata or India, the remaining six being Plakṣa, Śālmali, Kuśa, Krauñca, Śāka and Puṣkara (Vide *Agni P.* 108. 1-3)

2. A forest tract lying between the Godāvarī and Narmadā rivers in the South and a scene of many episodes in the Rāmāyaṇa.

Thus O excellent sage, there are four different types of holy centres.

No one, even the Yogin, knows the different types. O Nārada, it behoves you to hear about them attentively.

Many persons who profess to be scholars hear and recount. But some meritorious person knows how to speak and hear by virtue of his own good qualities.

Nārada said :

20-22. I wish to hear factually their difference and features, on hearing which one attains perpetual liberation from all sins. O Brahmā, in the beginning of the Kṛta age[1] there is no other means except resorting to holy centres which bestows the desired results with least amount of strain. O Creator, there is no other speaker or knower equal to you. You are born in the navel lotus of Viṣṇu. You are born ahead of all.

Brahmā said :

23. These six rivers in the south of the Vindhya are glorified, viz. Godāvarī, Bhīmarathī, Tuṅgabhadrā, Venikā, Tāpī and Payoṣṇī.

24. Bhāgīrathī, Narmadā, Yamunā, Sarasvatī, Viśokā and Vitastā are dependent on the Himālayan ridges.

25-33. These are the holiest rivers. They are cited as the holy centres.

The holy centres surrounded by the following Asuras are the Āsura holy centres: Gaya, Kolāsura, Vṛtra, Tripura, Andhaka, Hayamūrdhan, Lavaṇa, Namuci, Śṛṅgaka, Yama, Pātālaketu, Madhu and Puṣkara. They are auspicious.

O Nārada, the saintly holy centres are those holy centres frequented by the following sages: Prabhāsa, Bhārgava, Agasti, Nara, Nārāyaṇa, Vasiṣṭha, Bharadvāja, Gautama, Kaśyapa, Manu and others.

The human holy centres are those created by the following human beings: Ambarīṣa, Hariścandra, Nahuṣa, Rāma, Kuru, Kanakhala, Bharata, Sagara, Aśvayūpa, Nāciketā and

1. The first of the four ages of the world during which righteousness has a complete sway.

Vṛṣākapi the suppressor of foes. O brahmin, they are holy centres created by them for their own fame, benefit, prosperity etc.

Wherever there are holy centres that have sprung up themselves anywhere in the three worlds they are called Daiva holy centres. They call them Puṇyatīrthas.

The different holy centres have been mentioned by me.

What is not dug up by anyone is called Devakhāta (dug up by gods). O sage, the different holy centres have been briefly recounted by me to you. Merely by knowing them man is released from all sins.

CHAPTER TWO

Śiva's Marriage

Nārada said :

1. The holy centre that is presided over by three deities is the most excellent of all holy centres. Kindly recount to me its form and different types in detail.

Brahmā said :

2. The other holy centres or sacred regions and sacrifice or other holy rites are effective only as long as the holy centre presided over by three deities, is not visited.

3-5. Resorting to Gaṅgā yields greater benefit than holy rites, fasts and Kṛcchra rites. Kṛcchra[1] rites should be performed in holy centres. O sage, holy centres purify all objects, oneself, mother, father etc. Except in holy centre presided over by the three deities there cannot be any remission in sins. Remembered, seen or touched it yields all desired objects. This Gaṅgā is the most excellent of all rivers. It bestows all desired things. It is presided over by three deities, O excellent sage. Listen to its origin.

1. A common word for several types of austerities involving bathing, fasting, worship and other prescribed religious observances.

6. Ten thousand years before, when Devas were ascendant Tāraka[1] became very powerful. He became very arrogant due to the boons granted by me.

7-8. The great glory as well as wealth of Devas was taken away by that powerful demon. Thereafter, Devas along with their leader Indra sought shelter in the lord of the worlds, the great grandfather of the Universe, who was lying in the milk-ocean. With their palms joined in reverence Devas who had none else to approach said to Viṣṇu:

Devas said :

9. O lord, you are the saviour of the worlds. You increase the fame of Devas. O lord of all, O source of origin of the Universe, O lord with the three Vedas for your form, obeisance to you.

10. You alone are the creator of the world, destroyer of Asuras and lord of the worlds. O Jaganmaya (who are identical with the Universe), you are the cause of creation, sustenance, and destruction.

11. In the whole of the three worlds, there is no other saviour to the embodied beings under the storm and stress of adversities. O lotus-eyed one, excepting you there is none to quell the three kinds of distress.[2]

12. You are the father and mother of the universe. O lord, you are easily accessible through service. Be pleased, O lord, save us from great dangers. Say, who is the destroyer of our distress excepting you ?

13. You are the primordial maker. You are the Boar, Fish and Tortoise.[3] When fear overwhelms us you protect us by assuming different forms.

14. O lord Hari, we have no other refuge. Our lordship has been taken away. Our women have been disgraced. We have been rendered homeless. O lord, why don't you protect us?

---

1. A demon who after propitiating Śiva by his penance became a great terror to the world and was ultimately killed by Skanda.

2. The three kinds are ādhyātmika, ādhidaivika and ādhibhautika or those due to diseases and other bodily causes, those due to super-natural agencies and those caused by natural calamities.

3. Three well known incarnations of god Viṣṇu.

Brahmā said :

15. Then the lord of Lakṣmī, who lies on the serpent Śeṣa, said to them: "Whence has this danger and fear come over to you? Please speak out without any tension." Then they said to the lord of Lakṣmī in regard to the Asura Tāraka.

Devas said :

16-17. A terrible danger from Tāraka has overwhelmed us. It causes hairs to stand on end. We are not capable of killing him in battles or by curses or austerities. He will meet death from a child who is not yet ten days old. Hence, O lord, let action be taken with regard to him.

Brahmā said :

18-20. Again Nārāyaṇa said : "O Devas, I am not very powerful. He cannot be killed by me or by my child or by Devas. Tāraka, the scorcher of the worlds, will meet death from that extremely powerful child who may be born of lord Śiva. Hence, let us all go, O Devas, along with sages in order to strive for the marriage of lord Śiva. This is the first attempt that should be made by us who are powerful enough for that."

21-22. After saying "So be it" Devas went to the excellent mountain Himavān full of jewels and to Menā the beloved wife of Himavān. All of them said this to Himavān and his wife:

23-25. "Dakṣa's daughter who is the mother of the worlds, who is Śiva stationed as Śakti, who has various forms in the world such as Buddhi (intellect), Prajñā (intelligence), Dhṛti (courage), Medhā (faculty of comprehension), Lajjā (bashfulness), Puṣṭi (nourishment) and Sarasvatī (Speech) and who sanctifies the worlds shall enter Menā's womb in order to achieve success in the affairs of Devas. On being born that mother of the Universe will become Śiva's wife. She will protect all of us as well as you."

Brahmā said :

26. Himavān approved of the scheme of Devas. Menā became extremely enthusiastic and said "Let it be so".

27. Then the mother of the Universe was born as Gaurī in the abode of Himavān. She was engaged in meditation of

Śiva. She was his beloved. She considered him as her ultimate resort.

28. Devas said to her: "Enter penance for Īśa". Then Gaurī performed penance on the ridge of the mountain Himālaya.

29-30. Again Devas took counsel with one another. They said: "How can Īśa meditate on her? Does he meditate on the Ātman or anything else? We do not know. How can the lord of Devas be made to fix his mind on the daughter of Menā? Some means should be employed in regard to this. Thence you will derive excellence."

Then the highly intelligent Bṛhaspati of liberal intellect said:

Bṛhaspati said :

31. The intelligent Cupid who wields the flowery bow and excites people must hit the quiescent Śiva by means of splendid flowery arrows.

32. Pierced by the arrows the three-eyed lord may fix his mind on her. Then the lord will certainly marry her.

33. The arrows of the victorious Cupid have never been ineffective anywhere. So when the mother of the Universe gets married a son will be born to her.

34-35. That son born to the three-eyed lord will kill Tāraka. Give unto Kāma, Vasanta the storehouse of flowers as an assistant. He delights the minds of everyone.

Brahmā said :

36. Saying "So be it" Devas, the suppressors of their enemies felt relieved. They sent Cupid and Spring to Śiva.

37. Holding his bow and accompanied by Spring and his consort Rati, Cupid hurried to perform that very difficult task.

38-39. Holding the bow and arrows he stood in front of Śiva and began to think "Shall the lord Śiva, the preceptor of the worlds, be pierced? I am the conqueror of universe. But are my arrows firm in regard to him?"

He was reduced to ashes by Śiva by his fiery eyes.

40-44. In order to watch the same activity steadily Devas came there. Listen to the surprising event that happened then. Devas looked at Śiva. Even as they glanced at Cupid, they saw him reduced to ashes and they were frightened. With the palms joined together Devas eulogised the lord.

Devas said :

Great fear of Tāraka has overwhelmed us. Make the daughter of Himavān your wife.

Brahmā said :

Lord Śiva whose mind had been pierced, immediately acted according to the entreaties of Devas. It is the nature of noble souls that they do not consider their own welfare while they make sacrifices for the sake of others.

Devas sent Arundhatī, Vasiṣṭha, the discus-bearing Viṣṇu and me for the arrangement of the wedding.

In this manner the alliance between Himavān and Śiva, the lord of the Universe, was effected.

CHAPTER THREE

Gift of a Water Vessel to Brahmā

Brahmā said :

1-4. The wedding took place on the excellent Himālaya mountain which is wonderfully bedecked in different kinds of jewels, which is full of various sorts of trees and creepers, which is frequented by different birds, which is encompassed by rivers, lakes, tanks, wells, which is frequented by Devas, Gandharvas,[1] Siddhas,[2] Cāraṇas,[3] Yakṣas[4] and others, which is richly endowed with splendid wind, which was the sole cause of excessive merriment, which is surrounded by Meru,[5] Mandara,[6] Kailāsa,[7] Maināka[8] and other mountains and which is

1. Semi-divine beings skilled in singing and music.
2. A group of semi-divine beings of great purity and holiness.
3. The panegyrists of gods.
4. A class of semi-divine beings who attend on Kubera, the god of wealth.
5. A mythical mountain and abode of celestial beings.
6. Another mythical mountain used by gods and demous as a rod for churning the ocean.
7. A Himālayan peak on which resides god Śiva.
8. Another mountain which escaped when Indra planned to cut off wings which all mountains are supposed to have previously.

23. Distressed by hunger they went on eating dry soil day and night. They dug up hurriedly and rushed to the nether world.

24. On hearing that the powerful princes, the sons of Sagara who had accomplished their tasks had come (to the nether world) the asuras became frightened and they went near Kapila.[1]

25. Kapila the extremely intelligent sage was sleeping in the nether world. Formerly, a most important task of Devas had been accomplished by him.

26. He had achieved that success by continuous work without any sleep. Therefore he was tired. When the task had been accomplished the glorious Kapila said to Devas, "Give me a place for sleeping."

27-29. They gave him the nether world. Again, the sage said to Devas : "If a fool wakes me up he will be immediately reduced to ashes; then only, will I lie down in the nether world; if not I won't sleep at all."

When Devas said "So be it" he began to lie down there.

The asuras who knew his power and who were endowed with Māyā (witchcraft) planned to slay Sagara.

30-31. The asuras were afraid even without being fought. They hurried to the place where the extremely furious sage Kapila was lying. They hurriedly tethered the horse near his head. They stood watching silently a little away from the place eager to see what would happen.

32. Then the sons of Sagara entered the nether regions. They saw the tethered horse and the man lying down.

33-35. They considered him the person who took the horse by force and spoiled the sacrifice.

Some of them said then, "Let us kill this fellow and take the horse back".

Some said, "Let us take away this tethered sacrificial animal. Of what avail is this fellow !"

Then other heroic persons said—"We are kings. We are administrators. Let us waken this fellow who has committed the crime and kill him with our heroic power."

---

1. A celebrated sage and propounder of the Sāṁkhya system of philosophy. He is said to be the son of Karandama-Prajāpati and Devahūti. The Brahmāṇḍapurāṇa (ch. 93) mentions him as an incarnation of Viṣṇu.

All these were present there, viz. the oceans, rivers, serpents, mothers of the worlds etc. along with vegetable kingdom and seeds.

Ilā [Earth] carried out the function of productivity, the herbs performed the work of growth, Varuṇa performed the work of drink, Kubera performed the work of charitable gifts; Agni performed whatever was desired by the lord of worlds.

13. The eternal Viṣṇu performed worship separately in different places. The Vedas accompanied by their secret principles gave charming instructions.

14. The celestial damsels danced. The Gandharvas and Kinnaras[1] sang. O excellent sage, Maināka held fried grains (for the sacrifice).

15. The invocation of holy water was performed inside the house, O Nārada. The couple, the most excellent among Devas sat on the altar.

16. After setting the holy fire ablaze duly and performing the sacrifice with fried grains, O son, the couple went round the rocky slab duly.

17. During the course of touching the slab, Śiva urged by Viṣṇu, touched the toe of the right foot of the goddess with his hand.

18. Performing the sacrifice there near Śiva, I saw her. My semen got ejaculated due to my evil mind on seeing the toe.

19. In the entire three worlds, who is not deceived by Cupid? Defiled and ashamed, I scattered the ejaculated semen in small droplets.

20. From the minute particles of my semen the Vālakhilyas[2] were born. Then there was a great commotion caused by Devas. Overwhelmed by shame, I stood up from my seat and started.

21. Even as Devas watched silently, O Nārada, I went ahead. On seeing me go, Mahādeva spoke to Nandin:

Śiva said:

22. Call Brahmā here. I shall make him free from sin.

1. Horse-headed celestial musicians dwelling in Kubera's city.

2. Pigmy sages no bigger than half a thumb, numbering 6000 and residing in the solar region.

Even if other people commit offences good people take pity on them. They have sympathy for them in their minds. This is the nature of worldly objects. They delude even great scholars.

Brahmā said :

23-25. After saying this, Lord Śiva accompanied by Umā began operations. The lord of the worlds did this due to his sympathy for me and desire for the welfare of the worlds. Listen to it attentively, O Nārada.

"The Earth and Waters shall become the means of redemption of sinners from their sins. I shall extract their ultimate essence that is holy." After declaring this the lord extracted their essence.

26-27. He made the Earth into a water-jar and poured water into it. With great effort he chanted *Pāvamānya*[1] and other hymns and consecrated them. The lord who dispels sins remembered Śakti who sanctifies the universe and invoked her there. Then the lord of the worlds said to me, "Take this water-jar.

28. Indeed the waters are goddesses and mothers. The Earth is another mother. So both of them are the causes of existence, creation and destruction.

29. It is here that Dharma is established. It is here that the eternal sacrifice is established. It is here that enjoyment and salvation, mobile and immobile beings are established.

30. By remembering it the mental sin perishes. By bowing to it the verbal sin perishes. By bathing, drinking and performing the holy ablution, the physical sin perishes.

31. This alone is nectar in the world. There is nothing greater in sanctity than this. O Brahmā, take this water-jar consecrated by me with holy Mantras.

32. Whoever remembers or drinks the water herein attains all desired things. Take this water-jar.

33. Of all the five elements, water is the element of great effect. This water is the best among all those waters. Take this water-jar.

34. O Brahmā, by touching, remembering and seeing the

1. The verses in the ninth *Maṇḍala* of the *Ṛgveda* relating to Soma Pavamāna; also known as 'Pāvamānī'.

water herein, which is very splendid, holy and sacred, one is liberated from sin."

35-36. After saying this the supreme lord gave me the water-jar. Then Devas joyously spoke to their lord. There was great exhilaration there. Cries of victory rang the sky.

During the wedding festival of the lord I saw the tip of the foot of the mother. Due to this sin I attained the state of a fallen fellow. The merciful father gave me Gaṅgā water kept in the holy jar. It is holy and sanctifying even by remembering.

CHAPTER FOUR

How Gaṅgā Entered the Matted Hair of Śiva

Nārada said :

1. Goddess Gaṅgā stationed in your water-jar increased your merit. O lord, tell me in detail how it came to the mortal world.

Brahmā said :

2-3. There was a great asura named Bali. This enemy of gods was invincible. He was incomparable in regard to virtue, fame, protection of subjects, devotion to elders and preceptors, truthfulness, virility, power, renunciation and forbearance in the three worlds.

4. On seeing his prosperity increased Devas became worried. They spoke to one another, "How will we conquer Bali ?"

5. While he was ruling over the kingdom of the three worlds dispelling thorns, there were no enemies, no ailments, no anxieties in any way.

6. While Bali was ruling over the kingdom, none of these was seen even in dream, viz., famine, evil, denial of God, wickedness.

7. Devas did not have place or happiness because they were pierced by the arrows of his prosperity; they were severed by the sword of his renown, their limbs were cut by the spear of his command.

8. Keeping their jealousy in front they talked to one another. With their body set ablaze by the fire of his fame they were agitated. They approached Viṣṇu.

Devas said :

9. O lord of the worlds, O lord holding conch, discus and club, we are distressed. Your lordship always holds weapons for our sake.

10-17. Our misery is this much even when you are our lord, O lord of the Universe. How can the head of those who bow down to you, bow down to asuras ?

Mentally, physically and verbally, we have sought refuge in you alone. Having your feet alone as our shelter how can we bow down to Asura?

We worship you by means of great sacrifices. We eulogise you, O Acyuta, by means of words of praise. Having you alone as our shelter, how can we bow down to Asura?

Devas with Indra as their leader always depend upon your vigour and power. Having acquired our status bestowed by you, how can we bow down to Asura ?

Through the form of Brahmā you are the creator. You protect us as Viṣṇu. You are the annihilator through your power of Rudra. How can we bow down to Asura ?

Lordship and glory is the cause of everything in the world. Without it (life) is useless. O lord of Devas, with our prosperity dispelled how can we bow down to Asura ?

You are one without a beginning. You are the creator of the universe. You are one without an end. You are the preceptor of the universe. How can we bow down to this Asura ?

Our limbs have been nourished by your lordship and glory. After conquering the three worlds with our strength we shall become stable, O lord of Devas. How can we bow down to Asura ?

Brahmā said :

18. On hearing these words, the slayer of the asuras spoke with reference to the tasks of the Devas.

Vāsudeva said :

19-20. This asura Bali is my devotee. He cannot be conquered by Devas or Asuras. Just as you all are persons to be nourished by me so also Bali is to be nourished by me. Without a battle, O Devas, I shall take away his kingdom which extends to the three worlds. I shall bind him by means of words with miraculous power and give the kingdom unto you all.

Brahmā said :

21. After saying "so be it" Devas went to heaven. The holy lord, the lord of Devas entered the womb of Aditi.[1]

22. When he was born there were great festivities. The lord of sacrifices was born, O brahmin, as Vāmana.[2]

23-27. In the meantime, O brahmin, Bali the most excellent of all strong men made preparations for the horse sacrifice. He was accompanied by his priest Śukra who was conversant with the Vedas and Vedāṅgas.[3] He was sanctified by important sages. While the sacrifice was going on, while Bali went on with the performance of sacrifice, while chief of the sages performed the duties of a Ṛtvij,[4] while Śukra functioned as the chief priest, while Devas, Gandharvas and Nāgas were seated in order to receive their respective share in the sacrificial offerings, while these words were being exchanged, viz. "Let it be given", "Let it be partaken of", "Let the worship be performed separately", "It is complete", "Again it is filled up" etc., Vāmana who was singing Sāman verses came slowly to that place. Vāmana who was wearing ear-rings and holding an umbrella came to the sacrificial hall.

28-31. He began to praise the sacrifice. Vāmana had assumed the form of a brahmin. He was the lord Daityasūdana (the slayer of Daityas). He was the bestower of benefits of sacrifice and austerities. He was the slayer of asuras. Bhārgava (a descendant of Bhṛgu, i.e. Śukra) recognised him and then in a hurry spoke to the king, the king who had great splendour, who was a conqueror with the duties of Kṣatriya, who was a donor of riches with devotion, who was the most excellent of all powerful men, who was initiated in the sacrifice

1. The mother of gods.
2. The dwarf incarnation of Viṣṇu.
3. Subjects necessary for the study and proper understanding of the Vedas, eg. Śikṣā (Phonetics), Nirukta (Etymology) etc.
4. A priest officiating at a Vedic sacrifice. There are usually four such priests, viz. Hotṛ, Adhvaryu, Brahman and Udgātṛ.

along with his wife, who was meditating on Viṣṇu, and who was pouring oblations separately. Śukra who was the most powerful in the family of Bhṛgu and who was extremely intelligent spoke to the king:

Śukra said :

32-33. This brahmin who has the size of a dwarf and who has come to your sacrifice, O Bali, is not really a brahmin. It is true that he is the lord of sacrifices, the sanctifier of sacrifices. He who is greater than the greatest, who is the great Man, has come here to request you. Only after taking counsel from me should it be given by you, O lord.

Brahmā said :

34-35. Bali the suppressor of enemies said to his preceptor, Bhārgava thus.

Bali said :

Blessed am I because the lord of sacrifices is coming to my house so unexpectedly. If he requests me anything after coming here, of what avail is my cogitation ?

Brahmā said :

36. So addressed by Śukra, his priest, Bali, accompanied by his wife, went to that place where the leading brahmin Vāmana, the son of Aditi, was present.

37-40. With palms joined in reverence he said, "Why have you come ? Tell me that". Then Vāmana said : "A piece of ground measured by three steps should be given to me for staying. I do not wish for anything else."

After saying "So be it" he poured a stream of water from the pot embellished with different jewels. Thereafter, he gave the Earth to Vāmana even as the chief sages were watching, even as the priest Śukra was watching. While the illustrious Devas were watching he gave the Earth to Vāmana. While the asuras were watching cries of "Victory" rose up, in the sky.

41. Vāmana said slowly : "Hail to you, O king, Be happy. Grant me the measured ground, the three steps that have been promised."

42-44. "So be it", said the lord of asuras, "Let it be taken". Even as these words were uttered, even as he was watching

Vāmana, something wonderful happened. The lord of sacrifices increased in size so much that the moon and the sun came up to the breast and the Devas over the head. In exploit and size he increased, lord Acyuta, who has no end, who is the maker of the worlds and who identifies himself with the universe. On seeing him, the king of asuras who was humble and who was accompanied by his wife, said to the lord:

Bali said :

45. O Viṣṇu, O lord of worlds identifying with the Universe, take the steps as many as you can. O lord of Devas, O creator of the Universe, it is I who have conquered in every respect.

46. At the very same time when he was saying this Śukra too said this very earnestly: "O lord of kings, due to my intelligence you have already been propitiated before." As he spoke thus, Viṣṇu of great sacrifice said:

Viṣṇu said :

47. O lord of Daityas, of great arms, O king of Daityas, I shall take steps. See.

As he said so, he (ie. Bali) said again and again, "O Viṣṇu, take the steps."

Brahmā said :

48. After standing firmly on the back of the tortoise he placed a step in the sacrificial hall of Bali. He, the eternal lord, placed the second step over the whole world.

49. Then he said to Bali: "O lord of Asuras, there is no place for the third step. Where shall I place the third step? Give me the ground."

Laughingly Bali said with palms joined in reverence. He was accompanied by his wife.

Bali said :

50-52. The entire universe has been created by you, O lord of Devas. I am not a creator. Due to your fault it has become too small, O lord of cosmic identity.

Still, I have never uttered a lie, nor will I ever utter a lie proving me to be a man of truthful, statement. Step on my back.

Then, the lord who is worshipped by Devas, whose form is evolved by the three Vedas, became pleased.

He said, "Choose a boon. Welfare unto you, O lord of Ḍaityas, I am pleased with your devotion."

Brahmā said :

53-54. He said to the lord of the Universe—"O Trivikrama (one who took three steps), I do not beg anything of you."

Viṣṇu who was pleased granted him whatever was desired by his pure mind viz., the lordship of the nether worlds, the future status of Indra, the overlordship of Indra and a great deal of imperishable fame.

55-57. After granting all this to Bali, Lord Vāmana placed Bali, the enemy of Devas in nether worlds along with his son and wife. He gave the kingdom of Devas to Indra as at the time of its origin.

In the meantime he went back to his region honoured by Devas.

O highly intelligent one, that second step of Viṣṇu, my father, became my abode. On seeing my abode I thought:

58. "What is that work which shall be auspicious in this second step of Viṣṇu whereby my water-jar shall become excellent ?"

59-63. The water bestowed by the enemy of Tripuras is highly meritorious. It is excellent. It bestows boons. It is calm. It is highly conducive to tranquillity. It is splendid. It bestows splendour. It is eternal. It yields worldly enjoyment and salvation. It is in the form of the mother of the worlds. It is nectar. It is pure panacea (for all ills). It is holy. It is sacred. It is worthy of worship. It is the greatest and the most excellent. It is conducive to splendour. By remembering it sanctifies the worlds. What if it is seen ? Remaining pure, I shall utilize that water as the libation to my father.

Thinking that, I took that water and used it for *argha* (offering).

The water for *Argha*, that was consecrated by the recitation of *Mantras* fell on Viṣṇu's foot. That water fell on the Meru and flowed to the Earth in four ways.

64-68. The waters flowed in four directions, viz. East, South, West and North.

By means of his matted hair, Śaṅkara caught hold of the water that flowed towards the South.

The water that flowed towards the West went back to the water-jar.

Viṣṇu caught hold of the water that flowed towards the North.

The sages, Devas, manes and the guardians of quarters caught hold of the auspicious water that flowed towards the East. Hence it is called the most excellent.

The waters that reached the Southern quarter are the mothers of the worlds. The waters that flowed from the foot of Viṣṇu are conducive to the welfare of brahmins and the mothers of worlds. Thus they became cause of prosperity by remaining within the matted hair of Maheśvara. By remembering their power one would attain all desired things.

CHAPTER FIVE

Vināyaka and Gautama

Nārada said :

1. How the River Gaṅgā stationed in the water-jar reached the matted hair of Lord Śiva, has been heard. Kindly tell me how it reached the mortal world.

Brahmā said :

2. O highly intelligent one, there are two divisions in the waters stationed in the matted hair of Maheśvara, because of two persons who took them away.

3. One part that is well known in the world was brought by the brahmin Gautama who used to perform holy rites, donate charitable gifts and practise meditation after worshipping Śiva.

4-5. The other part was taken away, O extremely intelligent one, by the powerful Kṣatriya monarch Bhagīratha after propitiating Śaṅkara by means of penances and holy rites. Thus O excellent sage, the Gaṅgā had two different forms.

Nārada said :

6. For what reason was Gautama the conveyor of the water stationed in the matted hair of Maheśvara? Tell me, by which Kṣatriya was it brought.

Brahmā said :

7. For your pleasure, O dear one, I shall recount in detail how the river was brought by the brahmin or the other one.

8. O sage of great lustre, Gaṅgā became the beloved of Śambhu at the very time when Umā became the beloved of the lord of Devas.

9-10. Śiva was thinking about the means of dispelling my sin. Accompanied by Umā the glorious lord observed the goddess particularly. Since he was indulgent in pleasant activities he created the excellent juice. It was excellent because he was fond of its beauty and sweetness, feminine qualities as well as holy nature, and

11. Gaṅgā was the most beloved of all, O excellent brahmin. He kept her on his head (as a token of honour). Since Umā knew this, Maheśvara was always worried over it.

12. Gaṅgā alone came out of the matted hair for some other reason. Śiva had concealed Gaṅgā in his matted hair.

13-14. On knowing that she (Gaṅgā) was held by him in his head, Umā was not able to bear it. On seeing her stationed in the matted hair, again and again Gaurī spoke to her lord in anger thus: "Send her away, O lord of aesthetic taste." However, the lord declined to send her away.

15. On account of that misery Umā said "Oh, I am helpless."

On reflecting that the lord was concealing Gaṅgā in his matted hair, she spoke these words in secret to Vināyaka, Skanda and Jayā.[1]

16-17. "This lover, the lord of Devas will never forsake Gaṅgā. Now she too is the beloved of my lord. How will my lord abandon her, his beloved?" After reflecting thus many times, Umā spoke to Vināyaka.

Pārvatī said :

18. The lord will never abandon Gaṅgā even if attempted

1. Wife of Puṣpadanta, a gaṇa (attendant of Śiva).

by Devas, Asuras, Yakṣas, Siddhas, including yourself, kings or others.

19-20. Either I shall go to Himavān and perform penance once again or I shall entrust the job to holy brahmins who have dispelled their sins by practising austerities. Requested by them Gaṅgā may go to the Earth.

Brahmā said :

21-23. On hearing these words of his mother Gaṇeśa, the lord of obstacles said to his mother:

"It is proper to consult my brother Skanda and Jayā (and do everything). We shall do that whereby my father will cast off Gaṅgā from his head."

O brahmin, in the meantime there was a drought lasting for twenty four years. It caused great fright to all living beings in the mortal world. Then the whole universe consisting of mobile and immobile beings perished.

24-27. (There was great disaster everywhere) except the sacred hermitage of Gautama that bestowed all desired things.

Formerly, I desired to create the mobile and immobile beings, O dear son. A sacrifice was performed by me on the mountain Devayajana. Thereafter that mountain became well known as Brahmagiri associated with my name.

That Gautama has resorted to that excellent mountain and is staying there ever since. Neither mental worries nor physical ailments, neither famine nor absence of rain, neither fear nor grief, neither poverty nor misfortune are ever heard of in his excellent and highly meritorious hermitage on the auspicious Brahmagiri.

28. Excepting his hermitage in no other place the offering was made to Devas or manes. O dear son, there was neither a donor nor a Hotṛ[1] nor a person performing sacrifices.

29. The propitiation of Devas in heaven was accomplished only when the brahmin Gautama made offering or performed a sacrifice.

30. Sage Gautama became well known in the world of Devas and in the mortal world. People knew that he alone was the donor and the enjoyer of pleasant things.

1. An officiating priest reciting Ṛgvedic hymns during a sacrifice.

31. On hearing about this the sages of different hermitages enquired about the hermitage of Gautama and went there.

32. Sage Gautama devoutly nourished all those sages as if they were his disciples, sons or fathers.

33. Whatever was desired by them was provided by him. The sage rendered service to all of them in the proper order, in accordance with their ability and in a manner befitting them.

34-35. At the bidding of Gautama, the herbs and other vegetables became the mothers of worlds. Again Brahmā, Viṣṇu and Maheśvara were propitiated by him. Then the herbs and other vegetables grew up and were used by the people then and there. They were thought of and sowed by the power of penance of Gautama.

36-38. Whatever was thought of by Gautama was realised. All prosperities were achieved. Everyday Gautama addressed the sages like sons, disciples or fathers. He asked them, "What shall I do for you?". He nurtured them for many years as a father would do his sons. Thus, O dear son, Gautama acquired great renown.

Then Vināyaka spoke to his mother, brother and Jayā.

Vināyaka said :

39-42. Mother, the brahmin Gautama is being sung about in the abode of Devas: "Gautama has done that which can be achieved by Devas only with effort." O goddess, thus the power of penance of the brahmin has been heard by me. Dear mother, that brahmin may be able to dislodge Gaṅgā stationed in the matted hair after worshipping the three-eyed lord by means of penance. He alone can plead to the beloved of my father, who is stationed in the matted hair of my father. Some means should be employed so that the brahmin may plead to her. Due to his power the excellent Gaṅgā will descend from his head.

Brahmā said :

43. After saying this to his mother, the lord of obstacles[1] went to the place where the lean Gautama who was wearing

1. Lord Gaṇeśa who is supposed to be the creator as well as the remover of obstacles is propitiated at the commencement of all important undertakings.

the holy thread was present. He was accompanied by his brother and Jayā.

44-46. After staying for a few days within the precincts of Gautama's hermitage, the lord of obstacles said to the brahmins: "We must not stay there. Let us go to our own abodes, clean and pure hermitages. We have been nourished by Gautama's food. Let us ask sage Gautama". After discussing among themselves thus the excellent sages took leave of the sage. Due to his fond feelings he prevented the sages severally.

Gautama said :

47. Gautama said humbly with palms joined in reverence: Stay here alone ye all. O leading sages, I shall serve your feet.

48. While I stand by here, ready to serve you all, it is not proper for you, Devas on the Earth to resort to another hermitage.

49. In my opinion this hermitage alone is the holy penance grove for all. O sages, please do not go to any other hermitage.

Brahmā said :

50. On hearing these words of the sage, Vināyaka remembered his duty of causing obstacles (in secret). With palms joined in reverence he said to the brahmins.

Gaṇādhipa said :

51. We have all been bought over by the food offered to us. Why then should Gautama not forbid us? We are not allowed to go to our own abodes by peaceful means.

52. Nor does this excellent brahmin who has helped us deserve any punishment. Hence I shall endeavour in an intelligent manner. Let that be approved of by you all.

Brahmā said :

53-56. Then the brahmins replied: "Let it be done for helping this brahmin with a desire for the welfare of the world. Do anything which will do good to all the brahmins."

On hearing the words of the brahmins Gaṇādhipa (Lord of gaṇas or attendants of Śiva) approved of them and said.

Vināyaka said :

What is particularly good for Gautama is being done.

Brahmā said :

Vināyaka of liberal mind coaxed and cajoled the brahmins again and again. He bowed unto them. He took the guise of a brahmin himself. Gaṇeśvara who sided with his mother habitually, said to Jayā.

Vināyaka said :

57. O Lady of splendid face, do everything in such a manner as no one else comes to know. Assume the form of a cow and go to the place where Gautama is present.

58. Consume the paddy. O beautiful lady, destroy them and distort them. If you are beaten, or shouted at or even looked at do something (by way of retaliation). Bellowing loudly remain in a struggle between life and death.

Brahmā said :

59-60. Vijayā (Jayā) who sided with Vighneśvara did so. Jayā assumed the form of a cow and went to the place where Gautama was present, eating the paddy plants (on the way). Gautama saw her. On seeing the cow in a state of aberration, the brahmin prevented her by a blade of grass.

61. On being forbidden by him, the cow cried aloud and fell down. When the cow fell down there was a great hue and cry.

62. On hearing the cry and on seeing the action of Gautama the brahmins became distressed. Keeping Vighnarāja at the head the brahmins said.

The Brahmins said :

63. All of us are going away from here. We should not stay in your hermitage. We all had been nurtured by you like a son. O leading sage, we are taking leave of you.

Brahmā said :

64. On hearing these words of the brahmins who were determined to go from there, he was as though struck down by the thunderbolt. He fell down in front of the brahmins.

65. The brahmins said to him: "See this goddess mother of the Rudras, the beloved deity of the worlds sanctifying them, fallen on the ground.

66. When due to the power of fate, this cow whose form and features are like those of gods and holy centres has fallen down O excellent sage, what remains for us to do is to go away.

67. If we continue to reside in your hermitage (the merit of) the holy rites performed by us will dwindle down and waste away. O brahmin, we do not have any other asset. We are only ascetics whose only assets are their penance.

Brahmā said :

68-72. Standing humbly in front of the brahmins, Gautama said.

Gautama said :

Your holinesses alone are my refuge. It behoves you to make me pure.

Brahmā said :

Then Lord Vighnakṛt (Gaṇeśa, the creator of obstacles) surrounded by the brahmins, said.

Vighnarāja said :

This cow neither dies nor lives. In this extremely doubtful situation we shall mention the expiation and the goal.

Gautama said :

This cow will never gain sense. She will certainly die. How will this cow get up? It behoves you to tell me the way of expiation. Undoubtedly I shall do everything.

The Brahmins said :

73. This intelligent (brahmin) will speak in accordance with the opinion of all of us. His statement is (as good as) our statement. It should be considered authoritative by you, O Gautama.

Brahmā said :

74. Induced by the brahmins as well as the powerful Gautama, Vighnakṛt (i.e. Lord Gaṇeśa) in the guise of a brahmin spoke these words to all.

Vighnarāja said :

75. I shall speak truthfully on behalf of all. Let the sages as well as Gautama accept my suggestion.

76. We have heard that the water that had been in the jar of Brahmā born of the unmanifest one, is now staying within the matted hair of Lord Śiva.

77. Bring it quickly by means of austerities and holy rites. O holy sage, pour that water over this cow that has fallen on the ground. After that all of us shall stay in your house as before.

Brahmā said :

78. When that leading brahmin said thus in the assembly of the brahmins, there was a shower of flowers there. Cries of "Victory" rose up. Then the humble Gautama spoke these words with palms joined in reverence.

Gautama said :

79. Let the desire in my mind be fulfilled due to my power of penance, by the grace of Fire god, by the grace of gods and Brahmā as well as by your grace.

Brahmā said :

80. After saying "Let it be so," the brahmins took leave of the leading sage and went to their abodes that were now rich in food and water.

81. When those brahmins had gone, Gaṇeśvara returned accompanied by his brother and Jayā. After fulfilling his task he was extremely delighted.

82-83. After the brahmins had returned, after Gaṇeśa had gone, the excellent sage Gautama whose sins had been dispelled by his penance, began to ponder over the same incident. "What is this that has befallen me?" After a great deal of reflection the brahmin understood it by his powerful intuition.

84-88. He came to the firm conclusion that the affair was made-up for the task of the gods. "I consider everything conducive to welfare. It is a help unto the worlds. It is (a task) most pleasing to Śambhu and Pārvatī. It is the task of bringing, Gaṅgā on the Earth. There is no sin in me at all". Thinking thus in his mind, the excellent brahmin became extremely delighted. After consulting his wife the excellent brahmin said: "After propitiating the bull-bannered three-eyed lord of the worlds, I shall bring the excellent river. I shall delight Pārvatī, the consort of Śiva. The co-wife of the mother of the Universe is stationed within the matted hair of Maheśvara." After determining thus in his mind the excellent sage Gautama departed from Brahmagiri with a desire to please Śambhu who was staying in Kailāsa, who is worshipped by the mighty Devas and whose power is most terrible.

CHAPTER SIX

Descent of Gautamī

Nārada said :

1. After going to the peak of Kailāsa what did the holy lord, Sage Gautama do? Did he perform any penance? What excellent method did he adopt for attaining the goal?

Brahmā said :

2-3. After going to that mountain, O dear son, Sage Gautama controlled his speech. On the excellent mountain Kailāsa he spread Kuśa grass and sat thereon with purity of mind and body. Then he sang this hymn. While Maheśvara was being eulogized there was a shower of flowers.

Gautama said :

4. (Lord Śiva) accompanied by Umā assumes eight cosmic bodies that are always beneficial to the people. It is to bestow the desired enjoyment of worldly pleasures to those who seek it that the lord assumes these bodies. Hence the people eulogize the lord as the Great God.

5. Īśvara assumes the body of the Earth for this purpose viz. in order to create happiness by means of its own objects of pleasure and to sustain the entire (universe consisting of) mobile and immobile beings. It is conducive to the prosperity of the universe and its increase.

6. The form of waters (of Śiva with eight cosmic bodies) is for creation, sustenance and annihilation of the Earth and also in order to provide for support to the Earth. For granting happiness and piety to the people, Śiva of tranquil body assumed the form of waters that is well established in the universe.

7. Śiva's cosmic bodies of Sun, Moon and Fire caused the following viz., the demarcation of the units of time, the oozing current of nectar, sustenance, creation and destruction of living beings and joy, happiness and progress of the subjects.

8. The form of Īśa viz. Vāyu is evolved for the following purpose. It is for creating prosperity, movement, power, imperishable things, the proper arrangement of the living beings and for the accomplishment of their joys. Certainly, O holy lord, you alone are responsible for this.

9. Without mutual differences there cannot be action and piety, a thing that is one's own and not one's own, neither directions nor atmosphere, neither heaven nor Earth, neither worldly pleasures nor salvation. Hence, O Īśa, this ethereal body of yours.

10. (This ethereal body) assumes the form of word. In order to establish virtue the Vedas are divided into Ṛk, Yajus and Sāman. In the world (i.e. among non-Vedic sacred literature) the Gāthās (songs), Smṛtis, Purāṇas etc. (also flourish).

11. The various ancillary objects pertaining to sacrifice constitute the sacrificial body of Śiva. The sacrifice and the instruments of sacrifice, the form of the Ṛtvik, time, space and result, O Śambhu, you are all these things. They say that your sacrificial body is the ultimately real entity.

12. You are everything. You are the maker, donor, surety, charitable offering, the omniscient witness, the great Puruṣa, the supreme soul and the ultimate reality. You are everything. Of what avail are the verbal outpourings?

13. You are not pointed out by the Vedas and other sacred literature or preceptors. Nor are you accessible by means of intellect etc. You alone are unborn, unmeasurable and the lord expressed by the word Śiva. You alone are the Truth. O holy lord, obeisance unto you.

14. (Defective Text) Once Śiva saw his Prakṛti in unison with the Ātman as "This is my asset." At that same time, the Prakṛti that cannot be imagined or argued upon stood separate. The lord of cosmic form is one of unimaginable power.

15. The eternal Śiva whether possessed of all excellent virtues or devoid of any trait is the power of the creator of the

Universe. At every creation she becomes increased in purity. It has occupied the reason, its own reason.

16. Production, sustenance, increase and destruction of food—these are the eternal laws of nature. There is nothing which the beloved of Śiva cannot accomplish.

17. It is the Mother, the mother of the universe, the beloved of Śiva accompanied by Umā of grand and excellent renown for whose sake the living beings give food and wealth and perform penances and virtuous rites.

18. Even Indra yearns for her benign glance. One shall acquire auspiciousness from her names. Pervading the Universe she makes it free from impurities. That Umā has always a form similar to the form of the Moon.

19. It is due to her grace that the pleasures of intellect, eyes, consciousness and mind of all living beings beginning with Brahmā, whether mobile or immobile, become fruitful. The beautiful wife of the preceptor of the world is the goddess of speech.

20. "The mind of even the four-faced lord (Brahmā) has become defiled. Why not that of other creatures." Thinking thus, the goddess should perform the descent of Gaṅgā by means of different methods in order to sanctify the universe.

21. By means of all testimonies and by going through the Vedic passages, people came to believe in the lordship of Śiva. They performed all pious rites and enjoyed all worldly pleasures. This is the perpetual power and glory of Śiva.

22. The things to be accomplished, the most excellent and pleasing to be evolved, the rite, the performer of the rite and the instruments of the rite are expressed in the Vedas and found in the world—those are said to be the achievements of the primordial lord.

23. It is the Lord of Umā who must be meditated upon. After attaining him the good Yogins are not reborn. They are liberated. After meditating upon the excellent Brahman and the great Pradhāna[1] it is lord Śiva who is the essence.

---

1. The primordial matter, the inert stuff of the universe as opposed to spirit, more usually known as Prakṛti.

24. As and when Śambhu assumes the forms of the immeasurable Māyā[1] for the welfare of the universe, you too assume forms befitting contact with him. O Mother, that is your chastity.

Brahmā said :

25-26. As he was eulogising thus the bull-bannered lord, accompanied by Umā, appeared in front of him. The glorious lord Śambhu accompanied by Gaṇesa and his retinue went in front of him and spoke these words in delight.

Śiva said :

27. What shall I give you, O Gautama? I am delighted at your devotion, eulogy and splendid holy rites. You may ask anything, even for those things that are not easily accessible to the gods.

Brahmā said :

28. On hearing these words of Śiva having the universe for his body, Gautama was overwhelmed by the tears of delight. Expert in making statements, Gautama thought thus.

29. O fate ! O piety ! O the worship of brahmins, O the wonderful way of the world ! O creator, obeisance to you.

Gautama said :

30. O lord of Devas honoured by the gods, if you are pleased with me give me the splendid Gaṅgā stationed within your matted hair. O lord with the Vedas for abode, obeisance be to you.

The Lord said :

31. What has been requested for by you is for helping the three worlds. Rid of fear from every quarter you may request for something that will be helpful to yourself.'

Gautama said :

32. Indeed it is this that I choose. Let those devotees who eulogise you and the goddess by means of this hymn be prosperously endowed with all desired things.

Brahmā said :

33. "So, be it", said the lord of Devas who was delighted, "Free from all ailments you may request for other boons from me."

1. The cosmic power which creates illusory appearances.

34-45. Thus urged by the lord, Gautama said to Śaṅkara with joy:

"O Śaṅkara, let brahmin slaughter and other sins perpetrated mentally, verbally or physically be destroyed the by mere ablution in this river in any place upto the sea where it flows. It shall be the holiest of all holy rivers.

"O Hara, merely by remembering thus let there be that merit which is acquired in other holy rivers during the lunar and solar eclipses, during vernal and equinotical transit of the sun or during his northern and southern transit or during the holy occasion of Vaidhṛti.[1]

"In Kṛta[2] Yuga penance was praiseworthy, in Tretā it was the sacrificial rite, in Dvāpara, sacrifice and charitable gifts, and charitable gifts alone in Kali age.

"Yugadharmas (the virtues peculiar to certain Yugas or eras) and Deśadharmas (the virtues peculiar to certain countries) are honoured in accordance with the contact of the particular country or time unit.

"O Hara, merely by remembering this, let there be that merit which is acquired elsewhere by means of ablutions, charitable gifts and other observances.

"Wherever this river flows till the time it reaches the sea you must also be there. Let this be my most excellent boon.

"O Śiva, let these persons realize salvation, viz. those who come within ten Yojanas (i.e. 120 Kms) of this river even if they are great sinners, the manes who come here for bathing and other people who take bath.

"On one side stand all holy rivers whether in heaven or mortal world or nether world and on the other side stands this river. Still this river shall be the better one.

"Enough of this, O Śambhu, obeisance to you."

Brahmā said :

46-47. On hearing those words of Gautama Śiva said: "So be it. A holy centre greater than this has never been, nor will there ever be. It is truth. It is truth. It is truth. It is well

1. A particular position of the sun and moon.

2. The first of the four cosmic ages having a duration of 1728000, 1296000, 864000 and 432000 human years equivalent respectively to 4800, 3600, 2400 and 1200 divine years.

established in the Veda. Gautamī is the holiest of all rivers." After saying this the lord vanished there itself.

48. Then after the lord who is honoured by the worlds, had gone, Gautama became full of power. He grew matted hair. Leading the Gaṅgā, the most excellent of all rivers, he entered Brahmagiri surrounded by Devas.

49-50. Then, when Gautama came there, O Nārada, with matted hair, there was a shower of flowers. The leading Devas, the highly fortunate sages, brahmins and kṣatriyas came there, honouring that brahmin with cries of "Victory". They were joyous.

CHAPTER SEVEN

Glory of the Holy River

Nārada said :

1. After leading the Gaṅgā from the matted hair of Maheśvara and coming to the holy mountain Brahmagiri, what did Gautama do?

Brahmā said :

2-3. The pure Gautama of wholly controlled mind, led Gaṅgā. He was honoured by Devas and Gandharvas, the residents of the mountains. He placed his matted hair on the top of the mountain. Remembering the three-eyed lord, that excellent brahmin said to Gaṅgā with palms joined in reverence.

Gautama said :

4. O mother born of the matted hair of the three-eyed lord, O goddess bestowing all desired things, forgive. You are calm. Go happily, carry out what is conducive to the welfare of all.

Brahmā said :

5. On being spoken to thus by Gautama, the Gaṅgā who assumed a divine form and wore a divine garland and unguent, said to Gautama.

Gaṅgā said :

6. Where shall I go? To the abode of Devas, or to the water-jar or to the nether worlds? It is known that you are truthful of speech.

Gautama said :

7. O goddess, you have been requested by me for helping the three worlds. You have been given to me by Śambhu. O goddess, let it not be otherwise.

Brahmā said :

8-9. On hearing the words of Gautama, Gaṅgā accepted the suggestion offered by the brahmin. It divided itself into three for flowing in heaven, Earth and the nether worlds. In heaven it flowed in four channels, in the mortal world it flowed in seven channels and in the nether worlds it flowed in four channels. Thus it had fifteen different channels.

10. Everywhere it has the power of everyone of the channels. It destroys all sins. It bestows all desired things always. It is thus alone that she is sung about in the Vedas.

11. Human beings see only the part of Gaṅgā that flows over the mortal world and not that which flows over the nether worlds. Nor do the human beings of ignorant intellect see Gaṅgā flowing in heaven.

12. Till Gaṅgā reaches the Sea, it is one of divine nature. On being bid farewell by Gautama, it went towards the Eastern Sea.

13. Then Gautama the great among the sages circumambulated Gaṅgā, the splendid mother of the Universe frequented by Devas and Sages.

14-16. At the outset Gautama worshipped the three-eyed lord of Devas and then determined in his mind, "I shall take bath near the banks" Immediately after being remembered, the lord who is an ocean of mercy appeared in front of him. With palms joined in reverence and being humble due to devotion he asked the three-eyed lord Śiva how the holy ablution should be performed.

Gautama said :

17. O Maheśāna, lord of Devas, with a desire for the

welfare of the worlds tell me about the rules and injunctions regarding ablution in the holy centres.

Śiva said :

18-20. O great sage, listen to all injunctions regarding Godāvarī. At the outset, Nandi (a holy rite) and other rites should be performed after cleaning the body. The brahmins should be fed and their permission obtained. Maintaining celibacy they should go to the river, avoiding conversation with fallen persons.

He whose hands and feet and mind are well controlled, he who has learning, penance and renown enjoys the benefit of holy centre (and ablution therein).

21. The devotee should abandon vicious nature. He should closely abide by his own duty. He should massage the limbs of the tired people. He should give them food in the proper manner.

22-23. He should give garments and blankets to good people who may happen to be poor. He should be listening to divine stories of Hari as well as those connected with Gaṅgā. A person who goes on pilgrimage abiding by these injunctions, will obtain the benefit of holy centre duly.

The three-eyed lord said another thing to Gautama surrounded by the sages.

24. The holy centres are within distances of two hands of one another. O Gautama, I am present everywhere and I am the bestower of all desired things.

25. Gaṅgā is the bestower of merits and salvation of men at Gaṅgādvāra, the place where Gaṅgā rises, Prayāga and at the place where it falls into the ocean.

26-29. Narmadā, the excellent river, is in the mountain Amarakaṇṭaka. Yamunā joins Gaṅgā at Prayāga and Sarasvatī joins it at Prabhāsa.

O Nārada, the following holy centre is the bestower of salvation. It is the place of meeting of three rivers viz., Kṛṣṇā, Bhīmarathī and Tuṅgabhadrā.

The river is the bestower of liberation at the place where Payoṣṇī joins it. But this Gautamī, O dear one, is the bestower of liberation everywhere at my bidding. It will give salvation to all men always through the holy ablution.

Some holy centres are extremely meritorious on certain occasions when there is the advent of Devas. But Gautamī is a holy centre unto everyone on every occasion.

30. Plunging into and performing ablution in the Gaṅgā for sixty thousand years is on a par with taking bath once when Bṛhaspati (Jupiter) is in the Leo (zodiac).

31. It is rare that men are able to take bath in Gautamī when the Jupiter is in the zodiac Leo (i.e. it is highly meritorious then). (It is holy because) Rāma stepped into it and particularly so because he resorted to this holy centre.

32. When the sun is in the Leo zodiac the rivers Gaṅgā, Narmadā, Yamunā, Sarasvatī, Bhīmarathī and others come (to the river Gautamī) for taking bath.

33. When the sun is in the Leo zodiac if foolish persons avoid Gautamī Gaṅgā and go to other rivers for ablution they are sure to fall into hell.

34-36. Within a distance of two hundred Yojanas, O most venerable among sages, there will be three and a half crores of holy centres. O Gautama, this Gaṅgā belonging to Maheś-vara, is called Gautamī, Vaiṣṇavī, Brāhmī, Godāvarī, Nandā and Sunandā. It is the bestower of desired objects. It is brought by the force of splendour of a brahmin. By mere remembrance it destroys all sins. It is always dear to me. Of all the five elements it is the water that has attained most excellence.

37-38. The waters in the holy centres are said to be the holiest. Among those holy rivers Bhāgīrathī is the most excellent. Among different channels of Bhāgīrathī, Gautamī Gaṅgā accompanied by matted hair which was brought by you is the most excellent. There is no holy centre which is more auspicious than this either in heaven or on Earth or in the nether worlds. O sage, this holy centre is the bestower of all riches.

Brahmā said :

39-40. O dear son, what has been recounted thus to the noble Gautama, by the delighted lord himself has been narrated to you.

Thus that Gautamī Gaṅgā is considered greater than the other rivers. The form of that river has been mentioned to you. Have you any desire to hear about anything else?

CHAPTER EIGHT

The Descent of Bhāgirathi

Nārada said :

1-2. O lord, most excellent one among Devas, two types of channels of Gaṅgā have been mentioned. One of them that has been brought by the brahmin has been narrated. The other type is stationed in the matted hair itself, of the lord of Devas. Tell me how it was brought down to the earth.

Brahmā said :

3. There was a king born of the family of Vaivasvata Manu[1] and in the family of Ikṣvāku. O sage, his name was Sagara and the ocean takes its name Sāgara from him.

4. He was a performer of sacrifices. He was devoted to distribution of charitable gifts. He always thought about piety and good conduct. He had two wives devoutly attached to their husband.

5-6. He had no progeny. So he was anxious. He invited Vasiṣṭha (the family priest) to his abode and worshipped him. The king asked him as to how he could have progeny. On hearing his words, Vasiṣṭha meditated and spoke to the king.

Vasiṣṭha said :

7-9. O king, be devoted to the worship of sages together with your wives.

Brahmā said :

After saying this, O brahmin, the sage went back to his abode.

Once a great ascetic came to the abode of that saintly king. He worshipped that sage. The sage who was extremely pleased

1. The seventh Manu who was the son of Sūrya and father of Ikṣvāku, the founder of the Solar Race of Kings.

said to him. "O extremely fortunate one, tell me the boon you wish to have." On being told thus he chose sons.

10. That sage said to the king, "To one of your wives a son will be born and he will sustain the family. To the other wife there will be born sixty thousand sons."

11. When the sage went away after bestowing the boon, thousands of sons were born. The king performed horse and other sacrifices and distributed plenty of gifts to the deserving.

12. In one horse sacrifice the king got himself duly initiated. He employed his sons along with their armies in the work of protecting the horse.

13. Getting a loophole somewhere Indra took away the horse. Those sons searched for the horse but could not find it.

14-15. The sons of Sagara were sixty thousand and they were experts in different tactics of warfare. Even as they were watching, the asuras took away the anointed horse and went to the nether region. The sons of Sagara could not see the asura who had employed black magic.

16. Not being able to see the horse, the powerful sons of Sagara wandered here and there. Even then they did not find the horse.

17. They went to the world of gods then. Searching the mountains, lakes and forests, they did not see the horse then.

18. The holy rite for the safe journey and other similar auspicious rites were performed by the officiating priests on behalf of the king. Unable to see that beautiful creature, the king became worried.

19. Wandering (here and there) the sons of Sagara went to the world of Devas in their search for the horse. The horse was not there.

20. Thereafter the sons of the king came to the Earth and searched the mountains and forests. There also they did not see the horse then.

21. In the meantime a divine voice was heard there saying, "O sons of Sagara, the horse is kept bound in the nether world and not anywhere else."

22. On hearing this the sons of Sagara became desirous of going to the nether world. They dug up the Earth all round.

23. Distressed by hunger they went on eating dry soil day and night. They dug up hurriedly and rushed to the nether world.

24. On hearing that the powerful princes, the sons of Sagara who had accomplished their tasks had come (to the nether world) the asuras became frightened and they went near Kapila.[1]

25. Kapila the extremely intelligent sage was sleeping in the nether world. Formerly, a most important task of Devas had been accomplished by him.

26. He had achieved that success by continuous work without any sleep. Therefore he was tired. When the task had been accomplished the glorious Kapila said to Devas, "Give me a place for sleeping."

27-29. They gave him the nether world. Again, the sage said to Devas : "If a fool wakes me up he will be immediately reduced to ashes; then only, will I lie down in the nether world; if not I won't sleep at all."

When Devas said "So be it" he began to lie down there.

The asuras who knew his power and who were endowed with Māyā (witchcraft) planned to slay Sagara.

30-31. The asuras were afraid even without being fought. They hurried to the place where the extremely furious sage Kapila was lying. They hurriedly tethered the horse near his head. They stood watching silently a little away from the place eager to see what would happen.

32. Then the sons of Sagara entered the nether regions. They saw the tethered horse and the man lying down.

33-35. They considered him the person who took the horse by force and spoiled the sacrifice.

Some of them said then, "Let us kill this fellow and take the horse back".

Some said, "Let us take away this tethered sacrificial animal. Of what avail is this fellow !"

Then other heroic persons said—"We are kings. We are administrators. Let us waken this fellow who has committed the crime and kill him with our heroic power."

---

1. A celebrated sage and propounder of the Sāṁkhya system of philosophy. He is said to be the son of Karandama-Prajāpati and Devahūti. The Brahmāṇḍapurāṇa (ch. 93) mentions him as an incarnation of Viṣṇu.

Uttering these harsh words they kicked the sage with their feet.

36. Then Kapila the excellent sage stared at the sons of Sagara with great fury. With his anger he reduced them to ashes.

37. Then all the sons of Sagara were burnt up. But the king Sagara who was initiated to the sacrifice did not know these things.

38-39. It was Nārada who informed noble Sagara about the abode of Kapila, the situation of the horse, the aberration of asuras and the annihilation of the sons of Sagara. But the anxious king did not know what he should do in the circumstances.

40-42. This king had another son who was well known as Asamañjas. Due to his foolishness, he used to hurl down boys and citizens into water. Having been informed by the citizens collectively the king understood his wickedness. He became furious and told his ministers, "Let this Asamañjas, who has forsaken the duty of a Kṣatriya and killed children be banished from the kingdom."

43. On hearing those words of Sagara, the ministers hurriedly abandoned the son of the king. Asamañjas went to the forest.

44-45. (The King thought thus) "All my sixty thousand sons are destroyed by the curse of the brahmin in the nether world. One (who remained) has gone to the forest. Now what shall I do?"

Asamañjas had a son who was well known as Aṁśumān. The king called that boy and told him the task on hand.

46. Propitiating Kapila, the boy Aṁśumān gave the horse to Sagara. Thus was the sacrifice completed.

47. His son was a brilliant and virtuous king named Dilīpa. His intelligent son was well known as Bhagīratha.

48. On hearing about the sad end of all of his grandfathers he became very distressed. The humble prince asked the great king,

49. "How shall I accomplish the expiation of the Sagaras?" The king said to Bhagīratha, "Dear son, Kapila knows it".

50. On hearing his words the boy went to the nether world. After bowing down to the sage, he intimated everything to him.

51-52. That sage meditated for a long time and said to Bhagīratha, "Propitiate Śaṅkara by penance, O excellent king, and splash your ancestors with the water stationed in the matted hair of Śiva. Then you as well as your ancestors will become satisfied."

"I shall do so", said he to the sage. After bowing down to him he said again.

53-54. "Where shall I go ? O excellent sage, tell me everything what I should do".

Kapila said :

Go to the excellent mountain Kailāsa and eulogize Maheśvara. Perform penance according to your capacity. Then you will attain your desired object.

Brahmā said :

55. On hearing the words of the sage that boy whose activities were those of children bowed down to the sage and went to the mountain Kailāsa. Becoming pure (in mind and body) he decided to perform penance. (Then) Bhagīratha said :

Bhagīratha said :

56. O lord, wearing crescent moon, I am a boy and my intellect too is puerile. I do not know anything. Even then, be pleased, O lord.

57. I bow down to Śiva who is worthy of being worshipped, O lord of the immortals, for the welfare of those who are devoted to my welfare and who help me mentally, physically and verbally (even for) once.

58. May Śiva bring about things desired by those by whom I have been begot and nurtured, those whose Gotra (lineage) is the same as mine and those whose duties are also the same. I bow down to lord Sīva with the crescent moon on his head.

Brahmā said :

59. Even as he was eulogising thus Śiva appeared in front of him. Urging him to choose a boon as he pleased, he said to Bhagīratha.

Śiva said :

60. O Bhagīratha of great intellect, what cannot be given by

Sādhyas[1] and Devas will certainly be given by me to you. Tell me without fear.

Brahmā said :

61-63. The delighted Bhagīratha bowed down to lord Śiva and said.

Bhagīratha said :

In order to sanctify my ancestors, O lord of Devas, give me the excellent river stationed within your matted hair. Everything will be complete thereby.

Brahmā said :

Maheśa smiled and said to Bhagīratha.

Śiva said :

64-68. O son, she is given unto you by me. O dear, of good vow, eulogize her once more.

Brahmā said :

On hearing the words of the lord, Bhagīratha of pure mind performed penance for that purpose. With devotion he eulogized Gaṅgā.

He attained her grace too, like a mature man although he was only a boy. Leading Gaṅgā derived from Maheśvara he went to the nether world. He intimated everything to the noble sage Kapila.

After establishing Gaṅgā in the manner mentioned before and strenuously circumambulating her he spoke with palms joined in reverence.

Bhagīratha said :

69. O goddess, my ancestors have fallen as a result of the curse of sage Kapila. O mother, it behoves you to save them therefrom.

Brahmā said :

70-73. "So be it", said the divine river who helps everyone. In order to help the worlds and to sanctify the ancestors, parti-

1. A class of inferior deities who, according to Viṣṇupurāṇa, were the grandchildren of Dakṣa-Prajāpati.

cularly in order to fill up the sea drunk up by Agastya[1], in order to destroy sins merely by being remembered, the divine river did what she was told by Bhagīratha. She splashed the princes, the sons of Sagara who had been reduced to ashes by the curse of brahmin, in the nether region. She filled up the holes dug up by the Sagaras, the river flooded the mountain Meru and stopped. The young king spoke to her thus:

74-77. "You must remain in the land of holy rites."

Saying "So be it" she came to Himālaya. From that holy mountain, she came to the subcontinent Bhārata. From its middle the holy river flowed towards the eastern sea. Thus this river Gaṅgā brought by a Kṣatriya, O great sage, has been mentioned to you.

This same river belongs to Maheśvara, Viṣṇu and Brahmā. It is sacred. Bhāgīrathī the divine river is stationed on the peak of Himavān.

Thus, the water stationed within the matted hair of Maheśvara attained two forms. To the south of the Vindhya, Gaṅgā is called Gautamī. In the north of the Vindhya, she is called Bhāgīrathī.

CHAPTER NINE

The Holy Centre Varāha

Nārada said :

1. My mind is not satiated by listening to the stories mentioned by you. The predilection of my mind is to listen to the benefit of the holy centres separately.

2. At the outset recount to me in proper sequence how Gaṅgā was brought by the brahmin. Tell me the holy benefit of the holy centres separately in the proper sequence together with its legends.

1. The sage Agastya drank up the ocean because, according to Mahābhārata, the latter was hiding demons who could be killed by the gods only after this act of Agastya.

Brahmā said :

3. I am not able to recount entirely the benefit, greatness and the individual importance of the holy centres. Nor are you capable of listening to it.

4-6. Still I shall recount something. Listen to it attentively, O Nārada.

After bowing down to the three-eyed lord, I shall briefly speak about the holy centres mentioned by sages and the words of the Vedas.

O sage, the place where the three-eyed lord revealed himself is the holy centre named Tryambaka. It is the bestower of worldly pleasures and salvation. Another holy centre is "Varāha" which is well known in the three worlds.

7-8. I shall describe its features as well as how Viṣṇu's name came to be associated with it.

Formerly a Rākṣasa well known by the name of Sindhusena, harassed and defeated Devas. Taking away sacrifice he reached the nether region.

When sacrifice went over to the nether world the Earth became devoid of sacrifice.

9. When sacrifice perishes one shall have neither this world nor the other. At that time, the situation was thus.

Following the enemy Devas entered the nether region.

10-12. With Indra as their leader they were not able to conquer him. Approaching Viṣṇu the Purāṇa Puruṣa (lit. the primeval male) they intimated to him the evil action of the Rākṣasa viz., the entire destruction of sacrifice.

The Lord said:

Assuming the physical body of a Boar along with the conch, discus and mace in hands I shall go to the nether region and bring the holy sacrifice after killing the leading demons.

13-16. May Devas go to heaven. May your mental fever disappear.

Brahmā said :

It was by that path whereby Gaṅgā reached the nether regions, O dear son, that the discus-bearing lord hurried to Rasātala (nether world) after breaking through the Earth.

The glorious lord in the guise of a Boar killed the Rākṣasas and Dānavas residing in Rasātala. He held the great sacrifice in his mouth. The lord in the form of a Boar, the enjoyer of sacrifices, the conqueror of enemies, came out of Rasātala by the same path whereby Viṣṇu had entered it.

17-18. There, on the mountain Brahmagiri, Devas waited for Hari. Coming out by that path he came to the Gaṅgā-sravaṇa (the current of the river Gaṅgā). He washed his blood-stained limbs, O Nārada, with the water of Gaṅgā. Therefore it became (well known as) Varāhakuṇḍa.

19-22. Hari, the most excellent one among Devas, placed in front of Devas the sacrifice he had kept in his mouth. It was thus that the sacrifice was born of his mouth.

Thereafter the sacred ladle is called the most important part of sacrifice. Its form became that of a Boar for another reason.

Hence the holy centre Varāha is the holiest Tīrtha. It bestows all desired things. Performing the holy ablution and charity at that place bestows the benefits of all sacrifices.

If anyone stands there and remembers his ancestors or does any meritorious deed, his manes will be free from all sins. They shall attain Heaven.

CHAPTER TEN

Kapotatīrtha

1. I am not competent to recount to you the greatness of Kuśāvarta. Merely by remembering it one's purpose is accomplished.

2. The holy centre well known as Kuśāvarta is the bestower of all desired things unto men. It has been stirred up by Kuśa[1] by the noble Gautama.

3. The sage brought the river after stirring it with Kuśa. Performing ablution and offering charitable gifts there bestows satisfaction to the manes.

1. A sacred grass used in religious rites; also known as darbha in older texts.

4-7. Nīlagaṅgā which is the most excellent of all rivers comes out of the Nīlaparvata (Blue mountain).

If a man of mental and physical purity performs ablution etc., whatever holy rite he performs, know that all those are everlasting. They bestow satisfaction to the ancestors.

The excellent holy centre Kapotatīrtha is well known in the three worlds.

O sage, listen. I shall tell you about its form and features, which will do you great good.

On Brahmagiri there was an extremely terrible hunter.

He used to harass brahmins, ascetics and other decent men as well as cows, birds and animals. That sinning soul of this nature was inclined to become furious and was a speaker of untruth.

8-10. He was of a terrible shape and size. He was very fierce. His eyes were blue. His arms were short. He had deformed teeth. He had lost his nose and eyes. His legs were short but his belly was huge in girth and he was short in height. His arms were small. He was utterly deformed and his voice resembled the braying of a donkey. He had a noose in his hand. He was evil-minded and sinful. He wielded the bow ever and anon.

O Nārada, his wife and children too were like him. Urged by his wife, he entered the dense forest.

11. That sinner killed animals and birds of many forms. Some of them, both living and dead, he put inside a cage.

12. He returned home scorched and distressed due to hunger and thirst after wandering through many places.

13-14. After the months of spring season on an afternoon, the sky was suddenly overcast with clouds. There was a rumbling sound of thunder. A violent gust of wind blew, showering hailstones. It was extremely terrible due to heavy downpour. As he went ahead, the tired hunter could not even know his path.

15. As the sinful fellow was too tired, he could not know, where it was water and where it was land, where was a deep pit and where the path was right, where to take shelter and in which direction he should move.

16-17. He thought thus:"Where am I going? Where should I stay? What shall I do? Like the god of death I am the extractor of vital airs of all living beings. The spirit that causese ven my death has come, viz. the shower of hailstones. I do not see anyone who can save me. No rock, no tree nearby."

18-20. After thinking thus in diverse ways the hunter saw a tree nearby in the forest. It was like the lord of the forest, like the moon among the stars, like a lion among animals, like a householder among the persons of various stages and like mind among sense-organs. It was the saviour of living beings. The tree was splendid and excellent, embellished with branches and tender sprouts and leaves. With his clothes drenched in water, that hunter resorted to that tree and sat beneath it.

21. He thought of his wife and children wondering whether they were alive or not. In the meantime the sun also set.

22. There was a pigeon on that excellent tree. He was surrounded by his wife, sons and grandsons. He had resorted to the same tree.

23. He lived there happily well-contented, delighted and free from fear. Many years passed by since that bird began to live there.

24-28. His wife who was chaste was highly pleased with him. His hollow cavity in that excellent tree was not at all affected by water or wind. That pigeon lived there along with his wife and children. On that particular day both of them, the he-pigeon and the she-pigeon had, by chance gone out in search of prey. The he-pigeon returned to the tree. As ill luck would have it, dear son, the she-pigeon was caught alive by the hunter. The he-pigeon looked at the children separated from their mother. On observing that a terrible downpour was going on, that the sun had set and that his hollow was a void he began to lament.

29. The king of pigeons was not aware that the she-pigeon was bound and kept in the cage. The he-pigeon began to sing in praise of his beloved.

30. "Even now my beloved wife, the source of my welfare, who increases my joy, the mother of my virtue and the controlling mistress of my body, has not come back.

31. It is she alone who assists me in the acquisition of virtue, wealth, love and liberation. When I am pleased she laughs; when I am angry she tries to wipe off my misery.

32. She is a comrade unto me; she helps me by her counsels. She abides by my words and suggestions. Even after the sun has

set, my beloved wife, the source of my welfare, has not come back.

33. She does not know any holy rite, mantra, god, virtue or asset other than me, her husband. Her husband is her holy rite; her husband is her life; her husband is her Mantra. She is fond of her husband.

34. Even now my beloved, the source of my welfare has not come back. What shall I do? Where shall I go? Is this my house? Without her it appears to be a forest.

35. In her company my house is full of splendour and glory. Even if it is terrible, it is splendid. Even now she does not come back. By her presence alone this place is a home.

36-37. Without her I cannot remain alive. For her I shall even forsake my body. But what will my children do? I will be deprived of my religious rites now."

Even as he was lamenting thus, the she-pigeon who was in the cage heard his lamentation. On hearing it she spoke thus to her husband from within the cage.

The she-pigeon said :

38. O bird of great intellect, I am here imprisoned (and) helpless. I have been brought here by the hunter bound by ropes and nooses.

39-40. I am gratified and blessed. My husband recounts my qualities. Undoubtedly I am contented.

When my husband is satisfied the deities are pleased with me. They are extremely pleased. Otherwise I would perish.

41. You are my deity. You are my lord. You are my friend. You are my ultimate resort. You are my holy rite. You are the great Brahman. You are my heaven. You are my salvation.

42. O my beloved husband, the cause of my welfare, do not be worried. Make your intellect steady and stable in virtue and piety. It is by your favour that different kinds of worldly pleasures have been enjoyed by me.

43. Do not have any grief or worry due to me. Keep your intellect steady and stable in virtue and piety.

Brahmā said :

44. On hearing these words of his beloved the he-pigeon got

down from the tree and went hurriedly to the place where the she-pigeon was in her cage.

45. On approaching, he saw his beloved, and the hunter as though dead. He said, "Now the hunter is motionless. I shall release you."

The she-pigeon said :

46-49. O extremely fortunate one, do not release me. Know that (the worldly) relationship is unstable. (The birds) that move about constitute the food of the hunters. One living being is the prey of another. I do not think that this hunter is guilty in any manner. Keep your consciousness of virtue steady.

To the twice-born, the fire-god is a preceptor. The brahmin is a preceptor unto all castes. Husband alone is the preceptor of women. The guest is a preceptor unto all. Certainly the goddess of speech becomes pleased with the people who propitiate the guest by means of delightful words. If food is given to him Indra will be pleased.

50. If his feet are washed the manes are pleased. If he is given food to eat, Prajāpati is pleased. By rendering service to him Lakṣmī can be propitiated along with Viṣṇu.

51-55. If he is offered a bed, the gods are pleased. Hence, let my guest be worshipped. If a guest is scorched by the glare of the sun and is tired and if he comes to one's house one should view him like a god. Indeed he is the bestower of benefits of all sacrifices.

Gods, manes and fires follow the exhausted guest. If he is pleased they also rejoice. If he is disappointed they are also disappointed.

Hence, O beloved husband, forsake misery in every respect and attain calmness. Keep your intellect auspicious and practise virtuous activities.

It is considered by all that rendering help or harassing persons is of great consequence. People render help to those who help them. But he who befriends those who harass him is a virtuous person.

The he-pigeon said :

56. O lady of excellent face, what has been said by you is

befitting us both. What you think is excellent. But I have something to be said. Listen to it.

57. There are some who fill their belly with thousands; others with hundreds and still others with tens. Some fill themselves with happiness. But we fill our belly with great difficulty.

58. Some hoard their wealth and grain in deep pits. Others hoard their wealth in big barns. Some keep their wealth in pots. But we keep our wealth in our beaks.

59. O splendid lady, how shall I honour and propitiate this exhausted guest?

The she-pigeon said :

60. Fire, water, splendid speech etc., can be offered to the guest. Grass, wood etc. should also be given to the suppliant. This hunter is distressed due to chillness.

Brahmā said :

61. On hearing these words of his beloved the king of birds ascended the tree and saw a fire burning far off.

62. He went to the place where the fire was burning and brought a burning splinter in his beak. He lit a fire in front of the hunter.

63. During the mid-night he dropped dry twigs, leaves and grass into that fire.

64. On seeing the fire blazing, that hunter who was distressed by cold warmed his exhausted limbs and attained happiness.

65. On seeing the hunter consumed by the fire of hunger, the she-pigeon said to her husband, "O highly fortunate one, release me.

66. I shall propitiate the distressed hunter with my own body. O dear one of good holy rites, attain the worlds belonging to those who have worshipped their guests".

The he-pigeon said :

67. O splendid lady, when I stand (i.e. when I am alive) this duty is not laid down for you. I shall be the one who propitiates the guest. permit me to be so.

Brahmā said :

68-69. After saying these words he circumambulated the fire three times remembering the four-armed lord Mahāviṣṇu who is the soul of the Universe, who is worthy of being sought refuge in and who is favourably disposed to his devotees. Saying "Eat as you please" he entered the fire. On seeing him cast off his life in the fire the hunter spoke these words.

The hunter said :

70. Fie upon this life of mine with a human body, for, this daring act has been undertaken for my sake by this king of birds.

Brahmā said :

71-72. The she-bird spoke to the hunter who said thus.

The she-pigeon said :

O highly fortunate one, release me. This, my husband is going far off.

Brahmā said :

73. On hearing her words the hunter released the she-pigeon from the cage hurriedly as though he was afraid.

74-78. After circumambulating the fire she sang to her dead husband.

The she-pigeon said :

Dying immediately after the husband is the greatest duty of women. This is the path laid down in the Vedas. It is honoured in the world.

Just as the snake-charmer forcibly takes out the snake from its hole, so also the woman who is accompanied by her husband shall go to heaven.

The woman who follows her husband shall stay in heaven for as many years as there are hairs in a man's body, viz. three and a half crores of years.

After bowing down to the Earth, gods, Gaṅgā, and trees and after consoling her children, she said to the hunter:

The she-pigeon said :

79. The woman who follows her husband shall stay in heaven for as many years as there are hairs on a man's body, viz. three and a half crores of years.

80. O highly fortunate one, it is due to your grace that such a thing has happened to me. Pardon my guilt for leaving my children. I shall go to heaven along with my husband.

Brahmā said :

81. After saying thus, the good mannered she-bird entered the fire. As soon as she entered the fire there was a cry of victory.

82. Then the pair were seen in the sky seated on an aerial chariot resembling the sun and extremely splendid. They were like gods themselves.

83-85. With great delight both of them spoke to the hunter who was surprised much.

The Couple said :

We are going to the abode of gods. We are taking leave of you, O highly intelligent one. The staircase leading to heaven for both of us is the guest in you. Obeisance to you.

Brahmā said :

On seeing them seated on the excellent aerial chariot, the hunter cast away his cage along with his bow. With palms joined in reverence he spoke.

The hunter said :

86. O highly fortunate ones, I am not to be abandoned by you. Something should be given to me who do not know anything. I am your guest here and thus should be honoured. It behoves you to recount to me the manner of my expiation.

The Couple said :

87. Go to Gautamī river, welfare be to you. Taking bath there for a fortnight you will be liberated from your sins.

88. After being liberated from your sins if you plunge into Gaṅgā again you will acquire the merit of a horse-sacrifice. You will become sanctified.

89-90. If you take a holy ablution in the excellent river Gautamī, you will abandon this defiled body. Mounting on an excellent aerial chariot, you will go to heaven.

Brahmā said :

91-94. On hearing their words the hunter did so. He became seated on an extellent aerial chariot. He assumed a divine form. He wore divine garlands and garments. He was eulogized by celestial damsels. The he-pigeon, the she-pigeon and the hunter proceeded to heaven. Such is the power of Gaṅgā.

Thenceforward that holy centre is well known by the name *Kapota* (pigeon). All the holy rites performed there, viz. bathing, distributing charitable gifts, worshipping the manes and all other holy rites such as Japa, Yajña, etc. are capable of giving everlasting benefit.

CHAPTER ELEVEN

Kumāratīrtha

Brahmā said :

1. Another holy centre is Kārttikeya pertaining to Lord Subrahmaṇya, well known as Kaumāra. Merely by listening to its name one shall attain nobility of birth and exquisite beauty.

2. When the asura Tāraka was killed and the three worlds became quiet and normal, Pārvatī spoke to her eldest son Kārttikeya with great pleasure:

3. "By my consent and the grace of your father, be delighted in your mind. Enjoy as you please the worldly pleasures in the three worlds, which are dear to your mind."

4. Thus addressed by his mother, Viśākha (Kārttikeya) the beloved of gods, sported about as be pleased with the wives of gods. The wives of gods also sported about.

5. While the wives of gods were being enjoyed, O Nārada, the heaven-dwellers were not able to prevent Kārttikeya.

6-7. Then Devas intimated to Pārvatī that act of her son. Though he was frequently prevented by his mother and Devas, the spear-bearing lord did not act according to their suggestions. The six-faced lord was so much attached to the women. Afraid of his curse, Pārvatī thought over the matter.

8-10. Again and again the goddess thought about this due to her affection for her son. In order to achieve the task of Devas she decided that the wives of Devas should be protected. If Skanda (Kārttikeya) attempted to sport with any lady Pārvatī made her look like herself. When the six-faced lord called the wife of Indra or Varuṇa and stared at her he saw the form of his mother in her.

11. He set her aside after a bow. Again he called another lady. Seeing his mother's form in her too he became ashamed.

12. Thus he saw in all women the form of his own mother. He saw the entire universe full of the forms of his mother. Thinking thus, he became free from all attachments.

13-14. He knew that it was his mother who started dissuading him from his actions. He thought thus: "If I am to be dissuaded from enjoyment of pleasures why was I persuaded to act so at the first instance? Whatever my mother did was only to make me a laughing stock." Hence, he was extremely ashamed and went to Gautamī.

15. (He then said) "Let this river whose form is also like that of my mother, hear my statement. Hereafter whatever has a feminine name will be considered by me like my mother."

16-17. On coming to know of this, Śaṅkara, the lord of the worlds, accompanied by Pārvatī stopped him. Then Subrahmaṇya said, "It has already taken place." Then the delighted lord began to think: "What shall I give?"

With palms joined in reverence Skanda said to his father again.

18-22. "I am commander-in-chief and the leader of gods and I am your son. O lord of Devas and the one who is worshipped by Devas, this much is enough. Why should there be other boons?

Or, if you are desirous of granting me a boon, I shall ask for the welfare of worlds and not of myself. O lord, it behoves you to permit me. Let the great sinners such as the defilers of preceptors' bed, be rid of their sins merely by plunging into this river. O lord of Devas, let even the low creatures attain excellent birth; let the ugly and the deformed be richly endowed with beauty by taking their bath here."

Brahmā said :

Saying "Let is be so" Śambhu approved of what was suggested by his son. Thenceforward that holy centre became known as "Kārttikeya". Taking bath and distributing charitable gifts there yields the benefit of all sacrifices.

CHAPTER TWELVE

The Kṛttikā Tīrtha

Brahmā said :

1. The holy centre next to Kārttikeya is known as Kṛttikā-Tīrtha. Merely by hearing about it one will acquire the benefit of drinking Soma juice.

2-3. Formerly, for quelling Tāraka, Fire god drank the semen of Śiva. On seeing him with the Semen within, O sage, the wives of sages desired for the same. Of the seven sages Vasiṣṭha's wife Arundhatī had her menstrual bath. Excepting her, the other six women became pregnant through the Fire god.

4-6. They had scorching experience in their menstrual bath. They shone splendidly. They consulted mutually: "What shall we do? Where shall we go? How can we attain merit?" After saying thus mutually they went to Gaṅgā and pressed themselves hard. The foetuses coming out of them floated in the water in the form of foam. Through water and wind they joined together. Thus the six-faced lord with a single body was born.

7. After causing the abortion of the foetuses the wives of sages went home. On seeing their deformed bodies the sages said :

8. "You may go. You may go quickly. It is not proper for women to be licentious." After saying this their husbands cast them off.

9-10. On being forsaken by their husbands, those six women became very miserable. On seeing them thus Nārada said: "By the names of Kārttikeya, Gāṅgeya (son of Gaṅgā), Agnibhava (born of Fire god) and Tārakāntaka (slayer of Tāraka) Śiva's son is well known. Go to him. Ere long he will become pleased and grant you worldly pleasures."

11. At the instance of the divine sage the Kṛttikās approached the six-faced lord and themselves intimated to him everything in the manner it had taken place.

12-16. Kārttikeya approved of them and said to them "All of you go to Gautamī. Take your bath and worship Maheśvara. I shall come there itself, and lead you to the abode of Devas". Saying "So be it" the Kṛttikās took their bath in Gaṅgā and

Gautamī. They worshipped the lord of Devas at the bidding of Kārttikeya. By the grace of the lord they went to their abode and were accepted by the sages.

Thenceforward that holy centre is called Kṛttikātīrtha. He who takes bath on the full moon day in the month of Kārttika, in conjunction with the Kṛttikā stars, acquires the benefit of all sacrifices. He becomes a virtuous king. He who remembers that holy centre or hears about it becomes rid of all sins and acquires long life.

CHAPTER THIRTEEN

Daśāśvamedha Tīrtha

Brahmā said :

1. O great sage, listen to the description of the holy centre of Daśāśvamedha[1]. Merely by listening to its name one shall acquire the merit of a horse-sacrifice.

2. The glorious Viśvarūpa of great strength was the son of Viśvakarman. Pramati was his son. His son was lordly Bhauvana.

3. His chief priest was Kaśyapa who was an expert in all wise lores. The brawny-armed Bhauvana, the ruler of the whole world asked him:

4. "O sage, I wish to perform a horse sacrifice simultaneously with ten horses."

He then asked his preceptor the brahmin: "Where shall I perform the sacrifice?"

5. He said : "O excellent king, there are Devayajanas (places for the worship of Devas) at different places where excellent brahmins performed great sacrifices."

6. Ten sacrifices were simultaneously performed by the priest. In that sacrifice in a group, a number of sages were employed as Ṛtviks.

7-8. Avoiding Devayajana, the priest had initiated the sacrifices in another place. Hence defects and obstacles over-

1. A sacred place in Kurukṣetra (MBh, Vanaparva, 9.14)

whelmed him. The sacrifices could not be completed. On seeing them the king was extremely worried. On observing the sacrifice incomplete the king spoke to the preceptor.

The king said :

9. Is it because of the defect of place, or of the defect of time, or my defect or your defect that the ten horse sacrifices have not become complete?

Brahmā said :

10. The grief-stricken king accompanied by his preceptor Kaśyapa went to Saṁvarta the elder brother of Bṛhaspati. They spoke to him.

Kaśyapa and Bhauvana said :

11. O holy sage, the bestower of honour, ten horse-sacrifices have to be performed simultaneously. Tell us about the place and the preceptor thereof so that all the ten will be completed.

Brahmā said :

12. The excellent sage Saṁvarta meditated for a while and spoke to Bhauvana: "Go to Brahmā. He will tell you about the preceptor and the place of sacrifice."

13. Bhauvana of great intellect came to me accompanied by the noble Kaśyapa. They asked me about the preceptor, place of sacrifice and other things.

14. Then O dear son, I spoke to Bhauvana and Kaśyapa: "O leading king, go to Gautamī. That place is highly meritorious for sacrifices.

15-16. This Kaśyapa alone is your excellent preceptor. He is a master of Vedas. By the grace of this preceptor as well as of Gautamī, with a single horse sacrifice and the holy ablution therein, O king, you will achieve the benefit of ten horse sacrifices."

17. On hearing it the king Bhauvana went to the banks of Gautamī with Kaśyapa to assist him. He got himself initiated for the horse sacrifice.

18-19. Then the horse sacrifice, the lord of Yajñas was begun. When it was completed, the king became ready to offer the whole of the Earth. Then an ethereal voice addressed the excellent king who was standing by after worshipping the brahmins, the Ṛtviks and Sadaspatis[1] (types of priests).

The Ethereal Voice said :

20-22. O king, everything has been given by you who are desirous of giving the whole Earth with mountains, forests and parks to Kaśyapa, your priest.

Eschew your desire to give the Earth as gift. Offer food that yields great results. There is no meritorious thing like the gift of food in all the three worlds particularly on the bank of Gaṅgā if it is given with great faith, O sage.

This horse sacrifice with many monetary gifts has been performed by you. You are satisfied, welfare unto thee. No worry need be felt.

Brahmā said :

23-25. Still Bhauvana wanted to give the Earth away as gift. The Earth said to him then again and again:

The Earth said :

O son of Viśvakarman, do not give me away. If a person goes to the banks of Gautamī and gives a morsel of food it is as good as though I have been given wholly. Why do you give me then, O Bhauvana? I shall sink into water. It behoves you not to give me.

Brahmā said :

26. Then Bhauvana became afraid. He asked, "What then, should be given?" Again the Earth addressed Bhauvana surrounded by the brahmins.

The Earth said :

27-28. Gingelly seeds, cows, money, grains—whatever is given on the banks of Gautamī is everlasting in its benefit. Why then, do you give me, Bhauvana? If a person goes to the banks of Gaṅgā and gives a morsel of food, it is as good as though I have been given wholly. Why do you give me then, O Bhauvana?

Brahmā said :

29-30. On hearing the words of the Earth Bhauvana, the ruler of the whole world, considered that it should be so. He

1. Lit. lord of the seat or sacrificial assembly.

then gave food to the brahmins on a big scale. Ever since then, people know it to be Daśāśvamedhika Tīrtha. By taking bath there, the fruit of ten horse sacrifices is acquired.

CHAPTER FOURTEEN

Paiśāca Tīrtha

Brahmā said :

1-4 Another holy centre is the Paiśāca Tīrtha. It is honoured by persons who expound the doctrine of Brahman. I shall recount to you its form and features. On the southern bank of Gautamī, at the side of Brahmagiri, O Nārada, there is a mountain Añjana. On that mountain, O excellent sage, there was an excellent celestial damsel Añjanā. She had a downfall due to a curse. Her face resembled that of a monkey. Her husband's names was Kesarī. Adrikā was another wife of Kesarī. She too was a celestial damsel who had a downfall due to a curse. Her face and head resembled those of a cat. She too stayed on the Añjana mountain.

5. Once Kesarī who was well known in the world went to the southern sea. In the meantime sage Agastya came to that Añjana mountain.

6. Both of them, viz. Añjanā and Adrikā worshipped the excellent sage Agastya duly and pleasingly.

7. Then the delighted holy sage said to them, "Let a boon be chosen". They said to Agastya, "O lord of sages, give us two sons.

8. They should be stronger than all others and more excellent too. They should be persons who render help to the whole world".

Saying "So be it", that sage went to the southern quarter.

9-12. Once Añjanā and Adrikā were singing, dancing and laughing on the top of the mountain.

The two Devas, Vāyu and Nirṛti saw them and smiled. They were overwhelmed by lust and they rushed to those ladies. They said, "We are Devas, the bestowers of boons. Be our wives".

They too replied, "Let it be so". They then sported about on the top of the mountain. Hanūmān was born of Añjanā and Vāyu. The king of Piśācas (evil spirits) named Adri was born of Adrikā and Nirṛti.

13-14. Then the ladies said, "Due to the boon of the sage sons are born to us. Our form is ugly and distorted. It is defiled at the head and face due to the curse of Indra. It behoves you to know about this." Then Lord Vāyu and Nirṛti spoke:

15. "By taking bath in Gautamī you will be released from the curse". After saying this the two delighted Devas vanished there itself.

16. Then, for the sake of pleasing his brother Hanūmān, Adri who had the form and features of a Piśāca took Añjanā, his mother and made her take her bath.

17-20. In the same manner Hanūmān took Adri whose form was that of a cat, to Gaṅgā and rushed to the banks of Gautamī.

Thenceforward that holy centre was well known as Paiśāca and Añjana. (Being) near the mountain of Brahmā that is auspicious. It yields all desired things. The holy centre Mārjāra extended to fiftythree Yojanas to the east. Away from the holy centre Mārjāra is the holy centre Hanūmanta and Vṛṣākapi. The confluence of Phenā is the bestower of all desired things. Its form, nature and situation is recounted there itself.

CHAPTER FIFTEEN

Kṣudhā Tīrtha

Brahmā said :

1. Listen attentively, O Nārada. The holy centre well known as Kṣudhā Tīrtha is being recounted. It is highly meritorious and it bestows all desired things to men.

2. Formerly, there was a sage Kaṇva. He performed penance and he was the most excellent among those who were conversant with the Vedas. Once wandering among penance-groves he was afflicted by hunger.

3-7 Gautama's holy hermitage was richly endowed with food and water. He saw himself hungry and Gautama prosperous. He noticed this incongruity and became detached. He thought, "Gautama is an excellent brahmin. I too am a person well-established in penance. Begging of a person equal to one in status is not proper. Even though I am overcome by hunger, even when my body is afflicted, I am not going to take food in the abode of Gautama. I shall go to Gautamī Gaṅgā and earn wealth". After deciding like this the intelligent sage went to the sacred Gaṅgā. After taking bath he sat on the Kuśa grass with controlled mind. He eulogized Gautamī Gaṅgā and Kṣudhā (hunger), the greatest distressing thing.

Kaṇva said :

8. Gaṅgā, obeisance be to you, the destroyer of agony and distress, and to you, O Hunger, the cause of agony and distress to all the people.

Obeisance O splendid one, born of the matted hair of Maheśāna.

Obeisance O Kṣudhā coming out of the mouth of great Death.

9. O Gautamī assuming a calm form in regard to meritorious souls and furious form in regard to the wicked souls ! O destroyer of the distress and sins of all, in the form of a river !

10. Obeisance be to you, the bestower of agony, distress and sin, to all in the form of hunger.

Obeisance O goddess, the cause of welfare and the suppressor of sins.

Obeisance O goddess, the cause of peace. Obeisance, O destroyer of poverty.

Brahmā said :

11. As he eulogized thus two forms appeared in front of him, one the charming form of Gaṅgā and the other the terrible form of Kṣudhā. After bowing down with palms joined in reverence, the excellent brahmin said.

Kaṇva said :

12. Obeisance be to you O Godāvarī, the cause of all auspicious things, O Brāhmī (belonging to Brahma), O Māheś-

varī (belonging to Maheśvara), O splendid Vaiṣṇavī (belonging to Viṣṇu), O three-eyed goddess!

13. Obeisance be to you, O Godāvarī, born of the matted hair of the three-eyed lord, the destroyer of sins of Gautama, O river that flows into the sea in seven channels!

14. O goddess Hunger obeisance, obeisance to you, O sinner unto all sinful persons, O destroyer of virtue, love and wealth, full of misery and greed!

Brahmā said:

15-17 On hearing the words of Kaṇva both of them were delighted and they spoke to the brahmin.

Gaṅgā & Kṣudhā said:

O (sage) of good holy rites, O cause of welfare, mention your desire. Choose boons.

Brahmā said:

Kaṇva bowed down to Gaṅgā and Kṣudhā in due order and said:

Kaṇva said:

18. O Gaṅgā, O goddess, give unto me wealth and all charming and cherished desires, long life, enjoyment of worldly pleasures and salvation.

Brahmā said:

19-23 After saying this to Gautamī Gaṅgā, the excellent brahmin said to Hunger.

Kaṇva said:

O hunger, O thirst, O wretched one, never be in me or in anyone born of my family. O extremely sinful and harsh one, go away.

This is another boon I wish for. If persons afflicted by hunger were to eulogize you with this hymn let them not have miseries of poverty.

Let those men who devoutly perform such sacred rites as holy ablution, charitable gifts, chanting of Japas etc. in this holy centre of great merit become rich. Another boon I wish for is this—If a person reads this hymn whether in the holy centre or in the house, let him not have the fear from poverty and miseries.

Brahmā said :

24. After saying "So be it" to Kaṇva both of them went to their respective abodes. Thenceforward that holy centre was called Kaṇva, Gaṅgā and Kṣudhā. O dear one, it dispels all sins and increases the delight of manes.

CHAPTER SIXTEEN

Indra-Tīrtha: Ahalyāsaṅgama-Tīrtha

Brahmā said :

1. The holy centre named Ahalyā-Saṁgama is one that sanctifies the three worlds. O excellent sage, listen to what happened and how it happened.

2. Out of great curiosity, O lord of sages, many types of beautiful girls possessing good qualities had been formerly created by me.

3-6. Among them I created a girl of exquisitely splendid features. On seeing that most excellent girl of great beauty in every limb, I thought thus, "Who is capable of nurturing this girl ? Neither among the Asuras nor Devas is there anyone who has the ability to nurture her". This was my thought. Then I gave that highly intelligent girl to Gautama for bringing her up—to Gautama who was an intelligent brahmin superior to all in good qualities, who possessed the power of penance, who had all characteristics and who was conversant with the Vedas and Vedāṅgas.[1]

7-9. "Protect and bring up (this girl), O excellent sage, till she attains the age of youth. When she attains youth, bring her back to me". After saying this I gave that girl of slender waist to Gautama. The excellent sage whose sins had been dispelled by penance took her and nurtured her duly. The ex-

1. Disciplines auxiliary to the study of the Vedas.

cellent sage without any aberration brought Ahalyā near me after bedecking her duly.

10. On seeing her, Indra, Agni, Varuṇa and other Devas told me severally, "O lord of Devas, she should be given to me."

11-15. In the same manner the sages, Sādhyas, Dānavas, Yakṣaṣ and Rākṣasas also approached me. On seeing all of them gathered together for the sake of that girl Indra became all the more enamoured in particular.

I remembered the greatness, majesty, and courage of Gautama and was surprised. Then this good thought occurred to me, "This lady of splendid face should be given to Gautama alone. She is not suitable for anyone. I shall give her to him alone." I thought in this way also, "The mind and courage of everyone has been stirred up by this girl."

Then Devas and sages uttered "Ahalyā". I too said so. Looking at Devas and sages I said loudly again and again:

16. This lady of beautiful eyebrows will be given to that person who circumambulates the Earth and thereafter approaches me sooner than others and not to anyone else.

17. On hearing the words uttered by me, Devas proceeded ahead in their circumambulation of the Earth.

18. After Devas had gone Gautama, the lord of sages, too made some effort like this for the sake of Ahalyā.

19. In the meantime, O brahmin, the divine cow Kāmadhenu[1] had partially delivered her calf. Gautama saw her thus.

20. Remembering "This is the Earth" be circumambulated her. Then he circumambulated the Liṅga[2] of the lord of Devas.

21-22. After circumambulating both of them Gautama the excellent sage decided thus—"Devas have not completed even one round of the Earth. I have completed two rounds." After deciding thus, that sage came near me.

23. After bowing down to me Gautama of great intelligence said to me, "O lotus-seated lord, the soul of the universe, obeisance be to you again and again.

---

1. The wish-fulfilling cow born at the churning of the ocean by the gods and antigods.
2. The phallic symbol of Lord Śiva worshipped in the form of a stone column.

24. O Brahmā, the entire Earth has been circumambulated by me. What is proper in this connection? O lord of Devas, you know it better yourself".

25. By meditation I understood it and said to Gautama: "The lady of beautiful eyebrows will be given to you alone. The circumambulation has been completed.

26-29. O brahminical sage, Dharma (Virtue) is inscrutable even to the Vedas. The divine cow having partially delivered her calf is (identical with) the Earth consisting of seven continents. If that divine cow is circumambulated, the Earth too has been circumambulated. By circumambulating the Liṅga one shall obtain the same benefit. Hence, O sage Gautama of good holy rites, I am pleased with your effort, courage, knowledge and penance. O great sage, this girl, the most excellent one in the world is given to you." After saying this, O sage, I gave Ahalyā to Gautama.

30-31. After the wedding had been celebrated, Devas came there slowly. They had completed their circumambulation of the Earth. They saw Gautama, Ahalyā and their union that increased their pleasure. On seeing this after their arrival, Devas were surprised.

32. When the rites connected with the wedding were over Devas returned to heaven. The jealous husband of Śacī (wife of Indra) glanced at her (longingly) and went to heaven.

33. Delighted in my mind, I gave the sacred Brahmagiri which is splended and which bestows all cherished desires, to the noble Gautama.

34-35. The excellent sage Gautama indulged in dalliance there along with Ahalyā. Indra heard about this gift of Brahmā to Gautama in the heaven itself. In order to see that hermitage, sage Gautama and his uncensured wife, Indra assumed the guise of a brahmin and came there.

36. On seeing the sage's splendid beautiful wife and wealth Indra felt jealous and an evil thought entered his mind.

37. O dear one, Indra who was full of lust did not realize the risk; he was not aware of the time and place or even the danger of curse from sage Gautama.

38-41. Arrogant due to his overlordship of the kingdom of the Devas, he was meditating upon her alone continuously. He felt his limbs scorched by the pangs of passion. He was always thinking thus, "How shall I make myself content? How shall I enter this hermitage?"

Though he stayed there in the guise of a brahmin he did not succeed in getting an opportunity to go inside.

Once the highly intelligent sage Gautama performed his morning rituals and went out of the hermitage along with his disciples. The excellent sage went out to visit the penance grove on the Gautamī river, the brahmins and different kinds of cultivated grains. Indra saw him going out saying (to himself) "This is the opportunity". He did what was pleasing to his mind.

42. Indra who was desirous of attaining pleasures assumed the form of Gautama. Looking at Ahalyā who was beautiful in every respect he spoke to her.

Indra said :

43. "I am attracted by your good qualities. Remembering your beauty I have begun to falter in my steps." Saying this and grasping her hand he went inside the hermitage.

44. Ahalyā did not know that he was a paramour. She believed him to be Gautama and indulged in sexual dalliance with him as she pleased. Meanwhile Gautama came there along with his disciples.

45. Everyday it was the custom of Ahalyā to welcome him as he returned speaking pleasing words to him and satisfying him by her graceful qualities.

46. On this occasion he was unable to see her. The highly intelligent sage Gautama considered it a highly surprising mystery. O Nārada, the people looked at the excellent sage standing at the door.

47. The watchman and the domestic servants at the hall of Agnihotra sacrifice were awestruck and surprised. They spoke to the excellent sage Gautama.

The Watchman said :

48. "What a mystery is this, O holy sage, you are seen both inside and outside. You entered the house accompanied by your beloved. You are outside also. Oh the power of your penance is wonderful! You can assume different forms at your will."

Brahmā said :

49-50. On hearing it, the sage was surprised. "Who has entered inside? Who is standing there? O dear Ahalyā, why don't you reply?" On hearing these words of the sage Ahalyā spoke to the paramour.

Ahalyā said :

51-53. "Who are you ? In the guise of the sage you have committed a sin". Saying this she hurriedly got up from her bed in great fear. Indra the sinner became a cat due to the fear of the sage.

On seeing his beloved Ahalyā outraged and defiled the sage said furiously, "What is this rash act? Why has it been committed?"

Although her husband said this, she did not say anything in reply because she was too much ashamed.

54. The sage saw a cat distressed by fear and moving about surreptitiously. He said to him, "Who are you? If you utter a lie I will reduce you to ashes."

55-58. With palms joined together in reverence, Indra said thus.

Indra said :

"O ascetic, I am the husband of Śacī, the breaker of towns, one who has been eulogized much. This sin has been committed by me. O sinless one, I have spoken the truth. O sage, I have committed an excessively despicable act. What is it that those whose hearts are pierced by the arrows of cupid do not do? O brahmin, O storehouse of compassion, forgive me, a great sinner. Good men are never harsh towards a person even if he has committed a guilt."

On hearing his words the brahmin said to Indra in great anger.

Gautama said :

59. "Sin has been committed by you due to your passion for the vagina. Hence become a person with a thousand vaginas in your body".

He said to Ahalyā also in anger, "Be a dry river".

60-63. (Defective text). Narrating her wrong action she tried to pacify him.

Ahalyā said :

"If women were to love other men even mentally they will be eternally doomed. They should treat all persons as their brothers. Be pleased, O holy sage, and listen to my words. He approached me assuming your form. These persons are my witnesses."

"It is so", said the watchmen, "Ahalyā speaks the truth".

The sage knew the truth by means of meditation too. Becoming calm he said to the chaste lady:

Gautama said :

64. "O fair lady, when you come into contact with the Gautamī, the chief of rivers, you will become a river and thereafter will regain your own form that is pleasing to me".

65-66. On hearing these words of the sage the chaste lady did so. Ahalyā the beloved wife of Gautama came into contact with the divine river. Thereafter she attained that form which had been created by me formerly.

Then, with his palms joined in reverence the king of Devas said to Gautama.

Indra said :

67-68. "O mighty among the sages, save me. Save me. A sinner (no doubt) but I have come to your house as a guest."

On seeing him fallen at his feet Gautama said mercifully: "I have been pacified by Devas, wishing to free you from my curse." Gautama the most excellent sage said:

Gautama said :

69-71. "By taking bath in the sacred holy centre Ahalyā Saṅgama, O husband of Śacī, you will be rid of your sins instantly and will become one with a thousand eyes".

I have witnessed both these surprising events, O Nārada, viz., the resurgence of Ahalyā and the transformation of Indra into a person with a thousand eyes.

Thenceforward that pure holy centre became well known as Ahalyā-Saṅgama and Indra-Tīrtha. It bestows all cherished desires on men.

CHAPTER SEVENTEEN

Janasthāna Tīrtha

Brahmā said :

1-4. There is still another holy centre well known as Janasthāna. It extends to four Yojanas. It bestows salvation on men even by remembering it.

Formerly, there was a king Janaka born in the solar dynasty. He married Guṇārṇavā (ocean of virtue), the daughter of the lord of waters (i.e. Varuṇa).

King Janaka married Guṇārṇavā, the generator of virtue, wealth, love and liberation. In view of her befitting good qualities she was really Guṇārṇavā (ocean of virtue).

Yājñavalkya the leading brahmin was the priest of that king. The excellent king asked his priest Yājñavalkya:

Janaka said :

5-7. Enjoyment of worldly pleasures as well as salvation—these two are the most excellent as declared by the greatest of sages. Enjoyment of worldly pleasures is excellent through men, maidservants, elephants, horses, chariots etc. But in the end all is sapless. It is salvation alone that bestows immortality and therefore salvation is more excellent than enjoyment. How can one attain salvation through enjoyment?

The attainment of salvation by eschewal of attachment is a strenuous task. Hence, tell me, O greatest of sages, how can salvation be easily achieved?

Yājñavalkya said :

8-9. O king, the lord of waters (Varuṇa) is your father-in-law and well-wisher. Hence, he can be your preceptor. Go to him and ask. He will instruct you in what is conducive to your welfare.

Yājñavalkya and Janaka went to king Varuṇa and unperturbed they asked him about the path of liberation in the proper order.

Varuṇa said :

10. Salvation is effected in two ways: (i) through Karmans (holy rites) and (ii) through Akarman (refraining from work).

The path decided in the Veda is this. Karman is more conducive to welfare than Akarman.

11. Everything including the four aims of life, is bound with Karman. It is not true that the path of salvation is obtained by Akarman alone.

12. All grains are obtained, O excellent king, through Karman. Hence Vaidic Karmans should be wholeheartedly performed by men.

13-15. Men obtain (enjoyment of pleasures) and salvation through that Karman. Karman is based on birth in the various stages in life.

O leading king, conversant with piety and bestower of honour, the four stages are realized through Karmans.

Among the four stages that of the householder is remembered as the bestower of merit. It is my opinion that enjoyment and salvation are possible in the householder's life.

Brahmā said :

16. On hearing this, King Janaka and Sage Yājñavalkya honoured Varuṇa and spoke these words again:

17. "What is that place, what is that holy centre, which bestows worldly pleasures and liberation? Tell us, O excellent Deva, you are omniscient. Obeisance be to you."

Varuṇa said :

18. In the whole of the Earth the sub-continent of Bhārata is the most meritorious. In the continent of Bhārata, Daṇḍaka is the most meritorious. Karman performed in that region is the bestower of worldly pleasures and salvation to men.

19. Among holy centres, Gautamī Gaṅgā is the most excellent. It bestows salvation. By means of sacrifice and charitable gifts performed there, one shall obtain worldly pleasures and salvation.

Brahmā said :

20. On hearing the words of the lord of waters, Yājñavalkya and Janaka went to their city after being permitted by Varuṇa.

21. King Janaka performed horse sacrifice and other holy rites. Yājñavalkya the leading brahmin made that king perform the sacrifice.

22-26. Resorting to the bank of Gaṅgā, king Janaka attained liberation through sacrifice. So also, many kings attained liberation by the grace of Gautamī. Thenceforward that holy centre is known as Janasthāna. Since it was the seat of many sacrifices, it is glorified as Janasthāna. It extends to four Yojanas. On being remembered, it dispels all sins.

One shall obtain all cherished desires. One shall even obtain salvation by taking bath or offering charitable gifts or by performing oblations to the manes or by remembering the holy centre or by approaching it or by resorting to it devoutly.

CHAPTER EIGHTEEN

Cakratīrtha

Brahmā said :

1. O Brahmin, there is a great holy centre well known as Cakratīrtha. By taking holy ablution there with devotion a man shall obtain the world of Viṣṇu.

2. O King, if one fasts on the eleventh day of the bright lunar fortnight and takes bath in the Gaṇikā Saṅgama one shall attain the everlasting region.

3. Even as I recount what had happened there formerly, listen to it.

There was a Vaiśya of plenty of wealth. His name was Viśvadhara.

4. When he was much advanced in age, O sage, an excellent son was born to him. He possessed all good qualities. He was very handsome. He was indulgent in sports. He was splendid in appearance.

5. The son who was dear to them more than their life passed away untimely. On seeing him dead the parents were afflicted by misery.

6-7. They became inclined to die along with him. They lamented: "O son, you were in the prime of youth. You were an ocean of virtue. Still you have been taken away by the sinful and evil-minded god of death. You are dearer to us than even our life breath".

8-10. On hearing their lamentation thus Yama's mind became overwhelmed by sympathy. On hearing the piteous cry of the couple, Yama abandoned his city and went to Godāvarī. Seated on its banks he began to meditate on Janārdana. Within a short while everywhere, all round, the subjects became old, very old. The whole Earth was filled with old people so much so that they began to say: "My ground extends this much. Let it be said. By whom was it filled?" No living creature died. The Earth was over-burdened.

11. Thereupon, O excellent sage, the goddess of Earth went to the place where Indra, the conqueror of enemies' cities, was seated along with the Devas. On seeing the Earth Indra bowed to her and said this.

Indra said :

12. O Earth, What is the purpose of your arrival here? May it be said.

Earth said :

13. O Indra, I am afflicted by a heavy burden, in the absence of death. I have come here to enquire about the cause thereof. May it be mentioned to me.

Brahmā said :

14-18. On hearing these words of the Earth Indra spoke these words.

Indra said :

If there is any cause, O Earth, it will be known by me. I am the lord of all Devas.

Brahmā said :

Then, on hearing his words the Earth said to Indra:

Then, let Yama be ordered so that he would annihilate the subjects.

On hearing these words of the Earth Siddhas and Kinnaras were ordered to bring Yama quickly, O great sage, by Mahendra. Thereafter all of them, Sidhas along with Kinnaras, immediately went to the city of Yama. There they did not see Yama. After returning hurriedly they made a report to Indra.

Siddhas and Kinnaras said :

19. O lord, although he was searched for all round strenuously, Yama was not seen by us in the city of Yama.

Brahmā said :

20. On hearing these words of Siddhas and Kinnaras, Savitṛ (the sun) who was his father was asked by Indra, "Where is Yama?"

The Sum said :

21. O Indra, Yama is now on the banks of Godāvarī performing a very severe penance. I do not know what the reason is.

Brahmā said :

22-23. On hearing these words of the Sun Indra became suspicious.

Indra said :

Alas ! Woeful ! O woeful ! My lordship of Devas has come to an end. Yama of evil activities performing penance at Godāvarī ! It is my opinion that he is surely desirous of seizing my position, O Devas.

Brahmā said :

24-25. After saying this, the celestial damsels were immediately summoned by Indra.

Indra said :

May this be quickly mentioned to me, who among you is capable of spoiling the penance of my enemy Yama who is performing austerities on the banks of the Gautamī river?

Brahmā said :

26. Even on hearing these words of Indra, O great sage, no one said anything. Then in great rage Indra said to celestial damsels.

Indra said :

27. No one has replied to me. Therefore we ourselves shall go. Let all Devas be ready. Let them, without any delay, come with their armies. We shall slay our enemy who is desirous of ruling over heaven by means of his penance.

Brahmā said :

28-30. When this was said, the army of Devas appeared there.

On coming to know about the motive of Indra, the discus-bearing lord Hari, the preserver of worlds, sent his discus for the protection of Yama. Where the discus appeared is the excellent holy centre Cakratīrtha.

Then Menakā who was suspicious about the outcome said to Indra:

31-32. "O lord of Devas, no one among us is capable of even looking at Yama. It is better to die at your hands than at Yama's. Amongst us, that harlot Kṣamā is proud of her beauty and youth. Request her and send her to dissuade Yama, if you, O lord, consider it necessary."

Brahmā said :

33. On hearing her words, Indra the lord of Devas, ordered Kṣamā after duly honouring her.

Indra said :

34. O harlot, go. Carry out my task, beautiful woman. If you fulfil it and return, you shall be as dear to me as Śacī.

Brahmā said :

35. On hearing the words of Indra, Kṣamā flew over the quarters. The beautiful lady came near Yama in a moment.

36. Brightening the ten quarters the lady came near Yama. She sang the sweet Hindolaka song in an exquisitely graceful style.

37-40. Then the delicate tremulous mind of Yama was moved. He opened his eyes filled (as though) with the fire of passion, O great sage, and stared at her although she was a hindrance to his welfare. Thereafter the lady immediately became melted and attained the state of a river. This harlot joined the river Gautamī. Her songs of praise were sung by the Gaṇas and Kiṅkaras. Due to the power of the holy centre she ascended to heaven. On seeing the harlot going to heaven seated in an aerial chariot, Yama of tremulous eyes was surprised very much.

Then the Sun came there and said to Yama:

The Sun said :

41. Carry out, dear Son, your duty of annihilating the subjects. See the wind that blows always, Brahmā who creates subjects, Earth that carries them and me who wander over the three worlds.

Brahmā said :

42-43. On hearing the words of his father, Yama said:

Yama said :

Surely I shall not carry on this despicable work. It does not behove you to command me to do this extremely cruel task.

44-46. On hearing the words of Yama the Sun spoke thus: "O Yama, how is your duty despicable ? It is proper for you to do (this work). Did you not see that that harlot on having plunged into the waters of Gautamī went to heaven immediately, even as the Gaṇas and Kiṅkaras were singing songs of her praise.

Oh son, severe penance has been performed by you. It is very difficult to do. I do not see its end. Hence go to your city."

47-49. On saying these words lord Sun took his bath and went to heaven. Yama too had his bath at the confluence and went to his city.

The slayer of the living beings cast off his doubts, O great sage. On seeing Yama go, the discus too went away to the place where Govinda embellished with the garlands of sylvan flowers, was present. The man who reads this or listens to this narrative shall obtain long life. All his adversities shall perish.

CHAPTER NINETEEN

Aśvabhānu Tīrtha

Brahmā said :

1-3. The two rivers Aruṇā and Varuṇā are very auspicious. Their confluence with Gaṅgā is also very holy, O excellent sage.

They bestow merit more than the lake Mānasa, the holy centre Prayāga and the river Mandākinī. Listen now to its origin which destroys all sins.

The eldest son of Kaśyapa, Āditya, is well known in the worlds. He is the eye of the three worlds. He has hot and powerful rays. He has seven horses to draw his chariot. He is honoured by the people of the world. Uṣā, the daughter of Tvaṣṭṛ, was well known as the most beautiful woman in the three worlds.

4. Unable to endure the severity of the heat of her husband, the beautiful woman of good waistline thought, "What should be done by me?"

5. The extremely intelligent Manu and Yama were her sons born of Vivasvān (Sun). The holy river Yamunā (too was her daughter). Listen to that incident which caused surprise.

6-8. She created her own shadow strenuously in the form of herself. Uṣā then said to her:

"Be like me. At my bidding, look after my husband and children. Till I come back, be the beloved of my husband. Neither to my children nor to my husband should you reveal this fact".

"So be it", said the shadow.

Uṣā went out of her abode.

9. After saying this she went ahead, desirous of peaceful form. After going home Uṣā mentioned everything to her father. Tvaṣṭṛ was surprised. Being fond of his daughter he said to her:

Tvaṣṭṛ said :

10. It is not proper on the part of a married woman to do as she pleases. How do your children and husband do? O gentle lady, I am afraid I may be considered uncultured. Go back to your husband's abode once again.

Brahmā said :

11. Thus urged by her father she said "No, No" again and again. She went to the Northern Kuru country for performing penance.

12. There she assumed the form of a mare and performed a severe penance. Uṣā steadily meditated upon her husband who was too fierce to be looked at.

13. In the meantime, O dear one, the shadow Chāyā who had assumed the form of Uṣā, cohabited with her husband. Children were born to her.

14-17. (The sons were) Manu Sāvarṇi and Śani. Viṣṭi, a wicked daughter, was also born. Chāyā behaved differently to her own children and the children of Uṣā. Yama therefore became angry. Yama the lord of southern quarter kicked his step. mother Chāyā who was behaving differently. In her excitement due to the wickedness of her step-son Chāyā cursed Yama, son of the Sun god.

"O sinner, may your foot become putrefied at my bidding." With his foot putrefied he went to his father crying. He informed Savitṛ of the entire episode.

Yama said :

18-21. O excellent Deva, she is not my mother because I have been cursed by her thus. A (true) mother never gets angry even if children act against her wish. I might have uttered something due to my stupidity. I might have done something mischievous. If she had been my mother she would not have become angry. Hence she is not my mother.

Mother is so called because everything child does, whether good or bad, becomes measured in her. O dear father, she stares at me everyday as though she would burn me. She speaks to me with words as ferocious as black fire. She is not my mother.

Brahmā said :

22-24. On hearing this from his son Sun began to think (and understood). "This is Chāyā and not Uṣā. Desirous of quietening me she is engaged in penance. The daughter of Tvaṣṭṛ is in the northern Kuru in the form of a mare."

On coming to know that she was there Lord Sun went thither

where his wife was staying. He himself assumed the form of a horse.

25-28. On seeing her in the form of a mare, the sun in the form of a horse rushed at her. On seeing the horse excited by passion and on hearing the sound, Uṣā the chaste lady hurriedly fled to the South. She had been meditating on her husband. She was afraid of being attacked by the horse. She did not know who it was. When the husband approached her she fled to the South in great hurry. "Who will be my saviour now, the sages or the Devas?" She thought herself. The sun in the form of a horse pursued his beloved who was running fast. Wherever Uṣā went the sun also went there.

29-31. If anyone comes under the influence of Cupid, what wicked thing does he not do? Facing the southern direction they crossed Bhāgirathī, Narmadā and other rivers, parks, forests and Vindhya mountain. Distressed with fear, the daughter of Tvaṣṭṛ went to Gautamī because she had heard that in Janasthāna there were sages who could protect her. After entering Gautamī, the mare went to the hermitage of sages.

32. The horse too came there. It was the Sun in that form. People who were staying in Janasthāna stopped that horse. Lord Sun, the husband of Uṣā, then cursed them in anger.

The Sun said :

33-36. Since you stopped me you will become banyan trees.

Brahmā said :

By their eye of knowledge the sages saw that he was the husband of Uṣā. Thereupon they eulogized the lord of Devas in great delight.

Even as he was being eulogized by the sages the Sun approached the mare sexually. The face of the horse came into contact with the face of the mare. After realising that it was her husband, the daughter of Tvaṣṭṛ shed the semen from her month. From their semen the Aśvins were born in the river Gaṅgā.

37-40. The following persons came there, viz. groups of Devas, Siddhas, sages, rivers, cows, medicinal herbs, groups of luminaries, holy chariot of the seven-horsed lord (i.e. Sun), Aruṇa the charioteer of the Sun, Yama, Manu, Varuṇa, Śani son of the Sun god, the holy river Yamunā, Tāpī, Mahānadī and father-in-law of the Sun (i.e. Tvaṣṭṛ). O sages, out of wonder, the rivers had assumed their respective forms. They came there to see this wonderful event. On realising his purpose Sun spoke to his father-in-law.

The Sun said :

41. O Tvaṣṭṛ, mount me on to the lathe and chisel off my splendorous parts for pleasing Uṣā who has performed excellent penance. O Prajāpati, you cut off my parts until she finds herself pleased.

Brahmā said :

42. After saying "So be it", Tvaṣṭṛ began to cut off the splendorous parts of the Sun in the presence of Somanātha. They know it as Prabhāsa.

43-47. The place where Uṣā in the form of a mare came into contact with her husband, the place where Aśvins were born, is called Aśvatīrtha.

It is also called Bhānutīrtha where there is the hermitage with five banyan trees. Tāpī and Yamunā came there to see their father (i.e. the Sun). The confluence of the rivers Aruṇā and Varuṇā with the Gaṅgā is splendid.

There are nine times three thousand (i.e. 27000) holy centres of Devas there severally pertaining to Devas who had come to that holy centre. All these holy centres are good. Ablution performed and charitable gifts distributed there bestow great and everlasting merit.

O Nārada, by remembring, reading and listening to this, man becomes rid of all sins. He becomes virtuous and happy.

CHAPTER TWENTY

Garuḍa Tīrtha

Brahmā said :

1. The holy centre named Garuḍa destroys all obstacles. I shall recount its power, O Nārada, listen to it attentively.

2. There was an extremely powerful son of Śeṣa named Maṇināga. Afraid of Garuḍa he propitiated Śaṅkara with devotion.

3. Then the lord Maheśvara, Parameṣṭhin became pleased. He said to the great Nāga, "O Nāga, choose a boon".

4. The Nāga said, "O lord, grant me the boon of freedom from Garuḍa".

"So be it", said Śambhu to him, "You shall have freedom from the fear of Garuḍa".

5. The Nāga who was not afraid of Garuḍa, the younger brother of Aruṇa, went out to the place near the milk ocean where Viṣṇu was taking rest.

6. The Nāga wandered here and there over the place which was pleasingly chill. He went to the place which was occupied by Garuḍa.

7. On seeing the Nāga moving about fearlessly Garuḍa seized him and took him off into his own abode.

8. By means of nooses, Garuḍa bound the mighty Nāga. In the meantime, Nandin said to Īśa, the lord of the universe:

Nandikeśvara said :

9. Certainly the Nāga has been either swallowed or imprisoned by Garuḍa, O lord of Devas. Hence he does not come. The nāga may not come out alive.

Brahmā said :

10-13. On hearing the words of Nandin and understanding the situation himself Śiva said:

Śiva said :

The Nāga has been bound and imprisoned in the abode of Garuḍa. Go quickly and tell the lord of worlds, Viṣṇu. At my instance, you, yourself, bring the Nāga bound by Garuḍa, son of Kaśyapa.

On hearing the words of lord Śiva Nandin went and intimated to the lord of Śrī, the ultimate resort of the world, Viṣṇu, (the details).

Pleased in his mind Nārāyaṇa spoke to Garuḍa:

Viṣṇu said :

14. O son of Vinatā (Garuḍa), give Nandin the Nāga at my instance.

Vainateya the bird understood it but said "No". In the presence of Nandin, Garuḍa spoke to Viṣṇu in anger:

Garuḍa said :

15-19. Other masters give their servants whatever is most pleasing to them but you do not do so. Instead you want to take away what has been acquired by me.

See, the three-eyed lord wishes to release the Nāga through Nandin. But you wish to give Nandin the Nāga captured by me.

I bear you always along the path. Hence something should be given to me by you always. It is not proper for you to say "Give" in regard to the Nāga acquired by me.

This cannot be the practice of good masters who wish to maintain good service. Good men give unto the servants. But you are one who takes away what has been brought by me.

O Keśava, it is through my power that you conquer the asuras in battles. In vain do you boast, I am extremely powerful.

Brahmā said :

20-24. On hearing these words of Garuḍa Viṣṇu the bearer of discus and club laughed in the presence of Nandin even as the guardians of the worlds were watching.

The extremely intelligent lord said this: "You have become lean by bearing me (regularly). It is due to your power that I conquer Asuras, O excellent bird."

After saying this, O brahmin, the lord of Śrī spoke this, with his anger calmed down: "Be quick. Bear the small finger of my hand, in the presence of Nandin."

Placing the small finger of his hand over the head of Garuḍa Viṣṇu said again:

"It is true that you carry me always. See to your duty, O bird."

When the finger was placed over his head the head penetrated into his belly and the belly went inside the foot and became smashed. Then, the distressed Garuḍa said piteously out of shame, with palms joined in reverence:

Garuḍa said :

25-28. Save me, save me, O lord of the universe, your

servant. You are the lord of all gentle and submissive worlds. You are the supporter and the supported also. Those who are powerful, forgive thousands of offences. All the sages call you merciful since you have great sympathy even for those who have committed offences.

O mother, residing in the lotus, O mother of the Universe, save me who am distressed. O Kamalā, fond of your son, save me who am miserable and wretched.

Brahmā said :

Then the merciful goddess Śrī spoke to Janārdana:

Kamalā said :

29. O lord, save your own servant Garuḍa who has been involved in adversity".

Thereupon Janārdana spoke to Nandin the attendant of Śiva:

Viṣṇu said :

30-31. Take the Nāga to Śiva along with Garuḍa. On being glanced at by Maheśvara and favoured by him Garuḍa will regain his own form.

Brahmā said :

After saying "So be it" Nandin went to Śiva along with the Nāga and Garuḍa and intimated everything to him. Śiva, who has the crescent moon on his forehead spoke to Garuḍa:

Śiva said :

32-33. O hero of long arms, go to Gaṅgā, Gautamī the sanctifier of worlds. She is calm and bestower of all cherished desires. After plunging into it you will regain your body and all cherished desires.

O bird, Gautamī, the bestower of all desired things, is the refuge for all living beings whose enterprises are ruined by adverse fate and who are tormented by all sins in hundreds and thousands of ways.

Brahmā said :

34-36. Garuḍa listened to his words with humility. He went to Gaṅgā. After plunging into it he bowed down to Śiva and Viṣṇu. Then the bird of golden complexion regained his adamantine body and great strength. Hurrying up, O excellent sage, the intelligent one went again to Viṣṇu.

Thenceforward that holy centre of Garuḍa became the bestower of all desires.

If a man of purity in mind and body performs the holy ablution, O dear one, everything becomes everlasting in its benefit. The centre is pleasing to Śiva and Viṣṇu.

CHAPTER TWENTYONE

Govardhana Tīrtha

Brahmā said :

1. Then there is the Govardhana Tīrtha which destroys all sins. It generates merits unto all ancestors. Even on being remembered it dispels sins.

2. Its power has been tested by me, O Nārada.

There was a certain brahmin farmer known as Jābāli.

3. Even at midday he never rested his bullocks. He hit them with his whip on their backs and sides.

4. On seeing those bullocks full of tears in their eyes, the cow Kāmadhenu, the mother of the worlds, said to Nandin.

5. Nandin too was distressed and intimated everything to Śiva. Śiva said to the Bull, "May whatever you say be fulfilled."

6-7. Backed by Śiva's permission Nandin withdrew all the bovine species. When all cattle had vanished in heaven and in the mortal world, Devas came to me in hurry and said: "It is impossible to live without cows". I then told them, "Go to lord Śiva and request him".

8. In the same manner they eulogized Śiva and intimated to him the matter under reference. Śiva said to Devas, "My Bull knows everything".

9-10. Those Devas spoke to the Bull, "Give us the cows and bullocks that are helpful to us".

The Bull said to Devas, "Let the sacrifice Gosava be performed. Thereby you will obtain all cows both divine and human."

Then the sacrifice Gosava was performed by Devas.

11-13. The sacrifice was performed on the auspicious banks of Gautamī. Then the cattle flourished. That holy centre was named Govardhana and it increased the pleasure of Devas. The holy ablution performed there, O excellent sage, yields the benefit of gifts of thousands of cows. We do not know what the benefit will be if any charitable gift is made.

By seeing Śiva, the lord of Devas, the presiding deity Gautameśvara, one attains heavenly world as long as the mountain Meru lasts on Earth.

CHAPTER TWENTYTWO

Pāpapraṇāśana Tīrtha

Brahmā said :

1. There is the holy centre named Pāpapraṇāśana (Destroyer of sins). It dispels the fear of sins. I shall recount it, O Nārada. Listen to it attentively.

2. There was a brahmin known as Dhṛtavrata. His wife was a young woman named Mahī. She was the most beautiful woman in the world.

3. Their son was named Sanājjāta. He resembled the sun in splendour. Death urged by Kāla, O sage, took away Dhṛtavrata.

4. Unable to see anyone to protect her, that beautiful widow with a young son went to the hermitage of Gālava.

5. After entrusting her son to him that woman deluded by sin wandered here and there over many countries leading a lecherous life.

6-10. Her son became the master of Vedas and Vedāṅgas in the hermitage of Gālava. Still, due to the faults of his mother he too became sexy and passionate.

There is a place known as Janasthāna. People of different castes stayed there. The lady Mahī resided there adopting the profession of a prostitute.

Her son too wandered over many countries as a lecherous debauchee. As time passed he too came to Janasthāna and lived there.

The son of Dhṛtavrata, the brahmin (Sanājjāta) was desirous of a harlot. The lady Mahī too wanted men who would lavishly spend money on her.

Due to the curious turn of fate the mother and the son had sexual union. She did not recognise her son nor did he recognize his mother.

11. Although their union lasted for a long time, the mother and the son did not know the real facts about each other.

12. Although the brahmin's actions were bad, he possessed a good mind due to the virtue of his father. Listen to this wonderful account, O Nārada.

13. Living a carefree life he did not abandon prayers pertaining to Brahman. After performing the morning prayers he worked for earning wealth.

14-15. With the power of his learning he earned a lot and gave everything to that harlot. He used to get up early in the morning and go to Gaṅgā. He performed all acts of cleanliness, ablutions, prayers, etc. After performing all those he used to bow down to brahmins and return home.

16-17. When he went to Gautamī in the morning he was invariably ugly. His limbs were all afflicted by leprosy. Impure fetid blood oozed out of his body.

When he returned after bath in Gautamī Gaṅgā, he used to have handsome features. He was calm. He resembled the fire god and the sun. He appeared like the sun in human form.

18-23. That brahmin himself was not aware of the two different appearances. The holy sage Gālava, devoutly attached to penance and pursuit of knowledge, had his hermitage on the banks of Gautamī and lived there in the company of other sages. The brahmin Sanājjāta took bath everyday in the holy river and bowed to Gālava at the very same place. After bowing to Gālava he used to go to his own place.

Gālava observed the physical features of Sanājjāta both before and after his bath and prayers. On seeing this Gālava was surprised and he thought there must be some reason behind this.

Once when this brahmin was about to leave after bowing to Gālava, the sage called him out of wonder and spoke to him.

Gālava said:

24. Who are you? Where will you go? What do you do? Where do you eat? What is your name? Where do you sleep? Who is your wife? Tell me.

Brahmā said :

25-29. On hearing the words of Gālava, the brahmin said to the sage:

The Brahmin said :

I shall tell you tomorrow decisively everything connected with the matter.

Brahmā said :

Saying this to Gālava, Sanājjāta went home. Taking food at night he went to bed with the harlot. Sanājjāta was taken by surprise on remembering the words of Gālava. He said to her :

The Brahmin said :

You are endowed with all good qualities. Though you had been a harlot yet you are a chaste lady (now). Our mutual love is quite befitting. Let it continue as long as we live.

Still I wish to ask you something. What is your name? Where is your family? What is your native place? Where are your relatives? Let everything be mentioned to me.

The Harlot said :

30-31. There was a pure initiated brahmin Dhṛtavrata by name. I am Mahī, his wife. My son had been left in the hermitage of Gālava. He was an intelligent boy known as Sanājjāta. Due to my previous defects I abandoned my family tradition. I am staying here as a carefree harlot, but, O brahmin, know me to be a brahmin lady.

Brahmā said :

32. On hearing her words he was hit in a vulnerable spot. He fell suddenly on the ground. Seeing him in this condition the harlot spoke to him.

The Harlot said :

33-36. What has happened, O excellent brahmin? Where has your love gone? What is that word uttered by me which has afflicted your mind so much?

Consoling himself by means of his own effort the brahmin spoke these words.

The Brahmin said :

My father was the brahmin Dhṛtavrata. I am his son Sanājjāta. This lady, my mother Mahī has come here by chance.

Brahmā said :

On hearing his words she too became excessively distressed. For the whole of that night both of them lamented.

Afterwards when the day dawned with the bright sun, the brahmin went to Gālava, the greatest among the sages, and intimated to him.

The Brahmin said :

37-39. O brahmin, I am the son of Dhṛtavrata. I have been nurtured by you and my sacred thread has been tied by you. O holy lord, this is Mahī my mother.

What shall I do. How can I expiate?

Brahmā said :

On hearing the words of the brahmin, Gālava spoke words of sympathy to the Brahmin:

"I am seeing everyday this uncommon feature of having two forms in you.

40. It was then that you have been asked about the news. Everything has been heard and understood by me. The evil action which you have committed has entirely perished in Gaṅgā.

41. By virtue of the sanctity of this Tīrtha, due to the grace of this goddess, you have been purified, O dear one, everyday. In this matter you need not worry at all.

42-43. Everyday in the morning your features appear sinful. Again I used to see your excellent form. When you come you are sinful. When you go you are sinless. I see this everyday. You have been made pure by the goddess now.

44-46. Now nothing remains for you to do. This mother of yours, O brahmin, who is known as a harlot, has repented much. She has refrained from committing sins. In regard to all living beings, love is natural. But due to the great merit resulting from association with good people, the turning away can be effected by the grace of fate. Due to the merit acquired by previous actions she has sufficiently repented.

47-49. By taking her holy bath in this Tīrtha she will become purified".

Accordingly both of them, the mother and the son did so, O Nārada. Due to the holy dip both of them were undoubtedly rid of their sins. Thenceforward they call that Tīrtha Dhautapāpa. It is known as Pāpapraṇāśana and Gālava. Whether it is a "Great sin" or a minor one, whether it is little or big this holy centre Dhautapāpa shall destroy everything. It yields good merit.

CHAPTER TWENTYTHREE

Viśvāmitra Tīrtha

Brahmā said :

1. To the south of it, O brahmin, is the very rare Tīrtha known as Pitṛtīrtha. It is pure. It dispels all sins.

2. They know this as Pitṛtīrtha, O brahmin, because it was the place where Rāma, the son of Daśaratha, propitiated his ancestors, in the company of Sītā.

3. If holy bath, charitable gift and water libation unto the ancestors were performed there everything attains an everlasting status. No worry need be felt in this respect.

4-5. The place where the great king Rāma, the son of Daśaratha, honoured the great sage Viśvāmitra along with the sages, the seers of reality, is the holy centre Viśvāmitra. It yields great merit. It is frequented by ages. I shall recount its features as cited by the expounders of the Vedas.

6-7. Formerly, there was a great drought, extremely terrible unto the subjects. The extremely intelligent Viśvāmitra went to the Gautamī, accompanied by his disciples.

On seeing his disciples, sons and wife very lean and afflicted by hunger the glorious sage became distressed and spoke thus to his disciples.

Viśvāmitra said :

8. Let something to eat, something to munch and crunch be brought, no matter what the quantity be, in whatever manner possible, from wherever it is available. Let it be brought as it is. Do not delay. You must go now itself. It must be brought in a trice.

Brahmā said :

9-12. At this bidding of the sage the hungry disciples set out in a hurry. Wandering here and there they saw a dead dog. Taking it they rushed back and offered the same to their preceptor. Saying "Good ! well done !" he grasped it with his hand.

"Cut the flesh of the dog. Wash it with water. Cook it duly after repeating the Mantras and perform Homa into the fire in accordance with the injunctions.

After propitiating Devas, sages, Pitṛs, guests, preceptors and others, all of us shall partake of the remainder", said the sage thus.

13-17. On hearing the words of Viśvāmitra, the disciples did exactly so. When the dog's flesh was being cooked, Agni the messenger of Devas went to the abode of Devas and intimated everything to them.

Agni said :

Dog's flesh has to be taken by Devas as it has been offered by the sage and it has occurred so.

Brahmā said :

At these words of Agni, Indra assumed the form of a vulture and flying through the sky took away the closed pot that was filled with the flesh.

On seeing that the disciples informed the sage about the vulture. "O excellent sage, the pot has been taken away by the senseless vulture".

Thereafter, the holy sage became furious. He was ready to curse Indra. On coming to know of this, Indra filled the pot with honey.

18. Indra in the form of a bird, thereupon, placed the pot filled with honey among the comets. Viśvāmitra became angry. On seeing the pot, the sage said thus furiously.

Viśvāmitra said :

19. "Give us the dog's flesh alone. You can take away the excellent nectar. If not, I shall reduce you to ashes."

Becoming frightened Indra spoke then.

Indra said :

20. "Perform the Homa of honey duly and drink it along with your sons. Of what avail is this unholy filthy flesh of a dog, O great sage?"

Visvamitra said :

21-25. No. If a single person, that is, I alone take it in, what is the benefit? The subjects are exhausted and distressed, O Indra. Of what avail is that honey (wine)? If the people get nectar I shall also consume the same. Or after the divine Pitṛs have consumed flesh, I shall partake of that. I do not speak untruth. Believe me.

Thereafter the frightened lord of thousand eyes called the clouds quickly and showered nectar. The brahmin Viśvāmitra propitiated Devas at first and the three worlds thereafter by means of holy nectar offered by Indra. He then partook of it along with his disciples and his wife.

26-28. Thenceforth that holy centre is mentioned as the bestower of great merit. It is the place where Indra came and where the nectar was offered without meat. It is a holy centre that bestows merit on men. The holy bath taken there and the charitable gifts offered yield the benefit of all sacrifices. Thenceforth that holy centre is remembered as Viśvāmitra, Madhutīrtha, Aindra, Śyena and Parjanya.

CHAPTER TWENTYFOUR

Śveta and other Tīrthas

Brahmā said :

1. The holy centre known as Śveta Tīrtha in the three worlds is very auspicious. On being simply remembered it rids people of all sins.

2. Formerly, there was a brahmin Śveta who was the dearest friend of Gautama. He stayed on the bank of Gautamī river and was engaged in the worship of guests.

3-5. He was devoutly attached to Śiva in thought, words and deeds. That excellent brahmin continued to meditate on and worship Śiva till the last days of his life. When his days were over, the messengers of lord Yama came there to take away that excellent brahmin devoted to Śiva, but, O Nārada, they were not able even to enter his abode. When the time passed away Citraka spoke to (the god of) Death.

Citraka said :

6. O Mṛtyu, why does not Śveta come yet? His span of life has come to an end. Nor have the messengers of Mṛtyu too come yet. Why ? This pazzles me.

Brahmā said :

7. The infuriated Mṛtyu thereupon went himself to the abode of Śveta. Seeing his messengers highly frightened and standing mum, Mṛtyu said, "What is the matter, O messengers?"

The messengers then said to Mṛtyu.

The Messengers said :

8. We are not able even to look at Śveta who is protected by Śiva. What terror can there be to those with whom Śiva is pleased !

Brahmā said :

9-11. Then Mṛtyu with the noose in his hand entered the place where that brahmin was worshipping Śiva. The brahmin was not at all aware of either Yama's servants or Mṛtyu himself.

On seeing Mṛtyu holding the noose and standing near

Śveta who was worshipping Śiva with devotion the surprised Nandin said :

Nandin said :

O Mṛtyu, what do you see here?

Mṛtyu spoke to Nandin.

Mṛtyu said :

12-15. I came here to take away Śveta. Hence I am looking for the excellent brahmin.

Nandin said :

Go out, go out.

Brahmā said :

Then Mṛtyu threw up the noose against Śveta. O great sages, Nandin then became angry. Nandin hit Mṛtyu with the baton given by Śiva. Mṛtyu fell on the ground. Then the messengers saw that Mṛtyu was struck down. They intimated the incident to Yama.

16-20. Then Dharma whose vehicle is buffalo and who controls all addressed his attendants and associates, viz. Citragupta, Kāla, Yamadaṇḍa, buffalo, ghosts and vampires, Ādhis, Vyādhis, ailments of eyes, belly and ears, the three types of fever, sins, and hells severally. "Hurry up, hurry up", said Yama to them and himself proceeded ahead, surrounded by these and others, to the place where Śveta the excellent brahmin was worshipping Śiva. On seeing Yama approaching, Nandin who was wielding his weapons said to Vināyaka, Skanda and Bhūtanātha (Chief of Ghosts) who was whirling a baton (to be ready). Then a fight ensued which terrified the worlds.

21. Kārttikeya pierced the servants of Yama by means of his javelin. He killed Yama, the powerful ruler of the southern quarter.

22-24. The followers of Yama who survived intimated this to Āditya. On hearing about that extremely wonderful event Āditya approached me accompanied by Devas and followed by the guardians of quarters.

Lord Viṣṇu, Indra, Agni, Varuṇa, moon, sun, Aśvins, Maruts and I—all of us went to Yama.

25-26. The powerful lord of the southern quarter was

lying dade on the bank of Gaṅgā. Seas, serpents, rivers and living beings came there in order to see Yama the lord of Devas and son of the god Sun. On seeing Yama with all his armies killed Devas became frightened. With palms joined in reverence they said to Śambhu.

Devas said :

27-30. You always possess the quality of being fond of your devotees and that of slaying the wicked. O primordial Maker, obeisance to you. O blue-throated lord, obeisance to you. O lord, fond of Brahmā, obeisance to you. O lord, fond of Devas, obeisance to you.

Yama and his attendants were unable to take away the brahmin Śveta whose span of life has come to an end, (because) he is your devotee. On seeing the great lord they remain contented. O lord, truly you possess the quality of being fond of your devotees.

Even Yama, the annihilator is not able to look at those persons who have sought refuge in you, the merciful lord. After realising this, O lord, they worship you with devotion.

You alone are the lord of worlds; you alone are the leader of worlds; without you none is competent? Excepting you who will be competent to make this arrangement?

Brahmā said :

31. Even as they were eulogizing him lord Śiva appeared in front of them. He asked them pleasantly: "What shall I give you?"

Devas said :

32-34. This is Dharma, the son of Vivasvat and the Controller of all embodied beings. He has been established in the arrangement of Dharma and Adharma. He is the guardian of southern quarter.

He does not deserve death. He is not an offender. He is not a sinner. Without him no work of the creator of Universe can take place.

Hence, O Lord of Devas, revive Yama along with his army and vehicles. O lord, a request can never be fruitless in regard to great men. It is certainly fruitful.

Brahmā said:

35. Then the lord said, "Certainly I shall revive him; undoubtedly I shall make Yama come back to life, if Devas agree to my suggestion now."

36. Then Devas said: "We shall do as you bid—you in whose control the entire Universe along with Hari, Brahmā and others function."

37-38. Then the lord said to Devas who gathered there: "Let not my devotee undergo death."

"No", said Devas, "In that case, O lord, the people including the mobile and immobile will become immortal. O lord, idential with the universe, then there will not be any difference between mortals and immortals."

39-42. Śiva said to them again: "You listen to my speech. We are the perpetual masters of our devotees, and the devotees of Viṣṇu who resort to Gautamī. Mṛtyu does not deserve that lordship and mastery. Yama should never discuss them nor talk to them. They should never be attacked by worries and physical ailments, etc. Those who seek refuge in Śiva are liberated at the very moment. They are worthy of being bowed to by Yama along with his followers." Then Devas said to lord Śiva, "Let it be so".

43-46. Then the holy lord spoke to Nandin, his vehicle.

Śiva said :

Sprinkle the dead Yama with the waters of Gautamī.

Brahmā said :

Then Yama and his attendants were sprinkled by Nandin. They woke up alive and went to their abode.

Viṣṇu and Devas stayed on the northern bank of Gautamī worshipping Maheśvara, lord of Devas.

47-50. On the northern bank the following numbers of holy centres were established: (a) eighty thousand, (b) fourteen thousand, (c) six thousand and (d) six thousand. Thus there were one hundred and six thousand holy centres on the northern bank. On the southern bank there came to be (a) six thousand, (b) thirty thousand holy centres. Thus there are thirty six thousand holy centres on the southern bank. O Nārada, the recounting of Śvetatīrtha is meritorious. The place where Mṛtyu fell down is called Mṛtyu Tīrtha. By merely remembering it one lives upto a thousand years. The holy dip and the offering of charitable gifts there destroys sins. If it is listened to, read or remembered it removes impurities. It yields worldly pleasures and salvation to the people.

CHAPTER TWENTYFIVE

Śukratīrtha and Mṛtasañjīvanī Tīrtha

Brahmā said :

1. The holy centre known as Śukratīrtha is conducive to the achievement of all Siddhis. It subdues sins and destroys ailments.

2-4. There were two great sages of excellent virtue, namely Aṅgiras and Bhṛgu. Their sons known as Jīva (Jupiter) and Kavi (Venus) were very intelligent and handsome. The sons were obedient to their parents. On seeing that their sons had had their initiation ceremony the fathers spoke to each other.

The sages said :

Only one of us need be the preceptor for our sons, maintaining discipline. Let one be the preceptor and let the other one remain carefree and happy.

Brahmā said :

5. On hearing this Aṅgiras said to Bhārgava quickly, "I shall teach them equally. Let Bhārgava remain carefree and happy."

6. On hearing these words of Aṅgiras the scion of the family of Bhṛgu said "So be it" and entrusted his son Śukra to Aṅgiras.

7. He taught both the boys separately on account of his unequal feeling towards them. After a long time Śukra spoke to Bṛhaspati.

Śukra said :

8. O preceptor, everyday you teach me with discrimination.

This discrimination between son and disciple is not proper on the part of a preceptor.

9. Only teachers of deluded thinking practise discrimination. There is no limit to the sins incurred by the persons of discriminatory feelings.

10. O preceptor, you have been well-understood. I shall bow down to you again and again. I shall go to another preceptor. It behoves you to permit me.

11. O brahmin, I shall go to my father. If he too were to have this discrimination, I shall go elsewhere. O lord, I take leave of you. Bid me depart.

Brahmā said :

12. After taking leave of his preceptor Bṛhaspati and on being permitted by him Śukra went from there thinking, "I shall go to my father only after I have acquired learning."

13. So "Whom shall I approach? Which preceptor will be excellent?" thinking thus he asked Vṛddhagautama of great intellect.

Śukra said :

14. Who can be my preceptor, O excellent sage? Tell me. I shall go to that person who is competent to be the preceptor of all the three worlds.

Brahmā said :

15. Old Gautama told him to approach Lord Śiva, the preceptor of the Universe, lord of the worlds.

Śukra said :

How can I see that lord of Devas ? Where can I propitiate him?

On being addressed thus, Gautama said.

Gautama said :

16. Remaining pure in mind and body on the Gautamī Tīrtha propitiate Śiva by means of hymns. Being pleased thereby the lord of three worlds will impart learning to you.

Brahmā said :

17. At those words of Gautama, the scion of the family of

Bhṛgu went to Gaṅgā. After taking a holy dip and becoming pure the boy began eulogizing Śiva.

18-21. "O Śambhu, I am seeking refuge in you, the sole refuge for the poor and the helpless. O lord with the crescent moon, I am a boy of puerile intellect. I do not know how to eulogize you. Obeisance be to you. I have been abandoned by my preceptor. I have neither friends nor comrades. In every respect you are the lord. O lord of the worlds, obeisance be to you. You are weightier than the weightiest and greater than the greatest. I am only a small boy. O lord identical with the universe, obeisance be to you. It is for the sake of learning that I have come to you. O lord of Devas, I do not know your way. Look at me with kindness. Obeisance be to you, O lord, witness unto the worlds."

Brahmā said :

22-23. Even as he was eulogizing thus the lord of Devas became pleased with him.

Śiva said :

Welfare unto you. Choose what you wish even if it were to be difficult of access unto Devas.

Brahmā said :

24-27. Śukra said to the lord of Devas, with palms joined in reverence and the mind greatly pleased.

Śukra said :

O lord, I beg of you that learning which is not accessible to the sages as well as Brahmā and others. You are my preceptor. You are my deity.

Brahmā said :

The excellent Deva granted unto suppliant Śukra the Vidyā called Sañjavanī which was unknown even to Devas.

Other Vidyās are secular. Vedic lore is known to many. When Śaṅkara is pleased what is it that remains unachieved.

28. After acquiring the great learning he went to his father. By virtue of his learning Śukra received honour. He became the preceptor of Daityas.

29-32. Afterwards Kaca, the son of Bṛhaspati acquired Vidyā from Śukra. The reason thereof was something very different. From Kaca, Bṛhaspati acquired this and from him Devas acquired it separately. It was this great Vidyā which they called Mṛtajīvanī.

The place where Śukra acquired that Vidyā after worshipping Śiva on the northern bank of Gautamī is called Śukratīrtha.

This Tīrtha is conducive to the increase of life and health. Holy dip and charitable gifts at that place bestow everlasting merit.

CHAPTER TWENTYSIX

Seven Thousand Holy Centres

Brahmā said :

1. The holy centre known as Indra Tīrtha destroys the sin of brahmin slaughter. Even by being remembered it destroys heaps of sins and masses of sufferings.

2. Formerly, when Vṛtra was slain, O Nārada, the sin of brahmin slaughter pursued Indra who was frightened by the very thought of Brahmin slaughter.

3. He, the slayer of Vṛtra, began to run here and there. Wherever he went the thought of Brahmin slaughter pursued him.

4-5. He entered a great lake and penetrated a lotus stalk. Assuming the form of a fibre Indra took his abode there. The slaughter-thought stood watching on the bank of the lake for a thousand divine years. During this whole period Devas remained without Indra.

6-7. Devas had consultations among themselves without excitement: "How can Indra be regained?" After thinking of the place of slaughter, I spoke to Devas: "Let Indra be sprinkled with the waters of Gautamī. After taking a holy dip he will be purified in his soul and will become Indra once again."

8-9. Accordingly they decided and went to Gautamī. Devas and sages were desirous of showering the lord after he had taken a holy dip. The infuriated Gautama spoke as Indra was about to be showered with the holy water.

Gautama said :

10. I will reduce to ashes all those persons who will shower the sinful Indra who had defiled the bed of his preceptor. Let Devas go away quickly.

Brahmā said :

11. On hearing the words of the sage Devas avoided Gautamī and hurried to Narmadā taking Indra with them.

12-13. They stood ready for showering Indra on the northern bank of Narmadā. As Indra was about to be showered, the holy sage Māṇḍavya said, "If the showering is performed I will reduce you to ashes." Then Devas worshipped Māṇḍavya by hymns and persuaded him by cogent reasons.

Devas said :

14. O sage, wherever Indra the thousand-eyed lord is about to be showered, a terrible obstacle crops up there.

15-17. Hence, O sage, the cause of our welfare, perform Śānti rite for quelling the evil. Be pleased to grant us boons. O sage; we shall offer you a place where you shall perform sacrifice ('Removal of dirt'). We shall give to you many other excellent things as well. Hence, it behoves you to permit. The place where the ablution of Indra is to take place shall be full of grains, trees and fruits. It will bestow all cherished things on men. There will never be drought or famine in this place.

Brahmā said :

18. Then Māṇḍavya, the excellent sage, honoured by the world agreed to it. The rites of ablution and purification were performed there with all ceremonials.

19-23. Then that land was called Mālava by Devas and sages when Indra was showered and purified. They brought Gautamī Gaṅgā and showered him again for the increase of merit. Devas, sages, I, Viṣṇu, Vasiṣṭha, Gautama, Agastya, Atri, Kaśyapa, Yakṣas and Nāgas and others performed holy ablution by that sacred water. Then I showered Indra with the water coming out of Kamaṇḍalu. Two rivers Puṇyā and Siktā arose therefrom and joined Gaṅgā.

24-27. Their confluences are well known. They are resorted to by sages. Thenceforth that holy centre is called Puṇyā-saṅgama Tīrtha.

At the confluence of Siktā (with Gaṅgā) the holy centre is called Aindra Tīrtha. Seven thousand splendid holy centres cropped up there. A holy dip and the distribution of charitable gifts at the confluence gives everlasting benefit. This must be realised. No worry need be felt on this account. He who reads this holy narrative or listens to it shall be rid of all sins of thought, words and deeds.

CHAPTER TWENTYSEVEN

Paulastya Tīrtha

Brahmā said :

1. The holy centre Paulastya Tīrtha is mentioned as one which fulfils all desires of men. I shall mention its magic power that gives lost kingdom back to one.

2. The eldest son of Viśravas who is now the lord of northern quarter was formerly richly endowed with all types of riches and achievements. He was the ruler of Laṅkā as well.

3. He had three step-brothers, viz. Rāvaṇa, Kumbhakarṇa and Vibhīṣaṇa. They were very powerful, endowed with unmeasured luster. They were his enemies as well.

4-5. They too were the sons of Viśravas but they were Rākṣasas (because they were born) of a Rākṣasī (ogress). Dhanada (Kubera), seated in the aerial chariot and accompanied by his step-brothers used to come to me everyday with great devotion and return after a while.

Rāvaṇa's infuriated mother spoke to her sons.

Rāvaṇa's mother said:

6-7. I shall die. I don't (care to) live, O sons, because of this disparity and dissimilarity.

Devas and Dānavas were mutual enemies (though) they were brothers (step-brothers). (Step-brothers) wish for each other's slaughter in pursuance of victory and prosperity. Hence, you are not at all desirous of victory, nor are you competent. You have no manliness. Aimless and useless is the life of that fellow who permits an enemy to be prosperous.

Brahmā said :

8. On hearing those words of their mother, O sage, the three brothers went to the forest and performed penance.

9-10. All these three obtained boons from me. At the instigation of their uncle Mārīca and their maternal grandfather and at the instance of their mother Rāvaṇa requested for Laṅkā. Due to their Rākṣasahood and the defects of their mother, there was a great enmity between the brothers.

11-13. Then a war between brothers ensued like the war between Devas and Dānavas. In the war Rāvaṇa conquered his quiet and calm elder brother Dhanada and captured the city of Laṅkā, the (aerial chariot) Puṣpaka and other things. He then proclaimed throughout the three worlds consisting of mobile and immobile beings: "He who offers refuge to my step-brother is liable to be killed by me."

Forsaken and ousted by his brother, Dhanada did not receive any support anywhere. He went to Pulastya his grandfather and bowed to him.

Dhanada said :

14-17. I have been ousted by my wicked brother. What shall I do ? Tell me what should be my support and refuge, the fate or a holy centre?

Brahmā said :

On hearing the words of his grandson Pulastya said:

Pulastya said :

Dear child, go to Gautamī and eulogize lord Maheśvara. There in the middle of Gaṅgā your wicked brother will have no access. You will attain prosperous achievement. Do so at my bidding.

Brahmā said :

18-19. Saying "So be it" Dhanada went to Gautamī accompanied by his wife, parents and the aged Pulastya. The lord of wealth took bath in Gaṅgā. Maintaining all holy rites he eulogized Śiva, lord of the lord of Devas, the bestower of worldly pleasures and liberation.

Dhanada said :

20-23. O Śambhu, you alone are the master of this Universe consisting of mobile and immobile beings. There is no one else. If anyone swaggers after slighting you out of delusion, he is worthy of being punished.

You sustain everything by your eight cosmic bodies. Everything exists (and functions) at your bidding. Still, non-scholars shall never attain you who are possessed of ancient glory and splendid refulgence.

Something was born out of her dirt and Ambā jokingly said: "O lord, this is your heroic son." You glanced at it and it became Vighnarāja. Oh, the (powerful) action of the glance of Īśa !

On seeing Kāma and Rati separated in their conjugal enjoyment Girijā's eyes were filled with tears. She spoke to Īśa about this. As a result of that, the bodiless Kāma acquired body and Rati acquired the fortune of conjugal bliss from the lord of Umā.[1]

Brahmā said :

24. Even as he was eulogizing thus, the three-eyed lord appeared in front of him and asked him to choose a boon as he liked. Out of excessive delight he did not utter a word.

25-27. Dhanada and Pulastya were silent. Lord Śiva was delighted repeating "O, choose the boon, O, choose the boon." Then an unembodied voice was heard there telling Maheśvara thus: "The status of the protector of wealth should be granted to

---

1. The reference here is to the episode of the burning of Kāma by Śiva's glance when he was trying to inspire Śiva with amorous thought for Pārvati at the instigation of gods at a time when Śiva was engaged in deep meditation. (vide Vālmiki Rāmāyaṇa, Bāla Kāṇḍa, Ch. 23).

Dhanada." It was only after knowing the silent wish of Pulastya and the father of Dhanada, that the voice made the splendid intention explicit.

28. The divine voice became auspicious. What should take place is like what has already taken place. What is about to be given is like what has already been given. What should be attained is like what has already been attained.

29-33. He who had a number of enemies and who experienced miseries worshipped Someśvara and acquired Liṅga, the lordship of a quarter, the mastery of wealth, vast liberal-mindedness, wives and sons.

On hearing that voice Dhanada spoke these words to the Trident-bearing lord of Devas: "Let this be so."

Saying "May it be so," the lord of Devas assented to the Divine voice. The lord then honoured Pulastya, sage Viśravas and Dhanapāla with holy boons and went away. Thenceforth, they know that holy centre as Paulastya Tīrtha or Dhanada Tīrtha or Vaiśravasa Tīrtha. It is holy and splendid. It fulfils all cherished desires. Holy dip etc. in these holy centres bestows much merit.

CHAPTER TWENTYEIGHT

Agnitīrtha

Brahmā said :

1. The holy centre known as Agnitīrtha is the bestower of the fruit of all sacrifices. It subdues all obstacles. Listen to the benefit of that holy centre.

2-4. The brother of Agni was well known as Jātavedas. He was the bearer of Havya.[1] He was the excellent clever brother of the Fire-god, very fond of him. As he was carrying Havya to gods and was at the abode of the sages on the banks of Gau-

1. Any substance, e.g. clarified butter, food etc. to be offered as oblation, to gods; opposed to 'Kavya' or what is offered to ancestors.

tamī, Madhu the powerful son of Diti killed him even as the chief Sages and Devas were looking on. When Jātavedas died, Devas did not get their Havya.

5 When his dear brother Jātavedas died, Agni was overwhelmed by anger. He entered the waters of Gaṅgā.

6 When Agni entered the waters of Gaṅgā, Devas and human beings cast away their lives because they are considered to be Agnijīvas (having their life in Agni).

7-8 Devas, sages, and Pitṛs went to the place where Agni had entered water. Saying "Without fire we will not be alive" they began to praise Agni particularly. On realizing that Agni had entered the waters the heaven-dwellers spoke pleasing words to him.

Devas said :

9. O Agni, resuscitate the lives of Devas by means of Havya and those of pitṛs by means of Kavya. By the cooking of food and the splitting of seeds resuscitate all human beings.

Brahmā said :

10-13. Agni said to Devas:

"My brother who was very strong has gone. O Devas, while your work is being carried out, my fate will be the same as that of my brother Jātavedas. Hence I am not enthusiastic enough to work for you. Jātavedas who always performed his duty, working for you, has met this fate. I do not know what mine will be. Moreover, I may not have the ability to move about from world to world. Even granting that I may have the ability for it, if your work is not regularly performed by me my fate might be the same."

Then, Devas and sages spoke with emotion.

14-15. "Longevity, love for work and ability to move about will be given to you. O carrier of oblations, we shall give you the Prayājas and Anuyājas (i.e. the benefits of these holy rites).

You are the excellent mouth of Devas. All Āhutis are first given to you. O excellent Deva, we shall partake of what is given by you."

Brahmā said :

16-19. Thereupon the Fire-god was pleased at the words of Devas. He attained the power to move about here and there. He was capable of carrying Havya to Devas and Kavya to Pitṛs. At the instance of Devas, Agni became powerful and fearless everywhere. He is called by the names Jātavedas, Bṛhadbhānu, Saptārci (seven-rayed), Nīlalohita (Blue-red), Jalagarbha (one who hid under water), Śamīgarbha (one who lies latent in Śamī tree), Yajñagarbha (one who lies concealed in Yajña).

Devas dragged Agni from under the water and performed Abhiṣeka. Thereafter Agni became Sarvaga (moving about everywhere). He got two abodes: one on this Earth and another in heaven. Then Devas went away to their abodes in the manner they had come.

This holy centre is called Vahnitīrtha.

20-22. There have cropped up some seven hundred Tīrthas of great merit. If a man who has controlled himself performs the rites of holy dip or distribution of charitable gifts in this Tīrtha, he attains the benefit of a horse sacrifice and even more. That will be splendid and without deficiency. Devatīrtha, Āgneyatīrtha and Jātavedasa are all there. There is a multicoloured Liṅga established by Agni. By visiting that lord one shall obtain the benefit of all sacrifices.

CHAPTER TWENTYNINE

Ṛṇamocana Tīrtha

Brahmā said :

1. Those conversant with the Vedas know the holy centre Ṛṇapramocana. I shall mention its features, O Nārada. Listen to it attentively.

2-4. There was a favourite son of Kakṣīvān named Pṛthuśravas. Due to his detachment he did not marry. Nor did he worship fire.

His younger brother was competent, but, O sage, due to his fear of incurring sin he did not marry before his elder brother.

Then the manes spoke separately to the elder and the younger sons of Kakṣīvān.

Pitṛs said :

5-7. Let the marriage be performed for removing the threefold debts.

Brahmā said :

Thereupon the elder one said: "No, what is the debt? By whom is it incurred?" The younger one said to the Pitṛs: "Due to the fear of sin, O intelligent ones, it is not proper for me to marry while I have the elder brother." The grandfathers thereupon spoke to both of them again.

Pitṛs said :

8-9. O sons of Kakṣīvān, both of you go to the holy Gautamī. Perform the rite of holy dip therein. The holy dip in Gautamī fufils all cherished desires. Go to Gautamī Gaṅgā which sanctifies the three worlds. Perform the rites of bath and libation in that river with due faith.

10-12. Gautamī is the bestower of all cherished things when it is seen, meditated upon or plunged into. There is no sort of restriction of place, time, caste etc. for plunging into it. The elder brother will be freed from the sin of indebtedness and the younger one will not incur the sin of marrying before the elder brother.

Brahmā said :

Then the elder brother Pṛthuśravas performed the holy dip and libation rites. He became free from indebtedness to Pitṛs. Thenceforth that Tīrtha is called Ṛṇamocana. O Nārada, by taking bath or distributing charitable gifts a debtor becomes free from all debts mentioned in Vedas and Smṛtis as well as ordinary debts incurred by him.

CHAPTER THIRTY

Kadrū-Suparṇā-Saṅgama Tīrtha

Brahmā said :

1. There are two holy centres viz. Suparṇāsaṅgama and Kādrava Saṅgama where lord Maheśvara has resorted to the banks of Gaṅgā.

2. The following holy puddles and deep pits are also there viz. Agnikuṇḍa, Raudra, Vaiṣṇava, Saura, Saumya, Brāhma, Kaumāra and Vāruṇa.

3. The river Apsarā joins Gaṅgā and that confluence is a holy centre. Merely by remembering that holy centre a man can be assured and become contented.

4. It quells all sins. Listen, O Nārada, attentively.

Formerly, Vālakhilyas, the great sages, were harassed by Indra. All of them spoke to sage Kaśyapa after giving a moiety of their penance.

Vālakhilyas said :

5. Beget a splendid son through whom Indra's arrogance can be quelled. We shall give you a moiety of our penance.

The sage said to them, "So be it".

6. That Prajāpati made Suparṇā pregnant. He made Kadrū the mother of Nāgas too pregnant.

7-8. Prajāpati who was desirous of going abroad told those two pregnant ladies, "You must not commit any offence. You must not go anywhere. For certain, you will be cursed if you to elsewhere."

Brahmā said :

9-13. After saying thus to his wives he went away. When their husband had gone, both of them went to the sacrifice of sages with purified mind. The sacrificial chamber was crowded with groups of brahmins. It was situated on the banks of Gaṅgā. Both of them were arrogant because of their youth and wealth. They were mad too. Though forbidden many times by the sages, the seers of truth, they spoiled the Havi offerings in the sacrifice. Who can prevent the misconduct and evil actions of women? On seeing both of them fallen in the evil path the brahmins became enraged and excited. (They cursed them thus) "Since you are clinging to the evil path you will become rivers. Thereupon Suparṇā and Kadrū became rivers.

14-17. Prajāpati Kaśyapa returned home after some time. He heard the details of the incidents in the sessional sacrifice and the curse of those two ladies. On hearing it he was perplexed and thought, "What shall I do?" He told the sages known as Vālakhilyas. They said to the brahmin Kaśyapa: "Go to Gaṅgā Gautamī and eulogize Maheśāna. They will then become your wives again. You go to that place in the middle of Gaṅgā where lord Maheśvara resides perpetually due to the fear of sin of brahmin slaughter, by the name of Madhyameśvara."

18. Saying, "So be it" Kaśyapa of holy rites took bath in Gaṅgā and eulogized Maheśvara, the lord of Devas, by means of sacred hymns.

Kaśyapa said :

19. He is the sole master of the three worlds but he has not the least feeling of pride of possession. May that Siddhanātha, the maker of the entire Universe and the husband of Śivā, be pleased.

20. You alone are competent to dispel the misery of all embodied beings, whether mobile or immobile, who have been scorched by the sun of therefold misery[1] and who run about here and there.

21. The three types of Yoga (contact) of Sattva etc. (Sattva, Rajas and Tamas) of Lord Śiva cannot be recounted even by Śakra and others. Considering Soma (i.e. Śiva) to be of diverse wonderful activities, an excellent person who is always devoted to charitable gifts is happy always.

Brahmā said :

22. Eulogized by these and other hymns, lord Śiva, the

1. The there well known miseries are ādhyātmika (caused by self), ādhidaivika (caused by supernatural beings), and ādhibhautika (caused by the great elements); the terms are interpreted with slight differences by different commentators.

beloved husband of Gaurī became pleased. Śambhu granted many boons to Kaśyapa.

23-24. To him who was seeking his wives the lord said: "The two wives of yours will have the forms of rivers. They will reach Gaṅgā, the most excellent river. Due to this mere contact they will regain their own bodies."

Due to the grace of Gaṅgā they became pregnant once again.

25. Then the noble-souled Prajāpati, became delighted on regaining his wives. He invited those brahmins who had resorted to the banks of Gautamī.

26. The delighted Prajāpati performed their Sīmantonnayana rite (parting of hairs on the head ritualistically). He fed the brahmins in accordance with injunctions.

27-29. The brahmins had their food in the abode of Kaśyapa. Kadrū was seated near her husband. Looking at the brahmins she squinted and winked her eye and laughed at them. They became excited (and cursed): "O sinful woman, let that sinning eye of thine with which you winked and laughed be split." Then Kadrū became blind of one eye. She is called the mother of serpents. Then the holy sage Kaśyapa pacified the sages.

30-33. They were pleased and said: "The Gautamī, the most excellent of rivers will protect one from thousands of crimes on being resorted to. Kaśyapa, the excellent sage, did so along with his wives. Thenceforth, they know that their confluence is a holy centre. The river Kadrū is all round and the river Sauparṇikā is in the East. The holy centre Jaṭādhara extends all round from the Kadrū to the east as far as the Sauparṇikā river. This holy centre is a bit holier than Vārāṇasī. It suppresses all sins. It bestows the benefit of all sacrifices."

CHAPTER THIRTYONE

Sarasvatīsaṅgama

Brahmā said :

1. The holy centre named Purūravas destroys all sins even on being remembered. Why not on being visited? Those who are conversant with the Vedas know it.

2. King Purūravas went to the abode of Brahmā. There, by chance he saw the divine river Sarasvatī laughing by the side of Brahmā. On seeing her richly endowed with beauty the king asked Urvaśī:

The King said :

3. Who is this beautiful saintly lady near Brahmā? She is the most excellent lady among all ladies (assembled here). She (seems to) illuminate this assembly.

Brahmā said :

4. Urvaśī said to the king: "This is the splendid divine river Sarasvatī, the daughter of Brahmā. She comes here daily and goes back."

On hearing it the king was surprised (and he said), "Bring her near me"

Brahmā said :

5-9. Urvaśī said again to the king who used to distribute plenty of monetary gifts.

Urvaśi said :

I shall mention everything to her and fetch her.

Brahmā said :

Then out of pleasure the king sent Urvaśī there. Urvasī then went and repeated the words of the king. Sarasvatī agreed to what was mentioned by Urvaśī. She promised saying "So be it" and went to the place where Purūravas was staying. He indulged in sexual dalliance on the banks of Sarasvatī for many years. Sarasvān was born as (her) son and his (Sarasvān's) son was Bṛhadratha.

10-12. I observed Sarasvatī going everyday to the abode of the king. I saw Sarasvān (her son). I saw evidences of similar activities with regard to other persons also. So I cursed her, "Be Mahānadī." Afraid of my curse Vāgīśā (Sarasvatī) went to the divine river Gautamī, who is the holy mother sanctifying the whole world, who was born of Kamaṇḍalu (water-pot), who is the suppressor of the three distresses and who is the bestower of pleasures here and hereafter.

13-16. After going to Gautamī, the divine river, she recounted (the story of) my curse from the beginning. Gaṅgā said to me: "It behoves you to make her free from the effects of the curse. It is not proper on your part to have cursed Sarasvatī. This is the nature of women because youthful women desire men. O Brahmā, all young women are naturally unsteady. O lotus-seated lord, you are the creator of the Universe. How is it, that you do not know this? Whom does not cupid deceive naturally?"

Then I withdrew the curse and said "Sarasvatī shall be visible too."

17-20. Due to that curse the river Sarasvatī is both visible and invisible in the mortal world.

Purūravas, the most excellent and virtuous king, went to the place where the divine river (Sarasvatī), agitated due to the curse, joined Gaṅgā. He performed penance and propitiated lord Siddheśvara. He acquired all cherished desires by the favour of Gaṅgā. Thenceforth that holy centre is called Purūravas. It is also called Sarasvatīsaṅgama and Brahmatīrtha. The lord there is Siddheśvara and the holy center bestows all cherished things.

CHAPTER THIRTYTWO

Review of the Greatness of Five Tīrthas

Brahmā said :

1. Sages know these five holy centres as very holy, viz. Sāvitrī, Gāyatrī, Śraddhā (Faith), Medhā (Intellect) and Sarasvatī.

2-4. By taking bath there and drinking water therein one is released from all sins. Sāvitrī, Gāyatrī, Śraddhā, Medhā and Sarasvatī—these were my eldest daughters. (Then) I created the most beautiful woman in the world, the most excellent among all.

On seeing her, O excellent sage, my mind became deranged. I was desirous of seizing her and on seeing what I was going to do that lady fled.

5. That maiden assumed the form of a hind and I became a stag then. In order to save virtue, Śambhu became a hunter of the stag.

6. Those five daughters of mine (also) became afraid of me and went to Gaṅgā, the great river. Thereupon Maheśvara went ahead for the sake of saving virtue.

7. Then Hara, the hunter of stag, took up his bow and arrows. Īśa said to me, "I will kill you."

8-11. I desisted from that (evil) action and gave the maiden to the Sun. The five daughters beginning with Sāvitrī assumed the forms of rivers and flowed together. Again they came near me to the heavenly world. The place where these rivers joined the divine river Gaṅgā came to be called Pañcatīrtha. All confluences are holy. Sarasvatī (is the most important of) these five rivers. Holy dip, distribution of charitable gifts, whatever a man does in those rivers yields all cherished things. It yields salvation through Naiṣkarmya (cessation of activities). The holy centre of Mṛgavyādha is also there. It bestows all objects on men. It has the benefit of heaven and salvation. It yields the benefit of Brahmatīrtha.

CHAPTER THIRTYTHREE

Śamī and other Holy Centres

Brahmā said :

1. The holy centre well known as Śamītīrtha subdues all sins. I shall narrate it. Listen to it attentively, O Nārada.

2. There was a Kṣatriya named Priyavrata. He was the most excellent of all conquerors. He was initiated for a horse sacrifice by his preceptor on the southern bank of Gautamī.

3-6. Vasiṣṭha was the priest of that king of powerful arms. When that horse-sacrifice wherein the sages were the Ṛtviks (officiating priests), began, a Dānava named Hiraṇyākṣa came to that sacificial chamber. Devas with Indra as their leader became frightened on seeing that demon. Some of them went to heaven. Havyavāṭ (Fire-god) entered the Śamī tree. Viṣṇu went to the Aśvattha (the holy fig tree), Bhānu (Sun-god) went to the Arka plant. Śiva went to the Vaṭa (Banyan) tree. Soma (Moon) went to the Palāśa tree. Havyavāhana (Fire-god) went to the waters of Gaṅgā. The Aśvins (Twin gods) took the sacrificial horse (and fled). Yama turned himself into a crow.

7. In the meantime, the holy sage Vasiṣṭha took up a Yaṣṭi (thick stick) and commanded demons to stop.

8. Then the sacrifice began to function again. The Daitya who had his own intrinsic strength went away. Thereafter these holy centres became auspicious. They bestow the benefits of ten horse-sacrifices.

9. The first holy centre is Śamītīrtha. The second holy centre is Vaiṣṇava. The other holy centres, viz. Arka (belonging to Sun-god), Śaiva (belonging to Śiva), Saumya (belonging to Moon-god) and Vāsiṣṭha (belonging to Vasiṣṭha) are the bestowers of all cherished things.

10-12. When the elaborate horse sacrifice had been completed Devas and sages became pleased. They spoke to Vasiṣṭha, Priyavrata the sponsor of the sacrifice, those trees and Gaṅgā with great joy: "These have gone here and there for the fulfilment of horse-sacrifice. The holy centres bestow the benefit of horse sacrifice." Devas said thus. Therefore by taking holy dip and distributing charitable gifts in these holy centres, one surely attains the benefit of a horse sacrifice.

CHAPTER THIRTYFOUR

Twenty-two Thousand Holy Centres

Brahmā said :

1-2. Listen to the names of some holy centres I am going to recount now. They are Viśvāmitra, Hariścandra, Śunaḥśepa, Rohita, Vāruṇa, Brāhma, Āgneya, Aindra, Aindava, Aiśvara, Maitra, Vaiṣṇava, Yāmya, Āśvina and Auśana.

3. There was a king born in the family of Ikṣvāku, named Hariścandra. The sages Nārada and Parvata came to his abode. After receiving them with great hospitality Hariścandra said to the two sages:

Hariścandra said :

4. The whole world undergoes sufferings for the sake of a son. What is it that one gets from a son? A son may be wise or foolish, excellent or middling.

Brahmā said :

5-9. Parvata and Nārada spoke to Hariścandra:

Nārada and Parvata said :

The reply can be one, hundred or thousand. O king, all the replies are good. Still this is being mentioned. O excellent king, to a person without a son the other world does not exist. (He cannot expect to go there.) To that person of ill luck this world too does not exist (i.e. he cannot be happy here too). O ruler of men, a person who takes bath at the birth of his son shall derive the benefit of holy bath at the end of ten horse sacrifices. By obtaining a son one attains prestige. (One may become) the most excellent among the immortal beings. (What) the Devas get through nectar, the brahmins and other castes get through a son. A son releases his father and grandfathers from the three debts.[1]

10. Of what avail is (the vow of taking in only) roots and water? Of what avail is the practice of growing beard and moustache? Of what avail is penance without a son? O great king, a son is said as one leading to heaven and salvation.

11. Son alone is the other world, virtue, love and wealth. Son is liberation, the great light. He is the person who takes all embodied beings (across the ocean of worldly existence).

12. Without a son, O leading king, heaven and salvation are very difficult to achieve. In the world, it is the son who is the most conducive to the achievement of virtue, love and wealth.

13-15. A charitable gift given or a sacrifice performed without a son is fruitless. It appears to me that life itself, without a son is fruitless. One gets relief from debts to the manes through a son by whom people are redeemed from sins. If a father sees the face of a live son born to him he gets pleasure. By seeing a son, a father obtains all those enjoyments and pleasures that can be had in the mortal world or in heaven. Hence there is nothing else in the three worlds as desirable as a son".

On hearing these words the king was extremely surprised and he spoke again to the two sages.

Hariścandra said :

16. Tell me how I can obtain a son. I am willing to go anywhere and perform any rite, whatever be the means thereof. By manly endeavour, repetition of Mantras, performance of sacrifices or distribution of charitable gifts a son should be got by me.

Brahmā said :

17-19. They said to the excellent king Hariścandra who

---

1. The three well known debts are: (1) Ṛṣi-ṛṇa or debt to the sages, which one discharges by the study of Veda; (2) Deva-ṛṇa or debt to the gods, which is discharged by performing worship and sacrifice; and (3) Pitṛ-ṛṇa or debt to the manes, which is discharged by procreation of a son. Evidently these great debts or obligations aim respectively at acquisition, dissemination and advancement of knowledge, preservation of religious and moral values, and perpetuation of the human race.

was seeking a son, after meditating deeply for a short while: "O bestower of honour, go to Gautamī. There the lord of waters fulfils whatever excellent wish one has in mind. Varuṇa has been glorified by sages as the bestower of everything. On being delighted he will grant you a son at the proper time, sooner or later."

On hearing this, the excellent king carried out the suggestions of the sages.

20. Resorting to the banks of Gautamī he propitiated Varuṇa. Varuṇa who was pleased said to Hariścandra:

Varuṇa said :

21. O king, I shall grant you a son. Being issueless you have performed holy rites; certainly a son will be born to you if you are prepared to offer him in sacrifice.

Brahmā said :

22-23. Hariścandra said to Varuṇa, "I shall sacrifice him".

Hariścandra then prepared the holy offering pertaining to Varuṇa. The king then gave it to his wife. Thereafter a son was born to the king. When the son was born, the lord of waters, the most excellent among the eloquent ones, spoke.

Varuṇa said :

24-28. The son should be sacrificed today itself. Do you remember your former promise?

Brahmā said :

Hariścandra said this to Varuṇa who approached him duly:

Hariścandra said :

A sacrificial animal becomes fit for sacrifice after it passes ten days. Thereafter I shall perform the sacrifice.

Brahmā said :

On hearing the words of the king, Varuṇa agreed and returned home. When the boy passed the tenth day he approached the king once again and said, "Perform the sacrifice".

The King said to Varuṇa :

O lord of waters, the sacrificial animal without teeth is useless. Go now and come when the boy cuts his teeth.

29-31. On hearing those words of the king the lord of waters went again. When the teeth were cut, O Nārada, and the boy was aged seven years, Varuṇa said to the king again, "Perform the sacrifice". The king said tò Varuṇa, "O lord of waters, these teeth will fall off. Other teeth will come up. Then I shall perform the scrifice. Please go away now." Varuṇa went away. When the new set of teeth grew up, O Naradā, he said to the king, "Perform the sacrifice". The king said to the lord of waters.

The king said :

32. If a Kṣatriya happens to be the sacrificial animal, the same will be the most excellent one, if he knows the science of archery.

Brahmā said :

33-35. On hearing those words of the king, Varuṇa went to his own abode. When Rohita became efficient in the use of miraculous weapons, when that suppressor of enemies became conversant with the Vedas and scriptures, when the sixteen year old Prince Rohita was crowned as heir-apparent, the delighted Varuṇa went to the place where the king and Rohita were present. Varuṇa said to the king, "Sacrifice your son".

36. The king said, "yes". After saying so, the king said to the Ṛtviks and his eldest son Rohita, within the hearing of Varuṇa :

Hariścandra said :

37-38. Come on my great hero, come on my son, I shall sacrifice you unto Varuṇa.

Brahmā said :

Then Rohita asked his father, "What is this?" The father explained everything in detail in the manner it had happened. Even as Varuṇa was listening, Rohita said to his father :

Ròhita said :

39. I am pure. I am in a hurry. At the very outset, O great

king, I shall perform the sacrifice unto Viṣṇu, the lord, of the worlds, along with the Ṛtviks and the priest, Varuṇa being the sacrificial animal. It behovès you to grant permission for the same.

Brahmā said :

40-43. On hearing those words of Rohita the lord of waters was overwhelmed by great anger.

Taking up his divine bow and seated in his chariot without any discomfort Rohita went to the forest on the banks of Gaṅgā where Hariścandra, the lord of men, had propitiated Varuṇa and obtained a son. In the meantime the infuriated Varuṇa made king Hariścandra suffer from dropsy. Five years elapsed and as the sixth year was running, the prince heard about the ailment of the king.

44-46. He then thought thus: "Though I was born to my father I had been the cause of distress unto him. What benefit did he derive from me? Now what shall be my duty?"

On the banks of Gaṅgā the prince saw holy sages. He saw the most excellent sage known as Ajīgarta. He was wandering on the banks of Gaṅgā accompanied by his three sons and wife. He had no means of subsistence. On seeing him the prince bowed to him and spoke:

Rohita said :

47-49. How is it that you appear to be gloomy, lean and lacking in sustenance?

Brahmā said :

Ajīgarta said to prince Rohita:

Ajīgarta said :

I have no means for supporting my family. I have many dependents to be fed. We will die without food. Tell me. What shall we do?

Brahmā said :

50-53. On hearing it the prince spoke to the sage:

Rohita said :

What is it that you have in mind? Tell me, O most excellent one among the eloquent ones.

Ajigarta said :

I do not have gold, silver, cows, grains, garments etc., O great king. Therefore, I do not have any means of subsistence. I have three sons and a wife. I am the fifth one. There is no one to buy anyone of us in exchange for food.

Rohita said :

54. O Ajīgarta of great intelligence, what will you take from me? Tell me truthfully. You need not say anything else. Indeed, brahmins are truthful in speech.

Ajigarta said :

55. Take one of the three sons, or me, or take this (woman) my wife. We shall keep alive by this sale.

Rohita said :

56. Of what avail is your wife? O intelligent one, of what avail are you, an old man? Give me a youthful son of yours, whomsoever you may wish to give.

Ajigarta said :

57. O Rohita, I will not sell my eldest son Śunaḥpuccha. The mother will not sell the youngest one. Hence I shall sell Śunaḥśepa, the one between these two. Tell me the amount (you wish to give) for him.

Rohita said :

58. A sacrificial animal has to be kept ready for Varuṇa. (He must be) a man of superior qualities. If you are willing to take a price in exchange, tell me truthfully, O great sage.

Brahmā said :

59. Saying "So be it" Ajīgarta fixed a thousand cows, (measures) of grains, gold coins and clothes as the price of his son. "O Prince", he said, "give the excellent things (to me), I shall give my son to you".

Brahmā said :

60. Saying "So be it" Rohita too gave him money and clothes. After giving it, Rohita went to his father along with the son of the sage. He informed his father about the son of the sage bought for a price.

Rohita said :

61-67. Perform the sacrifice unto Varuṇa with (this) animal. You be free from your ailments.

Brahmā said :

Then after the words of his son Hariścandra said:

Hariścandra said :

The Vedas say that Brahmins, Kṣatriyas and Vaiśyas should be protected by the king. Indeed, excellent brahmins are especially the leaders of all castes. They are persons worthy of being worshipped even by Viṣṇu. Where are persons like me? By slighting and dishonouring them, kings will be faced with the destruction of their family. Brahmins are identical with the holy centres. They are identical with Devas. They are the saviours of persons about to fall into hell. After making them sacrificial animals how can I pretend to protect miserable persons. It is not proper that I should make a brahmin the sacrificial animal. It is better to die of ailments. I will not make a brahmin the sacrificial animal at all. Hence, dear son, go happily along with the brahmin boy.

Brahmā said :

68-70. In the meantime an etherial voice spoke thus:

The Ethereal Voice said :

O great king, go to Gautamī along with your Ṛtviks and priests as well as this brahmin's son who is the sacrificial animal and Rohita, your son. The sacrifice has to be performed by you without killing Śunaḥśepa. The sacrifice shall of course be complete there. Hence, go, O king of great intellect.

Brahmā said :

71-74. On hearing that voice the excellent king hastened

to Gaṅgā along with sage Viśvāmitra, his priest Vasiṣṭha, sage Vāma as well as other sages. After reaching Gautamī Gaṅgā he got himself initiated for the human sacrifice. He prepared the altar, pavilion, sacred pit etc. and erected the Post for the sacrificial animal and other things as well. After everything was ready and the sacrifice began Śunaḥśepa, the sacrificial animal, was tied to the Yūpa (post) along with the chanting of Mantras. On seeing him sprinkled with water Viśvāmitra said this:

Visvāmitra said :

75-79. Visvāmitra said to Devas, sages, to Hariścandra and particularly to Rohita: "May all of you free this Śunaḥśepa the excellent brahmin boy. O Devas, to whom the offering is to be given in the sacrifice, let not this sacrificial animal, Śunaḥśepa, the excellent brahmin boy, be offered to you, in the sacrificial fire along with fats, hairs, skins and the flesh consecrated by the chanting of Mantras. Let the leading brahmins be sprinkled over with water. Let them go to Gautamī and take their bath there. Let them eulogize Devas severally by chanting Mantras and hymns. Engaged in auspicious things let them rejoice. Let sages and Devas, partakers of offerings, protect this boy."

Brahmā said :

80-81. The sages said, "So be it". The excellent king agreed. Śunaḥśepa went to Gaṅgā, the sanctifier of the three worlds. After taking bath, he eulogized those Devas, the partakers of offerings. Even as Viśvāmitra stood listening, the delighted Devas said to Śunaḥśepa.

Devas said :

82-84. Let this, sacrifice be complete without killing Śunaḥśepa.

Brahmā said :

Varuṇa specifically spoke (so) to the excellent king.

Then the human sacrifice of the king, known in all the worlds, was completed. Thus by the grace of Devas, the sages of holy centre, the sacrifice of the king was completed.

85-92. Viśvāmitra honoured Śunaḥśepa in the midst of

assembly. After honouring him in the presence of Devas, he made him the eldest of his sons. The sons of the intelligent Viśvāmitra who did not accept the status of Śunaḥśepa as the eldest son were cursed by Viśvāmitra. He honoured those sons who accepted his status as the eldest son and granted them boons. Thus this narrative has been recounted by me. All these incidents happened on the southern bank of Gautamī. At that place many well known sacred holy centres praised by Devas and others cropped up. Listen to their names from me, O sage of excellent intellect.

They are Hariścandra, Śunaḥśepa, Visvāmitra, Rohita and others. They are twentytwo thousand holy centres. Having a dip therein and distribution of charitable offerings bestow the benefit of a human sacrifice. O excellent sage, the greatness of this holy centre has been described. He who reads this or causes this to be read or listens to this with devotion shall get a son if he has no son. He gets other things too pleasing to his mind.

CHAPTER THIRTYFIVE

The Twentyfive Confluences of Various Rivers

Brahmā said :

1. The holy centre known as Somatīrtha is one that increases the pleasure of Manes. Listen attentively to the extremely sacred incident that happened there, O Nārada.

2. Formerly Soma (Moon) full of nectar had been the king of Gandharvas and not of Devas. Then Devas approached me and said :

Devas said :

3. Formerly Soma, the bestower of vital airs on Devas, had been taken away by Gandharvas. Not able to meditate on him, sages and Devas became extremely distressed. Let some strategic means be employed so that Soma can be ours.

Brahmā said :

4. Vāk (Sarasvatī) said to Devas: "The Gandharvas are madly passionate over women. O Devas, it behoves you to bring Soma after giving me to them."

5. The immortal ones replied to Vāk: "We are not competent to give you away. It is impossible to live without Soma, nor is it possible to live without you".

6-13. Again Vāk said to Devas: "I shall come here again. A way should be thought out. Let an excellent sacrifice be performed on the southern bank of Gautamī. If Devas are prepared let them come there for sacrifice. Gandharvas are always fond of women. Exchange me for Soma".

"So be it", said Devas who firmly agreed to what was said by Sarasvatī. Through the messengers they invited Devas, Yakṣas, Gandharvas and Nāgas severally to the sacred mountain. Thereafter, O sage, the name of that mountain became Devagiri. There came Devas, Gandharvas, Yakṣas, Rākṣasas, Siddhas, sages and the eight species of inferior gods.[1]

While the great sacrifice was being performed by the sages on the banks of Gautamī, the thousand-eyed lord surrounded by Devas, spoke in the presence of Sarasvatī after honouring Gandharvas.

Indra said :

Exchange the nectar-souled Soma of yours for Sarasvatī.

Brahmā said :

14. At the instance of Indra those Gandharvas, passionate over women, gave Soma to Devas and took Sarasvatī.

15-19. Devas possessed Soma and Gandharvas possessed Sarasvatī. While she stayed there she secretly came near Devas everyday saying, "Let it remain a secret". That is how, O Nārada, Soma was bought. While buying Soma one should speak in a low tone. Thereafter Devas possessed both Soma and Sarasvatī. The Gandharvas had neither Soma nor Sarasvatī.

For the sake of Soma all the following came to Gautamī:

---

1. 'Devayonayaḥ' is demi-gods or inferior gods such as Ādityas, Vasus, Viśvedevas etc.

cows, Devas, mountains, Yakṣas, Rākṣasas, Siddhas, Sādhyas, sages, Guhyakas, Gandharvas, Maruts, Nāgas, medicinal herbs, Mothers,[1] Guardians of quarters, Rudras, Ādityas, Vasus, Aśvins and other Devas who deserve a share in the sacrifice.

20-21. Twentyfive rivers, O sage, have joined Gaṅgā. The place where the entire ghee offering was given is called the holy centre of Pūrṇā. As mentioned before, the rivers that joined Gautamī have holy centres in their names. Now listen to holy centres with their names O Nārada.

22-27. The holy centres are: Somatīrtha, Gandharva, Devatīrtha, Pūrṇatīrtha, Śāla, Śrīparṇā-Saṅgama, Ilāsaṅgama, the holy confluence of Kusumā, Puṣṭisaṅgama, the auspicious Karṇikā Saṅgama, Vaiṇavī Saṅgama, Kṛśarāsaṅgama, Vasavīsaṅgama, Śivaśaryā, Śikhī, Kusumbhikā, Upārathyā, Śāntijā, Devajā, Aja, Vṛddha, Sura and Bhadra—all these joined Gautamī. These and many other rivers, the holy rivers in the world, went to the Devaparvata mountain for the sake of Soma. Others also came to the sacrificial pavilion. Those holy rivers joined Gaṅgā in due order.

28-31. Some of them were in the form of rivers flowing east; some in the form of rivers flowing west, others in the form of lakes and still others in the form of streams. All these holy centres are severally well known. Taking bath in them, or performing Japa, Homa and Pitṛtarpaṇa (water libation to the manes) fulfils all cherished desires of men. It gives enjoyment and salvation. The people who read about these or remember them become liberated from all sins and go to lord Viṣṇu's regions. Twenty rivers have been mentioned between Pūrṇā and Pravarā. Then there are five divine rivers, my daughters. All together twentyfive of them have been described thus.

1. 'Mātaraḥ' is divine mothers or female energies of great gods, e.g. Brahmāṇī, Māheśvarī, Vaiṣṇavī, Aindrī etc.

CHAPTER THIRTYSIX

Amṛtāsaṅgama and other holy centres

Brahmā said :

1. Mahānadī is an excellent river. Its confluence is called Pravarā-Saṅgama. Lord Siddheśvara presides over this holy centre. He renders help unto all his devotees.

2. There was an extremely horrible fight between Devas and Dānavas. (Later on) there was mutual love and amity too between them, O great sage.

3. They went to the mountain Meru. Devas and Dānavas consulted one another. They wished for the welfare of each other.

Devas and Daityas said :

4. It is possible to obtain immortality through nectar. Let us make the excellent nectar and drink it. We shall become immortal.

5-6. We shall join together and protect the worlds. Abandoning fight we shall attain happiness. Fighting is a cause of misery. With pleasure and avoiding jealousy, we shall enjoy riches earned by us. Loving treatment is always pleasant to us.

7. What has happened to the contrary should never be remembered. The pleasure that one derives from absence of enmity is not obtained even by our rule over the three worlds or by acquiring a higher position or even in salvation.

Brahmā said :

8-9. Thus becoming friendly to one another Devas and Dānavas joined together with great delight and churned the Ocean. They made the Mandara mountain their churning rod and Vāsuki the rope. Devas and Dānavas churned the ocean.

10. Therefrom the holy nectar dear to Devas came out. When the holy nectar was produced they said to one another:

11-13. "We shall go to our abodes. We have done our duty. We are tired. Let this be distributed among all in an equitable manner. In an auspicious hour when all have assembled together, O excellent Devas, let this holy nectar be distributed." After saying thus Daityas, Dānavas and Rākṣasas went away. After they had gone Devas began to consult one another.

Devas said :

14. Our enemies, our suppressors have gone after confiding in us. The nectar should not at all be given to them.

Brahmā said :

15-18. Bṛhaspati agreed and said to Devas thus:

Bṛhaspati said :

Drink this nectar in such a manner that our enemies do not become aware of it. This is the secret advice to defeat our enemies. Those who are conversant with the science of politics know that the enemies are to be hated in every respect. The enemies are never to be trusted. They should never be told (any secret). They should never be consulted. Nectar should not be given to them. They are likely to become immortal thereby. When those enemies, Daityas, become immortal we will not be able to defeat them. Therefore the nectar should not be given to them.

Brahmā said :

19-21. After consulting each other thus, Devas said to Bṛhaspati:

Devas said :

Where shall we go? Where shall we have secret counsel? Where shall we drink it? Where shall we stay? We shall do that alone first. O Bṛhaspati, tell us.

Bṛhaspati said :

Let the immortal beings go to Brahmā and ask him the great expedient in this matter. He alone is the knower, donor and speaker (thereof).

Brahmā said :

22-27. On hearing the words of Bṛhaspati Devas came near me. After bowing down to me they intimated to me what had transpired.

O son, at the instance of Devas I went to Hari along with

Devas. Everything was then mentioned to Viṣṇu and Śambhu the remover of poison.

Viṣṇu, Śambhu and I went to the cave of Meru along with Devas, Gandharvas and Kinnaras without the knowledge of Asuras. After making Hari the watchman we sat for drinking Soma juice.

Āditya was the person to take note of those who partook of Soma. Soma was the distributor of share of nectar and the discus-bearing lord was the watchman. Neither Daityas nor Dānavas nor Rākṣasas knew it except Rāhu the highly intelligent son of Siṁhikā. He drank the Soma juice. Rāhu who had acquired efficacy to assume any form he desired entered the place.

28. He assumed the form of Deva and held the drinking bowl. On realising that it was a Daitya, the Sun-god intimated to Soma.

29. Soma gave nectar to that Daitya who had the form of a non-Daitya but informed Viṣṇu.

30. By means of his discus, Viṣṇu lifted the Daitya who could manage to gulp nectar. Viṣṇu cut off his head immediately. But, O dear one, that head became immortal.

31-32. The body bereft of head fell on the Earth. The body that had touched the nectar fell on the southern bank of Gautamī, O great sage, and shook the Earth. The body too became immortal, O son, and that was mysterious.

33. The body was dependent on the head and the head was dependent on the body. Both of them became immortal. This demon became extremely powerful. Devas thought:

34. "(if) the head were joined to the body it will eat all Devas. Hence we shall destroy at first this body which has come down to the Earth". Then all the excited Devas said to Śaṅkara:

Devas said :

35. Destroy the demon's body that has come down to the Earth, O lord, excellent among Devas. You are the ocean of mercy and the saviour of those who seek refuge in you.

36. Kindly do something so that the body of the demon does not join the head.

Brahmā said :

37-38. Īśa sent his excellent Śakti, the goddess Mother, the protectress of the worlds, along with the "Mothers". The goddess held the weapons of Īśa. She was full of the energy of Īśa. Desirous of eating it up she went to the place where the body came down to the Earth.

39. Devas pacified the head alone there itself on the Meru. The body fought with the goddess for many years.

40-41. Rāhu said to Devas : Pierce my body at the very outset. The excellent juice is within it. Extract it from the body. When the juice is separated, the body shall be reduced to ashes. Hence do that at the outset.

Brahmā said :

42. On hearing these words of Rāhu Devas became pleased. They performed his consecration. "Be pleased. Be the most excellent of all planets."

43-46. At the instance of Devas, Śakti who is mentioned as Īśvarī, pierced the body of the lord of Daityas. Equipped with the power of Devas she immediately extracted the excellent nectar outside. After placing that body there Ambikā devoured it. Ambikā of great strength is called Kālarātrī and Bhadrakālī. The excellent juice, the most excellent juice of all juices that had been placed there, oozed out and became the river Pravarā. She took in the nectar too that had been extracted and placed.

47-48. Then the excellent river Pravarā was born. It is auspicious and nectarous. It was born of the body of Rāhu and is fully endowed with the Śakti of Rudra. It is the most excellent and beautiful of all rivers. It is induced by nectar. There are five thousand meritorious holy centres there.

49-51. Worshipped by Devas Śambhu himself stayed there. The delighted Devas gave unto the divine river excellent boons, severally: "Whenever Śambhu, the lord of Devas, is worshipped, you too shall be worshipped with a desire for the welfare of worlds. O goddess, stay here. O goddess of juice, stay here, always bestowing all (spiritual and worldly) achievements.

52-56. You will be the bestower of cherished things on being eulogized, glorified or meditated upon. At the behest of deities all the desires will be fulfilled, the desires of those who bow down to you with devotion and de ire for anything whatsoever.

Sages call this Nivāsapuram (city of residence) since the eternal residence of Śiva and Śakti has taken place there. The highly delighted Devas gave excellent boons to Pravarā. The confluence of Pravarā with Gaṅgā is the favourite of Devas. It has been described to you. Worldly pleasures and salvation will be obtained by all who take their holy dip therein. Whatever they desire in their minds will be realised even if it happens to be inaccessible to the gods".

After granting this, Devas went away.

57-58. Thenceforth, they know it as the holy centre of Pravarā Saṅgama. The place where the Śakti was induced by the Lord of Devas is called Preritā. It is also well known as Amṛtā. In this manner Pravarā is a great river. Know that a holy dip and distribution of charities etc. at the confluence of Pravarā is of everlasting benefit. It yields pleasure to the Manes.

CHAPTER THIRTYSEVEN

Description of seventeen holy centres

Brahmā said :

1. The holy centre where Śiva is called Vṛddheśvara is named Vṛddhā Saṅgama. I shall describe it in detail. Listen to it. It destroys sins.

2-3. There was a sage belonging to the family of Gautama, named Vṛddha. He was a sage of great penance. When the brahmin was a boy as the son of Gautama (scion of the family of Gautama) he had no nose. He was born without a nose. Hence he had an ugly form. Due to the lack of worldly attachment he wandered to various holy centres in the land.

4. Since he was shy and modest he had no contact with any preceptor. Since he was bashful and reserved he had no opportunity to learn along with other pupils.

5. With great difficulty (somehow) he was initiated into the study of Vedas by his father Gautama. After doing so much Gautama set out on a journey.

6. Thus, much time elapsed. The brahmin was supported by the brahmin mother. That Gautama had no opportunity to study the Vedas.

7. Gautama did not engage himself in a regular study of any scriptures. But he observed vows regularly and performed rites in sacred fires.

8-10. He was brahmin only by name, by the practice of Gāyatrī and the performance of holy rites in sacred fire. He maintained his brahminhood with this much alone. O sage, Gautama the noble brahmin continued to perform holy rites in the fire and repeated the Gāyatrī Mantra. O son, Gautama became long-lived. His span of life increased but he could not get a wife. There was no one to offer him his daughter (in marriage).

11. He was wandering about in the holy centres in various places in different forests and holy hermitages.

12. During the course of his wanderings, Gautama came to Himālayas. There he espied a beautiful cave overgrown with creepers and branches of trees.

13. The great brahmin sat down there and decided to stay. Entering within he saw an excellent woman.

14. She was a lean old woman with flaccid limbs. She was a virgin practising celibacy and performing penance. She was staying in isolation there.

15. On seeing her the excellent sage stood ready for making obeisance to her but she prevented him.

The old woman said :

16. You are about to become my Guru (preceptor). It does not behove you to salute me. Longevity, learning, wealth, fame, virtue, heavenly enjoyment etc. of a person, perish if a Guru were to bow down to his disciple.

Brahmā said :

17-18. Gautama who was surprised (at this remark) spoke to her with palms joined in reverence:

Gautama said :

You are a saintly old lady superior to me in qualities. I am younger in age with lesser knowledge and learning. How can I be your Guru?

The old woman said :

19-23. In this connection, O sage of good holy rites, I shall narrate to you what happened long ago.

The son of Arṣṭiṣeṇa was known as Ṛtadhvaja. He was a meritorious, intelligent and heroic Kṣatriya devoted to the duties of Kṣatriyas. Once, attracted by a desire for hunting, Ṛtadhvaja went to a forest. He took rest in this cave. He was a clever, intelligent youth surrounded by a large army. As he was taking rest, a celestial damsel, the daughter of the king of Gandharvas, known as Suśyāmā saw the excellent king. On seeing her the king became enamoured of her and she too began to love him. O sage of excellent intellect, the king indulged in sexual dalliance with her. As his passionate love was fully satisfied the great king took leave of her and went back home.

24. I was born of that Suśyāmā, O sage of great intellect. As she was about to go back to heaven, O sage, my mother said this to me:

Suśyāmā said :

25-30. O gentle lady, he who enters this cave will become your husband.

The old lady said :

After saying this, O sage of great intellect, my mother expired. You are the only man who has entered this cave. Never has anyone else entered it. My father performed penance after ruling over his kingdom for eighty thousand years. Then he went to heaven. After my father had gone to heaven, O great sage, my brother ruled over that kingdom for ten thousand years and then died. But I remained here itself. O brahmin, I have never been wooed by anyone else. I have neither father nor mother. O brahmin, I am mistress of myself, a Kṣatriya girl waiting ready (for you). Hence, O brahmin, accept me who have been seeking a man and observing the holy vows.

Gautama said :

31. O gentle lady, I am aged a thousand years. You are older than I. I am a boy. You are an old lady. Hence, our mutual union is impossible.

The old lady said :

32-34. You have been indicated formerly as my husband. No one else is accepted by me to be my husband. You have been granted to me by Brahmā. Hence, it does not behove you to disown me. Or, if you do not desire me in spite of the fact that I am undefiled and ever prepared to follow you, I shall abandon my life even now in your presence. To all embodied beings death is far better than the non-acquisition of what is desired. There is no end to sins if one abandons persons attached to one.

Brahmā said :

35-37. On hearing the words of the old lady, Gautama said:

Gautama said :

I am devoid of penance. I do not possess good learning. I am poor and without possession. I am not a suitable bridegroom for you. I am deformed and bereft of worldly pleasures. I have no nose. What shall I do? I have neither learning nor penance as my asset. Hence first, O splendid lady, you should make me handsome and bestow on me good learning. Afterwards you can carry out what you have stated. Thereupon, the old lady said to the brahmin:

The old lady said :

38-39. Goddess Sarasvatī has been propitiated by me, O brahmin, by means of penance. So also the Waters of beautiful form and Agni the bestower of comeliness. Hence, goddess Speech will grant you learning and Agni, the beautiful god, will grant you a lovely form.

Brahmā said :

40. After saying this to Gautama the old lady pleaded (fire god) and made him handsome as well as learned.

41. Thereafter, Gautama who became learned, handsome and brilliant married the old lady. With great pleasure he sported with that charming lady for many years in the cave. He was happy and delighted in his mind.

42-43. While the couple stayed happily in their cave on the mountain, O most revered sage, sages Vasiṣṭha, Vāmadeva and others who had been wandering over sacred holy centres reached that cave.

44-45. On coming to know about the arrival of those sages, Gautama accompanied by his wife welcomed them with great hospitality. Some of them laughed at them. Some of those sages, boys proud of their youth, as well as men of middle age saw the old lady as well as Gautama and laughed.

46-48. They saw that the old lady was lean and lanky with hairs over the body. Her lips were hanging down. Her ears were broad like the winnowing basket. Her teeth, nose and hairs were all too long. She was infirm with her physical form shattered and decaying. They saw that Gautama was equipped with learning, good fortune, brilliance and comely features. On seeing this (disparity) some of those childish sons of sages began to laugh. On seeing her the narrow-minded disciples said smilingly:

The sages said :

49. Is this your son or grandson, old lady? Who is this Gautama? Tell us the truth, O gentle lady.

After saying this those brahmins laughed.

50-54. (They went on saying thus) "O saintly lady, truly the fruit of penance has been said to be powerful. By means of penance one attains peace and tranquility. If one is incompetent one is faced with exhaustion. O splendid lady, only he who views (everyone) with equanimity has peace and tranquility. Truthful speech amounts to the protection of what has been acquired in the course of many births.

Of what avail is profuse speech now. It is practically meaningless and worthless. You alone are blessed lady endowed with good fortune in this world. Tell us (is it not so?).

Your sins have been burnt by austerities you have practised. You have been glorified by your exertion in performing penance.

In this world, you have become lean and emaciated by practising austerities and subjugating your sense-organs, by worshipful hospitality to the guests and the nursing and nurturing of your son. Let not the body be nourished by accumulating sins.

55-60. Mercifulness, charitable gift, penance, truthfulness, cleanliness, subjugation of sense-organs, worshipful hospitality to the guests, quiescence, protection of sons etc.—by means of all these you are maintaining your duty. If anyone has only such activities as are conducive to the acquisition of what is required by his belly, he is considered certainly fit to be confined to hell. O beautiful lady, tell me who is that woman who endures all miseries? Who is that woman who is on a par with a dog (for miserable life)? A woman even of good eyebrows should be considered unholy if she is devoid of husband and sons. O splendid lady, certainly you are endowed with virtue because of your continuous hospitality to the guests. You are feeding brahmins with cooked food. Although you are very old and bereft of your husband you are still virtuous and splendid. Although you are deformed (physically) you must be considered beautiful. Although you have no wealth you are still rich. Penance has been performed by you with good concentration. Ekāṅguṣṭha (standing on a single toe) and similar other severe and difficult penances have been performed by you.

61. Lord of Lakṣmī (i.e. Viṣṇu) has been worshipped very well by you in your previous birth with devotion. Good charitable gifts have been distributed, sacrifices with good monetary gifts have been performed (by you.)

62. Holy centres have been duly visited and plenty of gifts have been given and much has been sacrificed. Hence Gautama, the knower of the Vedas has been obtained by you as son.

63. He is conversant with all the principles of Vedas and Vedāṅgas; he is well read in all the scriptures. A son (like) Gautama is very difficult to obtain even by the merit of all the three worlds.

64. (Defective Verse) Is he your great-grandson, grandson or son ? Or is he your daughter's son? Sesamum seeds are causes of satisfaction through a son but in the case of daughter's son they are like those kept in a leather bag.

65-66. O old lady with plenty of penance, through this boy you will attain the great region of Viṣṇu or a pure befitting family (in the next birth). In this matter no worry need be felt."

Thereupon some of the disciples of sages said in surprise: "A youthful woman is poison unto an old man but a young man is like nectar unto an old woman. Oh, the conjunction of desirable and undesirable things has been seen by us after a long period."

Brahmā said :

67. Thus spoke some of them even as the couple were listening to their talk.

After saying this and after receiving due hospitality the great sages went away.

68. On hearing the talk of the sages the couple were ashamed and sorry. The highly intelligent Gautama in the company of his wife asked Agastya the great excellent sage:

Gautama said :

69. What is that land or holy centre where happiness can be had? What is that place which bestows worldly pleasures and salvation? O highly intelligent one, tell me quickly.

Agastya said :

70-71. These words have been heard by me from the sages who had been narrating the same: "All desires are realised in Gautamī river". Hence go, O sage of great intellect, to Gautamī, the destroyer of sins. I shall follow you. Do as you please.

Brahmā said :

72-73. On hearing these words of Agastya Gautama and the old lady went there. That holy sage performed penance along with his wife. He eulogized lord Viṣṇu and Śambhu. The holy sage propitiated Gaṅgā on behalf of his wife.

Gautama said :

74. Like a tree unto the travellers in the desert, O Śiva, you in the company of your consort are the sole refuge unto those persons who are distressed in this world.

75. You entirely remove the sins of all living beings—high and low. O Kṛṣṇa, you are like the cloud to the planets that wither due to drought.

76. O Gautamī, you are the ladder leading to the fort of Vaikuṇṭha that is difficult of access. You are the river of nectar. Be the refuge of seven (? worlds) coming beneath.

Brahmā said :

77. Then the delighted Gautamī, worthy of being sought refuge in, spoke to Gautama who was accompanied by the old woman, who had sought refuge in her and who was in great distress.

Gautami said :

78-80. Pour my water over your beloved wife after consecrating it with Mantras. Pour the water out of pots sanctified with Mantras and other modes of worshipful service. She will then become beautiful with all her limbs rendered youthful. She will have conjugal felicity, fascinating eyes and good traits. She will attain beautiful physical form. Your beautiful wife shall pour water over you. That being done you will have all good traits in full and you will attain a beautiful form.

Brahmā said :

81. At the instance of Gaṅgā they said 'yes' and did as they were told. Both of them obtained beautiful form by the grace of Gautamī.

82. The water used for pouring became a river; it became well known, O excellent sage, by the name of the old woman.

83. It was known as 'Vṛddhānadī.' Similarly, Gautama was called 'Vṛddhagautama'. He was so called by the sages staying along with them.

The old woman said to Gautamī Gaṅgā in visible form :

Vṛddhā said :

84-85. O goddess, let this river be called Vṛddhā after my name. Let its confluence with you be an excellent holy centre. By means of holy dip, charitable gifts, Homas etc., let it be conducive to the increase of beauty, good fortune, wealth, sons and grandsons. Let it bestow longevity, health and welfare. Let it give victory and increase pleasure. Let it sanctify the manes.

Brahmā said :

86. "Let it be so", said Gaṅgā to the old lady, the beloved wife of Gautama. The Liṅga installed by Gautama is glorified by the name Vṛddhā.

87-88. The excellent sage attained great joy there itself along with the old woman. The holy dip and charitable gifts there are the bestower of all desired things.

Thereafter, that holy centre is called Vṛddhā Saṅgama.

CHAPTER THIRTYEIGHT

Sixteen thousand holy centres

1. The holy centre named Ilātīrtha is one that brings about spiritual achievement of men. It sanctifies men who commit (even) such (heinous) sins as brahmin slaughter etc. It bestows all cherished things.

2. Once a ruler of men named Ila born of the family of Vivasvān (Sun) went to the hunting forest along with a large army.

3. He wandered over the forest infested with beasts of prey, full of birds of various shapes and sizes and rendered beautiful by the branches of trees.

4. Wandering over the forest with his mind inclined to the sport of hunting the excellent king determined to stay there. Ila said to his ministers:

Ila said :

5. All of you go to the city looked after and protected by my son. May you all look after the welfare of the land, treasury, army, kingdom as well as the Prince.

6-7. Let Vasiṣṭha too go like my intelligent father accompanied by his wives. I shall stay in the forest maintaining sacrificial fires. I shall stay here with a few horses, elephants and men who can enjoy forest pleasures and who are skilled in the sport of hunting. Let all others go back to the city from here.

Brahmā said :

8-10. Saying "So be it" they went away. King Ila himself went to the mountain Himavat slowly. Staying on the Himavat full of jewels the king saw a cave wonderfully studded with different jewels. A certain Yakṣa leader known as Samanyu lived in that cave on that beautiful excellent mountain. His wife Samā was devoted to her husband and eagerly engaged in rendering service to him.

11-16. That highly intelligent Yakṣa roamed about here and there in his forest as he pleased, accompanied by his wife. He sported about dancing and singing. Though he had assumed the form of a deer the Yakṣa could know (whatever happened there). But Ila did not know that the cave was (used as residence by and) under the protection of the Yakṣa. That abode of the Yakṣa was large and wonderfully embellished with many jewels. There the king stayed surrounded by a large army. He stayed in the abode all alone. The Yakṣa who was accompanied by his wife and who had assumed the form of a deer was furious over this trespass. He thought thus: "I am not strong enough to defeat Ila. If I request him he is not likely to give my abode back to me. My abode has been taken away by him. How can I kill this arrogant fellow in battle?" After thinking thus he (wanted to) send his own heroic followers, the bow-bearing Yakṣas.

Yakṣa said :

17. Defeat king Ila in battle, Ila who is arrogant because he possesses elephants. It behoves you to do that which will make him leave and go elsewhere from my home.

Brahmā said :

18-21. At those words of the Yakṣa leader all those Yakṣas proud and undaunted in battle went to Ila and said: "Go out of this cave-home. Otherwise, you will be defeated in battle and have to run out of this". At those words of the Yakṣas, the emperor fought with them in anger. After defeating the Yakṣas, he stayed there for ten nights. With his abode taken away and with his servants killed the Yakṣa leader assumed the form of a deer and stayed in the forest along with his wife. Worried over the situation he spoke to the Yakṣiṇī, his beloved wife in the form of a doe.

Yakṣa said :

22. O beloved, how will I conquer (this king) who is strong, invincible, proud on account of glory and heroism, blind due to arrogance and very much attached to the sport of hunting?

Yakṣiṇī said :

23. Tell me, O loved one, is there any means of subduing his arrogance? If my words (or deeds) can help, tell me. I shall do that.

Yakṣa said :

24-25. O lady of excellent waist, there is a means of subduing the arrogance of the king. O lady of great fortune, do that whereby the pride of this king is driven away. It will be splendid and pleasing to me.

O blessed lady, go to that place where this silly king is staying.

26-27. There you reveal yourself in front of Ila after assuming the form of a hind, O splendid lady. Draw king Ila to the forest known as Umāvana. O lady of good fortune, attract that king who is staying in my abode and who is very much attached to the sport of hunting. Let the evil-minded one attain the form of a woman.

28. O beloved, this king is evil-minded and is indulging in vices. He will fall into adversity through this. This is the means thereof that has been thought of by me.

29. The kingdoms of all kings come to an end through the increase of sins and indulgence in vices. Assuming the form of a charming hind lead him on to the forest Umāvana, O lady of good eyebrows.

30. If this king gets in there he will undoubtedly become a woman. O gentle lady, this should be done by you. It is not

proper for me because I am a man. You are a woman and a Yakṣiṇī besides.

Yakṣiṇi said :

31. How is it that you should not go to the excellent forest Umāvana? What will be the harm if you go there? Tell me that briefly.

Yakṣa said :

32. Śiva roamed about as he pleased on the excellent mountain, Himavat accompanied by Umā and followed by Devas and his Gaṇas. Once Pārvatī said to Śaṅkara standing alone in an isolated place:

33-35. "This is the nature of women that they would love to have sexual dalliance in secret. Hence, O lord of Devas, give me a fixed place well guarded at your behest and known as Umāvana.

O lord, excepting you, Gaṇeśa, Kārtikeya and Nandin whoever enters this place should be turned into a woman."

36. Order was accordingly given by the delighted lord with the Moon on his crest. What is it that a man does not do, on being lovingly requested by his beloved? Hence I should not go to the excellent Umāvana.

Brahmā said :

37. On hearing the words of her husband the Yakṣiṇī who could assume any form as she pleased and whose eyes were large, became a hind and appeared in front of Ila.

38-40. The Yakṣa remained there alone. The king espied the hind. On seeing the hind the king who was particularly attached to the sport of hunting started by himself and followed the hind seated on his horse. She (the Yakṣiṇī) attracted the king who was overwhelmed by (the spirit of) hunting and gradually went to that forest called Umāvana. In some places (on certain occasions) she became invisible and in some places she revealed herself.

41. Standing still, sometimes walking and running as though

she was afraid, that hind of roving eyes dragged him on to the forest of Umāvana.

42-46. Following closely riding on his horse he reached that forest Umāvana. On realising that he had entered Umāvana, the Yakṣiṇī who could assume any form she desired abandoned the form of the hind and assumed a divine form. She stood near an Aśoka tree with one of her hands resting on its branch. The young maiden Samā who had assumed a divine form and who had applied (over her body) sweet smelling divine unguents (was delighted) because she had achieved her object. The tired king Ila was searching for the hind with rolling eyes. Fully remembering what her husband had said she smilingly looked at the king and said to him.

Samā said :

47. O delicate-limbed one, O young maiden, O Ilā, where are you going alone seated on a horse and dressed like a man. Whom will you follow?

Brahmā said :

48-52. On hearing (himself addressed by) the name 'Ilā' the king became furious and rebuked the hind. Still the Yakṣiṇī said, "O Ilā, what is it you are looking for?" On hearing (himself addressed by) the name 'Ilā' the king who was seated on the horse holding the bow and who had conquered the three worlds became angry and showed her the bow. Again she said to the noble-souled king: "O Ilā, see for yourself. Tell me thereafter whether I am speaking the truth or lying". Thereupon the king surveyed himself and saw the pair of protruding breasts between his arms. He became bewildered wondering what had happened to himself.

Ilā said :

What has happened to me? Surely you must know it clearly. Tell me everything precisely. Tell me, O woman of holy rites, who you are.

The Yakṣiṇī said :

53. Samanyu, my husband, stays in an excellent cave of

the Himālayas. He is the lord of Yakṣas. He is prosperous. I am his wife, a Yakṣiṇī.

54-56. It was his Yakṣas who had been killed by you out of delusion without a formal fight. It was in his splendidly cool cave that you had been seated. In order to make you come out from the same, I assumed the form of a hind and entered the forest Umāvana. You too entered it. Formerly, Maheśvara had declared: "The ignorant man who comes within this range will acquire womanhood". That is why you have attained womanhood. It does not behove you to grieve over this. Even a mature person cannot know the mysterious future.

Brahmā said :

57. On hearing the words of the Yakṣiṇi (the king) seated on the horse fell down. After pacifying him the Yakṣiṇī said again:

Yakṣiṇī said :

58. You have once for all become a woman. It does not behove you to strive to regain manhood. Learn the arts befitting women. Learn all these things such as the graceful charms of a woman, the elegance and coquetry of a woman, nay, all the activities of a woman.

Brahmā said :

59-60. After attaining all those accomplishments Ilā said to Yakṣiṇī :

Ilā said :

Who will be my husband? What is my duty? How can manhood be attained again? Mention this to me who am particularly distressed. There is no better thing conducive to welfare than the suppression of grief of distressed people.

Yakṣiṇi said :

61. There is a son of the Moon named Budha (Mercury). O extremely fortunate lady, to the east of this forest is the hermitage of that youth of great handsome features.

62. It is through this path that the planet Budha goes to meet his father, Moon, and also to pay respects to him everyday.

63. When the quiescent Budha goes (along this way) reveal yourself to him. O fortunate lady, on seeing him you will fulfil all your cherished desires.

Brahmā said :

64. After consoling her the Yakṣiṇī of splendid eyebrows vanished. She also reported the matter to her husband, the Yakṣa, who became happy on hearing it.

65-67. The army of Ila that had been stationed there, went away. Ilā stayed in the forest Umāvana singing, dancing and pursuing activities of feminine interest. She pondered over the ways of Karman. Once while Ilā was dancing, the intelligent Budha saw her on his way to meet his father. On seeing Ilā, Budha halted on his way, approached her and said thus:

Budha said :

68-70. Be my wife and become comfortably placed in my abode as the most beloved of all women.

Brahmā said :

With great devotion Ilā approved of the suggestion of Budha and did accordingly. She remembered the earlier statement of the Yakṣiṇī and therefore, O sage, became satisfied.

After taking her to his excellent home Budha indulged in sexual dalliance with her with great pleasure. In every respect she pleased her husband. After the lapse of a great deal of time the delighted Budha spoke to his beloved:

Budha said :

71-75. What is it that you wish that I should give you, O gentle lady? What is that delightful thought that lurks in your mind?

Brahmā said :

The moment he made that statement Ilā spoke to Budha, the son of the Moon, who was her delighted lover: "Give me a son".

Budha said :

This semen of mine is infallible as well as one that is the

outcome of great delight. Hence you will have a son who will be a Kṣatriya well known all over the world. He will be the founder of Lunar dynasty. He will be like the Sun in brilliance. He will be on a par with Bṛhaspati in intelligence. He will be equal to the Earth in forbearance. He will be like a lion in vigour and vitality in the battle-field. In anger he will be on a par with the Fire-god.

Brahmā said :

76. At the nativity of the noble son of Budha, there were cries of "Victory" everywhere in the abode of Devas.

77. When the son of Budha was born the great Devas came there. With great joy, O highly intelligent one, I too came there.

78-79. The moment he was born, the boy made a highly pitched loud sound. Hence the sages and Devas who had gathered there said, "Since his sound was loud (Purū—loud, great; Rava—Sound), he shall be Purūravas". Delighted in their minds they named him so.

80. Budha taught his son all the splendid arts of a Kṣatriya. At that time Budha taught his son the science of archery along with its practical application.

81. Like the moon in the bright half of the lunar month he grew up very fast.

Once that highly intelligent boy noticed that his mother Ilā was overwhelmed by sorrow. He humbly bowed down to Ilā and said :

Aila said :

82. Budha, my father, is your beloved husband, O mother. I, your son, am skilful. Wherefore then do you have this mental anguish?

Ilā said :

83-84. It is true, dear son, that Budha is my husband and you, my son, are a mine of virtues. I have never experienced any worry on account of my husband or son. Still, O highly intelligent one, I am worried because I frequently recollect a former misery.

Then he said to his mother:

Aila said :

85-86. Tell me at once, my dear mother.

Brahmā said :

Ilā spoke to him thus: "It is a secret. How can I tell you? Still I shall tell you, my dear son, since the son is the ultimate resort of parents. A son is the exceedingly splendid ship for those who are about to sink in the ocean of misery."

Brahmā said :

87-89. On hearing those words of his mother the humble son placed her feet on his head and said to her with choking words with his eyes filled with tears: "If a son does not remove the difficulty of his parents by means of remedies (at his disposal), then, alas, his birth and life are futile. Though alive, he is (no better than) dead. Holy rites such as resorting to pilgrim centres, distribution of charitable gifts, performance of sacrifices, penances and other things are meritorious only when they are performed by a person who has pleased his parents. Speak out, my dear mother, all those thoughts that lurk in your mind as they are."

She spoke to her son with the lower lip hanging loosely down on account of her hot breaths. Excited like one about to be drowned in the ocean of misery she narrated everything in the manner it had occurred.

90-96. She narrated all these details: The family of the Ikṣvākus born of the Solar dynasty, her own birth therein (as a man), her name (as a man), his dear sons and wife, his priest Vasiṣṭha, his own region, departure to the forest, sending off his priest and ministers back to the city, of his indulgence in the sport of hunting, entry into the cave of the Himālayas, access to the abode of the leading Yakṣa, entry into the forest of Umāvana and the complete transformation into a woman, the statement of Yakṣiṇī that no man was permitted to enter the place as ordered by Maheśvara, the granting of boon, the contact with Budha, love and the birth of a son. These and other things she completely narrated. After hearing everything Purūravas spoke to his mother: "What shall I do? What shall I do to earn merit? If you are satisfied with this much that is enough, O mother. If there is anything else in your mind please tell that also to me."

Ilā said :

97-98. I would wish for the excellent manhood. I should like to regain the excellent kingdom and the coronation of my sons, especially that of yours. I should like to do all these, viz. to give charitable gifts, to perform sacrifice and to be on the path of salvation. I wish to do everything by virtue of your favour my dear son.

The son said :

99. I am asking you the means whereby you will attain manhood. Tell me exactly whether it is through penance or through some other means.

Ilā said :

100. Dear Son, go and ask Budha your father. He knows everything precisely. He will advise you what is conducive to your welfare.

Brahmā said :

101. At those words of his mother, Aila immediately went to his father. After bowing down to him he asked him what he and his mother should do.

Budha said :

102-103. I know Ila, O highly intelligent one. I know he was transformed into Ilā. I know how he entered the forest Umāvana and also the command of Śambhu. Hence the redemption from the curse shall be only through the favour of Śambhu and that of Umā. Only by propitiating them can the curse be removed and not otherwise.

Purūravas said :

104. How can I see that lord as well as mother Umā? Shall it be through any holy centre or through penance? Father, mantion this at the outset.

Budha said :

105. Dear Son, go to Gautamī. The glorious Śiva who dis-

pels curses and bestows boons stays there always accompanied by Umā.

Brahmā said :

106-110. On hearing the words of his father Purūravas became delighted. Wishing for the manhood of his mother, hurrying to perform penance, the intelligent (son of Budha) went to the Gautamīgaṅgā that sanctifies the three worlds, after bowing down to the Himālaya mountain, his mother, father and preceptor. Ilā and the son of Moon followed their son who went ahead. From the excellent mountain Himavat all of them came to Gautamī.

They took their holy bath there and performed penance for a short while. Thereafter, they recited the splendid euology of Bhava, the lord of Devas. Listen to the order of their euologies. Budha euologized first, then Ilā and then their son Purūravas eulogized goddess Gaurī and Śaṅkara.

Budha said :

111. Let those two deities be my refuge; those two deities who take delight in the sound of the girdle, who resemble the natural gold, who have good features and who are worshipped by Skanda and Gaṇeśvara. They are worthy of being sought refuge in.

Ilā said :

112-113. Let Śāṅkarī and Śaṅkara be my refuge. Meditating upon those two deities, the embodied beings who have been scorched by the forest fire of the three types of worldly distresses, attain the greatest beatitude immediately.

I am distressed. My mind has been afflicted. There is no one other than you to protect me from suffering, distress etc. O lord, your feet are extremely meritorious and worthy of being sought refuge in. Let them be by my refuge.

Purūravas said :

114-115. Gaurī and Hara are worthy of being sought refuge in by the entire universe. They are the immanent souls of the universe. This entire (visible universe) rises from, prospers in and finally merges with those two deities. Let them be my refuge.

In the course of a great festival Devas said, "O Īśa, touch and hold the feet of the daughter of the lord of mountains". As soon as this was said they were lovingly held by Śiva. Let those two feet be my refuge. They are worthy of being sought refuge in.

The eminent goddess said :

116. What is it that you all wish to have? What shall I grant you all—tell me. You have performed that which is difficult even unto Devas. Welfare unto you all. Be satisfied, for you have done your duty.

Purūravas said :

117. King Ila had unwittingly entered your forest, O Ambikā (Mother). O goddess of Devas, forgive him. It behoves you to grant him manhood.

Brahmā said :

118. "So be it" said the goddess to all of them, the goddess who abided by the opinion of Bhava. Then the lord who is always devoted to the utterances of the goddess said:

Śiva said :

119-122. Let this king regain his manhood merely by taking a holy plunge here.

Brahmā said :

Water oozed out from the body of Ilā as she took her holy dip. Whatever she had acquired from Yakṣiṇī, such as dance, music, graceful charms etc. entered the waters of Gaṅgā along with the continuous flow of water and the following rivers issued forth: Nṛtyā (Dance), Gītā (Song) and Saubhāgyā (Conjugal Felicity). They also joined Gaṅgā. These three confluences are very holy. Holy plunge and charitable gift in these confluences bestow the benefit of the kingdom of Devas.

123. After regaining manhood by the favour of Gaurī and Śambhu Ila performed the Vājapeya sacrifice for the achievement of great prosperity.

124-125. That excellent king brought all these: his priest Vasiṣṭha, his wife and sons, his ministers, his army, and his treasury. Then he established a kingdom in the Daṇḍaka with the four types of military units. There that city became well known after the name of Ila.

126-128. This charming town in the valley of Sahya surpasses even the city of Mahendra.

After getting fed up with the enjoyment of worldly pleasures in that excellent city he crowned his sons born previously, in the kingdom that had come to him by succession in the Solar dynasty. Afterwards he sprinkled (the holy water) on Aila with great affection saying, "Let this (boy) be the founder of the Lunar dynasty (and) a glorious king."

O sage, (in fact) he became more intelligent and excellent than all others (and so) the eldest.

129-131 Sixteen thousand holy centres grew up in the places where the splendid sacrifices were performed by king Ila, where he met the sons after regaining his manhood and where the rivers arising from the faculty of dance, music, conjugal felicity, auspiciousness etc. bastowed by Yakṣiṇī joined Gaṅgā, O Nārada. The holy centres grew up on both the banks. O dear one, Śambhu is called Ileśvara here. Holy dip, charitable gifts etc. in them bestow the benefit of all sacrifices.

CHAPTER THIRTYNINE

Cakra Tīrtha

Brahmā said :

1. The holy centre famous as Cakratīrtha destroys sins of brahmin-slaughter etc. because it was here that lord Hari obtained his discus.

2. The place where Lord Viṣṇu stood and worshipped Śaṅkara for the sake of discus is mentioned as Cakratīrtha.

3-6. By merely listening to it one is freed from all sins.

Once Dakṣa began a sacrifice. When Devas had gathered, lord Śiva was slandered and insulted by Dakṣa in the assembly of Devas. The great lord was slighted. Dakṣa's mind was so polluted that he wantonly neglected to invite the lord of Devas. Satī, the daughter of Dakṣa, heard the reason for not inviting Śiva when it was mentioned by Ahalyā. The goddess of Devas became angry. "I shall destroy my father who is a sinner. I will not forgive him at all", said she on hearing the derogatory remarks made by her father against her husband.

7-9. "Where is the limit to the sins of those women who listen to the censure of their husbands. Whatever may be his nature or status the husband is the ultimate resort of women. What doubt is there then in regard to Mahādeva, the lord of everything, the preceptor of the Universe? His censure has been heard by me. I shall therefore not hold on to this despicable body. I shall cast off this body."

After saying thus that goddess of Devas, the highly chaste lady, was overwhelmed by great fury and she blazed.

10-12. With thoughts directed towards Śiva alone she abandoned her body through yogic power.

Meheśvara heard everything from Nārada. On hearing it he became angry. He asked Jayā and Vijayā[1] and both of them said that Dākṣāyaṇī's (Dakṣa's daughter's) (ultimate wish) was the destruction of the sacrifice of Dakṣa.

On hearing this, Maheśvara went to the place of sacrifice surrounded by his terrible Gaṇas. He went along with the senior Bhūtas (ghosts).

13. That sacrifice sponsored by Brahmā and Devas was entirely surrounded by them. It had been guarded with purity of mind by Dakṣa, the sacrificer.

14. It had been looked after from all round by Vasiṣṭha and other formidable sages. It had been well protected everywhere by Indra, Ādityas, Vasus and others.

15-16. It had been embellished with the Vedas, Ṛk, Yajus

---

1. According to Vāmana Purāṇa, Jayā was a daughter of sage Gautama by Ahalyā in addition to Jayantī and Aparājitā. Vijayā was presumably another name of either of the latter two.

and Sāman as well as the utterances of Svāhā. It had been adorned all round by Śraddhā (Faith), Puṣṭi (Nourishment), Tuṣṭi (Satisfaction), Śānti (Peace), Lajjā (Bashfulness), Sarasvatī (Speech), Bhūmi (Earth), Dyau (Heaven), Śarvarī (Night), Kṣānti (Forbearance), Uṣā (Dawn), Āśā (Hope), Jayā (Victory), Mati (Intellect) as well as others.

17-19. It had been constructed by Viśvakarman and the noble Tvaṣṭṛ. It was splendidly flourishing with cherished desires (fulfilled) through these divine cows that showered anything anyone desired, viz. Surabhi, Nandinī, Kāmadhuk and Kāmadohinī. There were the trees and creepers of Kalpa, Pārijāta, Kalpalatā etc. In fact whatever is the most covetable thing was present in that sacrifice there. It was well protected by Indra, Pūṣan and Hari themselves.

20. These utterances were heard all round, viz. "Let this be given," "Let this be eaten"; "Let this be done", "Stay here happily". Thus the sacrifice of Dakṣa had been honoured.

21-24. It was Vīrabhadra accompanied by Bhadrakālī who went ahead. He was full of sorrow and anger in his mind. Afterwards holding the spear and Pināka bow Mahādeva followed bedecked by the great Bhūtas (spirits). Those spirits encircled the sacrifice all round Maheśvara. They destroyed the sacrifice. A great commotion ensued there. Some of them fled. Some went to Śiva and began to eulogize the lord of Devas. Some were angry with Śaṅkara. On seeing the sacrifice destroyed thus Pūṣan came there.

25. After uprooting the teeth of Pūṣan Vīrabhadra routed Indra in a trice. O brahmin, he pierced and split the eyes of Bhaga.

26. Again, he whirled the Sun-god with his arms and hurled him down. Thereupon, all Devas sought refuge in Viṣṇu.

Devas said :

27. Save us, save us, O lord with the club in hands, from the danger arising from the leader of the Bhūtas. There is a certain Gaṇa (attendant) of Maheśvara. He is the leader of Pramathas. Even as Hari was watching the entire sacrifice pertaining to Viṣṇu the entire sacrifice was destroyed.

Brahmā said :

28. In order to kill the leader of Bhūtas the discus was discharged by Hari. As it advanced and approached him the leader of Bhūtas grasped it.

29. When the discus of Viṣṇu was grasped, the guardians of the quarters went away due to fear. On seeing the sacrifice (destroyed) and Devas in that (agitated) state the Patriarch Dakṣa eulogized lord Śiva with devotion.

Dakṣa said :

30-35. Be victorious, O Śaṅkara, lord of Soma (Moon). Be victorious, O omniscient one. Salutation to you. Be victorious, O Śambhu the benefactor, be victorious. Salutation to the lord identical with time or God of Death. O primordial maker, salutation to you. O blue-throated one, salutation to you.

O lord fond of Brahman, salutation to you. O lord in the form of Brahman, salutation to you. O lord, Parameśvara of three abodes, obeisance to the three-formed lord. O lord having all as your form (or Multiformed one), obeisance to you. O lord, the support of the three worlds, the bestower of cherished desires, obeisance to you, who can be realized only through Vadānta. Obeisance to you, the supreme soul. O lord with sacrifice for your form, obeisance to you. O lord, the abode of sacrifice, obeisance to you. O lord, the bestower of sacrifice, salutation to you. O the conveyor of sacrificial offerings, obeisance to you. O lord, obeisance to you, the destroyer of sacrifice. Obeisance to you, the distributor of benefits, O lord of universe. Save me, save me. O lord, fond of those who seek refuge in you. O lord, you alone are the refuge of devotees as well as non-devotees.

Brahmā said :

36. As he eulogized thus, Maheśvara became pleased with him and said to him, "What shall I give you"? (He replied) "O lord, let my sacrifice be complete".

37. "So be it" said Maheśvara, lord of Devas, Saṅkara, the soul of all living beings and the ocean of mercy.

38. After making the sacrifice of Dakṣa complete, O sage, and after saying thus the lord vanished along with his Bhūtas.

39-40. Devas went away to their respective abodes in the manner they came.

Then once a great battle ensued between Devas and Daityas. Therein Devas became afraid of Daityas. With complete devotion Devas eulogized Viṣṇu, the lord of Śrī in the following words:

Devas said :

41-42. Indra and other Devas perform penance seeking the benign side-glance of Lakṣmī. We seek refuge in that lord, who has become Brahman and to whose feet Lakṣmī is devoted.

In all the three worlds there is none equal or superior to Nṛsiṁha whose vehicle is Garuḍa. With great sympathy, let that lord of Devas protect all of us who have sought refuge in him from great dangers.

Brahmā said :

43. Thereupon the lord holding the conch, discus and club became pleased and said to them: "What for have all of you come? I shall do it for you."

Devas said :

44. O slayer of Madhu, Devas have an excessive danger from Daityas. Hence, O Lord, try to save them.

Brahmā said :

45-46. Hari said, "O Devas, my discus has been caught hold of by Hara. What shall I do? The discus is gone and all of you have fallen into misery. Yet your protection will be afforded by me. Let all Devas go back.

Brahmā said :

47. Then, after Devas had gone Viṣṇu prepared himself to get the discus. After going to Godāvarī he began the worship of Śambhu.

48. With great devotion Viṣṇu performed the daily worship of the consort of Umā with a thousand divine sweet smelling golden lotuses.

49. "Obeisance, the Pināka-bearing Maheśa, who removes great danger in the forest of worldly existence and who fulfils all cherished desires".

50. By means of this Mantra and with the mind endowed with devotion lord Viṣṇu worshipped Śiva, the lover of Bhavānī.

51-52. As the worship proceeded something happened between them. Listen to that. The lotuses were found to be one short of a thousand. When Viṣṇu noticed the shortage he dislodged his own eye and offered Arghya.[1] Taking the vessel of Arghya containing a thousand lotuses and meditating on Śambhu, Hari who had no other refuge, offered Arghya.

Viṣṇu said :

53. O lord, you alone know the innermost feelings of men. You alone are refuge and overlord. What doubt can be there ?

Brahmā said :

54. Speaking thus with tears welled up in his eyes he got himself merged as though with Īśvara. Then Śambhu appeared in front of him, accompanied by Bhavānī.

55. He embraced Hari closely and filled him with various boons. He got back his original eye as well as discus.

56-58. Then all Devas eulogized Hari and Śaṅkara. They eulogized Gaṅgā the most excellent of all rivers as well as the bull-bannered lord. Thenceforth that holy centre is remembered as Cakratīrtha. Merely by listening to it one is freed from all sins. He who performs the rites of holy dip, charitable gifts and libation to the manes, shall be rid of all sins. He will attain heaven along with the ancestors. This holy centre can be seen with a mark of discus even today.

CHAPTER FORTY

Cakreśvara and other Holy Centres

Brahmā said :

1-4. The holy centre Pippala comes after Cakratīrtha because the lord here is called Cakreśvara and it was from here

1. Things such as water, honey etc. offered to deities, guest etc. as a token of respect.

that lord Hari obtained his discus. The place where Viṣṇu himself stood and worshipped Lord Śaṅkara for getting the discus back is cited as Cakratīrtha. They know the place as Pippala where Śambhu became pleased with Viṣṇu. Even Śeṣa is not competent to narrate its glory. Listen, O Nārada, to the reason for the name Pippaleśa given to Cakreśvara. Listen to it with devotion because what is mentioned in the Vedas is being recounted by me.

5. There was a famous sage named Dadhīci. He was endowed with good qualities. His wife was a chaste lady of noble birth and highly intelligent.

6. She was the sister of that lady well known as Lopāmudrā. She was famous by the name Gabhastinī and glorified as Vaḍavā.

7. She was the beloved wife of Dadhīci. He performed penance regularly along with her. Dadhīci was devoted to the duties of a householder and he always maintained the sacred fire.

8. He resorted to Gaṅgā and was devoted to the propitiation of gods and guests. He was fondly attached to his wife. He was as calm as Agastya.

9-10. Due to his spiritual power Daityas and Dānavas came to that region, O great sages. It was there that Agastya too had his hermitage. After defeating Daityas who came for attacking them Devas, Rudras, Ādityas, twin brothers Aśvins, Indra, Viṣṇu, Yama and the Fire-god came there.

11. They were excessively delighted by their victory. They were eulogized by the Maruts. On seeing Dadhīci, the great sage, the leading Devas bowed down to him.

12. With great delight, Dadhīci welcomed and honoured Devas severally. Accompanied by his wife he thereafter performed the duties of a householder to them.

13-14. Devas were asked about their welfare and general happiness by him. They chatted with him. Devas who were delighted in their minds bowed down to sage Dadhīci who was made happy by his wife and who was seated there.

Devas said :

15. What is it that is difficult to be obtained by us, O sage,

in this world since a sage like you, the very Kalpa tree[1] in this world, is kind to us.

16. This alone is the benefit of all living men, O excellent sage, viz., the holy plunge in the holy centres, kindness to all living beings and meeting with people like you.

17. Listen, O sage, to what is being said by us out of affection.

We have come here after defeating Daityas and killing Rākṣasas.

18. We are happy, O brahmin, and especially so since we see you here. We have no use for our weapons. Indeed, we are not capable of carrying them.

19-20. We do not see, O leading sage, a place fit enough for keeping these weapons. If they are kept in heaven, Daityas will take them away. If they are kept in nether regions they will (surely) take them away. Hence, the weapons are being placed, O bestower of honour, in your sacred hermitage.

21. There is no fear at all here, O brahmin, from Dānavas and Rākṣasas. This is a sacred place well protected at your behest. There is no one equal to you in the power of penance.

22-24. O most excellent one among the knowers of Brahman, we have conquered our enemies. Daityas have already been killed. We don't need our weapons any more. They have become burdensome since they have fulfilled their purpose. The place worthy of placing them is near you, O leader among sages. Along with our lovely maidens we shall enjoy divine pleasures in the heavenly park, Nandana. Therefore, we shall go (now) along with Indra. We have fulfilled our tasks and we shall go to our respective abodes. As for the protection of weapons, let them be guarded by you. Therefore, bid us farewell. You are capable of holding and guarding them.

Brahmā said :

25-30. On hearing their words, Dadhīci said to Devas : "Let it be so", although he was prevented by his wife who said thus : "What (have we to do) with the affairs of Devas ? In

1. The divine wish-fulfilling tree obtained by the churning of the ocean (Vide Agnipurāṇa, Ch. 3).

fact, it has an adverse effect. Of what avail is indulgence in the other people's affairs to those who have understood scriptures, who abide by the supreme entity and who are free from attachment to the activities of the world. O sage, there is no happiness thereby either here or hereafter. Listen, O excellent brahmin, if the place (for keeping weapons) is given the enemies of Devas will hate us. If these weapons are lost or taken away, O great sage, Devas will become angry and turn into our enemies. Hence, O excellent one among the knowers of Vedas, this excessive affectionate attachment to other people's objects is not proper. As long as the material kept in deposit exists there is friendship, but once it is lost or taken away they will become our enemies. If one has power to give away things in charity, he should give them to the needy without any thought. If not, good people should help others by speech, thoughts and acts. But keeping things belonging to other peoples is repudiated by good people. Therefore, my dear husband, get rid of (these weapons) immediately."

Brahmā said :

31-34. On hearing these words of his beloved wife the brahmin said thus to his wife of splendid eyebrows.

Dadhīci said :

Having given consent at first to Devas, O gentle lady, saying "No" to them will not give me any pleasure.

Brahmā said :

On hearing these words of her husband the beloved wife (of Dadhīci) remained silent, thinking "Excepting the fate nothing else is capable of doing anything to men." At that opportune moment the excellent Devas deposited those highly shining weapons, bowed down to the great sage and went to their abodes. After depositing their weapons in a safe place Devas became contented.

When Devas had gone, the excellent sage lived in great delight while practising virtue in the company of his wife.

35. A long time elapsed. A thousand years according to the reckoning of Devas passed away. Devas neither spoke

about their weapons, O great sage, nor did they seem to think about them.

36. Dadhīci said to Gabhasti : "O gentle lady, Asuras are powerful, behaving inimically toward me. Devas do not appear to be desirous of taking away their weapons deposited with us. Tell me what is proper in the circumstances."

37. She said to her husband humbly: "It has already been said, dear lord. You know what is proper in this situation. The powerful Daityas, who have increased their efficiency and who are endowed with the power of penance will take away these weapons".

38. Therefore, Dadhīci did thus for protecting weapons. He washed those weapons with holy water inspired with Mantras. The water absorbed the essential splendour of all the weapons and Dadhīci drank this holy water.

39. Deprived of their intrinsic splendour those weapons gradually wasted away as time passed by.

Then at last Devas came and said to Dadhīci : "Great danger from our enemies has befallen us.

40-41. Give back those weapons, O excellent sage, which had been kept with you by Devas."

Dadhīci said : "Due to the fear of asuras and also due to the fact that you did not come for a long time, the weapons have been liquefied and drunk by me. They can be said to be stationed in my body. What is proper in this situation, you may please say".

On hearing what was mentioned by him, Devas spoke to him thus with great humility.

42. "O leading sage, give us the weapons. Can you say 'Yes' or do you refuse ? Without them we will be lost for ever. Our enemies are powerful. Where shall we go ?

43. Neither in the mortal world, nor in the nether world, nor in the heaven, O dear one, is it possible for us to stay today. You are an excellent brahmin. Moreover, you are endowed with (the power of) penance. It is not proper to say anything else in your presence."

44. The brahmin said then : "You may take the weapons assimilated in my bones. There is no doubt about this."

Devas said to him : "Of what avail is this to us ? Without the weapons the great Devas have become 'effeminate' ".

45. Again, the excellent sage said : "I shall abandon the spirits animating my body (as) I am endowed with the power of Yoga. You may make weapons out of my bones (as they have merged with them). Let them be excellent ones with excellent forms."

46. "Do so", said Devas in reply to Dadhīci who resembled Fire-god and who was never deficient in intrinsic power. At that time the wife of the sage was not there in the vicinity to say pleasing words to him, O great sage.

47-48. Not seeing her, but afraid of her, Devas said to the brahmin : "Do so quickly". With pleasure the sage cast off his vital spirits (ordinarily) very difficult to abandon, saying to them : "Use this body as you please. Let all Devas be pleased with my bones. What have I to do with this body ?"

Brahmā said :

49-50. Having said thus the noble-souled sage seated himself in the Padmāsana ("lotus pose"). He fixed his eyes at the tip of his nose. He was as pure as the light. By his yogic power he gradually led the vital air along with the gastric fire, to the inner portion of Daharākāśa (the ethereal portion in the cavity of the heart). He fixed his intellect in Brahman which is immeasurable, which is the highest in status and which should be meditated upon. He attained identity with Brahman.

51. On observing that his physical body had become lifeless Devas in their hurry, said to Tvaṣṭṛ, "Make a number of weapons immediately".

52-53. He said to them: "O Devas, how should it be done? This terrible body is that of a brahmin. I am afraid and incompetent to make weapons. If the bones are torn off I shall make excellent weapons from them quickly."

Thereupon, Devas said to bullocks in their great hurry:

Devas said :

54. O bullocks, to facilitate your work your faces are made adamantine in a trice by Devas for getting weapons. Tear off the body of Dadhīci and give the pure bones now.

Brahmā said :

55. At the instance of Devas they did so. They licked the bones clean and gave them to Devas. Devas of brave valour and strength hurriedly went to their abodes and so did the bullocks.

56-57. After making the weapons of gods the noble Tvaṣṭṛ went away hurriedly.

Then, after some time, the wife of the sage who was of good conduct, who had been the beloved wife of her husband, who was gentle and who had a boy in the womb came there. She held in her hand a pot full of water. She was on her way back after worshipping Umā. Carrying fruits and flowers she came quickly eager to see the sacred fire, her husband and the hermitage.

58. On her way, her necklace slipped from her neck and fell on the ground. The bangle also fell down from her wrist. Her right eye throbbed. Seeing all these omens she became distressed in her mind.

59-61. "What calamity is going to befall me immediately?" She pondered thus in her mind. While she was coming home, the fall of a meteor prevented her from proceeding. She came to the hermitage in great bewilderment but did not see her husband in front. Wondering where could he have gone she asked the Fire-god. The Fire-god mentioned everything to her in detail—the advent of Devas, request for the bones of the sage, the collection of the bones and their departure. On hearing everything she became distressed. Due to agitation born of misery she fell on the ground. Slowly she was consoled by the Fire-god. She said to Fire-god:

62-63. "I am not capable of cursing the immortal beings. What shall I do ? I shall enter fire."

Brahmā said :

After checking her anger and grief for her husband the chaste lady then spoke these righteous words :

64-67. "Everything that is produced in this human world is destructible too. It should not be bewailed. Meritorious men abandon their lives in protection of cows, brahmins and Devas. Blessed are those living beings who, after obtaining an efficient body endowed with virtue in this world that whirls like a wheel, abandon it for Devas and Brahmins. All the vital airs of every embodied being are sure to go away. There is no doubt at all in this. After realizing this, those masterminds cast them off for brahmins, cows, Devas and the distressed beings. I had dedicated myself to him. Though prevented by me he agreed to keep the weapons. Who knows the mind of the creator whose activities are beyond the comprehension of men of mortal world ?"

Brahmā said :

68-69. After saying this, she duly worshipped the sacrificial fires along with the skin and hairs of her husband. She slit open her stomach, took out her son from the womb and held him in her hand. After bowing to Gaṅgā, the Earth, plants and trees in the penance grove and medicinal herbs, she entered the hermitage (once again).

She said :

70. This boy is bereft of his father, mother and other relatives born of his family. May all the groups of living beings, the gurdians of quarters and medicinal herbs protect him.

71. Those who view and protect a boy bereft of his mother and father without any distinction from their own children are certainly to be honoured and saluted even by Brahmā and others.

Brahmā said:

72-73. After saying this the lady with her mind devoutly directed towards her husband cast off her son. She placed the boy near the holy fig-trees with the sacrificial vessel (in her hand). She circumambulated the fire and entered it. She went to heaven along with her husband.

74. The trees in the hermitage and the residents of the forest who had been nurtured by the sage Dadhīci like his own children, began to cry.

75. The animals, the birds and the trees, all of them said to one another. "We cannot live without him. Nor can we live without that mother".

The trees said:

76-78. Only those men are blessed and contented who give natural and continuous affection to the children of the parents who have gone to the next world. Formerly the sage and his wife had been treating us in a manner which (our own) father and mother were not habituated to. Fie on us. We are sinners. It is certain that hereafter, to all of us, this boy is Dadhīci, this boy is the mother. This is the eternal virtue.

Brahmā said:

79. After saying thus the medicinal herbs, plants and trees approached king Soma (i.e. the Moon) and requested for excellent nectar.

80. Soma gave them excellent nectar. They gave the boy the nectar that is dear to Devas.

81. Satisfied with this, the boy grew up like the moon in the bright half of the lunar month. Since he had been brought up by the Pippalas (fruits of the fig tree), the boy was (called) Pippalāda (the eater of Pippala fruits). After growing up he said to the Pippalas thus in great wonder.

Pippalāda said:

82. Men are born of men. Birds are born of birds. Plants and creepers are produced from seeds. No inconsistency is seen. How was I with hands, feet, vital breath etc. born of you?

Brahmā said:

83-84. On hearing his words the trees told him everything in the proper order viz., the death of Dadhīci, the entry of the chaste lady into the funeral pyre, the collection of bones by Devas etc. On hearing these details the boy was overwhelmed by sorrow and he fell on the ground.

85. He was consoled by trees by words endowed with meanings. On recovering he again said to those medicinal herbs, plants and trees :

Pippalāda said :

86-87. I will kill the murderers of my father. Otherwise it is unbearable to live. A real son maintains the friends and enemies of his father. He alone is the real son. Others are enemies in the form of sons. They say that friends of father redeem even the enemies.

Brahmā said :

88. The trees took that boy to the presence of the Moon. Those trees intimated the utterance of the boy to Soma (Moon). On hearing it, Soma spoke to Pippalāda :

Soma said :

89. Learn all the branches of knowledge in a formal way, my dear son. You will attain at my behest the power of penance, auspicious speech, heroism, handsome features, strength and intellect.

Brahmā said :

90-92. Pippalāda then said to the Moon humbly :

Pippalāda said :

I consider all these futile as long as I do not take revenge on the murderers of my father. Hence, tell me at the outset. In which land, on which occasion, by the help of which Deva or Mantra or holy centre can my ambition be realised, O excellent Deva ?

Brahmā said :

93. After meditating for a long time the Moon said: "Whether it is enjoyment of worldly pleasures or attainment of salvation, everything is attained undoubtedly from lord Maheśvara".

94. He said to the Moon again : "How will I see Maheśvara ? I am a boy with childish intelligence. I have neither skill nor power of penance."

The Moon said :

95-98. O gentle boy, go to Gautamī. Eulogize Cakreśvara Siva. Dear boy, with a very little effort, the lord will be pleased with you, the merciful lord will be pleased. Śambhu has been realised personally by Viṣṇu the powerful lord. He granted boons to Viṣṇu and the discus honoured by the Devas. Go there, O highly intelligent one. Go to the river Gautamī in the Daṇḍaka forest. The medicinal herbs know that holy centre

Cakreśvara. After going there eulogize Śaṅkara, lord of Devas, with full devotion. Delighted in his mind he will grant you all cherished desires.

Brahmā said :

99-100. At the instance of the Moon, O brahmin, the sage Pippalāda came to the place where Rudra, the lord of the universe, the bestower of Discus (was present).

Overwhelmed by a great sympathy the Pippalas (holy fig trees) took him to their penance groves. After taking his holy dip in Godāvarī and after bowing down to the lord of the three worlds, the pure Pippalāda eulogized Śiva with full devotion.

Pippalāda said :

101-107. I bow down to Śambhu the primordial lord in whom bold and self-possessed persons seek refuge earnestly for their salvation. Those self-possessed persons have cast off all worldly desires. They have renounced all actions. They have controlled their minds as well as vital airs.

He is the witness unto all. He is the immanent soul in everyone. He is the lord of all. He is the repository of all arts. Let that enemy of Cupid have mercy on me after understanding everything that is within my mind.

The Ten-headed (Rāvaṇa) had conquered the lords of the quarters. He shook the Kailāsa mountain honoured by Devas. He went down beneath the nether worlds when pressed down with toe (by Śiva). His body was bruised. On hearing his piteous cries the lord laughed along with the goddess and granted him pardon. Though the lord had been furious, yet he was pleased with him. In this manner, O Maheśvara, you are (sometimes) a donor unto (even) undeserving persons. Bāṇa became praiseworthy after performing the noble worship, beautiful and fascinating, unto the Moon-crested lord. By performing the daily worship he surpassed Indra in prosperity.

After conquering enemies and worshipping Devas Viśākha i.e. Skanda went ahead to bow down to his father. He became angry on seeing the lord of Gaṇas (i.e. Vināyaka) held in the lap. Lord Śiva took him (also) in his lap and laughed. Though he was seated in the lap of Śiva, the boy was reluctant to leave off the lap of his mother due to his childish innate nature. Unable to pacify his furious son Śiva assumed his half-female form.

Brahmā said :

108-109. Then the extremely delighted self-born lord spoke to Pippalāda.

Śiva said :

O Pippalāda, welfare to you. Choose any boon as you wish.

Pippalāda said :

110. My father of great renown who was never arrogant and who was truthful has been killed by Devas, O Mahādeva. So also my chaste mother.

111. O lord, after hearing in detail the death of both of them on account of Devas, I am overwhelmed by misery and anger. I am not eager to live.

112. Hence, grant me sufficient capacity to destroy Devas. In all the three worlds, you alone, O Moon-crested one, are worthy of being served by those who should not be killed.

Īśvara said :

113. O sinless one, if you are capable of looking at my third eye you will be competent to assail your foes.

Brahmā said :

114. Then he desired to look at the third eye of the lord but could not. Then he said to Śaṅkara : "I am not able".

Īśvara said :

115. O boy, do some penance so that you will be able to look at my third eye. Then you will undoubtedly attain your desire.

Brahmā said :

116-119. On hearing these words of Īśāna the son of Dadhīci of righteous soul decided to perform penance. Although he was a boy he engaged himself solely in meditation on Śiva like a powerful person, there itself for many years. Everyday he used to get up early in the morning, take his bath and bow down to the elders and preceptors in due order. He used to sit comfortably and fix his mind in the Suṣumnā (the tubular structure inside the spinal column) without thinking of anything else. By means of crossed arms he made the sign of Svastika over his navel. He forgot the world and its affairs. He thought of superior excellence of one position over another. He meditated on the splendour of Śiva. Pippalāda looked at the third eye of the lord. With palms joined in reverence in the form of a cup he humbly spoke thus.

Pippalāda said :

120-121. Formerly, this boon had been granted to me by Śiva, the lord of Devas. The lord of Devas had said that the moment I was able to see the brilliant splendour of the third eye, whatever I wanted would happen. Hence give me that which will bring about destruction of enemies.

122-123. At that very time, a voice said: "O highly brilliant one, your mother went to heaven after saying thus : 'Men who have forgotten what is conducive to their welfare, who are engaged in harassing others and whose minds wander here and there fall into the abysmal depths of hell.' "

124. On hearing that aerial voice, Pippalāda became angry. When the fire of pride and prestige burns within, advice regarding proper conduct is meaningless.

125-127. Kṛtyā, the female deity of destruction, said to him, "Give; Give". Since the brahmin was remembering Vaḍavā thus, Kṛtyā that came out of his eyes had the shape and features of Vaḍavā. She contained within herself plenty of fire for destroying all living beings. That Kṛtyā became one with fire within, in view of the fact that he was meditating on his mother with the child in the womb. Even as she came out she was extremely terrible. She was as terrible as the tongue of Mṛtyu (Goddess of death).

128. She said to Pippalāda, "What is my duty ? Tell me that". Pippalāda said to her, "Devour Devas, my enemies."

129-130. Saying "So be it," she caught hold of Pippalāda standing in front of her. He said, "O Kṛtya, what is this ?" She said, "What has been said by you is carried out by me. The body is made by Devas."

Thereupon, that frightened sage went to Śiva and eulogized that lord. Then Śiva said to Kṛtyā :

Śiva said :

131. O Kṛtyā, do not seize living beings remaining within a range of a Yojana (12 km) at my behest. Go far away from that place and do your duty.

Brahmā said :

132. That Kṛtyā which had the form of Vaḍavā stood at a distance of a Yojana to the East from the holy centre Pippala.

133-134. I big blaze of fire, capable of destroying the world, came out of her. On seeing it, Devas became afraid and approached Śiva. Eulogizing the lord, the frightened heaven-dwellers said to Śiva :

Devas said :

135. O Śambhu, protect us. The Kṛtyā and the fire born of it assail us. O lord of all, O bestower of protection from fear to the frightened persons, be our refuge.

136. O Śiva, you alone are the refuge to the creatures that are attacked from all sides, that are distressed and that are extremely wearied.

137. The Kṛtyā coming from the fire of your eye has been requested by the sage and she is desirous of destroying the three worlds. You are our protector and none else.

Brahmā said :

138-139. The lord of the universe said to them : "This Kṛtyā does not harass those who live within the range of a Yojana. Hence, you all, by day and night, remain here itself, O immortal ones. You will have nothing to fear from her.

Brahmā said :

140. Again, they said to the lord of Devas : "O lord honoured and worshipped by gods, how shall we live here after abandoning heaven granted by you ?"

Brahmā said :

141-143. On hearing the words of Devas Śiva said :

Śiva said :

Here is the Deva with eyes all round, the Deva who has faces all round, who always blows up with his rays and who is considered the father of all living beings. Let that lord Sun alone remain here directly in his visible form for ever. All others will be considered remaining here in his physical form.

Brahmā said :

144-148. At the instance of Śambhu Devas created (the Sun) from Pārijāta tree. Tvaṣṭṛ said to the Sun:

Tvaṣṭṛ said :

O lord of the universe, stay here itself. Protect these Devas yourself. We too shall stay here in the presence of Śambhu by means of our parts.

Brahmā said :

All round Cakreśvara, within a range of a Yojana, resorting to the banks of Gaṅgā the excellent Devas stood by. Each had a fourth of an Aṅguli (about 2.5 cms.) of the bank of Gaṅgā. They were three crores and five hundred, O excellent sage. Who is competent to speak about or hear the prosperity of these holy centres.

Thereafter, Devas spoke to Śiva.

Devas said :

149-155. O lord of Devas identical with the Universe, quieten Pippalāda.

Brahmā said :

Saying "O yes", the lord of the universe said to Pippalāda:

Śiva said :

Even if Devas are destroyed your father will not return. His life had been given by your father for the realization of the task of Devas. Who can be so kind to the wretched and the distressed in this world ? Similarly, O dear one, your mother, a chaste lady, has gone to heaven. No one is equal to her, not even Lopāmudrā (wife of sage Agastya) and Arundhatī (wife of sage Vasiṣṭha). Much fame has been acquired by your father due to whose bones Devas are victorious and happy for ever. An act of everlasting fame has been performed by your mother. Excellent fame spreading everywhere has been acquired by you, the son.

It behoves you to protect those who have dropped off from heaven for fear of your exploits. It behoves you to save the immortal ones who have fled because they were afraid of you. There is no meritorious deed superior to the protection accorded to the distressed.

156. A person who has gone to heaven lives in the other world without any malady for as many years as there are days when the fascinating fame prevails in human world.

157. Only those who have no fame are considered dead here. Only those who are devoid of renown are (considered) blind. Those who are not habitually liberal in gifts are eunuchs. Only those who are not invariably virtuous are to be pitied.

Brahmā said :

158. On hearing the lord of Devas the sage became calm. After bowing down to the lord he spoke with palms joined in reverence.

Pippalāda said :

159-163. I shall bow down to Śiva worthy of being worshipped by Devas and others for the welfare of these people and others too, viz. those who help me by words, thoughts and deeds and those who are engaged in actions conducive to my welfare. May lord Śiva do what these people wish, the people by whom I have been guarded and nurtured (as though) I belonged to the same family as theirs and I had the same qualities as theirs. I am bowing down to the Moon-crested lord for ever. O lord, O lord of Devas, let this holy centre be known all over the three worlds by the name of those by whom I have been brought up like my father and mother. If they attain fame I shall become free from indebtedness to them. If Devas admit that this holy centre is superior to other holy residences of Devas and all other holy centres on Earth, I shall condone the guilt of Devas for ever.

Brahmā said :

164. In the presence of the thousand-eyed lord (Indra) and others he spoke these words of fine sentiment and good syllables. Devas too agreed to the words uttered by the son of Dadhīci.

165. After appreciating the intellect, humility, learning, heroism, strength, truthfulness, filial devotion, and purity of emotions, Śaṅkara said to Pippalāda.

Śaṅkara said :

166. Dear boy, whatever cherished desire you have and whatever is pleasing to Devas you will attain. Speak out what is conducive to your welfare. Do not hesitate to speak out your mind.

Pippalāda said :

167. Those who take holy plunge in Gaṅgā and those who are virtuous, O Maheśa, and see thy lotus-like feet—let them attain their desires immediately. After their death let them attain the region of Śiva.

168. O lord, my father has attained your region. So also my mother, the Pippala and the immortal ones. After seeing the lord of lords they have attained happiness. Let them see you. Let them attain your region.

Brahmā said :

169. Saying "so be it" to Pippalāda, Maheśvara, lord of Devas spoke to him congratulating him along with Devas.

170. Devas were pleased after being freed from fear arising from him. All of them spoke this to the son of Dadhīci in the presence of Śiva.

Devas said :

171. Undoubtedly, what is liked by Devas has been performed by you. The behest of the lord of Devas, that embellishes the three worlds has been carried out by you.

172. O brahmin, what is requested for by you earlier is for others and not for yourself. Therefore, say something that you wish. We shall grant you something.

Brahmā said :

173. Devas repeated the same thing to the excellent brahmin again and again. After bowing down to Śambhu, the Pippalas and Umā, Pippalāda spoke with palms joined in reverence.

Pippalāda said :

174-179. I desire to see my parents who have always been the subjects of discussion by means of words. Blessed are those living beings in this world who are under the control of their parents, who are devoted to their service and who eagerly await their command.

After obtaining the sense-organs, the physical body, nobility of birth, capacity, intellect and the beauty of form, he, the son, shall be contented by utilising them in their service.

Seeing their own mother is easy even for animals and birds. Even that has become difficult for me. I ask you. Is it the result of my sins ?

(?) If it had been difficult of access to all (there would not have been any complaint). If it is easy of access to someone and not to others it is not proper. There is no other sinner than I.

O excellent Devas, if only I can get a glimpse of my parents I shall deem it as the fruit of my acts of thought, speech and body.

Who will be competent to count the great sins of those persons born in the world who cannot see their parents ?

Brahmā said :

180-183. On hearing those words of the sage, Devas consulted among themselves and said to him. "Surely you will see today your parents, the auspicious couple, seated in an excellent aerial chariot and eager to see you. Cast off your sorrow, covetousness and delusion, and pacify your mind". After some time, the excellent Devas said to the son of Dadhīci : "See. See your parents, the auspicious couple, are eager to see you. They are seated in an excellent aerial chariot. They have heavenly characteristics with golden ornaments. They are being fanned by the celestial damsels. They are eulogized by the Kinnaras."

184. On seeing his parents he bowed down to them in the presence of Śiva. Their eyes were filled with tears of pleasure. Somehow he spoke to them.

The Son said :

185. Other sons who perpetuate their families redeem their parents. But I am merely the cause of splitting the belly of my mother. Even though I am like this I shall look at them due to delusion. I am a wicked person with an evil mind.

Brahmā said :

186. On looking at them he could not speak anything further out of sorrow. Devas spoke to Pippalāda and his parents.

Devas said :

187. Blessed are you, dear son, whose fame has spread in the world and has gone up to heaven. The three-eyed lord has been directly perceived by you. Devas have been consoled by you. With you as son the excellent worlds will never dwindle down.

Brahmā said :

188. At that time a shower of flowers fell on his head from heaven. The shouts of "Victory" uttered by Devas arose, O great sage.

189. After bestowing blessings on his son and after bowing down to Śambhu, Gaṅgā and Devas along with his wife Dadhīci spoke to his son.

Dadhīci said :

190. Get yourself a wife. Have devotion to Śiva and serve Gaṅgā. After procreating sons and after performing sacrifices with due gifts, dear son, you can be contented. Thereafter, proceed to heaven for a long stay there.

Brahmā said :

191-192. "I shall do thus" said Pippalāda, the son of

Dadhīci. Along with his wife, Dadhīci consoled his son again and again permitted by Devas he returned to heaven.

With great bewilderment Devas said to Pippalāda.

Devas said :

193-199. Welfare unto you. Quieten Kṛtyā and the great fire arising from her.

Brahmā said :

Pippalāda said to them : "I am incapable of warding her off. I shall never utter a lie. You can yourselves speak to Kṛtyā.

On seeing me that highly terrible Kṛtyā will do just the opposite thing".

Devas went unto her and spoke to her and the fire, pleading for their being pleased for the sake of peace. Both of them said : "No. I have been created by the brahmin for devouring everything; so also the fire born of me. How can it be otherwise ? The five great elements and everything that is mobile and immobile must be kept in our mouth. There is nothing that remains to be mentioned."

After consulting me (Brahmā) Devas said again to both of them.

"Both of you devour everything in due order."

Vaḍavā then spoke to Devas thus. O Nārada, listen to it.

Vaḍavā said :

200-202. O excellent Devas everything is worthy of being devoured by me in accordance with your wish.

Brahmā said :

That Vaḍavā became a river, O sage, and joined Gaṅgā. The immortal ones call fire arising from her the primordial fire. It was extremely terrible and they know that it is the first of elements.

Devas said :

Waters should be considered the eldest. So also you are the first. Still, devour the eldest (ocean) according to what we say. Go and devour as you please.

Brahmā said :

203-205. Fire-god said to Devas : "There is water there. How can I go ? If you alone take me up to the vast sheet of water I shall go."

They said: "O Fire-god, in what way should your movement be ?

The Fire-god said to those Devas, "If a virtuous virgin places me in a golden pot and takes me to a place were I can move about myself (it shall be proper)."

On hearing those words of his, Devas said to the virgin Sarasvatī :

Devas said :

206-209. O Sarasvati, bear this Fire-god on your head and take him to the ocean.

Brahmā said:

Sarasvatī said to Devas: "I alone an unable to hold him. If I am helped by four others I shall carry him to the ocean quickly."

On hearing the words of Sarasvatī Devas spoke to Gaṅgā, Yamunā, Narmadā and Tapatī severally.

Accompanied by them she was able to carry him. After placing the Fire-god in a golden pot and carrying it on their heads they went to the ocean.

210-212. The five rivers (including) Sarasvatī brought the fire and placed it in Prabhāsa where Somanātha, the lord of Devas, the lord of the universe, the moon-crested lord is stationed along with Devas. The great fire presides over the place drinking water slowly. Then Devas spoke to Śiva, the most excellent Deva.

Devas said:

213-217. Tell us the way of sanctifying the bones of the cows as well as the bones of us.

Brahmā said:

Śiva then said to everyone: "By plunging into Gaṅgā scrupulously Devas and cows are released from their sins. There is no doubt about this."

Thereafter, the bones taken from the body of the sage were washed. Being washed there, they attained sanctity.

The place where Devas got rid of their sins is the holy centre Pāpanāśana (Destroyer of sins). A holy dip and distribution of charitable gifts there destroy even the sin of brahmin slaughter.

The holy centre where the cows were sanctified is cited as Gotīrtha. By taking a holy dip there the highly intelligent devotee shall obtain the benefit of a cow-sacrifice.

218. The place where the bones of that brahmin became sacred, O Nārada, should be known as Pitṛtīrtha. It is conducive to the increase of delight of the manes.

219-220 If the ashes, bones, nails or hairs of any living being, even if he has committed sin, were to fall into this holy centre he will stay in heaven as long as the moon, sun and stars exist. So, from the holy centre of Cakreśvara three holy centres are evolved, O Nārada. Then the sanctified cows and Devas spoke to Śambhu.

The cows and Devas said:

221-223. We shall go to our respective abodes. The sun is established here. As long as the sun stays Devas shall be established. O lord of worlds, it behoves you to permit it. The eternal sun is the immanent soul of mobile and immobile beings. The sun in the nature of a Deva has been established there by us where Gaṅgā, mother of universe, and the three-eyed Lord Śiva are established. The residence and the establishment of Devas shall be where the three-eyed lord is.

Brahmā said :

224. Taking leave of Pippalāda Devas went to their own abode. The Pippalas attained the everlasting (pleasures of) heaven after the lapse of some time.

225. The brahmin Pippalāda of great exploits established the position of trees in the overlordship of the field and worshipped Śaṅkara.

226. The courageous son of Dadhīci of fierce splendour married the daughter of Gautama and begot sons. He earned wealth and fame and attained heaven along with his friends.

227. Thenceforth that holy centre is called Pippaleśvara. It is sacred and it affords the benefit of all sacrifices. The very remembrance of it destroys sins.

228. What doubt is there then (that sins will be removed)

through holy dip and charitable gifts and by the visit to the Sun. Cakreśvara and Pippaleśa are the two names of the lord of Devas.

229-230. After knowing this along with the esoteric truth one shall achieve all cherished desires. That holy centre is called Pratiṣṭhāna because the sun is installed there and the abodes of Devas are established there. It is dear even to Devas. This narrative is very sacred. He who reads this narrative or listens to this or remembers it lives for a long time. He will be righteous and become wealthy. Remembering Śambhu at the time of death he will attain him as well.

CHAPTER FORTYONE

Nāgatirtha a Holy Centre

Brahmā said :

1. The holy centre well known by the name of Nāgatīrtha is auspicious. It bestows all cherished things. Here the lord is Nāgeśvara. Listen to the detailed description of the same.

2. In the city of Pratiṣṭhāna[1] there was a king known as Śūrasena. He was a prosperous intelligent king born of Lunar Dynasty. He was an ocean of virtue.

3. In the company of his beloved wife he made great efforts for getting a son. After a long time a serpent of very terrible features was born as his son.

4. Śūrasena, the king, nursed and brought him up. No man ever knew that the king's son was a serpent.

5. Excepting his mother and father, no one whthin or without knew (this secret). Neither the nurse nor the chief minister nor the priest knew it.

6. On seeing that terrible serpent the excellent king and his wife were acutely distressed everyday. (They thought) that having no sons is far better than having a serpent for a son.

1. (a) An ancient city near modern Allahabad, situated on the eastern side of the confluence of Gaṅgā and Yamunā. (b) The capital of Sālivāhana on the Godāvari.

7-8. There was a special thing in this instance. The great serpent used to speak like men. That serpent said to his father, "Perform the holy rites of tonsure as well as Upanayana (sacred thread) and the study of the Vedic texts. Till he studies the Vedas a twice-born is considered equal to a Śūdra."

Brahmā said :

9. On hearing these words of his son Śūrasena was extremely distressed. He fetched a certain brahmin and got the consecratory rites duly performed. After learning the Vedas the serpent said to his father.

The serpent said :

10. Celebrate my marriage, O king. I am desirous of a woman, O excellent king. This is my opinion that your duties will not be fulfilled otherwise.

11. One should beget sons in accordance with the injunctions of the Vedas and perform all consecratory rites. There is no redemption for one who does not become a father and perform such rites.

Brahmā said :

12-13. Being surprised the father said to that son with the shape of a serpent :

Śūrasena said :

Who will give his daughter in marriage to a person whose voice frightens even brave men ? Tell me my son. What shall I do ?

Brahmā said :

14-16. On hearing those words of his father the clever serpent said.

The serpent said :

There are many types of marriages of kings, O king, O ruler of men. Forcible abduction, with the use of weapons, is also a type of marriage. When the marriage of the son is celebrated the father can be contented.

If you are not celebrating my marriage I shall undoubtedly die in Gaṅgā.

Brahmā said :

17. On realizing the decision of that son, the excellent king without a (human) son called his ministers for discussing the marriage and said.

Śūrasena said :

18-22. My son Nāgeśvara is the heir apparent. He is an ocean of virtue. He has good qualities. He is intelligent. He is heroic. He is invincible. He scorches the enemies. If Nāga is seated in a chariot with his bow he becomes incomparable in the whole of the earth. His marriage is to be celebrated. I am becoming old. I want to be carefree after placing the burden of my kingdom on his shoulders. My beloved son will not get rid of his childish nature till he marries. Hence all of you approve of this. All of you, engaged in what is conducive to my welfare, may kindly make efforts for the celebration of his marriage. Once my son is married I will not have any worry at all. Those who have fulfilled their worldly duties place the burden on their sons and go to forest for performing penance.

Brahmā said :

23. On hearing the words of the king the ministers humbly joined their palms in reverence. Delightedly they spoke to the king of profound brilliance :

The Ministers said :

24. Your son is superior to all in virtue. You are renowned everywhere. Therefore in the matter of your son's marriage what is there to be deliberated upon ? What is there to be worried about ?

Brahmā said :

25. When the ministers said so, the excellent king of grave features did not mention to the ministers the fact that his son was a serpent. They too did not know it (from other sources).

26-28 The king said to them again : "Who shall be the bride richly endowed with virtues ? Who will be that prosperous king, born of a great dynasty and abode of good qualities, worthy of alliance with us ? Who is that heroic king whose alliance shall be praised by all ?

On hearing those words of the king the Chief Minister of great intellect, a man of noble birth and excellent conduct who was ever engaged in what was conducive to the welfare of the king and his affairs, spoke thus. He had understood the mind of the king and he was aware of his wishes.

The Minister said :

29. O great king, there is a king named Vijaya in the Eastern land. He has countless horses, elephants and jewels.

30. That intelligent great king has eight valorous sons. Their sister Bhogavatī is precisely like another Lakṣmī. She is a suitable wife unto your son, O king.

Brahmā said :

31-34. On hearing the words of the old Minister the king replied to him :

The King said :

How can his daughter be (the wife) of this son of mine ? Tell me that.

The old Minister said :

You have been understood, O great king. I have observed what (thoughts are there) in your mind. Permit me to carry out the duties of a Śūrasena (i.e. one who has heroic soldiers in his army).

Brahmā said :

On hearing the words of the old Minister, he honoured him with ornaments, garments and words (of praise). He then sent him with a great army.

35-41. He went to the Eastern land and met the great king. He addressed him by a variety of respectful words in accordance with the requirements of polity and strategic means. The highly intelligent (minister) made an alliance for the marriage of Bhogavatī, the daughter of the great king, and Nāga the intelligent son of king Śūrasena. The alliance was contracted through false and true utterances. He honoured the king with ornaments, garments etc. After receiving the due honour the king said then, "I shall give".

After returning from there the extremely intelligent old minister informed Śūrasena about the marriage proposal.

Afterwards when a great deal of time elapsed the highly intelligent old minister went there along with a great army. He was adorned with ornaments and garments. He went there quickly surrounded by all other ministers. The great intelligent minister, the old minister surrounded by other ministers spoke everything connected with the marriage to the great king.

The old Minister said :

42. The intelligent son of king Śūrasena, well known by the name of Nāga, the ocean of virtue, does not wish to come here.

43-44. The marriage rites of Kṣatriyas, O king, are of various types. Hence the marriage shall be through weapons and ornaments, O extremely intelligent one. Indeed Kṣatriyas and brahmins do speak the truth. So let this marriage through weapons and ornaments be permitted.

Brahmā said :

45-46. On hearing the words of the old minister the excellent king Vijaya considered the utterance of the minister and the king truthful. The king celebrated the marriage of Bhogavatī elaborately with a weapon (by proxy). Then he sent her in accordance with (the injunctions of) scriptures.

47-51. Vijaya who was much delighted entrusted his own ministers with many cows, gold coins, horses, etc. (to be given to Śūrasena). Those ministers with the old Minister at their head took her (the bride) to Pratiṣṭhāna and intimated to Śūrasena that she was his daughter-in-law. They conveyed the message of Vijaya too in so many words. They became contented after handing over to Śūrasena the different types of ornaments, maid-servants, garments and other things. King Śūrasena received with great honour those ministers of Vijaya who had arrived there along with Bhogavatī and bade farewell to them (after giving them some presents) so that Vijaya could be pleased.

52. The young maiden of excellent waistline, the youthful pretty daughter of Vijaya engaged herself in serving her father-in-law and mother-in-law everyday.

53-54. The great and extremely terrible serpent who was the husband of Bhogavatī was staying in a deserted house in an isolated place. It had been rendered splendid by means of jewels. Fragrant flowers had been scattered there. The abode was (thus) pleasingly cool. That serpent used to say to his father and mother again and again (thus) :

55. "Why does not my wife, the princess, come near me at all ?" On hearing these words of her son, the mother of the serpent said :

The King's wife said :

56. O Nurse, of great beauty and fortune, go quickly and tell Bhogavatī, "Your husband is a serpent". (Tell me) what she says thereupon.

Brahmā said :

57. After saying "so be it" and approaching Bhogavatī she said to her in secret very humbly. She said so in a manner fit for reporting an unprecedented thing.

The Nurse said :

58-63. O extremely fortunate lady of gentle manner, I know your husband to be a deity. Nowhere should this be mentioned by you that he is a serpent and certainly not a man.

Brahmā said :

On hearing these words of that (nurse) Bhovavatī said this.

Bhogavatī said :

Normally the husband of a woman of the mortal world is a man of the mortal world. A husband of the divine species is obtained only by merit.

Brahmā said :

She reported these words of Bhogavatī entirely to the serpent, the mother of the serpent and to the king in the due order. The king cried when she said this because he remembered the effect of Karmans. Bhogavatī said to the female companion mentioned before :

Bhagavatī said :

Welfare unto you. Show me my beloved husband. My (youthful) age passes in vain.

Brahmā said :

64-65. Then she pointed out that terrible serpent. Bhogavatī went to the bedchamber filled with fragrant flowers. On seeing her husband in secret (that is) the terrible serpent embellished with jewels, she immediately joined her palms together in reverence and spoke to her husband.

Bhogavatī said :

66. Blessed am I, honoured am I whose husband is a deity.

Brahmā said :

67-68. After saying this and remaining there on the bed the lady of slender limbs made the serpent sport about through songs delightful to serpents as well as contacts with his limbs. She pleased her husband by means of fragrant flowers and beverages. Due to her favour the serpent was able to recollect, O sage. After remembering everything perpetrated by fate the serpent said to his beloved wife at night.

The serpent said :

69. Though you are the daughter of a king, O my beloved wife, how is it that you are not afraid on seeing me?

She said (in reply) "Who is competent to transgress what is laid down by fate ? To women, the husband alone is the refuge."

Brahmā said :

70. Then the extremely intelligent and delighted Nāgendra said to his wife.

The serpent said :

71. I am pleased with your devotion. What is it that you desire ? What shall I grant you ? O lady of beautiful limbs, it is due to your favour that I have regained the ability of remembering everything.

72-74. Formerly I was a powerful serpent, a son of Śeṣa, coiled round the arm of Maheśvara. I was then cursed by the angry Pināka-bearing lord of the Devas. I was your husband, and you my wife named Bhogavatī. Once Śiva was delighted at the words of Umā in secret. Therefore he laughed boisterously. O gentle lady, I too laughed in the presence of the lord. Then Śambhu became angry and cursed me thus :

Śiva said :

75-78. You will be born of human womb. You will be endowed with knowledge and wisdom.

The Serpent said :

Then O gentle lady, Śambhu was pacified by you along with me. And this was said by him, O gentle lady : "You shall perform my worship in the Gautamī when you are in the form of a serpent. I shall endow you with knowledge and wisdom. Then you will be freed from the curse due to the grace of Bhogavatī." It is for this reason that I have acquired this state and you too, O lady of splendid face. Now take me to Gautamī and perform the worship along with me.

79. Then I will be released from the curse. Both of us shall go to Śiva once again. Śiva alone is the ultimate resort unto all distressed persons always.

Brahmā said :

80. On hearing the words of her husband, she went to Gautamī along with her husband. After taking bath in Gautamī she performed the worship of Śiva.

81. Then the lord became delighted, O sage, and granted them the divine form. The serpent took leave of his parents and got ready to go to Śiva's world along with his wife. On coming to know of it the extremely intelligent father said.

The father said :

82. The eldest son (of a king) holds the rank of Crown Prince. You are my only son. Hence rule over the entire kingdom. Beget many sons. After I proceed to the supreme abode, go to Śiva's city.

Brahmā said :

83-86. On hearing these words of his father the king of serpents said—"So be it". Along with his wife, father, mother and sons he ruled over the vast kingdom after attaining the beauty of Cupid. When his parents went to heaven he placed his sons in his own place. Accompanied by his wife, ministers and others he went to Śiva's city.

Thenceforth that holy centre is well known as Nāgatīrtha. A holy dip and distribution of charitable gifts in the place where lord Nāgeśvara was installed by Bhogavatī bestow the benefit of all sacrifices.

CHAPTER FORTYTWO

Mātṛtīrtha

Brahmā said :

1. The holy centre known as "Mātṛtīrtha" is conducive to all sorts of achievements of men. A creature is freed from all mental ailments merely by remembering that holy centre.

2. There was a terrible battle between Devas and Asuras. Devas were not able to conquer Dānavas in battle.

3. Then, along with Devas, I approached the Trident-armed lord standing in his abode. With my palms joined in reverence I eulogized him by reciting a number of prayers.

4-7. Devas and Asuras after mutual consultation came to an agreement that they should churn the ocean. O Maheśa, while they were churning there emerged Kālakūṭa (a virulent poison). Excepting you who else could have been competent to swallow it?

Cupid is competent to keep the three worlds under his control by means of his flowery weapons. He is worthy of being saluted by other Devas too. (Even he) met with destruction when he tried to extend his power over Hara.

O enemy of Cupid, after churning the ocean you gave to the heaven-dwellers the best thing, viz. the nectar, and yourself consumed the poison. This adds to your glory. It is certainly a greatness of yours.

Thereupon the three-eyed primordial lord was satisfied.

Śiva said:

8-10. I shall give you whatever is desired by you. May the excellent Devas speak out their needs.

Devas said :

We are in great terror of Dānavas. O bull-bannered one, come along with us. Kill our enemies. Save us, O lord, we are having a protector in you.

O Śiva, if you had not been a disinterested friend what could the miserable embodied beings have done ?

Brahmā said :

11. On being requested thus he went at the very same moment to the place where the enemies of Devas were camping. A fierce battle raged between Śaṅkara and the enemies of Devas.

12. Then the three-eyed lord became tired. Śiva (then) assumed the Tāmasa form. As he fought, drops of sweat fell from his forehead.

13. Having resorted to the Tāmasa form he killed Asuras. On seeing that form the Asuras went to the Earth from the top of Meru.

14. Killing all Daityas Hara too went to the Earth. Being, frightened, they went around here and there all over the Earth.

15. In the same manner Rudra too followed them in anger. In the same manner (as before) drops of perspiration fell down as Śambhu fought.

16. Wherever the drops of perspiration came into contact with the Earth, O sage, the Mothers with the features of Śiva were born.

17. All of them said to Maheśvara, "We shall devour Asuras". Then the lord surrounded by Devas said :

Śiva said :

18. Those Rākṣasas who came from heaven to the Earth

have reached the nether worlds (now). All of you hear my speech.

19. Let the Mothers go wherever the enemies go. Now, the enemies have gone to the nether worlds. They are afraid of me. Following these enemies all of you too go to the nether worlds.

Brahmā said :

20-23. Piercing the Earth, those Mothers went to the place where Daityas and Dānavas were hiding. The Mothers killed all those terrible enemies of Devas. Through the same path they returned to Devas. Ever since the departure of Mothers and till their return, Devas had been staying on the banks of Gautamī. This holy centre is called Pratiṣṭhāna because Mothers departed therefrom and Devas were firmly established there. It is holy and conducive to victory. Wherever Mothers were born there were separate holy centres called Mātṛtīrthas.

24-25. In different places there were holes leading to the nether worlds.

Devas granted boons to the Mothers: "Let them be worshipped in the world in the same manner as Śiva for ever." After saying this Devas vanished and Mothers remained there alone.

26-28. Wherever the goddesses Mothers stayed the places are known as Mātṛtīrtha. They are worthy of being resorted to even by Devas. Why not then by the human beings?

A holy dip, distribution of charitable gifts and water libation to Manes—everything has everlasing benefit in accordance with the utterance of lord Śiva.

He who listens to this narrative, reads or remembers this narrative of the holy centres of the Mothers shall become long-lived and happy.

CHAPTER FORTYTHREE

Brahmatirtha and other Holy Centres

Brahmā said :

1. There is another holy centre which is difficult of access even to Devas. It is known as Brahmatīrtha. It bestows on men worldly pleasures and salvation.

2-3. O excellent sage, when the hosts of Devas stood by (on the banks of Gautamī), when Daityas had entered the nether worlds and Mothers followed them, my fifth face having the terrible form of an ass said even as I was sitting in the midst of Devas.

4. "O Daityas why do you flee? You need not fear. I am coming quickly. I shall devour all Devas who come over here."

5. On seeing it preventing me and intending to devour in this manner all Devas became frightened and they spoke to Viṣṇu:

6. "Save us, O Viṣṇu, save us, O lord of Universe, cut off the face of this Brahmā".

The discus-bearing lord said to Devas : "I shall cut off the head with my discus.

7-8. But the moment it is cut off it will destroy the universe consisting of mobile and immobile beings. Hence, I shall tell you this secret. Let all Devas hear the entire thing.

The three-eyed lord is the proper person to cut off the head of Brahmā. He will hold it undoubtedly."

Then Śambhu was eulogized and addressed by me:

9. Sacrifice is transitory. It is incapable of according a visible benefit. It is not at all fruitful to the person who performs it. Thinking thus and deciding that one with matted hair was a sure guarantee for the gift of the fruit, people resorted to him and got realization.

10. Then the lord of Devas was pleased. For achieving the task of Devas and for rendering help to the people he spoke to Devas thus : "So be it".

11. After cutting off that fierce face of sinful nature that made hairs stand on ends, after cutting it off with his nails he said : "Where shall it be placed ?"

12-13. Then Earth spoke to Devas: "I am not capable of holding the head. I will be going down to the nether regions."

The Ocean said : "I am not capable of holding the head. I will go dry in a trice."

Then Devas said to Śiva : "This head of Brahmā must be held by you out of pity for the people."

14. "If it is not cut off the entire universe will be destroyed; if it is cut the result is the same."

After thinking thus Lord Śiva held the head of Brahmā in his hand.

15. On seeing that extraordinary and difficult task on the banks of Gautamī, Devas eulogized the lord out of love and devotion.

16. The extremely terrible head of Brahmā had been inimical to Devas. It had approached for devouring them. By the tips of his nails as sharp as a needle the crescent-crested lord plucked it off. Since there was danger in casting it off he held it in his hand out of compassion.

17. On seeing that super-divine activity, all those Devas who were standing near Brahmā eulogized the lord of Devas.

18. Thereafter that holy centre is known as Brahmatīrtha. Even today the form of Brahmā is one with four faces. It stands there.

19-23. He who sees only the head goes to the region of Brahmā.

The place where Rudra stood and cut off the head of Brahmā is the holy centre Rudratīrtha.

The place where the Sun stays directly in the form of Devas is the excellent Saurya Tīrtha. It is reputed as the bestower of benefits of all sacrifices. If one takes bath and visits the Sun, one does not take birth again.

The fifth head of Brahmā that was cut off by Mahādeva was installed in the holy centre Avimukta. By doing so he had done what is conducive to the welfare of Devas.

If a brahmin-slayer visits the head in the holy centre Brahmatīrtha and the skull of Brahmā himself installed in the holy centre Avimukta on the banks of Gautamī he becomes sanctified.

CHAPTER FORTYFOUR

Avighnatīrtha

Brahmā said :

1. The holy centre Avighna has been declared to be destructive of all obstacles. In this connection I shall narrate an incident. Listen devoutly, O Nārada.

2. On the northern bank of Gautamī a divine sacrifice was held but it could not be concluded due to some obstacles.

3. Then Devas spoke to Hari and me. Thereupon, I entered in meditation, saw the cause and spoke to them :

4. "This sacrifice is not concluded on account of certain obstacles created by Vināyaka. Hence, let Devas eulogize the primordial lord Vināyaka."

5. After saying "So be it" Devas took their holy plunge in Gautamī. On the banks of the river Devas eulogized Gaṇeśvara, the primordial lord.

Devas said :

6. We seek refuge in that Vighnarāja who is worthy of worship and bowed to by Devas and even by Śiva, Viṣṇu and Brahmā in all undertakings. He is worthy of being meditated upon.

7. There is no other deity equal to Vighnarāja in fulfilling wishes cherished in the heart. After coming to this conclusion, even the destroyer of Tripuras, Lord Śiva worshipped him at the time of slaying the Tripuras.[1]

8. May that Vighneśvara, son of Ambikā, bestow upon us freedom from obstacles immediately, in this great sacrifice. If he is meditated upon, the heart wishes of all embodied beings become fulfilled.

9. It was an occasion for merriment to the goddess when a son was born the moment he was conceived. Hence, while bowing down to Vighnarāja, the contented Devas spoke of him as "Sadyojāta" ("Born in a trice").

---

1. Literally, 'three cities', built by Maya for the Asuras out of gold, silver and iron and in Heaven, Sky and Earth respectively; they had the power to travel anywhere; said to have started tormenting Devas and so were burnt ultimately by Lord Śiva.

10. Gaṇādhinātha was given to amusement. At one time he had been lying on the lap of his mother. Although he was prevented by his mother he forcibly concealed the moon among the matted locks of his father.

11. He sucked the milk from the breasts of his mother. Still he was not satisfied. His heart had been rendered sour due to the jealousy of his brother. "Be Lambodara (pot-bellied)." Śambhu, thus, named Vighnarāja Lambodara.

12. Surrounded by Devas Maheśa said: "Start your dance." He was delighted by Gaṇeśa by the sound of his anklets. He then crowned his son as the lord of Gaṇas.

13. This deity holds the noose of obstacles in one of his hands. With the other he holds the axe placed on the shoulder. If he is not worshipped he causes obstacles, even to his mother. Who else is equal to Vighnapati?

14. In all undertakings for acquiring virtue, wealth, love etc., he is to be worshipped at the outset. He is worshipped by Devas and Asuras everyday. I bow down at first to that lord who is worshipped at the beginning of every rite and whose worship prevents destruction.

15. Achievement of benefits is befittingly effected by extending worship and entreaties unto him. In view of this the Mouse-vehicled lord takes excessive pride due to his independent power. He is fond of his brother. I worship that deity.

16. I seek refuge in Śrīgaṇeśa who is extremely delightful and who delighted his mother by means of exquisite dances and songs as well as all kinds of desires and sportful amusements.

17. I seek refuge in Śrīgaṇeśa who is made ever more powerful by his father's grace brought about for helping Devas in their fight against Asuras, and by eulogies and Mantras and the acts of obeisance (offered by devotees).

18. At the victorious campaign against Tripuras his father did an unusual thing (i.e. instead of being worshipped by his son he had to worship his son). I bow down to Gaṇeśa who has been worshipped by his father with pleasure and who brought about freedom to his father.

Brahmā said:

19-25. Thus eulogized by Devas Vighneśa spoke to them:

Gaṇeśa said :

Hereafter, all sacrifices, performed by Devas shall be free from obstacle by my favour.

Brahmā said :

When the divine sacrifice was completed Gaṇeśa spoke to Devas :

Gaṇeśa said :

Those who observe holy rites and enlogize me devoutly through this hymn will never experience the misery caused by poverty.

Let all be assured that all the undertakings of those persons who take their holy plunge here and who distribute monetary gifts in devont spirit, will be successful.

Brahmā said :

Simultaneously with this utterance Devas too said: "So be it". When the sacrifice was concluded Devas went to their abode.

Thereafter that holy centre is called Avighna. It bestows cherished desires and destroys obstacles.

CHAPTER FORTYFIVE

Śeṣatirtha and other Holy Centres

Brahmā said :

1. The holy centre known as Śeṣatīrtha grants all cherished desires. I shall describe its features which have already been stated by me.

2. The great Nāga (serpent) named Śeṣa was the lord of nether worlds. Surrounded by all Nāgas he went to Rasātala.

3. This lord of Nāgas was ousted (from Rasātala) by Rākṣasas, Daityas and Danujas who entered Rasātala. He therefore became agitated and spoke to me.

Śeṣa said :

4. Rasātala had been given by you to Rākṣasas as well as to me. They do not give me room. Hence, I am seeking refuge in you.

5. Then I said to him. "Go to Gautamī, O Nāga. By eulogizing Mahādeva there you will get everything you desire.

6. There is no other holy centre in the three worlds which can accord what you desire".

Induced by my suggestion the Nāga took his holy plunge in Gaṅgā carefully. With palms joined in reverence, he eulogized the lord of Devas.

Śeṣa said :

7-9. Obeisance to the lord of three worlds, the destroyer of Dakṣa's sacrifice. Obeisance to you, the primordial Maker. Obeisance to the lord identical with the three worlds.

Obeisance to the thousand-headed one. Obeisance to the lord carrying out the duty of annihilation. Obeisance to you having the form of Kāla. Save me, O Śaṅkara, Lord of everything, save me, O lord of Moon, O lord accompanied by Umā, O omnipresent one. O lord of the universe, obeisance to you; Give me whatever I desire in my mind.

Brahmā said :

10-14. Then the delighted Maheśvara granted boons desired by the Nāga. For the destruction of enemies of Devas—Daityas, Dānavas and Rākṣasas, he gave Śeṣa a trident. Then he was advised by Śiva, "Kill the leading enemies by means of this".

Along with the other Nāgas he returned to Rasātala and killed his enemies in battle.

After killing Daityas, Dānavas and Rākṣasas with his trident he returned to the place where Lord Hara, .Śeṣeśvara was present.

A crevasse appeared in the path whereby the king of Nāgas came from Rasātala to the place where the lord was present, in order to see the lord.

The holy water of Gaṅgā flowed through that crevasse. It is the bestower of great merit.

15-16. That water flowed to Gaṅgā. Beyond that is the confluence of Gaṅgā. There is a big sacrificial pit in front of the lord. At the place where the Nāga performed Homa a fire remained present always. The water became hot. It is here that we have the confluence of Gaṅgā.

17. After propitiating the lord of Devas the delighted Nāga of great fame attained what he desired from Śiva and went to Rasātala.

18. Thereafter that holy centre is called Nāgatīrtha. It is holy. It fulfils all desires. It destroys sickness and poverty.

19-20. It is conducive to longevity. It is holy and bestower of fortune. Through holy dips and distribution of gifts it yields salvation. He who listens and reads this with devotion, he who remembers this attains salvation. The place where Śiva handed over the trident to Śeṣa is the holy centre Śeṣeśvara.

There are altogether, O eminent sage, two thousand one hundred holy centres on the banks (of the river). They bestow all riches.

CHAPTER FORTYSIX

Vaḍavā and other Holy Centres

Brahmā said :

1-2. It is the fire Vaḍavā (lit. 'mare'; Vaḍavānala = submarine fire) that is known as Mahānala. The lord is called Mahānala and the river is called Vaḍavā.

Dear Sir, I shall describe that holy centre which dispels death, old age and other defects.

Formerly, the sages performed a sacrifice in the Naimiṣa forest.

3-4. The sages of great austerities made Mṛtyu (Death) as slaughterer.[1] When sacrifice went on with Mṛtyu as the slaughterer, no one died among the mobile and immobile beings. Excepting the sacrificial animals, O excellent sage, mortal beings attained immortality.

1. Śamitṛ is one who officiates in a sacrifice as a slaughterer of the sacrificial victim.

5. Therefore, heaven became void and the mortal world was overcrowded because they were neglected by Mṛtyu. Then Devas said to the Rākṣasas.

6. "All of you go to sacrifice. Destroy that great sacrifice of sages."

On hearing these words of Devas the Rākṣasas said to Devas:

7. "We shall destroy that sacrifice. But what is our benefit therefrom? No one engages himself in any activity anywhere on any occasion without a proper reason."

Brahmā said :

8. Devas said to Asuras: "You too will get the benefit of sacrifice (?). Hence you go to the excellent sacrifice of sages".

9. On hearing it they hurried to the place where the sacrifice was on in order to destroy it, especially at the instance of Devas.

10. On coming to know of it, the sages said to Mṛtyu: "What shall we do? At the instance of Devas the Rākṣasas have come here as the destroyers of sacrifice."

11-12. The residents of Naimiṣa forest discussed the matter with Mṛtyu. Accordingly, they abandoned their hermitage, O Nārada. They took with them only the sacred fire leaving the utensils behind for the successful conclusion of the sacrifice. They hastened to Gautamī Tīrtha along with the slaughterer.

13. After taking their holy plunge there they eulogized Maheśāna for their protection. With their palms joined in reverence they eulogized the lord of Devas.

The sages said :

14-17. We seek refuge in that Someśvara who sportingly created this universe; who is the creator and dispenser of the destiny of the three worlds; who has the cosmic form and who is beyond both the existing and the non-existing.

Mṛtyu said :

I seek refuge in that Śaṅkara, the lord of Devas, who creates, protects and destroys everything merely by his will.

I shall seek refuge in Śaṅkara who has great strength and

huge body; who has big serpents as his ornaments and who is the lord assuming a huge form.

Brahmā said :

Then the lord said : "What is it that you wish?"

Mṛtyu said :

18. O lord of Devas, a terrible danger has befallen us from the Rākṣasas. Protect our sacrifice. Protect us so that our sacrifice be concluded.

Brahmā said :

19. The lord did so. The three-eyed bull-bannered lord did so. With Mṛtyu as the slaughterer the sacrifice was concluded.

20. The immortal ones slowly came there for their respective shares in Havi offering. The furious sages said to them along with Mṛtyu.

The sages said:

21. Since Rākṣasas had been sent by you for destroying our sacrifice, let the sinful Rākṣasas be your enemies.

Brahmā said :

22-23. Thenceforth the Rākṣasas became the enemies of Devas. Devas and sages crowned Vaḍavā, the Kṛtyā,[1] saying, "You be the wife of Mṛtyu." The holy water that flowed at the time of coronation became the river Vaḍavā.

24-25. The Liṅga installed by Mṛtyu is known as Mahānala. Thereafter, they know this holy centre as Vaḍavā Saṅgama.

That holy centre where the lord is Mahānala yields worldly pleasures and salvation. There are altogether a thousand holy centres on the banks on either side. They give all desired things. By remembering them sins can be washed away.

---

1. A demoness or evil spirit created by black magic or born of sacrifice for destructive purposes.

CHAPTER FORTYSEVEN

Ātmatīrtha

Brahmā said :

1. The holy centre known as Ātmatīrtha yields worldly pleasures and salvation to men. I shall describe the efficacy of that holy centre where Śiva is called Jñāneśvara.

2. There was a son of Atri known as Datta. He was a favourite of Hara. He was the beloved brother of Durvāsas. He was an expert in all sciences and learning. He went to his father, bowed to him humbly and said.

Datta said :

3-6. How can I realize the Brahman? Whom shall I ask? Where shall I go?

Brahmā said :

On having the words of his son, Atri meditated and said.

Atri said :

Dear son, go to Gautamī and eulogize Maheśvara there. When he becomes delighted you will acquire knowledge from him.

Brahmā said :

Saying "So be it" the son of Atri went to Gaṅgā. He had purity and self-control. With his palms joined in reverence he eulogized Śaṅkara with devotion.

Datta said :

7. O overlord of Devas ! As ill luck would have it, I have fallen into the well of worldly existence. I am sunk in the mire of misery by delusion. I am enveloped by the darkness of ignorance. I am not able to realize the supreme soul.

8. I am pierced by the powerful trident of sins. I am torn asunder by the razor of worries and anxieties. I am scorched by the terrible heat of five sense-organs. I am wearied. Redeem me, O Somanātha.

9. I have been bound by the fetters of proverty. I have been damned by the scorching flames of fire of sickness. I have

been attacked by the serpent of Death. I am frightened much. What shall I do, O Śambhu ?

10. I have been extremely distressed by births and deaths, thirst and hunger, Rajas and Tamas. I have been overwhelmed by old age. O lord, see the condition in which I am placed today and be merciful.

11. I have been landed in difficulty severally by lust, anger, jealousy, arrogance, vanity and other faults. I have been pierced by them. O lord, like a true leader ward off these enemies of mine.

12. This is true that somebody will dispel the misery of some fallen fellow. Except from you, O Somanātha, I do not have even a sympathetic word anywhere.

13. It is only as long as I do not utter the words "Obeisance to Śiva" that I have to suffer from these, viz., anger, fear, delusion, misery, ignorance, poverty, sickness, lust and other similar vices and even death.

14. I am not virtuous. I am not devout. I am not discreet. I am not merciful. You are a donor. Hence, O lord, worthy of being sought refuge in, place the word 'Soma' in my mind.

15. I do not earnestly beg for the overlordship of Devas, O Somanātha. I request humbly for the presence of lotus-like feet of Śrīsomanātha in the middle of my lotus-like heart.

16. Even as I have been known to you as a sinner, listen to my submission. Let me be present always where the word "Śiva" is heard.

17. O consort of Gaurī, O Śaṅkara, O Somanātha, O lord of the universe, O storehouse of sympathy, O soul of all, where eulogies are offered thus, there some happy and successful person is sure to dwell.

Brahmā said :

18. On hearing the eulogy of Dattātreya, Lord Hara was pleased. Bhava, the creator of the universe, said to that Yogin, "I am the bestower of boons".

Ātreya said :

19. This is the boon I seek, O lord, worshipped by Devas,

viz. the knowledge of the soul, liberation, vast devotion[1] to you and the greatness of this holy centre.

Brahmā said :

20. "Let it be so", saying this Śiva vanished there itself. Thenceforth wise men know that holy centre as Ātmatīrtha. O Nārada, one shall attain salvation by taking holy dip there and by distributing monetary gifts.

CHAPTER FORTYEIGHT

Aśvattha and other Tīrthas

1. There are some other holy centres, viz. Aśvattha, Pippala and Mandatīrtha in the North. Listen to their excellence.

2. Formerly, the saintly lord Agastya of the southern quarter was induced by Devas to make a request to Vindhya mountain.

3-5. Surrounded by one thousand sages he approached Vindhya mountain abounding in trees of various kinds. With enumerable peaks Vindhya was trying hard to excel in height mountain Meru and the Sun. He had risen to a great height. Sage Agastya, the strong-willed husband of Lopāmudrā, was received with great acclaim along with other brahmins. The sage praised the mountain and spoke with the accomplishment of the object of Devas in mind.

Agastya said :

6. I am going on a pilgrimage, O excellent Mountain, along with these sages, the seers of truth. I am going in the southern direction.

7. O lord of mountains, give me the way, I beg of you. Accord me a hospitable welcome. Till I return you should stay thus.

8. It should not be otherwise. "So be it", said the excellent mountain surrounded by sages. Sage Agastya went in the southern direction.

1. The printed word Bhukti (enjoyment of pleasures) does not fit in the context. Bhakti (devotiou) seems to be the right word. (Ed.)

9. Slowly and slowly he went to Gautamī and got initiated for the sacrifice. Surrounded by sages he performed the sacrifice for a year.

10. There were two sinful sons of Kaiṭabha. They were Rākṣasas, the source of vexation to the virtuous. They were known in the abode of Devas as Aśvattha and Pippala.

11. Aśvattha disguised himself as the holy fig tree and Pippala assumed the form of a brahmin. Both of them were anxious to destroy the sacrifice.

12. The evil-minded Dānavas assumed the desired forms Aśvattha the form of a tree and Pippala the form of a brahmin.

13. Both of them harassed brahmins daily, O saint. Whoever touched Aśvattha was devoured by that tree.

14. Pippala, the younger Rākṣasa posed, as a chanter of Sāmans and devoured his disciples. That is why even today the chanters of Sāmans among the brahmins are devoid of compassion.

15-16. On seeing the brahmins dwindling in number the sages realized that they were being devoured by the Rākṣasa. The intelligent sages approached Śanaiścara (Saturn), son of the Sun-god, who was performing penance on the southern bank of Gautamī and observing the holy rites. They reported to him the (mischievous) activities of the two Rākṣasas.

17. The son of the Sun-god said to the sages : "I shall kill those Rākṣasas, O brahmins, when I complete my penance. With the penance (as yet) incomplete I am powerless to kill them."

18. Again, the sages said : "We shall give you the benefit of our penance".

On being told thus by the brahmins the son of Sun-god said to them, "It is done".

19. Saturn, the son of the Sun-god, approached the Rākṣasa in the form of a holy fig. Saturn was in the guise of a brahmin. As a brahmin he circumambulated the Rākṣasa.

20. As he circumambulated the Rākṣasa the sinful demon thought that he was an ordinary brahmin. He therefore ate him up by his power of Māyā.

21-23. After entering his body, Saturn looked at his intestines. On being looked at by Saturn the sinful Rākṣasa was reduced to ashes like a mountain struck down by thunderbolt.

After reducing Aśvattha to ashes he went to the other Rākṣasa who was equally the abode of sin and who had assumed the form of a brahmin. He approached the Rākṣasa with humility as a disciple would approach his preceptor.

24. As usual Pippala devoured Saturn, the son of Sun-god. When Saturn-entered his body he looked at the intestines in the belly of the Rākṣasa.

25-27. The moment he was looked at by Saturn the Rākṣasa was reduced to ashes. After killing both of them Saturn said : "What remains to be done now ? Let all sages tell me".

Then the sages with Agastya as their head became pleased. They granted boons to Saturn, the slow moving son of the Sun-god.

Being pleased, the powerful Saturn spoke to the brahmins :

Saturn said :

28. The tasks of the people will be accomplished when they touch the holy fig tree on my day after observing all holy rites. They will not have any trouble arising from me.

29. There is another boon : The tasks of the people will be accomplished when they take a holy plunge in the holy centre Aśvattha.

30-33. (The following Mantra is to be recited) "O holy fig tree, subdue immediately the throbbing of my eyes, the throbbing of my arms, the effects of bad dreams, vicious thoughts and suppress my enemies too."

On Saturdays men should get up early in the morning, O divine sage. They should meditate on Śiva. Repeating the above Mantra they should touch the holy fig tree. Thus the evil effects due to adverse planets will be dispelled.

Brahmā said :

Thereafter, they know this holy centre as Aśvattha and Pippala. There are other holy centres known as Saturn, Agastya, Sātrika, Yājñika and Sāmaga. Sixteen thousand and eight holy centres originated in this manner. A holy plunge therein and distribution of holy gifts yield the benefit of all sacrifices.

CHAPTER FORTYNINE

Somatīrtha

Brahmā said :

1. The holy centre Somatīrtha has also been mentioned by noble men. By taking a holy plunge and by distributing charitable gifts there, the benefit of drinking Soma juice can be had.

2. Formerly, the medicinal herbs were the mothers of worlds. They are honoured by all living beings. They are also my divine mothers. They are prior to all prior ones.

3. Virtue is rooted in them. So also the study of Vedas and sacrificial rites. All the three worlds, and their mobile and immobile beings are sustained by these.

4. All the ailments are undoubtedly cured by them. Food comes from them and all lives are saved by them. These medicinal herbs are worthy of being honoured by the worlds but being free from egoism they spoke to me.

Medicinal herbs said :

5-8. O most excellent Deva, give us a king. Give us our husband.

Brahmā said :

On hearing their words the medicinal herbs were told by me: "All of you will obtain a husband, a king, who will heighten your pleasure".

On hearing the word "king" they said to me again, O sage: "Where shall we go ?"

They were told by me, "May the mothers go to Gautamī. If she is satisfied you will have a king worshipped by the world."

O excellent sage, they went to the river Gautamī and eulogized her.

Medicinal herbs said :

9. O Gautamī, of meritorious waters, O beloved of Śambhū, if you had not come down to the Earth, could the people with miseries arising from their contact with different sins, have found it possible to live ?

10. Who knows the fate of persons on the Earth, O queen of rivers ? O mother Gaṅgā, you are the destroyer of their sins. You are easily accessible to them for ever.

11. O Gaṅgā, worthy of being honoured by the three worlds, O mother of the worlds, does anyone understand your real greatness ? Although his body is closely embraced by Gaurī, lord Śiva holds you on his head.

12. Obeisance to you, O mother, bestower of all desired objects ! Obeisance to you, O destroyer of sins, O goddess identical with Brahman ! Obeisance to you, O river, rising from the lotus-like feet of Viṣṇu ! Obeisance to you, O river rising from the matted hair of Śambhu !

Brahmā said :

13-16. Even as they were eulogizing thus the goddess said: "What shall I give you ?"

Medicinal herbs said :

O mother of the universe, give us a husband, a king of excessive splendour.

Brahmā said :

Then the river Gaṅgā spoke these words to the medicinal herbs.

Gaṅgā said :

I am of the nature of Nectar, the medicinal herbs are mothers of nectarous nature. I shall give you Soma (Moon) as your husband as he has nectar within.

Brahmā said :

17-20. Devas, sages, Moon and medicinal herbs accepted that proposal. Thereafter, they went to their respective abodes. Where the great medicinal herbs obtained the king of nectarous soul, the Moon, the dispeller of all distresses and sins, that holy centre is known as Somatīrtha. It bestows the benefit of drinking the Soma juice. If a person takes a holy plunge there and distributes monetary (and other) gifts his deceased ancestors will attain heavenly abode.

He who listens to this daily, or reads, or remembers it devoutly obtains a long life. He shall have sons. He shall be rich.

CHAPTER FIFTY

Dhānyatīrtha

Brahmā said :

1. The holy centre known as Dhānyatīrtha is the bestower of all cherished desires. It yields prosperity and welfare. It dispels all adversities.

2. After getting Moon as their husband, the medicinal herbs became joyous. They spoke these words liked by Gaṅgā and the entire world.

Medicinal herbs said :

3-5. There is a sacred legend in the Vedas which those who are conversant with the Vedas know.

He who, in the vicinity of Gaṅgā, gifts away a land full of plants, the land that is on a par with his mother, nay which is his own mother, shall attain all cherished desires.

If a man gladly and devoutly gifts away to a person in the form of Viṣṇu, Brahmā or Īśa a land full of plants, cows and medicinal herbs he will attain all cherished desires. Whatever is gifted is to be known as one of everlasting benefit.

6-7. The medicinal herbs have the Moon as their king. The Moon is the lord of the medicinal herbs. He who after knowing this gifts away medicinal herbs to a person who knows Brahman attains all cherished desires. He is honoured in the world of Brahmā.

Those very same medicinal herbs who were delighted and who had Moon as their king said again and again :

The medicinal herbs said :

8. O king, you redeem him who gifts us on Gaṅgā. You are the excellent one, O lord of herbs. The mobile and immobile beings are dependent on you.

9. The medicinal herbs conversed with king Soma: "O king you redeem him who gifts us to brahmins.

10. We are in the form of Brahman, we are in the form of vital airs. O king, you redeem him who gifts us to brahmins.

11. O king, you redeem him who successfully performs holy rites and who gifts us away always to brahmins. It is an adoration unto us.

12. Whatever is there in the world, whether mobile or immobile, is pervaded by us. O king, you redeem him who gifts us away to the brahmins.

13. O king, you redeem him who gifts away Havya or Kavya which is nectarous and which is consumed or something which is weightier.

14. O king, you redeem him who devoutly hears, remembers or reads this episode from the Vedic text."

Brahmā said :

15. That place on the banks of Gaṅgā where this episode had been told by the medicinal herbs in the company of Soma, the shining one, is called Dhānyatīrtha.

16. Thenceforth that holy centre is called (by such names as). Auṣadhya, Saumya, Amṛta, Vedagāta and Mātṛtīrtha.

17. A holy plunge, Japa, Homa, charitable gifts, libation to the Manes and gifting of food performed there are capable of bestowing endless benefit.

18. On both banks there are altogether one thousand six hundred holy centres which dispel all sins and increase wealth.

CHAPTER FIFTYONE

Vidarbhāsaṅgama and other Holy Centres

Brahmā said :

1. Vidarbhā-Saṅgama (the confluence of Vidarbhā and Gaṅgā) is holy. So also is Revatī-Saṅgama. What happened there I shall narrate. It is what those conversant with the Purāṇas knew.

2. There was a sage known as Bharadvāja. He was superior to others in penance. His sister Revatī was ugly in form. Her voice was disgusting.

3-6. On seeing her deformed and loathsome her brother, the valorous Bharadvāja was extremely worried. He had his splendid hermitage on the southern bank of Gaṅgā where he sat pondering thus : "To whom shall I give this girl, my sister of terrible features. No one will take her, but my sister has to be given away. Oh ! no one should have a girl who is the sole cause of misery, a veritable death at every step even to a living being !"

Even as he was pondering thus, an excellent sage came there to see Bharadvāja, a regular observer of vows.

7. He was a quiet young man of sixteen years with a splendid body. He was a mine of good qualities with subdued sense-organs. He was known by the name of Kaṭha. He bowed down to Bharadvāja.

8. Bharadvāja duly honoured that brahmin Kaṭha. Standing in front of him he asked Kaṭha the purpose of his visit.

9. Kaṭha said to Bharadvāja : "I have come to you as a student seeking learning and as a person desirous of seeing you. What is proper (in this situation) may be done."

10. Bharadvāja spoke to Kaṭha : "Study whatever you desire, such as Purāṇa, Smṛtis, Vedas and the various treatises on Dharma (virtue).

11. I know everything, O highly intelligent one. Speak something sweet. Do not delay. It is only through merits that one gets a disciple who is of noble birth, who is engaged in

piety, who is devoted to the service of his preceptors, who is proud (of his heritage) and who grasps what is heard."

Kaṭha said :

12. O brahmin, teach me, your disciple. I am devoid of sins. I am eager to serve you. I am your devotee. I am of noble birth and a speaker of truth.

Brahmā said :

13. Saying "So be it", Bharadvāja imparted to him all knowledge. After acquiring knowledge, Kaṭha was delighted and he spoke to Bharadvāja:

Kaṭha said :

14. O preceptor, I would like to give you your fee. Tell me what is thought desirable by you, even if it be a very rare thing. Obeisance be to you.

15. Even after acquiring learning if there are persons who, out of delusion, do not give a suitable present to the preceptor, they fall into hell and remain there as long as the Moon and stars shine.

Bharadvāja said :

16. Duly accept this girl. Make my sister your wife; you must treat her lovingly. I ask for this as my fee.

Kaṭha said :

17. A disciple should always be like a younger brother or son to his preceptor. A preceptor should be like a father. How can then there be an alliance here ?

Bharadvāja said :

18. You make my statement true. What I command you should be offered as Dakṣiṇā by you. Remembering everything, O Kaṭha, support and maintain Revatī with your mind directed to her.

Brahmā said :

19-22. Saying "So be it" Kaṭha grasped the hand of Revatī at the instance of his preceptor after she had been duly offered.

On seeing her Kaṭha worshipped Śaṅkara, lord of Devas there itself for the sake of Revatī's beauty as well as Śiva's favour. (As a result of that) Revatī became beautiful with all her limbs very fascinating. In beauty she became incomparable. The water of ablution performed by Ravatī flowed down and joined Gaṅgā. That turned out to be a river named after her. It is reputed as Revatī. It betows beauty and conjugal bliss.

23-26. Again with various kinds of Darbha grass he performed consecration by sprinkling water for attaining holy form and features. That water became the river Vidarbhā.

By taking a holy dip in the confluence of Revatī and Gaṅgā with great faith a man is freed from all sins and he is honoured in the world of Viṣṇu.

In the same manner, O sage, if a man takes a holy bath in the confluence of Vidarbhā and Gautamī, with full faith, he instantaneously attains worldly pleasures and salvation.

There are altogether a hundred holy centres on the banks of the river. They dispel all sins. They bestow all spiritual achievements.

CHAPTER FIFTYTWO

Pūrṇatīrtha and other Holy Centres

Brahmā said :

1. The holy centre well known as Pūrṇatīrtha is on the northern bank of Gaṅgā. Even when a man takes bath there without being aware of it he shall attain auspicious good things.

2. Which living being can (fully) describe the greatness of the holy centre Pūrṇatīrtha where (both) the discus-bearing lord and the Pināka-bearing lord stay.

3-6. Formerly, in the beginning of the Kalpa there was a king, son of Āyus named Dhanvantari. He performed horse-sacrifices as well as other kinds of sacrifices. He made numerous charitable gifts. He enjoyed worldly pleasures in abundance.

After realizing the unsteadiness of worldly enjoyment he experienced highest detachment. Dhanvantari thought: "If one performs penance, Homa or Japa on the top of a mountain, or beyond the ocean or on the banks of Gaṅgā or in the temples of Śiva and Viṣṇu ot particularly at any holy confluence all his holy rites will have everlasting benefit."

After coming to realize this Dhanvantari performed a great penance.

7. Dhanvantari who was richly endowed with wisdom and absence of worldly desire and who resorted to the feet of Bhīmeśa (the Awe-inspiring lord) performed an elaborate penance at the place where Gaṅgā joined the ocean.

8. Formerly, a great Asura (named Tamas) had been humbled by this king. He had fled from the battle-field out of fear and concealed himself in the ocean for a thousand years.

9. When after king Dhanvantari had gone to the forest his sons had begun to rule over the kingdom and the (old) king became disinterested (in worldly affairs) Tamas come out from the ocean.

10-11. The powerful Asura Tamas came to the banks of Gaṅgā where king Dhanvantari was continuously engaged in Japa and Homa and was eagerly pursuing the knowledge of Brahman. Thinking "I shall destroy my enemy who is performing a penance" Tamas came out from ocean.

12. "I have been ruined many times by this powerful king. I shall destroy this enemy". Thinking thus Tamas came out from the ocean.

13-14. By means of Māyā (power of deception) he had assumed the form of a young maiden of excellent eyebrows and fascinating appearance. Laughing, singing and dancing she came near the king.

On seeing her exquisitely charming in all her limbs for a long time (the king had been attracted by her). She had been quietly devoted to him and faithfully serving him with good behaviour. Then out of sympathy he spoke to her thus.

The king said :

15. O good lady, who are you ? Why are you staying in

this dense forest ? Whose sight makes you appear so delighted? Tell me who am asking you.

Brahmā said :

16-18. On hearing these words the young lady spoke to the king:

The young maiden said :

When you are here who else can be the cause of my delight? I am the royal splendour of Indra, O king. On seeing you fully endowed with love I am extremely delighted. Hence I am moving about in front of you again and again. I am inaccessible to all who are devoid of remarkable merits.

Brahmā said :

19-20. On hearing these words the king immediately abandoned his extremely difficult penance. He meditated upon her. He was rooted in her. She became his sole refuge. Then having destroyed his great penance Tamas vanished.

21-24. In the meantime I approached him in order to grant him boons. On seeing that excellent king fallen from the height of penance as though dead and much excited. I consoled him by means of various arguments (I told him) : "Your enemy named Tamas, O king, after having caused your fall from penance is now satisfied and gone away. It does not behove you to bewail. All young women without any difference whatsoever delight as well as harass men. Why then specifically that young woman evolved out of Māyā should not ?"

Then the king freed from perplexity and bewilderment said to me with the palms joined in reverence:

The king said :

25. How will I, O Brahmā, achieve my desired object ? What shall I do? How can I, O Brahmā, completely realise the fruit of penance ?

Brahmā said :

26-28. Then I replied to him : "Eulogize Viṣṇu the lord of Devas with all efforts. Then you will attain (spiritual) success. Indeed, he is the creator of universe. He is the primordial lord worthy of being known through the Vedas. He is the bestower of all desired objects. In the three worlds there is none else to bestow this on men".

That excellent king went to the Himālaya, the most excellent mountain. With the palms joined in reverence he devoutly eulogized Viṣṇu.

Dhanvantari said :

29-43. Be victorious, O Viṣṇu. Be victorious, O unimaginable one. Be victorious, O conquering one. Be Victorious, Acyuta (Unswerving one). Be victorious, O protector of cows, O Lord of Wealth. Be victorious, O Kṛṣṇa, O lord identical with the universe.

Be victorious, O protector of living beings, O lord. Be victorious. Victory unto the lord lying on the Serpent. Be victorious, O omnipresent one. Be victorious, O Govinda. Obeisance to the Maker of the universe.

Victory to the enjoyer (Devourer) of the universe. O lord, be victorious. Obeisance to the sustainer of the universe. Be victorious, O lord. You are the Sat (existing) and the Asat (non-existing). Be victorious, O Mādhava. (Obeisance) to the virtuous one.

Be victorious, O bestower of love. You are Kāma (Cupid). Be victorious, O Rāma, O ocean of good qualities. Be victorious, O bestower of nourishment. Be victorious, O lord of nourishment. (Obeisance) to the bestower of welfare.

Be victorious, O ruler of living beings. Be victorious, O lord of living beings. (Obeisance) to the prescriber of honour. Be victorious, O bestower of Karman. You are the Karman. Be victorious, O lord clad in yellow garment.

Be victorious, O lord of everything, you are everything, you are everything. Victory to one of auspicious form. Victory to the overlord of living beings. Be victorious. Obeisance to the knower of Vedas.

Be victorious, O bestower of birth. O (lord) stationed in creatures. O supreme soul, obeisance be to you. Be victorious, O bestower of salvation. You are salvation. Be victorious, O Keśava, the bestower of worldly pleasures.

Be victorious, O bestower of worlds, O lord of worlds. Be victorious, O destroyer of sins. Be victorious, O favourite of devotees, be victorious. Obeisance to the holder of discus.

Be victorious, O bestower of honour. You are honour. Be victorious, O (lord) bowed down to by the world. Be victorious, O bestower of virtue. You are virtue. Be victorious, O (lord) who has crossed the ocean of worldly existence.

Be victorious, O bestower of food. You are food. Be victorious, O lord of speech. Obeisance to you. Be victorious, O bestower of power. You are power. Be victorious, O bestower of boons, leading to victory.

Be victorious, O bestower of Yajñas. You are Yajña. Be victorious, O lord with eyes like the petals of a lotus. Be victorious, O bestower of charitable gifts. You are the charitable gift. Be victorious, O slayer of Kaiṭabha.

Be victorious, O bestower of fame. You are fame. Be victorious, O bestower of forms, O (lord) assuming forms. Be victorious, O bestower of happiness, O lord of happy soul. Be victorious, O sanctifier of sanctifiers.

Be victorious, O bestower of peace. You are peace. Be victorious, O lord born of Śaṅkara. Be victorious, O bestower of beverages. You are beverage. Victory to (the lord) having the form of blazing flame.

Be victorious, O Dwarf, O lord of wealth. Be victorious, O smoke-bannered fire. Be victorious, O lord of the form of the donor of the entire universe. Obeisance be to you.

You alone are competent for destroying the difficulties of living beings residing in the three worlds, O Śrīpuṇḍarīkākṣa (Lotus-eyed one), O storehouse of mercy, O Viṣṇu, place your hand on my head.

Brahmā said :

44. Lord (Viṣṇu) the wielder of conch, discus and club, the bestower of plenty and all cherished desires asked him to choose any boon he pleased as he eulogized thus.

45-47. Dhanvantari became delighted in his mind due to the granting of boon by the discus-bearing lord. The king humbly told Govinda, the lord of Devas who was standing in front of him for granting the boons : "The kingdom of Devas is desired by me. Once it is granted by you, O Viṣṇu, I shall attain contentment." Viṣṇu who was eulogized and worshipped vanished there itself. Accordingly the king gradually attained the suzerainty of Devas.

48-49. As a result of the fruition of various past Karmans the thousand-eyed lord Indra had been ousted from his post three times :

(1) once by Nahuṣa after the killing of Vṛtra,
(2) on the assassination of Sindhusena, and then
(3) when he outraged the modesty of Ahalyā for some reason.

50. By remembering these different incidents the lord of Devas became grief-stricken and anxious. He spoke these words to Vācaspati :

Indra said :

51-52. For what reason, O lord of speech, am I ousted from my kingdom every now and again ? Having no glory at all is far better for men than being pulled down from exalted positions again and again. Who knows for certain the mysterious ways of Karman of living beings ? None else is competent to know the secret of all living beings.

Brahmā said :

53-54. Bṛhaspati said to Indra : "Go to Brahmā and ask him. He is the knower of past, present and future. He will tell you how this has come about, O highly intelligent one".

Both of these highly intelligent ones came near me and bowed to me. With their palms joined in reverence they spoke to me thus :

Indra and Bṛhaspati said :

55. What it that fault, O lord, whereby the noble-minded husband of Śacī is being ousted from his kingdom ? It behoves you to dispel this doubt, O lord.

Brahmā said :

56. O brahmin, then I meditated for a long time and spoke to Bṛhaspati : "It is on account of the fault of Khaṇḍa-

Dharma (violation of one's duties) that he has fallen off from his kingdom.

57-60. Violation of one's duty is caused variously by : (1) the defects in place, time etc.; (2) misplacing of faith or wrong utterance of Mantras; (3) non-giving of monetary gifts due to someone; (4) gifting away bad articles; (5) slighting gods and brahmins. Such violation of duties by embodied beings inevitably causes excessive mental distress and loss of status. In regard to the men of disturbed minds even if a righteous action is performed it has harmful effects. It will not be capable of bringing about the fulfilment of tasks and peace of mind. When the performance of duty is imperfect will not the result be harmful ?"

61-63. O sinless one, the earlier incident too was described to them by me, viz., that there was the son of Āyus named Dhanvantari, who was glorious and liberal-minded; how obstacle was created by (the Demon) Tamas and how it was dispelled by Viṣṇu. The incidents of the previous birth and other similar things were also described by me.

On hearing this both of them were surprised. They said to me again :

Indra and Bṛhspati said :

64-67. By what means can that fault be counteracted, O excellent one among Devas ?

Brahmā said :

After meditating once again I spoke to them : "Let the thing that dispels defects and brings about spiritual achievements, that which redeems persons from miserable existence be listened to. It is the refuge of persons of distressed minds. It brings eternal bliss unto the living ones too.

Go to Gautamī, the divine river and eulogize Lord Viṣṇu and Lord Śaṅkara. In the three worlds there is no other means of purification than those two (lords) and that (river)."

O excellent sage, both of them went to Gautamī at that very time. They took their bath, visited Lord Viṣṇu and Lord Śaṅkara and eulogized them joyously.

Indra said :

68-73. Obeisance to Matsya (Fish), to Kūrma (Tortoise). Obeisance, obeisance to Lord Varāha (Boar). Obeisance, obeisance to Lord Narasiṁha (Man-lion), to Vāmana (Dwarf).

Obeisance be to (the lord) in the form of a horse. O Trivikrama, obeisance be to you. Obeisance be to the lord in the form of Buddha, in the form of Rāma and Kalki.

Obeisance to you, O lord. Obeisance to Ananta (Infinite one). Obeisance to Acyuta, obeisance to Jāmadagnya (Paraśurāma). Obeisance to you in the form of Varuṇa and Indra. Obeisance to you in the form of Yama.

Obeisance to the lord, to the supreme lord in the form of three worlds. You are omniscient, holding Sarasvatī in the mouth. Obeisance be to you.

You are Lakṣmīvān (Prosperous), therefore, O sinless one, you hold Lakṣmī in your chest. You are multi-armed, multi-thighed, multi-footed, multi-eared, multi-eyed and multi-headed. You are happy and after attaining you many have become happy.

O Hari, impurity, wretchedness and absence of glory trouble men, only as long as they do not seek refuge in you, the ocean of mercy.

Bṛhaspati said :

74-82. O Īśa, those desirous of liberation speak of you thus: You are the subtle supreme light in the form of the infinite. You are the Oṁkāra itself which is beyond Prakṛti. You are in the form of knowledge and bliss. You are all.

Even those who have no desire, O Lord, propitiate you by means of five great sacrifices.[1] Those persons who have achieved their desires enter your divine world which is beyond the ocean of worldly existence and which is your cosmic body.

They view all living beings with equality. In the six waves (i.e. the activities of six sense-organs including mind?)

1. According to Manu (3. 69-71), the five great sacrifices to be performed daily by every householder are : Brahmayajña or study/recitation of Vedic texts; Devayajña or sacrifice to the gods; Pitṛyajña or oblation made to the manes; Manuṣyayajña or honoring of guests; and Bhūtayajña or offering of food etc. to animats, birds etc.

they maintain calmness. By means of knowledge they forsake the fruits of action and by means of meditation they enter you, O Śambhu. Neither the pious duties pertaining to the castes nor the Vedas and scriptures, neither the path of meditation nor the practice of abstract contemplation (are suited to me). It is through devotion that I bow down to Lord Soma, Rudra, Śiva, Śaṅkara of quiescent mind.

Even a fool, O Śambhu, shall attain your body of the nature of liberation through devotion to your feet.

The excellent benefit acquired in jñānas, yajñas, penances, meditations and homas of great benefit, is this that one has a perpetual devotion to Someśvara.

O lord, in whom the whole universe dwells, devotion to you constitutes a series of steps to heaven and salvation that is always liked by all living beings and which is the fruit of everything seen and heard.

Wise persons do not mention the series of steps for the acquisition of the fruit in the form of attainment to your feet.

Hence, O merciful one, let me have devotion to you. I do not have the means of serving your form. In conformity with your greatness, O Īśa, have mercy on us, the sinners.

I bow down to Someśvara, the lord who is eulogized by Śrutis and Purāṇas thus : "You are both, the gross as well as the subtle. You are without beginning. You are the eternal one. You are the father and the mother. You are the existing and the non-existing."

Brahmā said :

83-88. Then the delighted Hari and Hara the lord of Devas said :

Hari and Hara said :

Let whatever you desire be chosen, any boon that may be extremaly inaccessible.

Brahmā said :

Indra said to the lord of Devas : "My kingdom is every now and again lost and regained. Let that sin be subdued so that I can be stable in my kingdom and everything belonging to me become stready. If the lords of Devas are well pleased everything will be steady for ever."

Saying "So be it" they approved of the words of Indra and they were extremely delighted. On seeing them (i.e. Indra and Bṛhaspati) a smile spread over their faces. Their forms were devoid of deficiencies. They stood without any support. They were free from aberrations. They were worthy of being sought refuge in by the worlds. Both of them were the bestowers of worldly pleasures and salvation.

Hari and Hara said :

89-92. This great holy centre has three presiding deities. The river Gautamī is the bestower of whatever is desired. Repeating the Mantra given below take a holy plunge in it with great respect. For the welfare of Mahendra, let Bṛhaspati perform purificatory ablution. Let him remember us both for the achievement of stability of riches. Here is a Mantra :

"Whatever good and meritorious deeds have been performed in this as well as in the previous birth let them attain perfection and completness, O Godāvarī, obeisance be to you."

If anyone repeats the above Mantra and takes a holy dip in Gautamī his holy rite shall attain perfection due to the blessings and favour of us both. He shall be freed from the faults committed in the previous births. He shall become meritorious.

Brahmā said :

93-94. Surendra and Dhiṣaṇa (Bṛhaspati) said "So be it" and did accordingly with great delight. The preceptor of the heaven-dwellers performed the great ablution of Indra.

The holy river that arose therefrom was called Maṅgalā. Its confluence with Gaṅgā is holy. It is the bestower of auspiciousness.

95-100. Viṣṇu identical with the universe was eulogized by Indra and he became visible. From the lord of the universe Indra obtained an idol as extensive as the three worlds. It is well-known by his name as "Govinda". A cow as extensive as the three worlds was obtained by that wielder of thunderbolt. It was given by Viṣṇu. Therefore, Indra became Govinda (one who got a cow). The kingdom of the three worlds was obtained by Indra from Hari (Viṣṇu), O sage. Therefore it became stable due to Maheśvara, lord of Devas.

The place where Bṛhaspati, the preceptor of gods, eulogized Maheśvara for the stability of kingdom of the noble-souled Devendra, became the holy centre well known as Govinda. The lord there is Siddheśvara and the Liṅga is worshipped by Devas. The confluence of the Maṅgalā is the holy centre Pūrṇatīrtha.

101-105. Beyond that is the holy centre well known as Indratīrtha as well as the centre well known as Bārhaspatya where the lord is Siddheśvara, Viṣṇu and Govinda.

A holy bath, distribution of charitable gifts and any other activity conducive to merit performed in these holy centres must be understood to bear everlasting benefit. They are very dear to the Manes.

He who listens to the greatness of that holy centre, he who reads and he who remembers it everyday regains lost kingdoms.

There are altogether thirtyseven thousand holy centres on both the banks, O the noblest among sages. They bestow all spiritual achievements.

There is no other holy centre yielding great benefit like the Pūrṇatīrtha. If any man does not resort to it his birth etc. are fruitless.

CHAPTER FIFTYTHREE

Rāmatīrtha and other Holy Centres

Brahmā said :

1. The holy centre known as Rāmatīrtha has the power of destroying the sin of brahmin-slaughter. Merely by remembering it, one is freed from all sins.

2-7. There was a king named Daśaratha. He was a Kṣatriya born of the dynasty of Ikṣvāku. Like Indra, the destroyer of cities (of enemies), he was strong, intelligent, heroic and well known in the world. Like Bali he was ruling over the hereditary kingdom. O highly intelligent one! he had three queens: Kausalyā, Sumitrā and Kaikeyī. These were of noble birth, blessed and endowed with beauty and excellent features. While that king, the ruler of Ayodhyā, was reigning over the kingdom, while Vasiṣṭha the most excellent one among the knowers of Brahman was his exclusive priest, there was neither sickness nor famine, neither lack of rain nor mental worries. The brahmins, Kṣatriyas, Vaiśyas and the Śūdras enjoyed pleasures. Men of all stages of life enjoyed bliss while that leading king, the scion of the family of Ikṣvāku, was ruling.

8. Quarrel arose between Devas and Dānavas for the kingdom. In that quarrel sometimes Devas and sometimes others gained the upper hand.

9-10. While it was going on thus, the three worlds became extremely afflicted, O Nārada. I then spoke to Daityas, Dānavas and Devas. But they did not act according to my advice. Again a great fight ensued between them.

11-14. Devas and Asuras went to Viṣṇu and Īśāna identical with the universe and spoke to them. Both of them replied to Devas, Asuras, Daityas and Dānavas, "Be stronger by means of penance and fight thereafter". They said, "So be it" and they went for penance with determination. Again Devas marched against Rākṣasas in a spirit of jealousy and rivalry. A terrible battle ensued. In that battle neither Devas nor Daityas nor Dānavas came out victorious. As the fight was going on, an unembodied voice said.

Ethereal voice said :

15-18. Only they will win to whom king Daśaratha offers help and not others.

Brahmā said:

On hearing this, both of them, Devas and Dānavas went ahead for victory. Vāyu came to the king hurriedly and said.

Vāyu said:

O king, you must come to the battle between Devas and Dānavas. This is well known that victory is there where Daśaratha is. Hence you must be on the side of Devas, so that Devas should be victorious.

Brahmā said :

19. On hearing those words of Vāyu, king Daśaratha said, "O Vāyu, I shall surely come. Go back assuredly".

20-21. When Vāyu had gone back, Daityas came to the king. They too said, "O lord, it behoves you to help us. O prosperous king Daśaratha, victory depends on you. It behoves you to help the lord of Daityas."

22. The king said, "I have been requested for help by Vāyu before and I have promised my help to Devas. Let Daityas and Dānavas go back."

23. The king went to heaven and did accordingly. He fought against Daityas, Dānavas and Rākṣasas.

24. Even as Devas were watching, the brothers of Namuci split the carriage-axle of the chariot of king Daśaratha with sharp arrows.

25. In his hurry and flurry the king did not know that the carriage-axle had been split, but Kaikeyī of excellent eyebrows who was by the side of the king noticed it, O Narada.

26-28. This was not intimated to the king by her. After seeing the axle broken, the woman of holy rites put her own hand in the wheel like the axle, O the noblest among sages. It was something very wonderful. Daśaratha, the most excellent among chariot-warriors, conquered Daityas and Danujas through his chariot in which she had placed her hand. He obtained many boons from Devas. Permitted by Devas he returned to Ayodhyā.

29. But in the middle of the way he saw his beloved wife. On seeing what Kaikeyī had done he became surprised much.

30. Then he granted her three boons, O Nārada. After acknowledging what was said by the king Kaikeyī spoke thus :

Kaikeyī said :

31-37. O great king, let these boons granted by you remain with you.

Brahmā said :

The great king gave the queen various ornaments. Accompanied by his beloved queen the victorious king went to his city happily in the chariot. When a proper occasion comes what is it that cannot be given to one's beloved.

Once king Daśaratha was wandering at night in a forest, surrounded by professional hunters. He stopped the flow of a river by discharging arrows. Although he knew that a king should be free from seven vices,[1] he did so under the urging of adverse fate. The king of great powerful arms entered a pit and killed the animals that came there for drinking water by means of his sharp arrows. Listen to the perversity of time.

When the king entered the pit an old man and his wife were speaking to their son. There was an old man on that excellent mountain. He had a son Śravaṇa by name. The Brahmin could neither hear nor see. His wife was also like that. They spoke to their son.

The parents said :

38-40. We are thirsty and the night is dark. Dear son, you, a (mere) child, constitute the entire life of us, old people.

Fie upon the life of blind and deaf old men ! Dear son, fie, fie upon the life of persons whose bodies are shattered due to old age !

Men should live only as long as they have wealth and strong body, as long as they can command without being thwarted. Otherwise, they should die in holy centres or similar places.

Brahmā said :

41. On hearing these words of the old people the son who was fond of his parents spoke thus, dispelling their misery with his sweet words:

The son said :

42-43. While I am alive why should you have such misery as this? Of what avail is a son who does not remove the mental agony of his parents through his own excellent conduct ? He

---

1. Manu (7. 45-48) has given two lists of *vyasanas* : (1) those arising from lust and (2) those arising from anger. Under the first he enumerates the following *ten*: hunting, playing the game of dice, sleeping during the day, calumny, promiscuous intercourse, intoxication, singing, dancing, music and idle rambling. Under the second the following *eight* are enermerated: deceit or crookedness of temper, rashness, seeking of other's discomfiture, envy, fault-finding, robbing of other's money or non-payment of just debts, use of abusive language, and inflicting of harsh punishment.

who acts to the contrary brings about grief and affliction to the whole family.

Brahmā said :

44-48. After saying this and pacifying his old parents the noble son bowed to them and placed them on the branch of a tree. The son of the sage took water-pot in hand and started. The sage did not know the king nor did the king perceive the sage. Both of them were in hurry. The brahmin entered the water and began to fill water in his pot bent downwards. The king took him to be an elephant and hit him with sharp arrows. Even a wild elephant should not be killed by kings. Although the king knew this he hit the brahmin thus. What is it that a person deceived by fate does not do? Struck at a vulnerable spot the miserable brahmin spoke these words:

The brahmin said :

49. By whom was this mean act committed causing misery to a good brahmin like me? O my father, I am not guilty of anything whatever.

Brahmā said :

50. On hearing these words of the distressed sage the king was stunned. Without any enthusiasm he went to that place slowly.

51-52. On seeing that excellent brahmin who appeared to be shining with his splendour he too became unconscious as though pierced by thorns. After steadying himself by his own efforts the king spoke thus:

The king said :

53-54. O the noblest among sages, who are you? Why did you come here? Say this to me who have committed a sin. Tell me the means of expiation.

O extremely intelligent one, the slayer of a brahmin should never be touched, should never be seen, not only by persons of higher caste but by Cāṇḍālas too.

Brahmā said :

55-60. On hearing the words of the king, the son of the sage spoke thus.

The son of the sage said:

My vital airs are about to come out. Hence, I shall say something in brief. Know that your Karmans are bearing fruit after realising your own wanton action.

I do not bewail for my own sake. My parents are very old. Who will assist them? They had me as their only son and they are blind.

Without me how will they live in this great forest? What an unfortunate fellow am I! There has come a break in my service to my parents.

O fate, what has been done by you by depriving me of my life!

Still, O king, take the pot with you and go there quickly. Give them water to drink lest they should die.

Brahmā said :

61-65. Even as he was saying this his life became extinct. The king threw down his bow and arrows. Taking up the water pot he hastened to the place in that great forest where the old people were staying. At that very time the old couple were talking to each other thus:

The old people said :

(Our son) is grief-stricken or angry. Or he is devoured by some animal. How is it that he has not come back? He is our only support. What shall we do without him? What will become of us?

There is no other son like him in this world consisting of mobile and immobile beings. Even when censured he does not disobey us.

Indeed our life is harder than adamant. We do not see him. Our life is entirely in his power. Still our vital airs do not come out quickly.

Brahmā said :

66. The old couple were talking together in that forest in this way. Meanwhile Daśaratha came to the place slowly.

67-71. On hearing the footsteps they thought their son had come.

The old couple said :

O dear son, why have you come after so much delay? You are our eyes. You are our ultimate resort. Why don't you speak, dear son? Are you angry with us, the blind old couple?

Brahmā said :

Grief-stricken as though he had been pierced with thorns, bewailing his own evil action, that great king spoke to them, O Nārada as though he was afraid : "Please drink the water".

On hearing the words of the king (they said): "This speaker is not our son. Who are you ? Say that first. We shall drink the water afterwards". Then the king said to them.

The king said :

72-75. Your son is there where there is an expanse of water.

Brahmā said :

On hearing that the distressed couple said : "Tell us the truth and not otherwise."

Thereafter, the king related everything precisely as it had happened.

On hearing this the old people fell down (and cried) :"Take us there. Do not touch us. The sin of touching a brahmin-slayer never perishes.

The excellent king took the old man along with his wife to the place where the son had fallen dead. Touching the dead body of their son they lamented.

The old couple said :

76. Just as our death has been brought about through separation from our son, so also, O sinner, you will meet with your death on account of separation from your son.

Brahmā said :

77-79. Even as they prattled thus, O brahmin, their life became extinct. Then the king cremated the old couple and the son of the sage together.

Thereafter the dejected king went to the city, O sage. He mentioned everything without any omission to Vasiṣṭha.

Indeed Vasiṣṭha was the ultimate resort to the kings of Solar Dynasty. After consulting excellent brahmins Vasiṣṭha mentioned to him the mode of atonement.

Vasiṣṭha said :

80-83. Call together Gālava, Vāmadeva, Jābāli, Kaśyapa and other (experts too) and perform a horse sacrifice with many monetary gifts.

Brahmā said :

King Daśaratha performed many horse sacrifices through brahmins. In the meantime, an unembodied voice said :

The Ethereal Voice said :

"Indeed, the body of king Daśaratha has become pure. He will become worthy of being communicated with. Sons also will be born to him. By the virtues of his eldest son the king will become free from sins.

Brahmā said :

84-88. Then, after a lapse of time through the help of sage Ṛṣyaśṛṅga sons were born to him. They were comparable to Devas. They were born for the achievement of the object of Devas.

Rāma was born of Kausalyā. Lakṣmaṇa and Śatrughna of Sumitrā and the most intelligent Bharata was born of Kaikeyī.

All of them were intelligent, loved by the king and obedient to the king.

Sage Viśvāmitra came to that king, O highly intelligent one. He begged for Rāma and Lakṣamaṇa for protecting Yajñas. The sage had already known their greatness.

The old king who had obtained the sons after a long time said "No" to him.

The king said :

89-90. Somehow in my old age, due to my good luck, my sons are born, O sage. They yield much pleasure to me. I shall willingly give up this kingdom along with my body, but not these sons.

Brahmā said :

91-96. Then king Daśaratha was advised by Vasiṣṭha.

Vasiṣṭha said :

Descendants of Raghu have never been taught to deny requests.

Brahmā said :

With great difficulty the king said to Rāma and Lakṣmaṇa.

The king said :

Both of you protect the sacrifices of Viśvāmitra, the brahminical sage.

Brahmā said :

Saying thus to his sons and heaving hot sighs with withered lips the king who wanted to do what is laid down in scriptures handed over the sons to Viśvāmitra.

Saying "So be it" and bowing down to Daśaratha again and again they went along with Viśvāmitra for protecting his sacrifices.

97-100. Then the delighted sage taught them various arts and science such as the Vidyā of Maheśvara along with the science of archery, the arts pertaining to the use of śastras and astras (ordinary and miraculous weapons), the secular arts partaining to the use of chariots, elephants, and horses, the arts of wielding clubs, and the discharge of weapons and their recall through Mantras.

After attaining Vidyās, Rāma and Lakṣmaṇa killed Tāṭakā in the forest for the welfare of forest-dwellers.

By the touch of their feet they made Ahalyā rid of her curse. They killed Rākṣasas, who had come for destroying sacrifices.

101-108. Both of them who had acquired all learnings protected sacrifices with bows in their hands.

After the sacrifice had been concluded the great sage Viśvāmitra went to visit Janaka along with Rāma and Lakṣmaṇa.

Prince Rāma demonstrated his wonderful skill in archery as approved by his preceptor, in the midst of kings.

Pleased with that Janaka gave Sītā who was not born of any womb and who was Lakṣmī herself.

The prosperous king Daśaratha who used to abide by the advice of Vasiṣṭha and others celebrated the marriages of Śatrughna, Bharata and others, O sage.

Then a long time passed. With the permission of his subjects and preceptor, the king decided to give kingdom to Rāma. Kaikeyī became agitated by jealousy and rivalry on being urged by bad luck in the form of Mantharā. She created obstacles by requesting for the kingdom on behalf of Bharata and for (Rāma's) exile to the forest. The king did not grant this. In order to make his father truthful in his statements Rāma entered the great forest along with Sītā and Lakṣmaṇa.

109-111. By his good qualities he had already won the hearts of good people. When Rāma who had no desire for the kingdom set out with the intention of residing in the forest, along with Sītā and Lakṣmaṇa, the distressed king Daśaratha was overwhelmed by sorrow. He remembered Rāma, Lakṣmaṇa and Sītā of many good qualities. Recollecting them Daśaratha gave up his life.

112-115. O highly intelligent one, when that king was in the world of mobile and immobile beings he had committed certain evil actions. As a result of the same he was led by the followers of Yama. There are many terrible awful hells, such as Tamisra and others in the abode of Yama. The king was then thrown into several hells one by one. He was cooked out, powdered and pounded. He was dried up, bitten and again and again burnt, O highly intelligent one. In these and other terrible hells the king was tortured.

116. Traversing his forest path Rāma came to Citrakūṭa. Three years elapsed there itself, O highly intelligent one.

117. Again he went in the southern direction to the Daṇḍaka forest. It is well known in the three worlds. Among all the countries that place is the most meritorious.

118-119. He entered that terrible forest frequented by Daityas. It had been abandoned by the sages because they were afraid of Daityas. By killing Daityas and Rākṣasas he rendered service to the sages and roamed about in the Daṇḍaka forest. In this connection I shall narrate an incident. Listen attentively, O Nārada !

120-129. Rāma was slowly proceeding ahead (in the forest). King Daśaratha was in the hell. When Rāma reached within five Yojanas of Gautamī Yama said to his servants :

"Rāma, son of Daśaratha, is advancing towards Gautamī. Now pull out of hell the king, the father of that intelligent Prince. Rāma's father should not be tortured in hell as long as he (Rāma) is within five Yojanas after crossing Gautamī.

If the messengers do not carry out these holy words of mine all of you will be sinking in the terrible hell.

Good men say that Gautamī is the great Śakti who is inseparably connected with Śiva. She is in the form of water. She is worthy of being honoured by Viṣṇu, Brahmā and Maheśa and should be saluted. The sin caused by transgressing her cannot be got rid of by anyone. If the son of any sinner were to think of Gaṅgā that sinner is set free from many an impassable hell and attains salvation. Then when the son is stationed near Gautamī, how can the father be tortured in hell by anyone ?

On hearing the words of the Lord of Southern Quarter, the servants of Yama took away from hell the king of Ayodhyā who was being cooked there. They spoke these words to him.

The Servants of Yama said :

130. Blessed are you, O great king, whose son is such a one as this. By whom is a good son who is a place of rest as it were both here and hereafter, obtained ?

Brahmā said :

131-136. After taking rest, the king spoke these words slowly to the servants:

The King said :

I was being cooked again and again in the awful hells. How was it that I have been dragged out of it so quickly ? It behoves you to mention it to me.

Brahmā said :

A certain (messenger) of calm mind from among them said this to the king :

The Messenger of Yama said :

This is a secret of the Vedas, scriptures, Purāṇas etc. kept with great effort. It is being revealed to you. It is the efficacy of the holy centre as well as your son. Rāma, your glorious son, has come to the banks of Gautamī. Hence, O excellent one among men, you have been pulled out from the terrible hell.

If Rāma along with Lakṣmaṇa were to remember you after taking bath in Gautamī, O excellent king, and if he offers balls of rice etc. you will be relieved of all sins and you will go to heaven.

The King said :

137. I shall go there and say to my sons what your excellencies have stated. You alone can be my refuge. It behoves you to accord me permission.

Brahmā said :

138. On hearing the words of the king, the servants of Yama gave him permission out of pity. The king went to his sons.

139-142. The body (that he had at that time) for undergoing torture was awful. He was frequently heaving sighs. Surveying himself and remembering the sinful deeds committed by him he became ashamed. He reached Gaṅgā after wandering about as he pleased.

After reaching the banks of Gautamī, Rāma and Lakṣmaṇa along with Jānakī duly took their bath.

On that day, the residents had nothing to eat on the banks of Gautamī.

On seeing it Rāma's brother Lakṣmaṇa became sad and he spoke to Rāma.

Lakṣmaṇa said :

143-146. We are the sons of Daśaratha. Your power is great. But we have no food to eat. The residents on the banks of Gaṅgā too have no food to eat.

Rāma said :

Dear brother, the Karman committed by us cannot be otherwise. When the world is full of food we are desirous of food.

O son of Sumitrā, we have not fed a brahmin.

O Lakṣmaṇa, those persons who, out of contempt, do not propitiate and worship Brahmins remain hungry for ever.

After taking bath and worshipping Devas sacrificial fire has to be lit and sacrifice should be performed. Then the lord will provide us with food at its own time.

Brahmā said :

147-152. While the brothers were talking together thus and observing the way of Karman king Daśaratha came to that place slowly.

Immediately after seeing him Lakṣmaṇa drew his bow in anger and said, "Stop Stop. Are you a Rākṣasa or a Dānava."

On seeing him coming nearer still he said "Go. Go away. The virtuous king Rāma, son of Daśaratha, is staying here. He is devoted to his preceptor. He is truthful. He renders service to Devas and brahmins. He is capable of protecting the three worlds.

Persons like you who commit sins have no entry into the place where Rāma stays. If, O sinner, you were to enter you will be killed."

On hearing these words of his son (the king) again and again meditated upon the result of evil action. With palms joined in reverence he gently called his daughter-in-law and sons and said with his face bent down.

The King said :

153-154. I am king Daśaratha, dear sons. Listen to my words. I have become distressed because I have been surrounded by three sins of brahmin slaughter. See my body split and cooked in hells.

Brahmā said :

Then with palms joined in reverence Rāma, Sītā and Lakṣmaṇa made obeisance to him. They prostrated before him on the ground and said :

Sītā, Rāma and Lakṣmaṇa said :

155-164. Dear father, O excellent king, of what action is this the result ?

Brahmā said :

He mentioned the three deaths of brahmins as they had happened.

The King said :

Dear sons, there is no atonement for the slayers of brahmins anywhere.

Brahmā said :

Overwhelmed by great sorrow they fell down on the ground. Remembering all these things such as the king, their exile, mother, father, the onset of sorrow, the course of fate, the fall into hell and similar things the prince fell unconscious. On seeing the king unconscious Sītā said :

Sītā said :

Noble persons like you do not bewail at the onset of sorrow. They think of remedies, supernatural or human. An adversity is never averted by persons who lament even in a thousand Yugas. Wise and far-sighted persons never become perplexed. Why then, O ruler of men, do you feel sad in vain ? Give (unto me) the sin of that slaughter, the terrible one, that occurred first. I shall duly perform the expiation for the sin resulting from the death of that brahmin who was sinless, who was the master of Vedas and Vedāṅgas, who was a doer of meritorious deeds and who was devoted to his father. I shall perform expiation in accordance with the injunctions of the scriptures. Both of you do not grieve over it. Let Lakṣmaṇa take up the second sin and you the remaining one.

Brahmā said :

165. These righteous words were uttered with firmness by Sītā. Both of them said 'So be it'. Then Daśaratha spoke :

Daśaratha said :

166. You are the daughter of Janaka, the knower of Brah-

man. You are not born of any (mortal) womb. You are the wife of Rāma. There is no wonder that you speak befittingly ?

167-169. But you need not undergo the least of strains. By the holy dip, distribution of charitable gifts and offerings of Piṇḍas on Gautamī I will be freed from the three sins of brahmin slaughter and I will go to heaven. What is befitting to your family has been uttered, O daughter of Janaka. Ladies of noble family take one across the sea of worldly existence. What is it that is difficult of access if Godāvarī favours.

Brahmā said :

170. Saying "So be it", preparations were made for the offering of Piṇḍas. But the slayer of enemies did not see any eatable thing to be offered as Piṇḍa. Then he spoke to Lakṣmaṇa.

171. Lakṣamaṇa said politely, "Here are Iṅgudi fruits" and in a moment oil cakes of Iṅgudi were brought.

172. Rāma sadly hesitated to decide on the offerings of Piṇḍa to his father at Gaṅgā through the oil cakes.

173-175. A divine voice was heard there saying, "O prince, get rid of your sadness. Why ? You are banished from the kingdom. You have come to the forest. You are penniless. You are devoted to virtue and you are not wicked. Hence it does not behove you to bewail.

He who is conceited on account of his wealth and performs religious rites on that basis, is a sinner.

Listen attentively, O Rāma, to what all the scriptures say.

O king, the deities should be propitiated by the same food as the devotee takes."

176-181. When the Piṇḍa was placed on the ground he did not see his father. Where the dead body fell there is the excellent holy centre Śavatīrtha. Even its remembering dispels deadly sins.

The following came there : Guardians of quarters, Rudras, Ādityas, and Aśvins. They were seated in their respective aerial chariots. In their midst their father shone like the sun. He had excessive lustre. He was seated on an excellent aerial chariot. He was being eulogized by Kinnaras. But Rāma did not see his father. Looking at Devas in their chariots Rāma said with palms joined in reverence, "Where is my father?"

Then a divine voice was heard addressing Rāma and Sītā.

"King Daśaratha is rid of three sins of brahmin slaughter. See him, O dear one, standing alone with Devas."

Devas also said to him :

Devas said :

182-185. You are blessed. You can rest contented. O Rāma, your father has gone to heaven.

Blessed is he who redeems his ancestors from hells. By that blessed one the three worlds are to be decked. See him, O mighty one, he is freed from sins. He has the lustre of the Sun. Even if he is endowed with all riches, a sinner can be compared to a burnt tree. Even a penniless fellow is looked at like the crescent-crested lord if he is meritorious.

Brahmā said :

On seeing his son the king showered blessings on him and said :

The king said :

186. O sinless one, welfare unto you. You can rest contented. I have been redeemed by you. In this world, blessed is that son who is the redeemer of his ancestors.

Brahmā said :

187. Devas said to Rāma, the most excellent among men : "Go, dear, go away happily for achieving the object of Devas".

Then, on hearing their words Rāma said to Devas.

Rāma said :

188-190. O Devas, what duty still remains to be performed by me for my elderly father ?

Devas said :

There is no river equal to Gaṅgā. There is no son equal to you. There is no lord on par with Śiva. There is no Mantra equal to Praṇava.

O Rāma, the tasks for the sake of your elders have been performed by you. O bestower of honour, all your ancestors have been redeemed by you. All go to their respective places. You too go away happily.

Brahmā said :

191-194. At those words of Devas Rāma, the elder brother of Lakṣmaṇa, became delighted along with Sītā. He was surprised on noticing the greatness of Gaṅgā. He said these words :

Rāma said :

Ah ! the power of Gaṅgā cannot be compared to anything in the three worlds. We are blessed because Gaṅgā, the sanctifier of the three worlds, has been seen by us.

Brahmā said :

With great pleasure Rāma installed Maheśvara. He worshipped Īśāna with the sixteen articles of worship with great devotion. Īśvara had thirtysix Kalās (digits) and requisite coverings. With palms joined in reverence. Rāma eulogized Śaṅkara.

Rāma said :

195-206. I bow to Śambhu, the ancient Puruṣa. I bow to the omniscient lord of vast expense. I bow to lord Rudra, that lord of never-ending capacity. I bow to Śarva. I bow with my head.

I bow down to that unchanging great lord. I bow to the consort of Umā, the preceptor of the worlds. I bow to that destroyer of poverty. I bow to that dispeller of sickness.

I bow to the lord of welfare, of unimaginable form. I bow to the lord in the form of the seed causing creation. I bow to that lord who is the cause of sustenance of this universe. I bow to the lord of destruction.

I bow to that unchanging lord fond of Gaurī. I bow to that eternal lord identical with the destructible and indestructible. I bow to the lord in the form of knowledge whose existence is incomprehensible and whose capacity is immeasurable. I bow to that three-eyed lord with my head.

I bow to the lord merciful to the living. I bow to the lord always terrifying. I bow to the donor of desired things. I bow to the lord of Soma, to the lord of Umā at the outset.

I bow to the lord with three Vedas for his eyes. I bow to that lord devoid of three forms. I bow to the meritorious lord beyond existing and non-existing. I bow to the destroyer of sins.

I bow to that lord engaged in the welfare of the universe. I bow to the lord who assumes many forms, who is the protector of universe; and who is the creator of Sat and Asat. I bow to the lord of universe.

I bow to the lord of sacrifices who bestows Havya and Kavya offerings. I bow to that lord who gives everything when propitiated, who is auspicious unto the worlds and who is the (ultimate) goal. I bow to my beloved deity who is fond of charitable gifts.

I bow to the lord of Soma who is not independent (i.e. bestower of fruits based on one's actions). I bow to that consort of Umā. I bow to that lord of victory. I bow to the lord of Vighneśvara and Nandī. I bow my head to that lord who is fond of his sons.

I bow to the lord who destroys sorrow and misery of worldly existence. I bow to the bearer of Moon. I bow to the supporter of Gaṅgā. I bow to Īśa worthy of being worshipped. I bow to the husband of Umā, the excellent one among Devas.

I bow to the lord whose pair of feet are worshipped by Devas and Asuras as well as by Brahmā, the primordial deity, Viṣṇu, Indra and others. I bow to the lord who wished for three eyes in order to see the eye-music of the face of the goddess (?)

I bow to Soma who is worshipped with the articles of worship, viz., mixture of milk, sugar candy, ghee, curds and honey, fragrant incense, lamps, flowers of various colours and different kinds of cooked food.

Brahmā said :

207. Then the lord said to Rāma accompanied by Lakṣmaṇa, "Welfare unto you. Choose the boons". Rāma said to the Bull-bannered lord.

Rāma said :

208. O Śaṅkara, let the undertakings of those persons come to a fruitful end, who devoutly propitiate you by means of this prayer, O excellent one among Devas.

209. Let those Manes, O Śambhu, who are fallen into the ocean of hell be sanctified by the offerings of Piṇḍas and let them go to heaven.

210. Whatever sin one has committed ever since the birth, by thoughts, words and deeds let it be immediately destroyed merely by taking bath here.

211. If, O Śambhu, anyone devoutly gives even a minute particle to the suppliants here, let that be of everlasting benefit to the donors.

Brahmā said :

212-213. The delighted Śaṅkara said to Rāma : "Let it be so". When the lord, the most excellent one among Devas, had gone, Rāma too, accompanied by his followers, slowly went to that place where Gautamī rose from. Thenceforth that holy centre is called Rāmatīrtha.

214. The place where the arrow fell down from the hand of merciful Lakṣmaṇa became the holy centre "Bāṇatīrtha". It dispels all adversities.

215-217. The place where the holy bath and the worship of Śaṅkara was performed by Lakṣmaṇa, became Lakṣmaṇatīrtha. So also is the case of Sītātīrtha. It is capable of dispelling sins of different types entirely.

Where Gaṅgā the sanctifier of three worlds, had a contact with the feet of Viṣṇu (i.e. Rāma) and where Rāma took bath that is the holy centre Rāmatīrtha. How can its special excellence be described ? There is no holy centre anywhere equal to that Rāmatīrtha.

CHAPTER FIFTYFOUR

Putratīrtha and other Holy Centres

Brahmā said :

1. The holy centre well-known as Putratīrtha is said to be a meritorious Tīrtha. Even by hearing its greatness one attains cherished desires.

2-3. I shall describe its qualities. Listen attentively, O Nārada. The sons of Diti[1] (Daityas) and the sons of Danu[1] (Dānavas) became week and exhausted. The sons of Aditi[1] became superior to them in every respect. Then Diti became overwhelmed by a spirit of rivalry on account of her misery due to separation from her sons. She approached Danu.

Diti said :

4-5. O gentle lady, our sons have become powerless. What shall we do ? In the world Karman is extremely powerful. See the progeny of Aditi. They are unafflicted. They are excellent. They have a good kingdom with fame and splendour of victory. They have vanquished all enemies. Their renown and virtue are increasing. They are capable of destroying my mental peace and delight. This inequality is in spite of the fact that the same person is our husband, the family is the same and the general features and duties are the same.

6. I will not survive this. I have become shattered on seeing the splendour and glory of the children of Aditi. I am dejected and am experiencing a peculiarly miserable condition on seeing the excessive prosperity of Aditi. Even if we enter the forest fire it is certainly conducive to happiness. The prosperity and glory of a rival should not be seen even in dream.

Brahmā said :

7. Even as the charming lady was saying thus with deep sighs and sad face the son of Parameṣṭhin who had been honoured and whose weariness had gone, said to her after consoling her.

Parameṣṭhin's son said :

8-12. O gentle lady, do not be grief-stricken; what is desired is achieved only by merit. Kaśyapa of noble features knows the means of achieving it. He will tell you, O chaste lady, should you be humble in every respect.

---

1. According to Mahābhārata, Ādiparvan, Diti, Danu and Aditi were daughters of Dakṣa Prajāpati and were married to Kaśyapa, grandson of Brahmā and son of Marīci.

Brahmā said :

Danu said to Diti as she was saying thus, O Nārada.

Danu said :

O gentle lady, satisfy your husband Kaśyapa by your good qualities. If your husband is pleased you will attain your cherished desires.

Brahmā said :

Saying "So be it" she satisfied Kaśyapa in every respect. The holy lord Kaśyapa, the Patriarch, said to Diti.

Kaśyapa said :

13-15. O Diti of good holy rites, what shall I give you ? What is it that you desire ? Choose it.

Brahmā said :

Diti said to her husband that she wished for a son endowed with good qualities, who would be the conqueror of the universe and who would be bowed to by all. She said thus humbly: "O father of Devas, I choose this gift that I shall become a lady with a valiant son in this world through the child that is born.

Kaśyapa said :

16. I shall impart to you a holy rite lasting for twelve years. It will yield good fruits. After the holy rite is concluded, I shall impregnate you, as you desire. Ambitions are realized only when one is free from sins.

Brahmā said :

17-19. On the suggestion of her husband the delighted Diti of wide eyes bowed to him and performed the holy rite imparted by him adhering to the instructions laid down by her husband.

How can living beings who shun visits to the holy centres, who are averse to distribution of charitable gifts to deserving persons and observances of holy rites realize their ambitious desires ?

After the holy rite had been duly performed Kaśyapa impregnated Diti. Again, he spoke to Diti, his beloved wife, in secret.

Kaśyapa said :

20-21. Since even the sages adhering to their penance do not attain what they desire if they disregard the ancillary rites as laid down (in the scriptures), O lady of pure smiles, what is censured should not be done. You must neither sleep nor move about during both the junctions (i.e. dawn and dusk). Do not keep your tresses loose.

22. O fortunate lady, one should not eat, sneeze or yawn during dawn and dusk when hosts of evil spirits gather together (and are very active).

23. These activities should always be pursued, especially laughter, with something to screen it with. You must never stand at the bounding edge of the house during dusk and dawn.

24. My beloved one, neither during the day nor at night should one step over the threshing rod, mortar, winnowing basket, pedestal, scabbard and other things.

25. One should not lie down with the head towards the north, especially at dusk and dawn. One should never utter a falsehood nor frequent other people's houses.

26. No man except one's husband should be looked at wantonly.

If you strictly adhere to these observances a son who will enjoy the riches of the three worlds will be born to you.

Brahmā said :

27-30. She promised the same to her husband who is worshipped by the world saying "So be it". Kaśyapa then went away, O brahmin, hither and thither amongst Devas. The foetus within Diti increased in size and strength since it had been meritoriously procreated.

Maya[1] Daitya had known all these things exactly through his miraculous power, Māyā. Maya had intimate and pleasant friendship with Indra. He went to Indra and intimated everything to him in secret, viz. the intentions of Diti and Danu, the holy vow, development of the foetus and its valour and all other things. All these Maya intimated to Indra out of love.

31. If merits of various kinds are acquired, it is possible to

1. The architect and artificer of the non-gods.

have a friend who is the sole abode of confidence, devoid of fear of any calamity.

Nārada said :

32. Maya the very powerful Daitya was the beloved brother of Namuci. How did then Maya become friendly with the slayer of his brother, O lord of Devas ?

Brahmā said :

33. Formerly, there was a very powerful leader of Daityas named Namuci. His enmity towards Indra was terrible. It caused hairs to stand on end.

34. Once Namuci, the heroic leader of Daityas, saw Indra abandoning the battle and going off. Then he pursued him.

35. On seeing him coming Indra became overwhelmed with fear. Leaving off Airāvata, Indra entered the foam in water.

36-40. The thunderbolt-armed Indra instantly killed his enemy through the foam. Namuci was slain and his younger brother Maya performed a great penance as an expiation for the annihilation of the brother's foe. He was able to secure Māyā (deceptive powers) of diverse kinds terrifying to the gods. By means of penance he secured boons from Viṣṇu, the ultimate refuge of all worlds. Then he became an efficient donor and lovingly delightful conversationist. Maya worshipped the sacred fires and the brahmins and waited impatiently for an opportunity to conquer Indra. From Vāyu Indra knew that Maya was a liberal donor unto the suppliants; that he was eulogized by the bards and that he was his enemy with the power of Māyā. Then Indra assumed the form of a brahmin and approached asura Maya who had started a strategic battle. He spoke to Maya again and again.

Indra said :

41. I am an excellent brahmin, O lord of Daityas. I have come to you as a suppliant after hearing that you are the most distinguished among the donors. Give unto me, a suppliant, the boon sought after.

Brahmā said :

42. Maya took him for a brahmin and said : "It has been given to you by me. When a suppliant is in front, do virtuous persons begin to ponder over (the subject begged for) whether it is too much or too little ?"

43-45. When this was said Indra replied, "I wish for friendship with you". Maya said again to Indra, "Of what avail is this, O excellent brahmin ? I have no enmity with you." Indra then said: "O Hail to Maya." Indra was then advised by the Daitya, "Speak out the truth". Thereupon Indra revealed to the Daitya his own body which was thousand-eyed. Then Maya who was extremely surprised said to Indra :

Maya said :

46-48. What is this ? You are the thunderbolt-armed one ! Friend, this is an action not befitting you.

Brahmā said :

Laughing and embracing him Indra said : "That is enough. Learned men achieve their desired object by any means whatsoever".

Thenceforward, O greatest of sages, Indra had great love for Maya and Maya too acted for the welfare of Indra.

49. Maya went to Indra's abode and intimated everything to him. Indra asked Maya, the expert in Māyā, "What am I to do ?"

50. Out of love Maya gave his Mā[illegible] to Indra. Indra was then delighted on acquiring it and said "O Maya, what should I do ? Tell me that."

Maya said :

51-52. Go to the hermitage of Agastya. The pregnant Diti stays there. You remain there for some days waiting on her. Holding the thunderbolt enter her womb and cut the growing foetus till it comes under your control or dies. Then the enemy will cease to exist.

Brahmā said :

53-55. Saying "So be it" and after honouring Maya Indra immediately went to Diti, his step-mother, in great humility. He began to serve that noble lady, the mother of Daityas. Diti was not aware of the real intention of Indra who was actually inimical. But the living entity that was inside the womb knew the intention of Indra. It was the unfailing splendour of sage Kaśyapa, inaccessible to enemies.

56-58. The thousand-eyed lord Indra was desirous of entering within. Holding his thunderbolt, he waited for an opportunity. Once he saw her sleeping at dusk with her head to the North. The thunderbolt-armed lord said to himself, "This is the opportunity" and he entered the belly of Diti : The living entity that was staying within, saw Indra holding the weapon and desirous of killing him. Then he said to the lord boldly:

The foetus in the womb said :

59. O thunderbolt-armed one, why don't you protect me, your brother. You are desirous of killing me. There is no other greater sin than killing (someone) outside battle.

60. (Killing) except in battle (is never just), O lord of large arms. O Indra, fight (with me) when I come out. Hence this is not proper on your part.

61. You are the person who has performed a hundred sacrifices; you are the thousand-eyed one; you are the husband of Śacī; you are the annihilator of the cities (of enemies); you are the lord of Devas armed with thunderbolt. O lord this is not proper on your part.

62. Or, if you are desirous of a battle, facilitate my coming out. O thunderbolt-armed one, shun this path.

63-64. Great men do not step on the evil path even though there may be an emergency. (I am) devoid of learning; I have no weapon. Nor do I have any collection of implements. O thunderbolt-armed one, you are learned. Aren't you ashamed in attempting to kill me ? Noble men never indulge in a despicable act.

65-68. Do you expect fame or merit by killing me? If brothers staying within the womb are deliberately killed, will it be an act of manliness ! If, on the other hand, you have any eagerness for fighting with me, my brother, (you can have it) undoubtedly.

After saying this he stood up there showing the fist to Indra. (He continued then.) This is the fruit, O Indra, of being a slayer of a brother or committing breach of trust. Why did you attempt to kill me? Does this yield any fame? Is there manliness in this? He by whose command the entire world consisting of mobile and immobile beings, functions has now become slayer of a boy ! He is trying to kill me.

Brahmā said :

69. Even as he was saying thus Indra cut the foetus with his thunderbolt. Neither greedy persons nor those who are blind with anger have any sympathy anywhere.

70-72. (The foetus) did not die. (The pieces) said sadly, "We are your brothers". Again he cut those pieces. They said, "O Śatakratu (one who has performed a hundred sacrifices), do not kill us, your brothers confidently resting in the mother's womb".

There is not even an iota of mercy in the minds of those persons whose intellects are affected by hatred.

He saw seven times seven (i.e. fortynine) pieces cut apart without any sign of emotion. All of them had hands, feet and life. On seeing this he was surprised.

73-76. The auspicious pieces stationed in the womb had many but similar forms. Those multiformed pieces began to cry. Indra said to them "Māruta" (Do not cry). They therefore became Maruts of extremely powerful splendour. Even while remaining within the womb they consulted one another free from all misapprehensions about Indra. They said to Agastya, the noblest among sages in whose hermitage their mother was staying :

"Our father and your brother esteems your friendship much, O sage. We know that you have a tender feeling for us. The thunderbolt-bearer Indra has done to us what even a Caṇḍāla does not do".

77-79. On hearing these words Agastya went there in excitement. He roused Diti who was distressed due to pain in the womb. The extremely infuriated Agastya cursed the husband of Śacī.

Agastya said :

O Indra, your enemies will always see your back in battle-field.

If enemies see the backs of self-respecting fighters as they flee from battle-field it is death unto them even though they are physically alive.

Brahmā said :

80-81. Angrily Diti cursed Indra who was within her womb.

Diti said :

O Indra, what has been committed by you is not an act of manliness. Hence this curse will take effect on you. You will be humiliated by women and ousted from your kingdom.

Brahmā said :

82. In the meantime the patriarch Kaśyapa came there. He became distressed on hearing from Agastya about the evil deed of Indra.

Indra who was within the womb spoke to his father like a frightened person.

Indra said :

83-84. I am afraid to come out because of Agastya and Diti.

Brahmā said :

The patriarch Kaśyapa who came near his wife saw the act of his son, his stay within the womb, and heard about the curses of Diti and Agastya. So he became distressed.

Kaśyapa said :

85. Dear son Indra, come out. Why did you commit this sin? Persons born of pure families do not become inclined towards sins.

Brahmā said :

86. The thunderbolt-armed one came out and spoke with his face downwards on account of shame. Physiognomy of men itself speaks out their good and bad deeds.

Indra said :

87-94. Undoubtedly I shall do what is said (by you) as conducive to welfare.

Brahmā said :

Then Kaśyapa came near me along with the guardians of the quarters. He told me everything that had happened and asked me (how to bring about) the normalcy of the womb of Diti, freedom of the thousand-eyed lord from the curse, the friendly alliance of all those (pieces) within the womb with Indra, their freedom from illness, absence of defects for the husband of Śacī and non-effectiveness of the curse given by Agastya, in due order.

Then I spoke these words to Kaśyapa, who was endowed with humility : "O Kaśyapa, O Prajāpati, bestower of honour, go immediately to Gautamī accompanied by Indra, Vasus and guardians of quarters. Take your bath there and eulogize Maheśāna in the company of everyone. Then by the grace of Śiva everything conducive to your welfare shall befall you."

Saying "So be it" Kaśyapa went to Gautamī then. After taking bath, he eulogized the lord of Devas by these words.

For the removal of all miseries only two things are well-known—the sacred river Gautamī and Śiva the merciful.

Kaśyapa said :

95-100. Protect, O Śaṅkara, O lord of Devas. Protect, O lord, bowed to by the worlds. Protect, O sanctifier, protect, O lord of speech with serpents for ornaments.

Protect, O virtuous one seated on the bull. Protect, O lord, with three Vedas as the eyes. Protect, O upholder of the Earth, O lord of wealth and glory. Protect, O Śarva with the elephant's hide for garment.

Protect, O lord, destroyer of three cities. Protect, O crescent-crested one. Protect, O lord of Yajñas, O lord of Soma. Protect, O lord, the bestower of cherished things.

Protect, O abode of mercy. Protect, O bestower of auspiciousness. Protect, O origin of everything. Protect, O protector, O Indra, lord of wealth.

Protect, O brilliant one. Protect, O lord of wealth bowed to by Brahmā. Protect, O lord of the universe. Protect, O lord of Siddhas. Protect, O perfect one, obeisance be to you.

O Śiva, O ocean of mercy, you alone are the refuge of the embodied beings whose minds are dejected due to the wanderings through the terrible forest of worldly existence.

Brahmā said :

101. Even as he eulogized thus, the bull-bannered lord appeared in front of him. He asked Kaśyapa, the patriarch, to choose a boon as he pleased.

102-103. Kaśyapa spoke these words very humbly to Śiva. He narrated in detail the evil deeds of Indra, the curse, the destruction of sons, the mutual enmity, the incurring of sins and curse by Indra. Then Vṛṣākapi said to Diti and Agastya.

Śiva said :

104-106. The Maruts who are your sons and who number fortynine shall be fortunate ones taking their shares in the Yajñas. They will always be accompanied by Indra and they will be joyous. Wherever Indra has a share in the Havis offerings in any sacrifice, Maruts will undoubtedly have priority therein.

107. No one will ever vanquish Indra when accompanied by Maruts. He will be victorious always. Stay happy for ever, O Patriarch.

108. From now onwards if persons commit fratricide unjustly they will meet with extermination of their family as well as other calamities for ever.

Brahmā said :

109-113. Śambhu emphatically said to Agastya, the noblest among sages :

Śambhu said :

O sage, do not be angry with the husband of Śacī. O extremely intelligent one, be calm. The Maruts have become immortal.

Brahmā said :

The delighted bull-bannered lord Śiva spoke to Diti also.

Śiva said :

You had thought thus : "Let a son be born to me who will be embellished with the riches of the three worlds" and then had strictly pursued the path of penance. That penance has now become fruitful to you. You have now splendid sons with numerous qualities. They have become strong and heroic. Hence cast off your mental anguish. O lady of beautiful eyebrows, be free from excitement and beg for other boons as well.

Brahmā said :

114. On hearing these words of the lord of Devas, Diti bowed to Śambhu with arms joined in reverence and said :

Diti said :

115. The birth of a son is a great event for parents in the world. It shall be particularly endearing to a mother, O lord, worshipped by Devas.

116. If that son happens to be one richly endowed with handsome features, heroism and valour (there is no doubt that he will be more endearing). Even one such son (is endearing). What to say when there are many such (sons) !

117. By virtue of your power my sons will be certainly strong and victorious. They are the true sons of the Patriarch and the brothers of Indra.

118-119. (They are valourous) due to the favour of Agastya and Gaṅgā. There will be auspiciousness, O lord, where there is your favour. What doubt is there in it ? I am contented. Still I shall submit this devoutly. Listen, O lord, to my words and do what is conducive to the welfare of the universe.

Brahmā said :

120-123. When she was told by the Maker of the universe, "Speak out", Diti humbly said :

Diti said :

The acquisition of a child in the world is very difficult, O lord, saluted by Devas. It is particularly pleasing to the mother. What to say if it happens to be a son !

If that son is endowed with good qualities, glorious and long-lived, of what avail is heaven, salvation or the status of

Parameṣṭhin himself? The acquisition of a virtuous son is always welcomed by the living beings desirous of benefits both here and hereafter. Hence let that benefit be conferred if one takes one's holy dip here.

Śaṅkara said :

124-126. It is fruit of great sins that one is unable to beget children. If a woman were to be barren or a man to be impotent that defect can be rectified merely by taking bath here. One shall take bath and offer fruits and recite this prayer and then one obtains a son as a result of the bath and charitable gifts performed for three months. A barren woman shall bear a son by taking bath here.

127-128. Any woman who has had her bath after menstruation shall bear a son if she takes her bath here. Within three months after conception a pregnant woman shall devoutly take her bath, offer fruits, visit me and eulogize me with this prayer. She will then give birth to a son who will be equal to Indra.

129. O Diti, listen. If persons do not beget sons due to offences committed against the manes or due to the fault of misappropriation of money, the following is the best atonement.

130. In such cases the person shall offer balls of rice, propitiate manes and gift away a bit of gold. Then he will certainly have a son.

131. The family of these persons does not flourish : those persons who take away or misappropriate money kept in trust, persons who conceal jewels or deny their existence, and those who do not perform the rite of Śrāddha.

132. This (holy river) shall be the resort of such guilty persons after their death. Children deserving praise shall be born to those living persons who perform pilgrimage to the holy centres.

133-136. The devotee shall take a holy bath at the confluence of Diti and Gaṅgā and worship lord Siddheśvara who is beginningless and unageing, who is extensive, whose body consists of existence, knowledge and bliss, who is the great lord served by the chiefs among Devas, sages, Siddhas, Gandharvas and Yogins, who is in the form of Liṅga, who is brilliant and who is free from illness. He shall worship everyday with all articles of worship. He shall be devout. He shall perform holy rites with full control over the limbs and sense-organs. He shall eulogize me by means of this prayer on the eighth and fourteenth days of the lunar fortnight. He shall gift away gold in accordance with his capacity. He shall feed brahmins. Whoever does these on the Gaṅgā shall obtain a hundred sons.

137-141. After attaining his cherished desires he shall go to the city of Śiva on death. Whoever eulogizes me by means of this prayer, wherever be he, shall beget a son within six months. Undoubtedly it is so even if she happens to be a barren lady.

Brahmā said :

Thenceforth that holy centre is cited as Putratīrtha. By taking bath there, by distributing charitable gifts and performing other similar rites there one shall attain all cherished desires.

The place where friendship with the Maruts took place is called Mitratīrtha. Since this holy centre rendered Indra sinless it is called Śakratīrtha.

Where Indra obtained his glory, that holy centre is named Kamalatīrtha. All these holy centres are the bestowers of all cherished desires.

"All will happen" saying this Śiva vanished. All (those assembled there) went away in the manner they had come, with contentment.

It is well known that there are a hundred thousand holy centres there that bestow merit.

CHAPTER FIFTYFIVE

Holy centres Yamatīrtha etc.

Brahmā said :

1-2. The holy centre well known as Yamatīrtha is the enhancer of the satisfaction of the Manes. It is sacred. It bestows all desired things seen and unseen. It is resorted to by all holy men. I shall recount its power that destroys all sins.

There was a powerful Pigeon well known as Anuhrāda.

3. His wife was a she-bird named Heti who could assume any shape she liked. Anuhrāda was the grandson of Mṛtyu and Heti his granddaughter.

4. As time passed on they begot sons and grandsons. His enemy was the powerful king of birds named Ulūka (owl).

5. His sons and grandsons were fiery and powerful. Between these two (sets of) birds there was a long-drawn enmity.

6-8. The hermitage of Pigeon was on the northern bank of Gaṅgā. The king of birds named Ulūka was on its southern bank. He resided there along with his sons and grandsons, O excellent brahmin. Those two strong sets of birds were antagonistic to each other. Surrounded by their strong sons and grandsons those powerful birds fought for a long time. Neither the owls nor the pigeons won or lost.

9. By propitiating Yama and his grandfather Mṛtyu, the Pigeon obtained miraculous Yāmya weapons and became superior to all.

10. Similarly, the owl propitiated Fire and became strong. A terrible fight ensued between them as they became excessively arrogant on account of their boons.

11-12. The owl discharged towards the pigeon a Fiery arrow. The pigeon hurled the noose of Yama at his enemy. He discharged the thick rod as well as the nooses of Mṛtyu. Again a fight ensued between them like the one between Āḍi (a kind of bird) and Baka (crane) formerly.

13-14. On noticing the fire closely approaching her husband in the course of that great battle, the chaste lady Heti, the she-pigeon, became extremely distressed. On seeing her sons being particularly enveloped by the fire, Heti approached the Fire-god and eulogized him through various utterances.

Heti said :

15-17. His mode of granting gifts and his form are not invisible. All the objects are his soul(?) It is through him that Devas partake of Havyas (sacrifical offerings). I bow down to that husband of Svāhā, to that enjoyer of Yajñas.

I seek refuge in that lord who is the mouth of Devas, who is the carrier of Havyas, who is omniscient, who is the performer of Homas on behalf of Devas, who is the messenger of Devas, who is the primordial lord and who has bright light as his asset. Inside the body he dwells in the form of vital airs and outside he is the bestower of cooked food. He is an instrument for the performance of Yajñas. I seek refuge in that Fire-god, the conqueror of wealth.

Agni said :

18. O she-pigeon, this miraculous weapon of mine that has been discharged in the course of the battle is infallible. Where should it be made to rest, O chaste lady. Tell me that.

The she-pigeon said :

19. Let the miraculous weapon rest in me—neither in my sons nor in my husband. O lord of Havyas, be truthful in speech. O Jātavedas, obeisance be to you.

Jātavedas said :

20-21. I am delighted at your words, O chaste lady, as well as at your devotion to your husband. O Heti, I shall bestow happiness on you and on your husband and sons. This miraculous fiery weapon of mine will not scorch you, your husband or your sons. Therefore, O she-pigeon, go happliy.

Brahmā said :

22. In the meantime she-owl saw her husband encircled by the nooses of Yama and struck by his rod. Being distressed and frightened she approached Yama.

The she-owl said :

23. People sympathise (with others) because they are frightened by you. Afraid of you they practise celibacy. Afraid of you, they do good actions. Afraid of you, they scrupulously cling to their duties.

24. It is because they are afraid of you that they refrain from destructive acts as they rush to the forest from the village; afraid of you they adopt gentleness; afraid of you they imbibe Soma juice; afraid of you steadfastly they hold on to the prac-

tice of distribution of charitable gifts of cooked food and cows; afraid of you they expound the principles of Brahman.

Brahmā said :

25-30. While she said this the lord of the southern quarter said to her :

Yama said :

Welfare unto you. Choose a boon. I shall give you whatever pleases your mind.

Brahmā said :

On hearing these words of Yama, that chaste lady said to him :

The she-owl said :

My husband is encircled by your nooses and struck by your rod. Hence, O excellent one among Devas, save my sons and husband.

Brahmā said :

Becoming sympathetic on hearing her words Yama said again and again :

Yama said :

O lady of splendid face, tell me a befitting place for the nooses and the rod.

Brahmā said :

31. She spoke to lord Yama : "O lord of the universe, let the nooses hurled by you enter me. Let the rod penetrate me."

Thereupon lord Yama sympathetically spoke to her again.

Yama said :

32-33. Let your husband and sons, let all of them come out alive and free from ailments.

Brahmā said :

Yama stopped the nooses and the Fire-god stopped the fiery missile. The two gods made the pigeons and owls happy. They said to the birds : "Let the desired boon be chosen".

The birds said :

34-40. Under the pretext of our hostility we have been able to have a view of both of you which is usually very difficult to achieve. We birds are sinful ones. O excellent ones among Devas, of what avail is a boon? If you two lovingly decide that a boon has to be given, we do not, for our own sake, request for the same. One who begs for one's own sake should indeed be pitied, O great Devas. Fruitful is the life of that person who always acts for the welfare of others. Fire, water, sun, earth and different kinds of food grains—all these exist for the sake of others. Good people too exist similarly for the sake of others. Brahmā and others are linked with death, and when this is realized, O lord of Devas, eagerness for the realization of one's own interest becomes fruitless. What has been fixed by Brahmā at the time of a man's birth can never be otherwise. Therefore creatures strain themselves in vain. Hence, we two shall beg for something auspicious for the welfare of the worlds, what is conducive to the good of all. Both of you may be pleased to agree to it.

Brahmā said :

41. For the acquisition of virtue and fame and with a desire for the welfare of the worlds, the two birds spoke to the lords well known in the world.

The birds said :

42-43. O lords of the worlds, let the two hermitages of us both be in the holy centres on either side of Gaṅgā. This is our foremost boon.

Whether the holy dip, charitable gifts, Japa, Homa and worship of the Manes are performed by a meritorious person or a person of evil actions, even if these are performed in a haphazard manner—let everything be meritorious and everlasting; this is our second boon.

The Devas said :

44-45. Let this be so. We are delighted to say another thing also.

Yama said :

There shall be no untimely death for seven generations in

the families of those persons who recite Yama's prayer on the northern bank of Gautamī.

46. The man who conquers his soul and recites everyday the prayer of Mṛtyu shall be the recipient of all riches.

47-49. He will never be tormented by eighty-eight thousand varieties of ailments. In this holy centre, O excellent birds, a pregnant chaste lady shall take holy dip for seven days within three months and a near-barren lady within six months. That lady shall give birth to a heroic son.That son will live for a hundred years. He shall be rich, intelligent and heroic. His sons and grandsons will flourish. By offering balls of rice and distributing charitable gifts the manes will attain liberation. By taking holy dip a man shall be free from sins committed by thought, speech and deeds.

Brahmā said :

50-53. Immediately after the statement of Yama the Fire-god said to the birds :

Agni said :

I shall bestow good health, prosperity and beautiful form on those persons who observe sacred rites and recite my prayer on the southern bank.

If this prayer is recited by anyone at any place and if this prayer is written down and kept in the house there can be no fear from fire.

If a pure person takes his holy dip and performs charity in the holy centre of Agnitīrtha, he will undoubtedly derive the benefit of Agniṣṭoma sacrifice.

Brahmā said :

54-56. Thenceforth learned men know that holy centre variously as Yāmyatīrtha, Āgneyatīrtha, Kapotatīrtha, Ulūkatīrtha and Hetyulūka Tīrtha.

There are three thousand three hundred and ninety holy centres there. Everyone is conducive to the attainment of salvation.

Those man who take their holy dip in them and practice charity become purified even after their death. They will be endowed with riches and sons. They will become splendid and attain heaven.

CHAPTER FIFTYSIX

The holy centre Tapastīrtha and others

Brahmā said :

1. The holy centre well known as Tapastīrtha excessively increases Tapas (power of penance). It bestows all cherished desires. It is sacred. It increases the happiness of the manes.

2. Listen to what happened in that holy centre. It is destroyer of sins. There arose a controversy amongst the sages as to the greatness of waters versus fire.

3. Some considered waters the most superior. Others considered fire the most superior. The controversy among the sages on the subject of fire versus water proceeded thus.

4-8. Without fire where can life exist ? It is so because fire is the very essence of life. It is the soul. It is offerings. Everything is born of fire.

The world is sustained by fire. Fire illuminates the world. Hence there is no greater deity than Fire-god. He alone is the inner light. He alone is the great flame. Nothing exists without fire whose abode is the entire set of three worlds. Therefore, there is nothing other than Fire-god which has the superiority over all other living beings. The semen deposited by a man in the womb of a woman has more power than its physical form. That power is of fire and not anything else. Indeed fire is the mouth of Devas. Hence they know none superior to this.

9-12. Others who expound the Vedas advocated the superiority of water. Indeed food is produced from water. Fire is produced from water. Everything is sustained by water. Waters are remembered as mothers. Those who know the ancient lore say that water is the very life of the three worlds. Nectar is produced from water. Medicinal herbs are possible only through water.

Thus some said that the Fire-god is superior. Others said that Waters are superior. Those expounders of Vedas, those sages who were voicing mutually opposed views approached me and said.

The sages said :

13-17. Tell us whether fire or water is superior. You are the lord of the three worlds.

Brahmā said :

I too said to all those sages, the regular performers of holy rites who came there : "Both of them are worthy of being worshipped in the world. The world is evolved out of both. Havya, Kavya and Amṛta are produced from both. Life in the world is sustained by both. The sustenance of the body (is through both). There is no special difference between the two. Their superiority is considered equal. This is my emphatic pronouncement that neither is superior to the other.

But the excellent sages considered that one of them must be superior. They were not satisfied with my words. Those sages went to Vāyu (the Wind-god).

The sages said :

18-22. Who is the superior of the two, O Vāyu? You are the vital air. Truth is rooted in you.

Brahmā said :

Vāyu said : "Fire is superior. Everything is founded on fire". Saying "No" amongst themselves those sages went to the Earth.

The sages said :

Speak the truth, O earth, as to who is superior. You are the support of the mobile and immobile beings.

Brahmā said :

The Earth humbly said this to the sages who came there.

Bhūmi said :

The waters, the eternal goddesses are the supports even unto me. Everything is born of waters. Hence superiority is well established in waters.

Brahmā said :

23. After saying 'No' amongst themselves the sages went to

the lord lying down in the ocean of Milk. By uttering prayers they eulogized the lord holding conch, discus and iron club.

The sages said :

24-27. We seek refuge in that true entity which knows the entire universe, future, present and that which is hidden in the cavity and which the entire set of three worlds of diverse and variegated forms enter on death. We seek refuge in that truthful entity which is imperishable, permanent, and immeasurable, which the sages mention as one that is comprehensible through the Vedas and those resorting to which obtain what they desire. The Yogins do not get the form of Viṣṇu which is (identical with) the elements and which is the most important entity in the universe consisting of the great elements. We, the sages, have come here to say it. O abode of the universe, tell us the truth. You are the immanent soul of all the embodied beings. You alone are everything, O lord, everything is in you. Still alas, no one anywhere knows you on account of the influence of Prakṛti (i.e. Māyā). No one knows you though you are within, without and everywhere and you convert yourself in the form of the universe.

Brahmā said :

28-29. Then the divine voice, the unembodied one, the support of the universe spoke.

Divine voice said :

Let both these (i.e. water and fire) be propitiated by means of penance, devotion and regular observances. That element can be said to be superior, from which one attains fulfilment first.

Brahmā said :

30-31. Saying "So be it" the sages worshipped by the worlds went away. They were weary, inwardly depressed and extremely detached.

All of them went to Gautamī, the sole mother of all the worlds, the sanctifier of the three worlds, for performing penance. They observed holy rites with self-control.

32. Then they were ready for the worship of the Water-god and Fire-god. Some were the worshippers of Agni and

some adhered to the worship of waters. Then the divine voice, Sarasvatī, the mother of the Vedas, spoke.

The Divine voice said :

33-35. Waters are the source or origin of fire. Purity, cleanliness are obtained through water. Without water how can the worship of fire be accomplished ? When water is made ready one becomes authorized to perform holy rites. A man becomes impure, dirty and unfit for holy rites till he faithfully plunges into cool waters, even if he be a scholar of the Vedas. Hence waters shall be the superior ones since they are remembered as mothers. Therefore, the superiority belongs to waters since they are the mothers particularly of fire.

Brahmā said :

36. Those sages, the expounders of the Vedas, heard these words. Thereupon they came to the conclusion that the superiority must be of the waters.

37. The holy centre where this happened, O Nārada, is called Tapastīrtha. The holy centre where the two Satras of the sages took place is called Satratīrtha.

38-40. It is also called Agnitīrtha. So also they know this as Sārasvata (Tīrtha). A holy plunge and the distribution of charitable gifts there is splendid and it bestows all cherished objects.

There are one thousand and four hundred holy centres there. They are the bestowers of merit. A holy plunge and distribution of charitable gifts here bestow heavenly pleasures and salvation.

The place where the doubts of the sages were dispelled by the divine voice is the source of the river Sarasvatī which flows into Gaṅgā. Who indeed could fully describe the glory of that confluence !

CHAPTER FIFTYSEVEN

Holy Centre Ārṣṭiṣeṇatirtha etc.

Brahmā said :

1. The holy centre well known as Devatīrtha is on the northern bank of Gaṅgā. I shall describe its power that destroys all sins.

2. There was a king well known as Ārṣṭiṣeṇa. He was endowed with all good qualities. The name of his wife was Jayā. She was just like another Lakṣmī.

3. His son was named Bhara. He was intelligent and a favourite of his father. He was an expert in the science of archery and the Vedas.

4-5. His wife was a beautiful lady well-reputed as Suprabhā. Thereafter king Ārṣṭiṣeṇa placed the responsibility of the kingdom on his son and took initiation for a horse sacrifice through the chief priest. He intended to perform the horse sacrifice on the banks of Sarasvatī.

6-10. The king was initiated by Ṛtviks and important sages devoted to (the study of) Vedas and scriptures. In the presence of the brahmins and the sacred fires, Mithu the valiant king of Dānavas, an evil-minded spirit of great exploit, destroyed the sacrifice and abducted the king, his wife and priest, O sage, and went hurriedly to the nether rigions.

When the excellent king was thus taken away and the sacrifice was destroyed the immortal ones and the Ṛtviks went away to their respective places. The son of the king's priest was a boy well known as Devāpi. The boy saw his mother but could not see his father. He was suprised and excessively distressed.

11-12. He asked his mother : "O mother, where has my father gone ? I would not like to live without him. Dear mother, tell me the truth. Fie, fie upon the life of those persons of evil deeds, bereft of their fathers. Dear mother, if you do not tell me I will enter water or fire".

13. The mother said to the son : "The king, his wife and the priest, your father, were taken away by a Dānava to the nether worlds."

Devāpi said :

14. Where was he taken? By whom was he taken ? How was he taken? In which rite? Who were all watching it ? What is the abode of the Dānava? Tell me.

The Mother said :

15. While Devas were watching, in the presence of the sacred fires and the brahmins, Mithu the Daitya abducted the king who had been initiated in the sacrifice to the nether worlds along with his wife and the priest.

Brahmā said :

16-17. On hearing those words of his mother Devāpi remembered his duty : "I will see Devas, fire, Ṛtviks and Asuras. My opinion is that my father should be sought among these and not elsewhere."

After deciding thus Devāpi spoke to Bhara the son of the king :

Devāpi said :

18-20. All those who have been taken to the nether worlds should be brought back by me through the power of penance, celibacy, holy rites, and sacred observances.

Of what avail is that wretch, whether alive or dead, who does not retaliate when a terrible insult has been inflicted. Rule over the entire Earth like your father Ārṣṭiṣeṇa. O king, my mother should be protected by you till my return after fulfilling my task. O Bhara, permit me to go.

Brahmā said :

21-23. After a careful deliberation Devāpi was addressed thus by Bhara.

Bhara said :

Achieve your puropse. Go happily. Do not have the least of worry.

Brahmā said :

Devotedly meditating on the feet of the king of immortals, Devāpi searched out the Ṛtviks and bowed to them severally. With the palms joined in reverence the boy Devāpi said.

Devāpi said :

24-26. The sacrifice should have been saved by you all. The sponsor of sacrifice who had been initiated therein, the priest and the wife of the initiated one should have been saved by you all. Even while you were all watching, O Ṛtviks, the king and others have been abducted by him after destroying the sacrifice. This is not proper. Still, I consider this (necessary). It behoves you all to return them devoid of all ailments. O leading brahmins, otherwise you will deserve a curse.

The Ṛtviks said :

27-28. In a sacrifice, the Fire-god should be worshipped at the outset. It is Agni who is the presiding deity here. Hence, we the servants of the sacrificial fires do not know (these things). That carrier of the Havyas (offerings) (i.e. the Fire-god) is the donor, the enjoyer, the remover and the maker.

Brahmā said :

29. Turning his back upon the Ṛtviks and worshipping the Fire-god, Devāpi duly intimated it to the Fire-god. (Then the Fire-god replied.)

Agni said :

30. Just like the Ṛtviks I too am a servant of Devas. I carry Havya to Devas. They are the enjoyers (and therefore) they are the saviours too.

Devāpi said :

31. I shall call Devas and carefully distribute their shares in the Havis to each. Hence, you go hurriedly towards them.

Brahmā said :

32. Devāpi approached Devas and bowed to each of them. He then intimated to them the statement of Ṛtviks, of the Fire-god and (his own threat of) curse.

Devas said :

33. When we are invoked by the Vedic Mantras by the Ṛtviks in the proper order we partake of our shares in the Havis. We are not otherwise free, O excellent brahmin.

34. Hence, we are the perpetual followers of the Vedas. We are induced by the Vedas. O brahmin, we are dependent. Therefore, intimate this to the Vedas.

Brahmā said :

35-36. Devāpi cleaned himself and then invoked the Vedas with care. He was endowed with (the power of) meditation and penance. The Vedas appeared before him.

Bowing down to them again and again he spoke to the Vedas. He intimated to them the statement of the Ṛtviks, the statement of Agni and the statement of Devas.

Vedas said :

37-41. We too are dependent, O dear one. We are the followers of Īśvara and subject to his control. He is the support of the entire universe, but he is not supported by anyone. He is unsullied. He is the sole abode of all power. He is the storehouse of all riches. He is the great god, the maker. He is Maheśvara, the annihilator. We are in the form of words and sounds, O brahmin. We speak, we know. It is our duty that we speak (i.e. explain) what you ask. We know by whom they were taken away. We know his name, his city and his power. We know that they have been eaten but they are not destroyed. We also know how you can acquire the capacity to get them back again, whom to propitiate and where (for the same purpose).

Brahmā said :

42-46. On hearing this he pondered for a long time and spoke to the Vedas.

Devāpi said :

O Vedas, be pleased to speak this alone immediately, entirely and truthfully. I shall get back all those who had been taken to the nether worlds. Adequate obeisance to them all. Obeisance be to you all.

The Vedas said :

O Devāpi, go to the Gautamī. There eulogize Maheśvara. The merciful lord (when) pleased will surely bestow on you what you desire. (When) eulogized lord Śiva will be pleased.

This is true, O extremely intelligent one. King Ārṣṭiṣeṇa, Jayā his chaste wife and Upamanyu your father—all of them stay in the nether worlds devoid of ailments, due to the boons bestowed by lord Śiva. Due to the boons bestowed by lord Śiva you will kill Rākṣasa Mithu and attain fame and virtue. This is possible. It is not otherwise.

Brahmā said :

47. At the instance of the Vedas the boy Devāpi went to Gautamī. The brahmin took his bath and having got the proper opportunity eulogized Maheśvara.

Devāpi said :

48. O lord of the chiefs of Devas, I am a mere boy. You are the preceptor of preceptors. I have no power to eulogize you befittingly. Obeisance be to you, O Śambhu.

49. The Vedas do not know you. Neither Devas nor sages. Neither Brahmā nor Viṣṇu. As you are so you are. Obeisance be to you.

50. You protect, O Maheśvara, those who are sinning souls, who are helpless, who are miserable, who are poor and who are sickly.

51. The heaven-dwellers who are worshipped by penance, holy rites and Mantras will give them the benefit ordained by you, O lord of the worlds.

52. (Even) beggars will turn out to be donors. Whatever they desire is not wanting at your door. You are the cause of this unique situation.

53. O preceptor of the universe, O lord, at the mere utterance of the word Śiva, you protect ignorant persons, sinners and those who are immersed in the ocean of hell.

Brahmā said :

54-56. Even as he was eulogizing thus, the three-eyed lord appeared in front of him and said.

Śiva said :

Tell me what boon (you wish to have), O Devāpi. Enough of your despondency, O boy.

Devāpi said :

O lord of the universe, I wish to redeem the king, the king's wife and the preceptor who is my father. I wish for the death of my enemy.

Brahmā said :

57. On hearing the words of Devāpi the lord of the universe said "So be it". At the behest of Śaṅkara, Devāpi got everything.

58. Calling Nandin, one of his Gaṇas, the merciful lord Śambhu sent him with his Spear, O Nārada.

59. Nandin went to the nether worlds and killed Mithu and the leading Asuras. Bringing his father and others he handed them over to them (Devāpi).

60. The horse sacrifice of the self-possessed Ārṣṭiṣeṇa was performed there. The Fire-god, Ṛtviks, Devas, Vedas and sages said :

Agni and others said :

61. Where Śambhu, the lord of Devas, the lord of the universe, favourably disposed towards his devotees appeared personally, O Devāpi, that place has become the holy centre Devatīrtha.

62-64. This holy centre shall be conducive to the destruction of all sins; it shall bestow all spiritual achievement; it yields merit and your fame shall be perpetual.

Brahmā said :

When the horse-sacrifice was concluded Devas granted them boons. After taking their bath they became contented and went to heaven. Thereafter fifteen thousand and hundred and eight holy centres cropped up on both the banks. Let it be known that a holy dip and distribution of charitable gifts there bestow excessive merits.

CHAPTER FIFTYEIGHT

Holy Centre Tapovanatīrtha etc.

Brahmā said :

1-2. The holy centres on the southern bank of Gautamī well known as Tapovana, Nandinī Saṅgama, Siddheśvara and Śārdūla are very holy. Listen to their details by merely listening to which one is rid of all sins.

3. Agni (Fire-god), Hotṛ was formerly the carrier of Havyas unto Devas. He got as his wife the beautiful daughter of Dakṣa named Svāhā.

4. She was childless in the beginning. She performed penance for a son. The Fire-god said to his wife Svāhā, the uncensured lady who performed elaborate penance and delighted the Fire-god.

Agni said :

5-8. Children will be born, O splendid lady; do not perform penance.

Brahmā said :

On hearing the words of her husband she desisted from penance. Excepting the words of husband nothing else fulfils the cherished desires of women anywhere.

Some time passed by. Terror from Tāraka increased. Kārttikeya was as yet unborn, although Maheśvara and Bhavānī had been indulging in amorous dalliance in secret for a long time. Devas became frightened and approached Agni. The heaven dwellers spoke to him thus for realizing the task of Devas.

Devas said :

9. O highly fortunate one, go to lord Śambhu worshipped by the three worlds. Inform Śiva that there is danger from Tāraka.[1]

---

1. A powerful demon who by the performance of severe penance had secured a boon from Śiva and had later became a great terror to gods; killed by Skanda who as a result of a divine planning was born to Śiva and Pārvatī.

Agni said :

10. One should not go to that place where a couple remain in secret communion. This is a general rule. What then with regard to the trident bearing lord ?

11. There is no deliverance from hell to that person who overhears the conversation of a passionate couple who remain in an isolated place indulging in frank carefree talk.

12. He is the master of all the worlds. He is Mahākāla wielding trident. By whom can he be looked at while he is staying in a secret place along with Bhavānī.

Devas said :

13. This is justifiable when a great danger is overshadowing us. What is the rule to be followed and mentioned elsewhere ? (i.e. This is an extraordinary situation) when there is great danger from Tāraka you are the Tāraka (redeemer).

14. The life of good men is meant for others especially (when they are immersed) in the ocean of great danger and terror.

Or you can go in another form (in disguise) and speak the words befitting (the role).

15. After intimating to Śambhu the words of Devas come back quickly. Then, Fire-god, we shall offer you worship (on behalf) of the two worlds.

Brahmā said :

16-18. At the instance of Devas the Fire-god assumed the form of a parrot and went to the place where the lord of the worlds was sporting with Umā. Then the Fire-god went ahead timidly in the form of a parrot. The carrier of the Havyas (Fire-god) could not go through the doorway. Then he went to the window sill and remained there with face turned down and trembling. On seeing him Śambhu in that secret place laughingly said to Umā.

Śambhu said :

19-22. See, O gentle lady, the parrot that is the Fire-god himself who has come here at the instance of Devas.

Brahmā said :

Pārvatī bashfully said to the lord, "O lord, enough". The lord of Devas called the Fire-god moving about in front of him. in the form of a bird and said, "O Agni, you have been recognised through various ways. Do not speak anything. Open your mouth. Take this in and carry it with you." After saying this lord Śambhu discharged a great deal of semen into the mouth of Fire-god.

With this semen within him Agni could not at all go.

23-27. Utterly tired, Agni sat down on the bank of Gaṅgā. He then discharged a greater portion of that semen into Kṛttikās wherefrom Kārttika was born.

The remaining portion of the semen of Śambhu that had been within his body, Agni split into two and deposited into his beloved wife Svāhā who was particularly eager to have a child. Formerly, she had been assured by saying "You will have children." Agni remembered this now and deposited the semen of Śambhu. Excellent twins were born of that semen discharged by Agni. They were Suvarṇa and Suvarṇā, unrivalled in the world in handsome features and beauty. It was pleasing to Agni and it perpetually increased the pleasures of the worlds.

28. Out of love Agni gave Suvarṇā (in marriage) to the intelligent Dharma. He made Saṁkalpā the beloved wife of his son Suvarṇa. Thus Fire-god performed the marriages of his son and daughter.

29-34. Due to the fault of the mutual intermixture of the semen both the children of Agni (became lax in sexual behaviour). The son Suvarṇa who could assume many forms, assumed the forms of the excellent Devas and indulged in sexual intercourse with the wives of Indra, Vāyu, Kubera, Varuṇa and the leading sages. If any lady was fond of any particular person he assumed the form of that person and indulged in amorous dalliance with that lady. In some places the son of Agni who had splendid form assumed the forms of husbands of chaste ladies and sported about with them fully satisfying (Cupid). On account of his action Suvarṇa became contented.

Although she was the wife of Dharma, the daughter of Svāhā named Suvarṇā became an adulteress. If any person had a beautiful wife pleasing to his mind, Suvarṇā assumed that form and sported about with those husbands whether human beings, Asuras, Devas or sages. She indulged in sexual sports with these and others endowed with beauty, munificence, stability and majesty and having the brilliance of her father (Agni). If any wife of any Deva gained his approbation, she used to assume the form of that lady and sport with him. By means of diverse ways and activities she used to attract his mind and achieve the fulfilment of her love.

35. On seeing these (amorous) activities of Suvarṇa and Suvarṇā, the son of Agni as well as the daughter of Agni, Devas and Asuras became angry and they cursed the son and daughter of Agni at that time.

Devas and Asuras said :

36-37. Since this act involving transgression (of moral laws) has been committed, since this sinful deed marked by deceitful behaviour has been done, O Havyavāha (the carrier of Havyas), your son shall become one of infidels and one going everywhere.

Similarly, Suvarṇā too shall not be steadfast to any single person. She shall not be satisfied with any one person. She will resort to many ignoble embodied beings of different species. This shall be the defect of your daughter.

Brahmā said :

38. On hearing these words of imprecation Agni approached me with great fright and spoke, "Tell me the mode of expiation for the children".

39-41. Then I said : "O Agni, go to Gautamī, After eulogizing Śaṅkara, O large-armed one, intimate to the lord of universe (everything).

O Agni, such a child as this has been born to you due to the semen of Maheśvara deposited in your body. Hence intimate to the lord these imprecations of Devas. For the protection of his own progeny Śambhu will do something conducive to their welfare.

42. Eulogize the lord and the goddess. Śiva will be pleased with your devotion. Then you will get the fulfilment of cherished desires in regard to your children.

43. Then at my instance, Agni went to Gaṅgā and eulogized Maheśvara by means of laudatory statements equal to the Vedas in importance.

Agni said :

44-47. He is the creator of the universe. He has the cosmic form. He is unsullied. He is the primordial maker and the self-born. I bow down to that lord of the universe.

I bow down to that three-eyed lord who becomes fire and annihilates; who is the creator in the form of water and who protects in the form of the Sun.

(Obeisance) to the lord who is the cause of satisfaction to Devas in the form of the (sponsor of sacrifice) and to the living beings by making neat arrangement in the form of Vāyu (wind) ; who protects in the form of Śiva; who is conducive to perpetual happiness (in the form of) Viṣṇu, and who accords space to the living beings in the form of firmament.

Brahmā said :

48. Then the delighted lord Śiva, the unchanging and the endless, asked Agni, worshipped by Devas to choose any boon he liked.

49. Humbly he said to Śiva, "Your semen is stationed in me. Due to that the handsome son Suvarṇa well known throughout the worlds was born.

50-51. Similarly, the daughter Suvarṇā was also born from it, O lord of the universe. On account of the defect of mutual interchange of semen, O Śiva, both the children have become defective due to the transgression of moral laws. Devas have cursed them. O lord, quell it."

On hearing these words of Agni Śiva said the following that is conducive to the outcome of auspiciousness.

Śiva said :

52-56. Due to my semen Suvarṇa of great expolit was born of you. Complete magnificence and all accomplishments will be bestowed upon this Suvarṇa by me. O Agni, listen to my words. He will become the sanctifier of the three worlds. He alone is the nectar in the world. He alone is the beloved of Devas. He alone is the enjoyment of worldly pleasures and salvation. He alone is Dakṣiṇā (monetary gift) in the sacrifice. He alone is the beautiful feature of everything. He is the preceptor of the preceptors. One should know that the excellent semen from me is the most excellent thing. Especially that which is deposited in you. What worry can there be in regard to that ? Without it everything is deficient. Due to it riches are perfect.

57. Men without Suvarṇa are dead though (physically) alive. A rich man though devoid of good qualities is worthy of being honoured, but not so a poor man though endowed with good qualities.

58. Therefore, there is nothing greater than Suvarṇa. So also this Suvarṇā though restless and fickle shall be excellent.

59-61. Everything deficient, if glanced at by her will become perfect. She is to be attained in the three worlds by means of penance, Japas and Homas. O Agni, her power and excellence is recounted a little. She will stay everywhere. She will wander about after coming there. Suvarṇā, Kamalā, shall be holy. From now onwards the merit of your children who loiter as they please shall be one like which has neither been nor will ever be.

Brahmā said :

62. After saying thus Śiva assumed the form of a Liṅga and remained there manifest with a desire for the welfare of the worlds.

63-65. After acquiring boons Agni became delighted along with his children, the son and the daughter. Suvarṇā, the daughter of Agni, remained joyous along with her husband Dharma. His son also remained jolly along with Saṁkalpā.

In the meantime O sage, Śārdūla, the lord of Dānavas, attacked and defeated Dharma and fraudulently abducted Suvarṇā, the daughter of Agni, the abode of fortune, conjugal felicity and graceful charms.

66-67. Suvarṇā well known throughout the world was taken to the nether worlds by him. Agni the carrier of Havyas and Dharma the son-in-law of Agni eulogized again and again Viṣṇu, the lord of the worlds, and intimated to him the matter on hand. They intimated to the powerful lord the matter on hand.

68-69. Lord Viṣṇu cut off the head of Śārdūla with his discus. The divine lady Suvarṇā, the most beautiful women in the world, was brought by the lord. She was the daughter of Maheśvara as well as the beloved (daughter) of Agni too. Viṣṇu showed her to Maheśvara, O Nārada. Maheśvara became pleased and embraced her again and again.

70-74. The place where the discus that shone brilliantly and cut off Śārdūla's head was washed is well known as Śaṅkara Tīrtha as well as Vaiṣṇava Tīrtha and Siddha Tīrtha.

In the place where Agni and the eternal Dharma attained great delight, in the place, O excellent sage, where tears of delight fell down a river named Ānandā and Nandinī arose. Its confluence with the Gaṅgā is sacred. Śiva is present there. In the very same confluence, Suvarṇā is manifestly present even today.

75-77. She is also well known as Dākṣāyaṇī, Śivā, Āgneyī, Ambikā, Kātyāyanī, Īśvarī and Jagadādhārā (support of the universe). She is the perpetual bestower of the cherished desire of the devotees. She adorns both banks. The place where Agni performed penance is the holy centre Tapovana. There are these and other holy centres on both sides. O sage! A holy dip and the distribution of charitable gifts in them is auspicious and it bestows all cherished desires.

78. There are fourteen thousand holy centres on the northern bank and sixteen thousand holy centres on the southern bank.

79. In different places, the holy centres have special marks of recognition. They have separate names as well. It has been briefly mentioned by me.

80. Whoever listens to this, reads or remembers this, will be perfect in all desirable respects.

81. If a man knows this and performs holy dip etc. there, he remains rich always and particularly righteous.

82-84. The holy centre to the west of Abjaka is known as Śārdūla. It is superior to all holy centres such as Vārāṇasī.

He who takes his holy bath there, salutes Pitṛs and Devas

and performs libations, becomes rid of all sins. He is honoured in the world of Viṣṇu.

Between Tapovana and Śārdūla there are many holy centres. The greatness of each and every one cannot be described by anybody.

CHAPTER FIFTYNINE

Holy Centres Indratirtha etc.

Brahmā said :

1-2. A holy bath and distribution of charitable gifts in these holy centres prevents return to the worldly existence. The holy centres are Indratīrtha, Vṛṣākapatīrtha, the confluence of Phenā where there is the holy centre of Hanūmanta, and the holy centre Abjaka where the lord is Trivikrama.

3. I shall mention what has transpired on the southern bank of Gaṅgā. On the northern bank there is the holy centre named Indreśvara. Listen with devotion observing holy rites with controlled senses.

4. The excessively arrogant enemy of Indra named Namuci was very strong. He fought with Indra. Indra removed his head with Phena (watery foam).

5-7. That foam of waters assumed the form of Vajra (thunderbolt) and it cut off the head of his enemy Namuci. Thereafter, the foam fell on the ground on the southern bank of Gaṅgā. After piercing the Earth it entered the nether worlds. The sacred water of Gaṅgā originating from the nether worlds came to the Earth's zone through the path pointed out by the thunderbolt. That water followed the river Phenā called after the name Phena, i.e. foam.

8. Its confluence with Gaṅgā is holy and well known throughout the worlds. It is conducive to the destruction of all sins like the confluence of Gaṅgā and Yamunā.

9-11. The holy centre where the step-mother of Hanumān became free from the state of a cat merely because of a holy dip there due to the grace of Viṣṇu is called Mārjāra. This has been previously recounted to you. It is also called Hanūmanta. The narrative has been mentioned before. It is also called Vārṣākapa and Abjaka. Listen to it with attention.

There was a strong ancestor of Daityas well known as Hiraṇya.

12. By performing penance he became invincible to all Devas. He became very terrible. His son also was very powerful, difficult to be conquered by Devas.

13-16. He was known as Mahāśani. His wife was Aparājitā. A long-drawn continuous battle ensued between him and Indra. On all occasions Mahāśani of great virility used to conquer Indra in the battlefield along with his elephant and hand him over to his father. After binding him he used to see him devoid of strength and forsake cruelty and hand him over to Hiraṇya. The father of Mahāśani was superior to Devas and he used to put Indra in the nether worlds under surveillance.

17. After conquering Indra Mahāśani marched against Varuṇa in order to conquer him. Varuṇa of great intellect offered his daughter to Mahāśani.

18. Varuṇa gave his own abode in ocean to Mahāśani. Friendship was generated between Varuṇa and Mahāśani in this way.

19-20. Varuṇa's daughter Vāruṇī married Mahāśani. In all the three worlds Mahāśani the great Daitya was incomparable in virility, fame, heroism and strength. When the universe was devoid of Indra, Devas had mutual consultation.

Devas said :

21. Viṣṇu alone shall be the person to restore Indra. He alone is the slayer of Daityas. He alone shall be the seer of Mantras. He will create another Indra.

Brahmā said :

22-23. After having consultation together thus, Devas intimated this to Viṣṇu.

Saying, "Mahāśani, the great Daitya, cannot be killed by me" Viṣṇu went to the lord of waters, Varuṇa, his father-in-law.

After going to Varuṇa, Keśava said to him about the defeat and discomfiture of Indra.

24-26. (He said) "You must do something whereby Indra comes out". At those words of Viṣṇu, O sage, the lord of the waters hurriedly went to the valorous Mahāśani, the husband of his daughter, and the son of Hiraṇya. Lord Varuṇa was excessively honoured by his son-in-law. The Daitya then humbly asked his father-in-law (the reason of) his arrival. Varuṇa mentioned to the Daitya the reason of his arrival.

Varuṇa said :

27-28. O mighty-armed one, give me Indra who has been conquered by you before. Dear friend, the overlord of Devas has been imprisoned in the nether worlds. He is worthy of our honour always. O slayer of enemies, give him to me. If the enemy is released (voluntarily) after being imprisoned, it will confer great glory on good men.

Brahmā said :

29-30. With very great difficulty the lord of the Daityas said "So be it" and gave to Varuṇa Indra, the husband of Śacī, along with his elephant. He appeared excessively majestic in the midst of Daityas. With diverse ways and modes of worship Mahāśani honoured Indra in the presence of the lord of Waters (Varuṇa).

Mahaśani said :

31. By whom have you been created, O Indra? Your valour is useless. Wherefore do you boast so much? You are being tormented by enemies in the battlefield. Still you continue to be Indra. This is ridiculous.

32. If any woman is imprisoned by a man it is proper on the part of her husband to set her free. Women are always dependent on men (So are you). O my good Indra, you shall also be a man!

33. You have been caught and imprisoned by me in the battle along with your vehicle. Your miraculous weapon (Thunderbolt) of uncontrollable power has been (cast off) somewhere. Fie upon your life! After being set free through the intercession of the lord of waters you still wish to live despite

the fact that you have lost the costly jewel, Cintāmaṇi, the park Nandana, the celestial damsels, fame, strength and everything that could be enjoyed by the lord of Devas.

34. "That which is the storehouse of fame is life, that which is antagonistic to fame is death"—even after knowing this, O Indra, how did you get yourself released through the intercession of the lord of Waters? Why don't you feel ashamed?

35. You were staying in heaven surrounded by Devas fanned by your beloved wife and eulogized by the celestial damsels. I think, indeed, bashfulness is afraid of you.

36. "You are the slayer of Vṛtra, killer of Namuci, breaker of cities; with the thunderbolt in your hand you have split the mountains". Thus Devas honour you. Hence, O victorious one! abandon all these.

37. How is it that the maker of people like you, the lord born of the imperishable lotus, did not get his heart broken? People like you continue to live, continue to mix with the people of the world even after getting insult and injury from enemies.

Brahmā said :

38. After saying this, the lord of Daityas gave Indra to the noble-souled Varuṇa. Thereafter, he said these words again.

Mahāśani said :

39. From now onwards Indra shall be the disciple and Varuṇa the preceptor—Varuṇa who is my father-in-law and through whom, O Indra, you have attained freedom.

40. In the same manner you shall behave like a servant unto Varuṇa. Otherwise, I will be obliged to imprison you and hurl you into the nether worlds.

Brahmā said :

41. After rebuking Indra thus and laughing again and again he took leave of Varuṇa and said (to Indra) "Go, go".

42. Indra then reached his abode completely overwhelmed by shame. He told his wife the details of his defeat and discomfiture at the hands of the enemy.

Indra said :

43. I have been told thus and treated thus, O lady of splen-

did face. O fortunate lady, tell me whereby I can console my soul.

Indrāṇi said :

44. O Indra, the slayer of Bala, I know the origin of Dānavas, their Māyā, mortification, grant of boons as well as their death.

45. Hence, I shall say for your satisfaction everything necessary for the death or defeat of that demon.

46. He is the heroic son of Hiraṇya. He is the powerful son of my paternal uncle (Puloman). Hence, he is my brother (cousin). He became arrogant due to the boons granted to him.

47. He propitiated Brahmā by means of penance and observances. He acquired a great power like this. What is it that cannot be achieved by means of penance?

48. Hence, no undue worry or wonder should be entertained by you. Listen. This must be pursued as it is overdue.

Brahmā said :

49-52. After saying thus, the daughter of Puloman said to Indra in great humility.

Indrāṇi said :

There is nothing which cannot be achieved by penance. There is nothing which cannot be achieved by sacrificial rites. There is nothing which cannot be achieved by devotion to Viṣṇu and Śiva, the lord of worlds. Again dear husband, this extremely splendid thing has been heard by me. O overlord of Devas, only women know the nature of women. Hence, O lord, there is nothing which cannot be achieved by the Earth and waters. It is through them only that penance or sacrificial rite can take place.

53. There too you shall go to that land which has become a holy centre. There you will attain all cherished desires by worshipping Viṣṇu and Śiva.

54. Again this has been heard by me. Only those women who are chaste ladies know everything. The world consisting of the mobile and immobile is sustained by them.

55. The forest of Daṇḍaka is in the middle of the Earth and is its essence. Gaṅgā, the mother of the universe flows there. O lord, worship Śiva there.

56-57. Or worship Viṣṇu, lord of the worlds, the lord who dispels the agony and the grievance of the wretched and the distressed. The sole refuge of helpless men who are drowned in the ocean of misery is lord Śiva or lord Viṣṇu or Mother Gaṅgā. There is no other refuge anywhere. Hence by all means satisfy these with mental purity and concentration.

58. By means of devotion, penance or prayer perform the rite of propitiation along with me. Then you will attain welfare by the favour of lord Śiva and lord Viṣṇu.

59. If a man performs a good rite unknowingly the lord gives him as much benefit as he deserves; but if he performs it knowingly it shall be hundred times more beneficial. If a man performs a holy rite along with his wife it has everlasting benefit.

60. In every performance of a man it is the wife who assists him. Even if the tasks are very small they are not fruitful without her.

61. If a man does anything alone he gets only half the benefit, but if he does it along with his wife, O lord, the man gets abundant benefit.

62. This idea occurs in the Vedas too, which say that one who has understood holy rites very well takes the help of his wife.

It is heard that there is one excellent river Gautamī in Daṇḍaka forest.

63. It subdues sins entirely. It bestows all cherished desires. Hence, go there along with me. Perform meritorious rites yielding great benefit.

64-66. Then you will get profuse happiness after slaying the enemies in battle.

Brahmā said :

Saying "So be it" the lord of hundred sacrifices went to Gaṅgā well known as Gautamī along with his wife and preceptor. He went to Gautamī, the mother of the universe, flowing in the middle of Daṇḍaka forest. The delighted Indra went there with an intention to perform penance unto Śambhu, the lord of Devas.

67. At the outset he bowed down to Gaṅgā. After taking the holy bath he joined his palms in reverence. Seeking sole refuge in Śiva he recited the following prayer :

Indra said :

68. May that Pināka-bearing lord be pleased with us—the lord who creates, protects and devours the entire universe consisting of the mobile and immobile beings through his own Māyā but does not get entangled in it; who is single, who is independent and who is of the nature of non-dual knowledge and happiness.

69. May that consort of Pārvatī be pleased with me, the lord whose reality even Sanaka and others conversant with the esoteric doctrine of Vedānta, do not know; who is the bestower of all cherished desires and who is the enemy of Demon Andhaka.[1]

70. The self-born lord created Brahmā and saw his terrible head. He plucked it off with the tips of his nails. He hurled it when it stuck to his nails and from it the three objects[2] of worldly existence, viz., virtue, love and wealth, originated.

71. Sin, poverty, greed, begging, delusion and adversity were born therefrom. Many other endless things also took shape from them. They became influential. They had the features of worldly misery. This entire visible world is pervaded by them.

72. On seeing everything, the lord of Devas became bewildered and said to the goddess : "The whole universe is crumbling down. O goddess of the worlds, protect it. O mother of the worlds, the sole refuge, O gentle lady, O fortunate one.

1. A demon with a thousand arms and heads, two thousands eyes and feet, so called because he walked like a blind man; killed by Śiva when he attempted to carry off the Pārijāta tree from Svarga.

2. *Trivarga*, i.e. the three supreme objects desired by worldly persons, viz., Dharma, Artha and Kāma. The fourth is Mokṣa or ultimate deliverance from the world of transmigration. All the four together are know as *caturvarga* i.e. four kinds of highest objects or *Puruṣārthacatuṣṭaya* i.e. four supreme objects of human endeavour.

73. O bestower of boons, the foundation of the universe, be victorious. You are the enjoyment of worldly pleasures, you are the concentration, you are the highest liberation. You were Svāhā, Svadhā, Svasti (hail), the primordial spiritual achievement, the speech and the intellect, O immortal goddess, devoid of old age.

74. At my behest you accord protection to the three worlds. They shall be created by you alone as variegated and wonderful as the one created by Prakṛti."

75. On being told thus by lord Śiva, the beloved wife of the lord became eager to embrace and chat lovingly to the lord. When she became tired she closely clung to half of the body of Śiva and discharged drops of sweat from the tips of her fingers.

76-78. From that, Virtue (Dharma) was the first to appear; then followed Lakṣmī, Dānam (charitable gift), good rain, the animals of rich variety, lakes, grains, flowers, fruits, the articles conducive to conjugal felicity, good bearing, dress and demeanour, great medicines linked with amorous toilet and sport, dances, songs, nectar, Purāṇa, Vedas, Smṛti texts, polity, food, beverages, weapons, scriptures, domestic utensils etc., miraculous arrows etc., holy centres, forests, sacrifices, social services, auspicious vehicles, splendid ornaments and elegant seats.

79-81. Due to contact with Bhava and on account of your fire, laughter, excellent perspiration, gentle talk and other secret activities and modes the world consisting of the mobile and immobile beings became devoid of sins, O goddess. Everything born therefrom also became so.

Happiness is abundant. Auspiciousness shines perpetually. This is because of your feelings, O goddess. Hence, O mother of the universe, O chief of the worlds, save me. I am afraid of worldly existence. There are some people who become silly due to abstruse arguments. Others get merged there. I bow down to that non-dualistic beautiful body of Śiva and Śakti.

Brahmā said :

82-86. Even as he was eulogizing thus, Śiva appeared in front of him.

Śiva said :

O Indra, what is that thing you desire and seek from me? Tell me the best thing that you require.

Indra said :

My enemy is very powerful. He appears like thunderbolt. I have been imprisoned, abducted, taken to the nether worlds and harassed in many ways. I have been pierced by words sharp like arrows. This endeavour of mine is for the purpose of killing him. For that purpose, O lord, O lord of worlds, give me that virility whereby I will be able to conquer my enemy. Grant me other things too which will destroy the enemy. If that person from whom defeat and discomfiture had been experienced, is destroyed, I will consider myself born again. Renown is better than victory and splendour.

Brahmā said :

87-93. Śiva said to Indra thus :

"Your enemy cannot be slain through me alone. Hence you propitiate Viṣṇu, the unchanging lord also. With your intellect concentrated on nothing else, propitiate lord Janārdana Nārāyaṇa, the sole refuge of the three worlds. Propitiate him along with your wife. Then, O Indra, you will acquire what is pleasing to you through him and through me".

Lord Maheśvara, the primordial Maker, said again :

"Practice of Mantras, penance and Yogic exercises bestow spiritual achievement even if they are carried on at any confluence. The sages know it. What then if these things are practised at the confluence of Gautamī with the ocean ! or in the caves of mountains or at the confluence of rivers !

There is a brahmin, a great sage named Āpastamba on the southern bank of Gaṅgā. His mind remains fixed on the feet of Mukunda. I am pleased with him also, O slayer of Bala. Therefore you propitiate the club-bearing lord along with your wife."

Brahmā said :

94-95. After taking bath in the sacred confluence of Phenā and the Gaṅgā he eulogized the lord on the southern bank of Gaṅgā along with Āpastamba. With great purity of mind he eulogized lord Janārdana by reciting various kinds of Vedic Mantras. He propitiated him through penance also.

96. Then Viṣṇu became pleased and spoke, "What should be given?"

Lord Indra said :

"Give me a slayer of my enemy".

97-99. Janārdana said to him, "Know that it is already granted."

By the grace of Śiva, Viṣṇu and Gaṅgā a person rose up from the water. He had the form of Śiva and Viṣṇu. He was having trident and discus in his hands. He went to the nether worlds and killed Mahāśani, the enemy of Indra. He is called Abjaka. He is Vṛṣākapi. He became a friend of Indra.

100. Though he was a resident of heaven, Indra used to follow Vṛṣākapi always. Seeing him attached to another person, Śacī became angry due to her love. The lord of hundred sacrifices laughingly consoled Śacī and said thus :

Indra said :

101. O Indrāṇī, I do not seek refuge except in my friend Vṛṣākapi. Either libation of water or the Havis offering in fire had been my favourite always.

102. I do not go anywhere else. My beloved one, I swear so by your body. O beautiful lady, it does not behove you to think suspiciously about me.

103. You are a chaste lady and my beloved one. You assist me in the performance of holy rites and advise me (on important matters). You have children. You are of noble birth. Who else can be my beloved ?

104-106. Hence, at your suggestion I reached the great river Gaṅgā. By the favour of the discus-bearing Viṣṇu, the lord of Devas, by the favour of Śiva, the lord of Bhūtas, by the favour of Vṛṣākapi, my friend Abjaka who was born of water and who is well known in the world. I have overcome my miseries, O fortunate lady. I am Indra here, the unfallen one. What cannot be achieved if a wife acts according to her husband's wish !

107. It may be difficult to attain liberation there (in a

householder's life) but, O splendid lady, the three things beginning with wealth (i.e. wealth, virtue and love) are possible. A wife who desires welfare in the two worlds is the greatest friend.

108. If she is of noble birth, if she always speaks pleasing words, if she is chaste, if she is richly endowed with good qualities and beauty and if she has equanimity during affluence and adversity, what is it that cannot be achieved by her in the three worlds!

109. It is because of your ideas that, my beloved wife, this auspicious thing has happened. Hereafter, I have to do only what is ordered by you and nothing else.

110. For practice of piety and attainment of other world there is nothing equal to a good son. To a distressed man there is no other curative remedy than his wife.

111. There is nothing like Gaṅgā for the attainment of salvation as well as for relief from sins. Listen to another thing also, O lady of splendid face.

112. There is nothing other than the realization of non-difference of Śiva and Viṣṇu for the achievement of virtue, wealth, love and salvation and for getting rid of sins.

113. Hence, O chaste lady, due to your intellect all these mentally cherished things have been obtained by the grace of Śiva, Viṣṇu and Gaṅgā.

114. It is on account of this that my position as Indra has become stable again by the power of my friend, I think. O beautiful lady, Vṛṣākapi who was born of waters and is my friend.

115. You are my perpetual dear companion. There is nothing more endearing to me.

Among holy waters Gautamī and Gaṅgā are the best and among Devas Hari and Śaṅkara are the best.

116. Hence, by the grace of all these I have acquired everything desired by me. This holy centre well known in the three worlds is pleasing to me.

117. Hence, I will request Devas for only this : Let them in due order permit this. Let the sages, Gaṅgā, Devas, Hari and Śaṅkara permit this.

118. O Devas, on either bank of the river, there is Śaṅkara in Indreśvara and lord Janārdana in Abjaka on the other side.

119. Viṣṇu, Trivikrama, directly sanctifies the Daṇḍaka forest. Whatever holy centres are in between are the bestowers of everything meritorious.

120-124. Merely by taking bath here all of them will attain liberation along with their ancestors of five generations. If anything is given to the suppliants here, even if it be as little as a sesamum seed, it accords everlasting benefit to the donors. It bestows all cherished desires. It yields salvation. The narrative of Viṣṇu and Śambhu is conducive to the attainment of wealth, fame, longevity, health and merit. It yields salvation through knowledge and holy dip. Those who read or listen to the glory of this holy centre shall acquire merit. They will attain the power of memory of Śiva and Viṣṇu that causes the total destruction of all sins. It is this, that even the sages who have conquered their sense-organs and mind, seek.

Brahmā said :

125-127. Devas and sages spoke to him, 'It will be so'.

There are, on the northern bank of Gautamī, seven thousand holy centres that bestow salvation and that are worthy of being resorted to by Devas, sages and Siddhas. Similarly, on the southern bank there are eleven thousand holy centres. Abjaka is mentioned as the heart of Godāvarī by great sages. It is the abode of rest of Īśa, Viṣṇu and Brahmā.

CHAPTER SIXTY

Āpastambatīrtha and other Holy Centres

Brahmā said :

1. The holy centre well known as Āpastamba is famous in the three worlds. A mere remembrance of it is capable of destroying all sins completely.

2. There was a highly intelligent sage of great fame named Āpastamba. His wife named Akṣasūtrā was devoted to the pious activities of her husband.

3. His son named Karki was extremely intelligent and was a knower of truth. The excellent sage Agastya came to his hermitage.

4. After worshipping Agastya the wise great sage followed by his disciples began to ask.

Āpastamba said :

5-6. O excellent sage, among the three Devas who is the one deserving worship ? From whom can we have worldly pleasures and salvation ? Who is the bestower of food ? Who is the infinite one, O brahmin ? Who is the deity of Devas? Which lord is worshipped by means of Yajñas ? Who is being sung about in the Vedas ? O great sage Agastya, speak out to dispel this doubt of mine.

Agastya said :

7. In the matters of virtue, wealth, love and liberation scriptures are said to be the authority. And among scriptures Vedas are considered to be the greatest authority.

8. The Puruṣa sung about by the Vedas is greater than the greatest. That which is destructible is Apara (not great)—The Amṛta (non-destructible) is called Para (great).

9. That which is Amūrta (unembodied) is Para and the Mūrta (embodied) is Apara which is of three kinds according to the distribution of attributes—Sattva, Rajas and Tamas.

10. The very same entity is called in three forms as Brahmā, Viṣṇu and Śiva. The greatest entity, the sole one, is the object to be known by the three Devas.

11. The spreading of the single one into many is due to difference in attributes and activities. The three forms arise for the good of the worlds.

12. Only he who knows the highest truth (or principle) is the learned one and not the other. He who speaks of difference (in the three forms) is called Liṅgabhedin (the splitter of Liṅga).

13. There is no atonement for that person who speaks of (real) difference between them. There is difference in the physical forms of the three Devas.

14. The Vedas are our authority in respect of the separate physical forms. The one that is formless is superior to them.

Āpastamba said :

15. By this (statement) I have not come to any fixed conclusion. In this respect too, let the secret doctrine be elaborated upon and explained quickly. That secret doctrine should be free from doubts and alternatives and it should be (important enough so as) deserving all riches.

Brahmā said :

16-18. On hearing this the holy sage Agastya spoke these words.

Agastya said :

Athough there is no difference amongst these Devas, still the achievement of everything is possible only through Śiva of the nature of happiness. Śiva is that excellent brilliance which is the cause of the universe. O sage, propitiate that lord alone with the utmost devotion. The annihilator of all sins is in the Daṇḍaka forest on Gautamī.

Brahmā said :

19-20. On hearing these words of the sage, he attained great pleasure. He asked : Which one yields worldly pleasures ? Which one yields salvation ? Is it the (one with form) or the one without form?

Which is the form for creation ? Which is the form for protection ? Who is the donor ? Who kills everything? What is it where all these things come to an end ?

Agastya said :

21. The form Brahmā has the characteristics of the creator, the form Viṣṇu is the protecting one, the form Rudra is destructive.

Brahmā said :

22. Āpastamba went to Gaṅgā and took his bath there. With self-control and holy observances he eulogized lord Śaṅkara, O Nārada, by means of this prayer.

Āpastamba said:

23-31. (Prayer)

I seek refuge in that Somanātha who is present in all living beings and who is fire in wooden pieces, fragrance in flowers, the future tree in seeds and gold in stones.

I seek refluge in that Somanātha who sportingly created this universe, who is the maker and dispenser of the destiny of the three worlds, who has the cosmic form and who is beyond both Sat and Asat (the existing and non-existing).

I seek refuge in that Someśvara by remembering whom an embodied being is not affected by the great curse of poverty, sickness etc. and those who resort to him obtain everything desired.

I seek refuge in that Someśvara by whom, after taking into consideration the Trayīdharma (the righteous activities laid down in the three Vedas), Brahmā and others had been assigned duties, by whom the body has been divided into two.

I seek refuge in that Somanātha to whom the obeisance sanctified by Mantras proceeds, to whom the Havis offered in the fire and the worship performed also go. It is the Havis handed over by him that Devas partake.

I seek refuge in that Someśvara than whom there is no greater or more excellent one, than whom there is nothing subtler and who is greater than the greatest.

I seek refuge in that Someśvara at whose behest the whole of this universe follows as if in a single action, the universe which is variegated and diversified, which is great and whose form is unimaginable.

I seek refuge in that Someśvara in whom there is superhuman power, the overlordship of everything, the states of being the maker and the donor, greatness, love, fame, happiness and the primordial virtue.

I seek refuge in that Someśvara who is perpetual refuge for all, who is worthy of being worshipped by all, who always loves a person who seeks refuge, who is always auspicious and who is the form of everything.

Brahmā said :

32-34. Then the delighted lord said to the sage, O Nārada, "(Seek anything) for your own sake or for others."

Āpastamba said to Śiva :

"Those who take their bath and visit lord Īśvara, the lord of the worlds should obtain their cherished desires".

"Let it be so", said Śiva to the sage. Thenceforward that holy centre is cited as Āpastambatīrtha. It is capable of dispelling the darkness of Avidyā that is beginningless.

CHAPTER SIXTYONE

Holy Centres Yamatīrtha and others

Brahmā said :

1. The holy centre Yamatīrtha is well known as the increaser of pleasure to the Manes. It subdues sins entirely. Listen to what happened there.

2. Here is the story. It is an ancient legend. There was a divine bitch, O sage, famous by the name Saramā.

3. She had two extremely excellent dogs as sons. They always followed people. They had four eyes. They had only the air for their food and they were the favourites of Yama.

4. She used to keep watch over the cows of Devas as well as the animals set apart for Yajñas. The Rākṣasas, Daityas and Dānavas followed her while she was watching.

5-6. The highly intelligent Rākṣasas tempted that bitch, the mother of the dogs, who was guarding (the cows), by means of agreeable words and gifts. The splendid cows kept as the sacrificial animals were taken away by the sinful Rākṣasas. Then the bitch gradually came to Devas and said.

Saramā said :

7-11. The Rākṣasas bound me with nooses and hit me with blows. The cows and the animals kept apart for the completion of Yajñas, O Devas, were taken away by them.

Brahmā said :

Immediately after hearing her words, Bṛhaspati said to Devas.

Bṛhaspati said :

This (bitch) has deformed features. I see her sin. Those cows have been taken away only with her connivance and not otherwise. This sinful bitch appears like a virtuous one by her bodily movements.

Brahmā said :

At the words of his preceptor, Indra hit the bitch with his foot. On account of that kick milk flowed out of her mouth.

Indra said :

O bitch, milk has been drunk by you. It has been given to you by Rākṣasas. Therefore, our cows have been taken away by them.

Saramā said :

12-13. It is not my fault, O lord. Nor is it the fault of anyone. O lord of Devas, there is neither guilt nor negligence on my part. It is on your arrival that the cows were taken away by them. Are you then to be blamed, O lord ? Your enemies are very powerful.

Brahmā said :

14-17. Then the preceptor of Devas meditated and understood her misconduct. (He said) "O Indra, it is true that she is to be blamed. She has sided with our enemies".

Then Indra cursed her : "O sinful woman, become a bitch in the mortal world; you have become a sinner but you committed this sin out of ignorance."

Then on account of the curse of Indra she was born in the mortal world due to her sin. As cursed by Indra she became very terrible.

The lord of Devas attempted to bring back those cows which were taken away by the Rākṣasas. He intimated this to Viṣṇu.

18-21. Viṣṇu got ready to kill Daítyas, Danujas and Rākṣasas who had taken away the cows. He took up his great bow

Śārṅga which is famous in the three worlds and which is the destroyer of Daityas.

Lord Viṣṇu who had conquered his enemies and who is worshipped by Devas and who is the lord of the universe stood in the Daṇḍaka forest with the bow Śārṅga in his hand. Viṣṇu killed the powerful Daityas, Danujas and Rākṣasas who were there and by whom the cows had been taken away. There the lord is well known as Śārṅgapāṇi.

22. Then Viṣṇu fought with the sons of Diti and the Rākṣasas. Frightened of Viṣṇu they went to the southern quarter, O great sage.

23-26. Then Viṣṇu the great lord followed them. He overtook them by Garuḍa, his vehicle. With the arrows as swift as mind discharged from the Śārṅga, Viṣṇu killed them on the northern bank of Gaṅgā. The enemies of Devas were annihilated by the powerful Viṣṇu. By the arrows of great velocity, having good sound and well-inspired by means of magical and mystical words, discharged from the Śārṅga those enemies of Devas were annihilated. The place where the cows were recovered is called Bāṇatīrtha. It is well known in the worlds as Vaiṣṇava and Gotīrtha.

27. In the southern bank of Gaṅgā the cows were set apart as the sacrificial animals. These cows had fled and the Devas herded them together on Gaṅgā.

28. In its middle they caused an island to be made as the place of rest for the cows. Through those cows the Yajña of Devas was celebrated on Gaṅgā.

29. The island of cows in the middle of Gaṅgā is called Yajñatīrtha. That spot of sacrifice of Devas is the splendid bestower of all cherished desires.

30. The (Divine power) of Gaṅgā assumes an embodied form, O sage of great splendour. It is a raft that takes one across the ocean of worldly existence which is worthless but boundless.

31. She is the Yogamāyā, the goddess of the universe, the bestower of freedom from fear on devotees. Beyond that, on the southern bank of Gaṅgā is the holy centre of Gorakṣa.

32-33. The two dogs, the sons of Saramā and the favourites of Yama, with four eyes each described to Yama the details of their mother's guilt and the (subsequent) curse.

After intimating this duly they asked Yama as to what they should do to bring about happiness and the removal of the curse.

34-36. The son of Sun (Yama) went to his father accompanied by them and related to him (everything). On hearing it the Sun said to his son: "Dear son, O excellent Deva, take your bath duly in the Gautamī Gaṅgā, the sole sanctifier of the three worlds in the Daṇḍaka forest. Take your bath with full faith, due concentration and mental purity. With great devotional feelings eulogize Brahmā, Viṣṇu, me and Īśa in due order. Your servants will attain satisfaction."

37-38. On hearing the words of his father, Yama was delighted in his mind. For pleasing him, Yama delighted in his mind, went to Gautamī for propitiating the two gods. With mental purity and concentration he propitiated the excellent Devas in Gautamī Gaṅga, the dispeller of sins.

39-40. Accompanied by the dogs the glorious lord of the southern quarters propitiated Sun-god and Brahmā on the southern bank. By himself the valorous Dharma propitiated Īśāna and Viṣṇu on the northern bank. He prayed to them for many boons which would do good to the worlds. They granted the excellent boon removing the curse of Saramā.

Yama said :

41. O Brahmā, Viṣṇu and Maheśvara, those who take their holy dip in these holy centres shall obtain their splendid desires for their own good as well as for others' good.

42. Those who take their holy bath in the Bāṇatīrtha and remember Śārṅgapāṇi Viṣṇu will never experience the miseries of proverty for ages.

43-45. If anyone with self-control and holy observances takes his holy bath in the Gotīrtha or Brahmatīrtha, bows down to Brahmā and circumambulates the island, it is as fruitful as the circumambulation of the Earth consisting of seven continents and holding rich resources within its bowels. If he gives a little sun to a brahmin and if he performs Homa with ạnything in the holy fire after reaching Devayajana, he shall attain plenty of benefit of horse sacrifice and other Yajñas.

46. If a man recites but once Gāyatrī, the mother of Vedas,

it is as much fruitful as though all the Vedas have been read by him. The person who has no desire (while performing all these holy rites) becomes worthy of liberation.

47. By taking holy bath in the southern bank and by worshipping goddess Śakti devoutly and duly one shall attain all cherished desires.

48. The Śakti of Brahmā, Viṣṇu and Maheśa is the mother in the form of the three Vedas. (One who worship her) attains all cherished desires. He shall be endowed with sons and riches.

49. If a man with self-control takes bath in the southern bank and sees Sun-god it is as fruitful as performing Yajñas with various monetary gifts.

50. He who takes his holy bath in the northern bank of Gaṅgā, bows down and sees Viṣṇu, attains the great region of Viṣṇu.

51-52. A man of self-control shall take bath in the Yamatīrtha and see the honoured Yameśvara. He shall then make the merit of Pitṛs everlasting, yielding benefits and conducive to the increase of their fame. By means of holy dip, charitable gift, Japas and eulogy even the manes of evil actions shall attain liberation.

Brahmā said :

53-58. There are eight thousand and three holy centres such as these, O Nārada. A performance of holy bath and charitable gift there yields everlasting merit.

The remembrance of these (holy centres) is meritorious and conducive to the destruction of sins of many births. By listening to their glory one's liberation shall be achieved along with that of the Pitṛs, and a reading of their narrative shall liberate one along with all the members of one's family. Their awful sins too will be destroyed at my behest.

The devotee shall perform holy bath and other rites there. He shall offer as charitable gift something with the soul under control. Then he shall perform the rites offering balls of rice to the ancestors. He shall bow down to these Devas. He shall obtain wealth, grains, fame, valour, longevity, health, riches, sons, grandsons, and a beloved wife. He shall obtain other desired objects also. He shall never be separated from his relatives. He shall be delighted in his mind. He will be honoured by his kinsmen. He shall redeem even the Pitṛs staying in hells. He will sanctify his family members. Accompanied by his beloved ones he shall remember Viṣṇu and Śiva at the time of death. Then he shall attain the blessed state of liberation as stated by those lords.

CHAPTER SIXTYTWO

Holy Centres Yakṣiṇisaṅgama etc.

Brahmā said :

1. The holy centre named Yakṣiṇī-Saṅgama yields all benefits. By taking bath and offering charitable gifts there one shall obtain all cherished desires.

2. One shall obtain the benefit of Satrayāga[1] merely by taking bath at the place where the lord is Yakṣeśvara who bestows worldly pleasures and salvation by granting his vision.

3-5. There was a sister of Viśvāvasu[2] named Pippalā. She went to the Satra of the sages residing on the bank of Gautamī. On seeing the sages there feeble and emaciated she laughed with great arrogance. She had (the temerity) to laugh at her elders. She repeated the Mantras firmly : "Let there be Vauṣaṭ. Let there be Śrauṣaṭ". She had repeated the Mantras with a wrong accent. Therefore, they cursed her: "Be a flowing river" Then she became the river famous as "Yakṣiṇī".

6. Then Viśvāvasu worshipped the sages and the three-eyed lord. Making the river join Gautamī he made it free from curse.

7-9. Thereafter that holy centre is remembered as Yakṣiṇīsaṅgama. By performing the rites of holy bath there and by giving charitable gifts one obtains all cherished desires. The place where Śambhu accompanied by Śivā became pleased with Viśvāvasu is the greatest holy centre Śaiva (pertaining to Śivā). It is well known as Durgātīrtha also.

1. Soma sacrifice lasting for more than twelve days.
2. A Gandharva chief.

It dispels all sins. It destroys all evil destinies and adversities. O great sage, it is the essence of all important holy centres. It is a holy centre praised by excellent sages. It bestows all spiritual achievements on men.

CHAPTER SIXTYTHREE

Śuklatīrtha and other Holy Centres

Brahmā said :

1. The holy centre well known as Śuklatīrtha is the giver of success in all endeavours to men. By merely remembering it one shall attain all cherished objects.

2. There was a sage named Bharadvāja who was extremely righteous and well-known. His wife was Paiṭhīnasī by name. She was the ornament of a noble family.

3. That chaste lady sat on the bank of Gautamī and prepared sacrificial offerings for Fire-god and the Moon as well as for Indra and Fire-god.

4. When the Puroḍāśa was being cooked a terrible demon was born out of the smoke. He was a terror unto all the three worlds. He was desirous of devouring the Puroḍāśa.

5. "Who are you destroying my Yajña out of anger ?" The sage Bharadvāja, the excellent brahmin, asked him immediately. On hearing the words of the sage the Rākṣasa replied to him.

Rākṣasa said :

6. O Bharadvāja, know me as (the demon) well known as Havyaghna. I am the eldest son of Sandhyā and Prācīna-Barhiṣ.

7. This boon has been granted to me by Brahmā : "Devour Yajñas as you please." My younger brother Kālī is strong and extremely terrible.

8. I am black. My father is black. My mother is black. So also my younger brother. I will destroy the sacrifice. I will cut off Yūpa (sacrificial post). I am the destroyer.

Bharadvāja said :

9. Let my Yajña be saved by you. Performing Yajña is my

favourite and eternal duty. I know you are a destroyer of Yajñas (but) save my sacrifice along with the brahmin (priest).

Yajñaghna said :

10. O Bharadvāja, understand this brief statement of mine. Formerly, I was cursed by Brahmā in the presence of Devas and Dānavas.

11-12. Then the lord, the grandfather of the worlds, was pacified by me. (He said) "When the excellent sages sprinkle you with Amṛta (Nectar), O Havyaghna, you will be free from the curse and not otherwise". O brahmin, if you do this whatever you desire you will get. This is not at all false.

Brahmā said :

13-15. Bharadvāja said again : "You are my friend, O highly intelligent one. Tell me that whereby my sacrifice can be saved. I shall do that. Devas and Daityas joined together and churned the milk ocean. They obtained nectar with great effort. How can that be easily accessible to us ? Please, if you are favourably disposed tell me that which is readily available."

On hearing the words of the sage the Rākṣasa said happily.

Rākṣasa said :

16-17. The water of Gautamī river is called Amṛta. Gold is called Amṛta. Ghee produced from cow's milk is also Amṛta, and Soma juice too is Amṛta. Sprinkle and shower me with these or at least with these three, viz. the water of Gaṅgā, ghee and gold. The water of Gaṅgā is superior to all. It is divine Amṛta.

Brahmā said :

18-23. On hearing this the sage experienced great pleasure. He took in his palm with great respect, the Amṛta, the water of the Gaṅgā and sprinkled the Rākṣasa with it. He sprinkled everything connected with the Yajña such as the sacrificial post, sacrificial animal and the circular platform of the sacrifice. When the noble-souled sage sprinkled, everything became white. The Rākṣasa became white. He who was dark in colour before became white in a moment. Bharadvāja the valorous one concluded his Yajña, bade farewell to the Ṛtviks and cast off the sacrificial post in the waters of Gaṅgā. Indeed the very same sacrificial post is in the middle of Gaṅgā even today serving as a token of that event. That Rākṣasa spoke to Bharadvāja again.

Rākṣasa said :

24-27. I am going, Bharadvāja. I have been made white. Hence those who take holy bath, offer charitable gifts or worship in this holy centre will realise their cherished desires. They will reap the fruit of this sacrifice, O sage. Their sins are destroyed by its mere remembrance. Thenceforth that holy centre is remembered as Śuklatīrtha. The door to heaven was kept open on the river Gautamī in the Daṇḍaka forest. On both banks there are seven thousand other holy centres. O noblest among sages, these holy centres bestow all miraculous powers.

CHAPTER SIXTYFOUR

Cakratirtha and other Holy Centres

Brahmā said :

1. The holy centre well known as Cakratīrtha destroys sins by mere remembrance. I shall recount its greatness. Listen attentively, O Nārada.

2. Seven sages with Vasiṣṭha as their leader are well-known, O sage. They resorted to the banks of Gautamī and began to perform Satrayajña.

3. When a terrible obstacle was started by the Rākṣasas there, the sages approached me and intimated to me the activities of the demons.

4-5. Then, O Nārada, I created the form of a young maiden, by means of Māyā. Saying, "By the mere sight of this (woman) the Rākṣasas shall perish", I gave that young maiden to the sages, O sage. At my instance, the sages went back taking Māyā with them.

6-8. That Māyā exists in physical form even today well known by the name of Muktakeśī (one whose tresses are loose). She is Ajā (unborn) and Ekā (single) and has black and red forms. She can assume any form as she pleases. She inflicts delusion in all the three world. On account of her power the excellent sages had peace of mind. They went to Gautamī, the excellent river, and got themselves initiated for the Yajñas once again. Again the Rākṣasas came there to destroy that sacrifice.

9. On seeing Māyā near the sacrificial ground the leading Rākṣasas began to dance, sing, laugh and cry.

10-11. The great Māyā of Maheśvara was excessively proud on account of her power. Among them there was the lord of Daityas named Śambara. He was valorous and he devoured the young woman of the form of Māyā, O Nārada. It was extremely surprising to those persons who had seen the power of Māyā.

12. When the sacrifice was being destroyed they sought refuge in Viṣṇu. Then Viṣṇu gave his discus for the protection of sages.

13. That discus chopped off the Daityas, Danujas and Rākṣasas in the battle. The leading Rākṣasas died on account of their fear of it.

14. That great Satra was completed by the sages. Sudarśana, the discus of Viṣṇu, was washed by the waters of Gaṅgā.

15-16. Thenceforth that holy centre is cited as Cakratīrtha. By taking holy bath and offering charitable gifts there one shall obtain the fruit of Satra sacrifice.

There are five hundred holy centres that dispel sins. Taking holy dip and the offering of charitable gifts in each of them yields liberation.

CHAPTER SIXTYFIVE

Vāṇisaṅgama and other Holy Centres

Brahmā said :

1. The holy centre Vāṇīsaṅgama is (to be) mentioned (next). The lord there is Hara (Śiva) Vāgīśvara (the lord of speech). That holy centre rids one of all sins. It bestows all cherished desires.

2-5. By taking holy dip and offering charitable gifts there one can dispel even the sin of Brahmin-slaughter.

There had started a dispute between Brahmā and Viṣṇu as to who was superior. In their middle Mahādeva appeared like a column of fiery flame. Dear son, a splendid divine voice spoke to them as they were arguing "I am great", "I am great."

"He who sees the limit to this (column of light) is superior (to the other one). Hence, it does not behove you to quarrel and argue over it." At its instance, Viṣṇu went below and I went up.

6. Then Viṣṇu returned quickly and sat near the column of light. Unable to reach the limit, O sage, I went farther and farther.

7-8. Then I became tired and returned to lord Īśa. At that time this thought occurred to me repeatedly. "The limit of this lord has been seen by me. Hence my superiority over Viṣṇu shall be clear."

Again, O highly intelligent one, I thought as follows :

9. "Even though I am afflicted how shall I tell a lie through the truthful mouths. Among the different kinds of sins there is no greater sin than telling a lie.

10-14. How will I tell an untruthful word?" I thought thus and created a fifth face terrible to look at like the face of a donkey. "With that I shall speak an untruthful word". After meditating thus for a long time. I told Viṣṇu, the lord of the worlds, who was seated there :

"The extremity of this (fiery column) has been seen by me, O Janārdana. Hence my superiority". Even as I was saying thus, both of them, Hari and Śaṅkara assumed a single form like the sun and the moon. On seeing them I was surprised and frightened. I eulogized both of them. Then the infuriated lords of the world spoke to Vāc (the divine voice) as follows :

Hari and Hara said :

O evil lady, you shall become a river. There is no greater sin than falsehood.

Brahmā said :

15. Then she became agitated and assumed the form of a river. On seeing it I was surprised and afraid. Then I told her thus.

16. "Since you uttered a lie, though stationed in the voice of Brahmā you shall become invisible. Undoubtedly you are sinful."

17. On realizing this curse, she bowed down to those two lords and eulogized them again and again pleading for freedom from the curse.

18. Those two lords of Devas who had been honoured by Devas and requested (by her) became pleased. Out of affection, Hari and Hara spoke to Vāc thus:

Hari and Hara said :

19. O gentle lady, the sanctifier of the worlds, O splendid one, when you get merged in Gaṅgā, your body shall become pure once again.

Brahmā said :

20-23. Saying "So be it" that divine voice joined Gaṅgā. That divine lady attained her own body after joining Bhāgīrathī and Gautamī. This was an achievement difficult even for gods. That bestower of merit is well known by the name Vāṇī when she joins Gautamī. In the Bhāgīrathī the same divine lady is called Sarasvatī. In both the places the confluence is well known and is honoured by the whole world, viz., the Sarasvatīsaṅgama and the Vāṇīsaṅgama. The divine (river) joined to Gautamī is the Vāṇī. Otherwise it is Sarasvatī.

24-27. The place where the divine voice worshipped lord Śiva, lord of Devas, and got rid of her curse is a holy centre honoured everywhere. Brahmā shook off his wickedness accrued to him due to his (untruthful) speech and went back to his residence.

Hence, a person who remains pure and takes a holy bath in the confluence and visits Lord Vāgīśvara shall attain salvation merely due to that. He who performs a holy rite such as charitable gift, Homa, fasting in the holy confluence, shall not be born again in the world. There are one thousand nine hundred holy centres on either side (of the holy river). They dispel sins accumulated in the course of different births.

CHAPTER SIXTYSIX

Viṣṇutīrtha and other Holy Centres

Brahmā said :

1. The holy centre well known as Viṣṇutīrtha (is being recounted now). Listen to what happened there. There was a sage well known as Maudgalya since he was the son of Mudgala.

2-5. His wife was well known as Jābālā. She had good sons. The father, sage Mudgala, was old and well known in the worlds. His splendid wife was known by the name Bhāgīrathī.

Maudgalya used to take bath in Gaṅgā early in the morning. He was regular in observing holy rites with self-control. O excellent sage, this was his daily routine. On the banks of Gaṅgā, the son of Mudgala used to invoke Viṣṇu by means of Kuśa grass, clay, Śamī flowers in his lotus-like heart by the method taught by his preceptor everyday.

6. When invoked by him, the consort of Lakṣmī, the lord of the universe holding conch, discus and iron club, came to him in a hurry seated on Garuḍa.

7. On being worshipped devotedly by that sage Maudgalya, the lord of the universe used to recount wonderfully variegated stories to Maudgalya.

8. Late in the afternoon Viṣṇu repeatedly told Maudgali—"Go back to your abode, dear one. You are tired."

9. On being told thus by lord Viṣṇu that brahmin went home. Then the lord of the universe went to his abode accompanied by Devas.

10-14. The learned Maudgalaya used to bring something to his house and give his wife money earned by himself. He was (mainly) devoted to the lotus-like feet of Mahāviṣṇu.

Maudgalya's beloved wife was a chaste lady and considered him as her ultimate goal. Greens, roots or fruits whatever was brought by her husband she used to cook very well and serve food unto the guests, her husband and her sons. She used to take her food only after they had been fed. She too used to perform holy rites with self-control. Everyday at night, when all had taken food, the delighted son of Mudgala used to recount to them the wonderful stories heard from Viṣṇu. A great deal of time passed by. The wife of Maudgalya, who had been surprised (on account of their sufferings) said to her husband in secret.

Jābālā said :

15-16. O highly intelligent one, when Viṣṇu comes near you ask the lord of the universe : "If Viṣṇu, honoured by Devas, approaches why should misery befall us?" The moment that lord is remembered old age, birth, death and sickness vanish; what then if he is seen !

Brahmā said :

17. Saying "So be it", on hearing the words of his beloved wife, Maudgalya worshipped Hari as usual. With palms joined in reverence he humbly asked him.

Maudgalya said:

18. When you are remembered, O lord of the universe, sorrow, poverty and sin vanish. But even when you are seen how is it that adversity still persists in me?

Śrīviṣṇu said:

19. All living beings everywhere and always enjoy or suffer the consequences of their own deeds. No one does anything good or bad to anyone.

20. The fruit is in accordance with the seed that is sown. Never and nowhere can mango be produced from a margosa seed.

21. How can they be befitting recipients of glory and wealth—they by whom Gautamī has not been served, Hari and Śaṅkara have not been worshipped and nothing has been given to the brahmins?

22. Nothing has been given by you to brahmins or to me. Only what is given goes over to the supreme soul.

23-24. One can very well become a purified soul by means of regular acts of cleanliness through clay, water, kuśa and Mantras or by causing emaciation of the body.

But nowhere can men attain worldly pleasures without offering charitable gifts. One becomes purified by performing holy rites. Then alone one becomes detached (i.e. loses interest in worldly pleasures).

25. Then his knowledge becomes unimpeded. Thereafter he becomes a liberated soul while still living. Through devotion to me at first, liberation is easy of access to everyone.

26. Worldly pleasures can be achieved by means of charitable gifts etc. or by alleviating the misery of all living beings. Or you will attain liberation, but you will not obtain worldly pleasures through devotion (alone).

Maudgalya said :

27-28. How can there be liberation through devotion? Liberation is rarer than worldly pleasures. If liberation is achieved, of what avail is anything else to the embodied beings? Liberation is worthy of being honoured by everyone more than devotion. O lord, who is identical with the universe, I would like to have it.

Viṣṇu said :

29-31. This is the difference, O brahmin. Whatever is given away to a brahmin or (other) suppliants after remembering me shall be given in return everlasting benefit. If without meditating upon me anything is given away it yields only an equivalent benefit. That is already given. It is not capable of contributing to our worldly enjoyment. Hence, O highly intelligent one, certainly give me something to eat or to a superior brahmin after resorting to the banks of Gautamī.

Brahmā said :

32-34. Maudgalya said to Viṣṇu : "I have nothing else to be given to you. The body etc. (which I have) is dedicated unto you." Then Viṣṇu, the lord of the universe, hastened to tell Garuḍa : "Bring an ear of corn here. He will offer that to me. Thereafter, he will obtain befitting worldly pleasures according to his choice." On hearing the command of his master the lord of birds did so.

35. Maudgalya who performed holy rites with self-control placed the grains of corn in the hand of Viṣṇu. In the meantime Viṣṇu spoke to Viśvakarman.

Viṣṇua said :

36. O highly intelligent one, all the cherished desires and

ambitions shall be fulfilled in the family of this sage up to the seventh generation of successors. They will have cows, gold, grains, clothes and ornaments.

Brahmā said :

37. Due to the power of Viṣṇu and Gaṅgā Maudgalya obtained all those things which embellish and contribute to mental satisfaction in the world.

38. On being told by Viṣṇu "Go home" Maudgalya went back. On seeing all riches and prosperity in his hermitage the sage spoke.

The sage said :

39. Oh the power of charitable gift ! Oh the remembrance of Viṣṇu ! Oh the power of Gaṅgā ! By whom could this great thing have been imagined?

Brahmā said :

40. In the company of his wife, sons, grandsons and kinsmen, Maudgalya enjoyed worldly pleasures and attained salvation along with his ancestors.

41-43. Thenceforth that holy centre is well known as Maudgalya and Vaiṣṇava. The holy bath taken and charitable gifts distributed there yield the benefits of worldly pleasures and liberation.

If somehow the holy centre is heard or remembered Viṣṇu becomes pleased with him. He shall be rid of all sins. He shall be happy.

There are eleven thousand holy centres on both the banks together. Through holy bath, offering charitable gifts, Japas etc. these holy centres bestow all riches.

CHAPTER SIXTYSEVEN

Lakṣmītīrtha and other Holy Centres

Brahmā said :

1. The holy centre well known as Lakṣmītīrtha is directly conducive to the increase of wealth and prosperity. O Nārada,

listen to the sacred narrative that destroys Alakṣmī (poverty, ignominy, etc.).

2-3. Dear sir, formerly there was a dispute between Lakṣmī and Daridrā (Poverty). They approached the universe as mutual antagonists. There is nothing in all the three worlds that is not pervaded by them. Both of them said to each other, "Superiority is mine," "Superiority is mine". Poverty said emphatically to Śrī, "It is I who am born earlier".

Śrīlakṣmī said :

4. I alone am the nobility of birth, good conduct and the very life of embodied beings. Even though (physically) alive, the embodied beings are like dead ones if they are bereft of me.

Brahmā said :

5-8. She was then told by Daridrā : "I am superior to all. Liberation is perpetually dependent on me. Love, anger, greed, arrogance and malice never stay where I am present; fear does not rise up. Madness, jealousy and haughtiness too never stay where I am present.

On hearing the words of Daridrā Lakṣmī replied to her.

Lakṣmī said :

9-14. Every creature embellished by me becomes honoured and worshipped. A man devoid of wealth is attacked by all even though he may be on a par with Śiva.

The following five deities present in the body immediately quit the body through the word "dehi" (Please give), viz., Dhī (Intellect), Śrī (Splendour), Hrī (Sublimated bashfulness), Śānti (Peace) and Kīrti (Fame).

Good qualities and venerability are present in one, only as long as one does not seek and beg of others. If a man becomes a suppliant where are his good qualities? Where is his venerability? A creature is the most excellent of all, the abode of all good qualities and worthy of being bowed to by all the worlds, only as long as he does not beg of others. This is a painful thing. The state of deficiency in wealth is (the result of) great sin of the embodied beings. People neither honour nor speak to nor even touch the man without wealth. Therefore, I alone am the most excellent one, O Daridrā, listen to my words.

Brahmā said :

15-17. On hearing those words of Lakṣmī Daridrā said :

Daridrā said :

O Lakṣmī, you are not ashamed to say frequently "I am superior". You enjoy with sinners always forsaking the excellent person (i.e. Viṣṇu). You are guilty of breach of trust. How can you boast of yourself ? In attaining you one does not derive as much happiness as repentance.

18. Men do not become so much terribly elated and haughty through liquor as through your mere presence, even if they be learned men.

19. Generally you take delight in sinners always. I reside always in deserving men of righteous conduct.

20-22. O Lakṣmī, I always reside in persons devoted to Śiva and Viṣṇu, in men of grateful nature, in calm and quiet men of good conduct, in persons eager to serve elders, in good men in learned men, in heroic men and in good men of well-developed intellect. Hence superiority abides in me. I will reside in pure brahmins, in mendicants, in persons who perform holy rites and are fearless. Now listen where you are stationed.

23-24. You cling to sinners who hover round kings (and serve them), in cruel persons, in wicked persons, in scandal-mongers, in miserly persons, in rogues of great aberration, in ungrateful persons of ignoble nature, in those who always violate rules of piety, in those who harass and betray even their friends, in those who are frustrated in their minds and in those who cause evil.

Brahmā said

25. Mutually arguing thus, both of them came to me. After listening to their statements they were told thus by me.

26. "The Earth is anterior to me. The waters are still anterior. Only women know the (intricacies of) dispute between women, none else.

27. Particularly, the waters arising from the special types

of water-pots (kamaṇḍalu) are better than all others. Even there the divine deity Gautamī will be able to say decisively.

28-30. She also is the dispeller of all agonies. She alone is the dispeller of all doubts."

They went to Earth along with waters at my instance. Accompanied by Earth and waters they went to the river Gautamī. The Earth and waters stated entirely to Gautamī the rival claims of the two (Lakṣmī and Daridrā) after bowing down to her. They intimated the statements of Daridrā and Lakṣmī in the manner expressed by them both. They put up the case as neutral observers or umpires.

31. Even as the guardians of quarters were listening, even as the Earth was listening, O Nārada, even as the waters were listening, Gautamī Gaṅgā spoke these words to Daridrā. Praising Lakṣmī, Gautamī spoke thus.

Gautamī said :

32-36. Everything that exists in the world consisting of mobile and immobile beings, is pervaded by Lakṣmī. Such things are: the splendour of Brahman, of penance, of Yajñas, of renown, of wealth, of reputation, of learning, of intellect, of Sarasvatī (speech), of enjoyment, of worldly pleasures, of liberation, of bashfulness, of forbearance, of forgiveness, of spiritual attainment, of contentment, of nourishment, of peace, of waters, of Earth, of Ego, of medicinal herbs, of the Vedas, of purity, of night, of heaven, of moonlight, of blessings, of hailings, of pervasion, of illusion and of the auspicious dawn. Whatever is beautiful in the following is the display of the power of lakṣmī: Brahmins who are bold, self-possessed, of great patience, and good, others of great erudition and who follow the path of salvation and worldly enjoyment.

37-39. Why go into so much detail ? The entire universe is pervaded by Lakṣmī. Whatever excellence is seen in anyone is the overwhelming power of Lakṣmī. There is nothing devoid of her. Aren't you ashamed to compete with her maliciously ?

Then Gaṅgā spoke these words to Daridrā. "Go away, Go away". Thenceforth, the waters of Gaṅgā are inimical to Daridrā (Poverty).

40-41. The harassment by poverty occurs only so long as Gaṅgā is not resorted to.

Thenceforth that holy centre has bceome an auspicious one that dispels Alakṣmī (ill fame and absence of affluence). By taking holy bath there and offering charitable gifts one shall be wealthy and meritorious.

O highly intelligent one, in that holy spot there are six thousand holy centres, frequented by Devas, divine sages and mortal sages and they bestow all spiritual achievements.

CHAPTER SIXTYEIGHT

Bhānutīrtha and other Holy Centres

Brahmā said :

1. The holy centre by the name Bhānutīrtha is well known as a giver of all powers and prosperity to men. I shall recount what happened there. It is conducive to the destruction of great sins.

2. There was an extremely virtuous king famous by the name Śaryāti. His wife was Sthaviṣṭhā. She was unrivalled in physical beauty in the whole world.

3. The priest of that king was a brahmanical sage born of the family of Viśvāmitra well known as Madhucchandas. He was the lord of persons of great self-control.

4. Accompanied by his priest, that king, that heroic lord of rulers of men went to conquer the quarters. After conquering the quarters and camping on the way back the king said to the priest of great dignity.

5-7. He asked thus : "O priest of majestic lustre, tell me the reason why you are dejected. In my kingdom you alone are the person worthy of being honoured by all. You have the excellent knowledge of all the branches of learning.

You have dispelled all sins. Then why do you appear to be one with the mind attracteb by something else ? Why are you devoid of happiness ? The (whole) of this world has been conquered. Great kings have been defeated. This is great occasion for rejoicing. Why should then you be lean and emaciated ? O most excellent twice-born of great dignity, tell me the truth".

After addressing Śaryāti the brahmin Madhucchandas spoke these pleasing words full of love.

Madhucchandas said :

8-10. Listen to my statement, O king, (as well as) to what was uttered by my wife. "We are going when there is still a Yāma (i.e. 3 hrs.)" (said by me). "The night—half of it has passed by" (said by my wife). (Now) my beloved who is the owner of this body who is awaiting me. On remembering those words of my beloved my body becomes parched and deied up. When there is an aberration caused by Cupid it is the beloved who can be the curative medicine for restoration.

Brahmā said :

The king who used to suppress his enemies laughed and said to the priest :

The king said :

11-13. You are my preceptor and friend. Why are you deceiving yourself? Of what avail is my advice, O extremely intelligent one, the bestower of honour? What love and attachment can noble persons have for the pleasure that is transitory, perishable and momentary ?

Brahmā said :

On hearing this the intelligent Madhucchandas said.

Madhucchandas said :

The three-fold objects of life (virtue, love and wealth) increase when there is mutual compatibility and consideration between husband and wife. What is usually a defect may be considered an ornament there, O king.

Brahmā said :

14-15. The king came back to his own land accompanied by the army. In order to test his (boasted) love he circulated this rumour in the city : "When king Śaryāti proceeded ahead in his conquest of quarters, a great Rākṣasa killed him along with his priest and went away to the nether worlds."

16-18. The king's wives, O excellent sage, began to enquire for confirmation. But on hearing the news from the messengers the wife of Madhucchandas died immediately. It was indeed extremely surprising. On seeing what happened in the city the messengers reported to the king as to what was done by the queens as well as by the beloved wife of the priest. The king was both surprised and distressed. He spoke to the messengers again.

The King said:

19. O messengers, go quickly. Preserve the body of that brahmin lady and spread the rumour that the king will be coming along with his preceptor.

Brahmā said:

20-21. When the king was worried in this manner an unembodied voice announced.

The Ethereal Voice said :

O king, Gaṅgā will fulfil your desire entirely. Gautamī subdues all mortifications on the Earth. She is sacred.

Brahmā said :

22-27. On hearing it Śaryāti resorted to the banks of Gautamī. He offered monetary gifts to brahmins and performed tarpaṇa rites unto the manes and sages. He then sent the excellent brahmin, the priest, to another holy centre after providing him with adequate funds. He told him thus : "Give money and other charitable gifts too to the members of the caravan." The king's idea was not to make the priest aware of what he was planning to do. When the noble preceptor, the descendant of Viśvāmitra had gone, the king sent away the entire army and entered the burning pyre on the banks of Gaṅgā after proclaiming as follows. The leading king addressed Gaṅgā, the Sun-god and Devas and said as follows : "If momentary gifts have been made by me, if Homa has been performed by me, if the subjects have been protected by me, let that chaste woman come back to life by that truth, by dint of (the balance of) my life."

After saying this, the excellent king Śaryāti entered the burning pyre. At the very same time the wife of the priest of that king regained her life.

28-32. The preceptor of the king heard about these incidents that caused him a great deal of wonder. He was wonder-struck on hearing that the king entered the burning fire; that this chaste wife who was dead regained her life; that it was for this special purpose that the king had sacrificed his own life. Thereupon he remembered his own duty. He mused thus : "Shall I too enter the burning fire ? Or shall I go back to my beloved wife ? Or shall I perform a penance here ?" Then the brahmin came to this decision: "I consider this alone as my duty as well as a meritorious deed. I shall first resuscitate the king and then go to my beloved wife. This alone shall be conducive to my auspiciousness."

Thereafter, he eulogized the Sun-god. There is no god other than the Sun-god who bestows all cherished desires.

Madhucchandas said :

33-34. Obeisance be to that Sun, who is liberation itself, who has unmeasured splendour, who is identical with the Vedas; obeisance to you, the lord who is the meaning of Oṁkāra (i.e. the mystic Mantra "Praṇava").

Obeisance to the lord without a form, to the lord with splendid form, to the lord possessing the three attributes and the three forms, to the powerful lord, the cause of birth, sustenance and destruction.

Brahmā said :

35-36. Then the delighted Sun revealed himself and spoke to him, "Choose your boon".

Madhucchandas said :

O lord of Devas, give me the king and my wife of sweet talk. Give me splendid sons and give the king excellent boons.

Brahmā said :

37-38. Then the lord of the universe gave Śaryāti his wife and other splendid boons. Everthing was full of weal. Then the king was extremely pleased. He went back to his kingdom, accompanied by the delighted priest. He was happy. That holy centre is remembered as a splendid one.

39-41. There are three thousand holy centres of good quality there. Thenceforth that holy centre is cited as Bhānutīrtha. It is well known by the names Mṛtasañjīvana (Reviving the dead) and Śaryāta. It is also called Madhucchandas. O sage, on being remembered it dispels sins.

A holy plunge there and offering of charitable gifts yields the benefit of all yajñas. It resuscitates the dead. It causes increase of longevity and health.

CHAPTER SIXTYNINE

Khaḍgatīrtha and other Holy Centres

Brahmā said :

1. The holy centre Khaḍgatīrtha is on the northern bank of Gautamī. By taking holy plunge there and offering charitable gifts a man attains salvation.

2. I shall tell you what happend there. Listen attentively, O Nārada. There was a brahmin well known as Pailūṣa. He was the son of Kavaṣa.

3. On account of the burden of maintaining a large family he began to run about here and there seeking wealth. But he did not get anything. Then he became detached from the world and lost interest in worldly affairs.

4. When the fate is extremely adverse and manly endeavour becomes futile nothing else lends support to a learned man except Vairāgya (freedom from passionate attachement to worldly things).

5-9. Thereupon, he began to sigh frequently and think thus : "I do not possess any hereditary wealth. I have many dependents to maintain. But the soul is proud. It cannot bear any stress and strain. Fie upon the doings of the evil fate !"

Once he got some job. In that job he did not get adequate

amount. Then he became dejected and detached (and said): "Service is prohibited. If at all there is anything (not prohibited) it is inaccessible (to me). Penance is very difficult to perform. Greed drags me forcibly towards evil activities. O Tṛṣṇā, it is out of ignorance that you have acted against me. Hence, obeisance be to you."

After thinking thus and after considering what he should do to sever all bondages the highly intelligent Pailūṣa spoke to his father.

Pailūṣa said :

10. O saintly lord, O dear father, tell me that means whereby I can allay anger and greed as well as cross (the ocean of) worldly existence that cannot be crossed, by the sword of perfect knowledge.

Kavaṣa said :

11. One shall seek perfect knowledge from Īśvara—so says the Vedic text. Hence, propitiate him. You shall obtain perfect knowledge from Īśvara.

Brahmā said :

12. Saying "So be it", Pailūṣa worshipped Īśvara for the sake of knowledge. Thereupon, lord Īśāna who was delighted granted him perfect knowledge. That (brahmin) of superior intelligence spoke these wise things, that bestow salvation upon the seeker.

Pailūṣa said :

13-17. The first enemy is Krodha (Anger). Even if it is ineffective (for others) it burns one's own body. By appeasing it by means of perfect knowledge one shall obtain supreme bliss.

Greediness is of different types. It is deceptive. It is binding. It causes sins. By killing it by the sword of perfect knowledge a man becomes happy.

Contact (with sensual objects) is a great evil even to Devas and others. So says the Vedic text. This contact is a great enemy of the soul though it is free from contact.

By destroying this by the sword of perfect knowledge one

shall attain identity with Śiva. Doubt is highly destructive. It causes the destruction of virtue and wealth.

By destroying it one shall obtain the greatest of one's cherished desires. Hope possesses one like a female vampire. It burns all happiness. By destroying it, one shall attain the state of liberated soul.

Brahmā said :

18-20. Then, after acquiring perfect knowledge he resorted to the banks of Gaṅgā. He got rid of delusion by perfect knowledge. Then he attained release.

Thenceforth that holy centre is remembered as Khaḍgatīrtha. (It is also known as) Jñānatīrtha, Kavaṣa and Pailūṣa. It bestows all cherished desires.

Great sages have mentioned about this and six thousand other holy centres. They dispel all sins and depressing agonies entirely and bestow what is desired.

CHAPTER SEVENTY

Anvindratīrtha and other Holy Centres

Brahmā said :

1. The excellent holy centre Anvindra is well known as Ātreyatīrtha also. I shall recount its efficacy. It is capable of giving back a lost kingdom.

2. Ātreya the lordly saint surrounded by Ṛtviks and sages began to perform Satras on the northern bank of Gautamī.

3-5. Agni the carrier of Havyas became his Hotṛ priest. The Maheśvarī sacrifice dedicated to the supreme lord was thus performed. The brahmin acquired prosperity thereby as well as the ability to move about everywhere. The great brahmin was then able to visit the heavenly world, the beautiful abode of Indra and the nether worlds as he pleased on account of the power of his auspicious penance.

Once, he went to heaven to the world of Indra.

6-10. There he saw the thousand-eyed lord, Indra, surrounded by the splendid Devas. He was being eulogized by the Siddhas and the Sādhyas. He was watching the excellent dance and listening to the sweet music. He was being fanned by the heavenly nymphs.

He was being worshipped by those leading Devas who sat near him. He was seated on a grand seat. He had kept his son, Jayanta, on his lap and he was accompanied by Śacī. He was the grandest of all and he had the satisfaction of experiencing the highest conjugal pleasure.

On seeing Mahendra who was worthy of being sought refuge in by the good men and who was the bestower of boons, the noble-souled leading brahmin was fascinated and deluded by the prosperity and glory of Indra. The sage desired for the kingdom of Indra.

After being duly honoured and worshipped by gods he came back to his hermitage. As contrasted with the extremely beautiful city of Indra that is filled with meritorious qualities and embellished by jewels when he saw his own hermitage that was lacking in gold and devoid of lustre the brahmin experienced great pain. Desirous of getting the kingdom of Devas immediately, the son of the great sage Atri spoke to his beloved wife.

Ātreya said :

11. When I remember the most sacred nectar and the various types of edibles there, the excellent seats, eulogy, charitable offerings, splendid assembly, miraculous weapons, clothes, city and parks, I am unable to eat the fruits and roots though they are excellent and well-consecrated.

Brahmā said :

12-13. Then the noble-souled sage empowered by his penance invoked Tvaṣṭṛ and spoke to him.

Ātreya said :

O noble-souled one, I should like to possess the state of Indra. Quickly reproduce the region of Indra here. If you refuse to obey me I shall undoubtedly reduce you to ashes.

Brahmā said :

14-18. At the instance of the son of Atri, the lordly creator of creatures, Viśvakarman hurriedly built Meru, the city of Devas, Kalpa trees, Kalpa creeper and the divine cow. He made splendid and variegated houses embellished with diamonds. He created a new Śacī who was free from blemish in respect of her limbs and who was as if the chamber of Cupid's sports. O wonderful ! he created within a moment the divine assembly chamber Sudharmā. He created the charming heavenly nymphs, (the horse) Uccaiḥśravas and the elephant Airāvata. He made thunderbolt and other weapons. (In fact) he made all Devas.

Though prevented by his beloved wife the son of Atri made (the new lady) resembling Śacī, his bride. At that time the son of Atri accompanied by the (other sages) beginning with Atri made weapons of the form of thunderbolt etc. He reproduced the dance, music etc. as was seen by him at the city of Indra. On acquiring all these things the great sage became extremely delighted in his mind.

19. The sensual objects are beautiful only for the nonce. Still, who does not have a desire for them ? On hearing about this, the Daityas, Dānavas and Rākṣasas became furious immediately.

20. They began to ask : "Why had Indra come to the Earth after forsaking heaven ? Was it for some secret enjoyment ? Hence we shall go there from here in order to fight the slayer of Vṛtra, whose Satra is not of long duration."

21. Then those Asuras came there and surrounded the son of Atri. After encircling the city built on the order of son of Atri and called by the name Indrapura, they began to attack Ātreya. On being tortured by the great onslaught of weapons he became afraid and spoke to Indra.

Ātreya said :

22-23. Even as he was born intelligent, Lord Indra embellished at first Devas by means of sacrifices. It is by his prowess that heaven and Earth are lifted aloft by the greatness of the lord protecting men.

Brahmā said :

After eulogizing Indra by the hymn the son of Atri spoke to his enemies.

Ātreya said :

24. I am not Indra. Nor Śacī is mine. This is not Indra's city. Nor does this park belong to Indra. He alone is Indra. He is the slayer of Vṛtra. He is the wielder of thunderbolt. He is the thousand-eyed lord. He is the suppressor of mountains. He is the thunderbolt-armed.

25. I am only a brahmin conversant with the Vedas and surrounded by scholars. I am stationed on the banks of Gautamī. Due to the evil fate I have committed an act which is no cause for happiness either today or in the future.

Asuras said :

26. O Ātreya, withdraw all these imitations of Indra. Happiness will befall you really. There is no necessity for worry.

Brahmā said :

27-28. Ātreya spoke again : "O highly fortunate ones, I shall definitely do as you say. As a token of truthfulness I shall touch the fire."

After saying this to the demons he spoke again to Tvaṣṭṛ.

Ātreya said :

29-30. O Tvaṣṭṛ, withdraw again the state of Indra that had been created by you out of love for me. Hasten to protect a brahmin. Give me once more my own state, my hermitage, the (old) animals and birds, trees, water etc., whatever had been here before. I have no use for those divine objects. Nothing that one irregularly acquires can be conducive to one's happiness.

Brahmā said :

31-33. Saying "So be it", Tvaṣṭṛ, lord of creatures, withdrew (everything). The Daityas went to their own abodes after making the land free from trouble.

Tvaṣṭṛ too went to his abode laughingly. Surrounded by

his disciples and accompanied by his wife, Ātreya resorted to the banks of Gautamī. He became delighted by performing penance. As a great sacrifice was being performed he became ashamed (on account of his former blunder) and spoke these words :

Ātreya said :

34-39. Oh the power of delusion ! Oh my mind's confusion ! Was the position of Mahendra obtained by me ? What had been committed by me formerly ?

Brahmā said :

As Ātreya was speaking thus out of his shamefulness Devas came to him and said :

Devas said :

O mighty-armed one, get rid of your bashfulness. You will have excellent fame. Those living beings who take bath in Ātreyatīrtha shall immediately become Indras. Merely by remembering it they shall enjoy happiness. Wise men say that there are five thousand holy centres there. They are glorified by the names of Anvindra, Ātreya and Daiteya. Holy plunge and charitable gifts there yield everlasting merit.

Brahmā said :

After saying thus Devas went away and the sage became contented.

CHAPTER SEVENTYONE

Kapilasaṅgama and other Holy Centres

Brahmā said :

1. The holy centre named Kapilasaṅgama is well known in three worlds. Listen, O Nārada, I shall tell the excellent and holy story.

2. There was a sage of very great fame named Kapila. He was a knower of philosophical truth. He was cruel sometimes

and kind and gracious sometimes. He was devoted to the performance of penance and holy rites.

3-4. As that excellent sage was performing penance after resorting to the banks of Gautamī, Vāmadeva and other sages came to him and said :

Vena had already been killed by the curses of these brahmins. But after his death there was anarchy and practice of virtue disappeared. At that time the sages approached the preceptor Kapila who was a Siddha and spoke thus:

The sages said :

5-9. When the Veda has gone, when holy rites are gone, what should be done, O leading sage ?

Brahmā said :

Then the sage Kapila meditated (for a short while) and spoke to the sages who came there.

Kapila said :

The thigh of Vena should be twisted and churned. Thereafter someone will come out of it.

Brahmā said :

The sages did likewise. They twisted and churned the thigh of Vena. From it was produced an excessively sinful and black being full of terrible strength. On seeing him the sages became afraid and said : "Be seated." Hence he became Niṣāda. From him the Hill tribes (Niṣādas) were born.

10-12 Then they twisted and churned the right arm of Vena, endowed with virtue. From it the glorious king Pṛthu was born. He had a loud voice. He was marked by all characteristics. He was endowed with the ability of Brahmā. Devas approached him, congratulated him and granted him excellent boons. They gave him miraculous weapons of good quality and their magic formulae. Then sages accompanied by Kapila spoke thus to Pṛthu.

The sages said :

13-18. Give food unto the living beings. Give them those medicinal herbs that had been swallowed by the Earth.

Brahmā said :

Taking up his bow, the excellent king spoke to the Earth.

Pṛthu said :

For the welfare of subjects, give me those herbs that have been swallowed by you.

Brahmā said :

The frightened Earth spoke to Pṛthu who had big eyes.

The Earth said :

The great medicinal herbs have been digested within me. How will I be able to give them ?

Brahmā said :

Then the furious king spoke again to the Earth.

Pṛthu said :

19-22. If you do not give them today I will kill you and take away the great medicinal herbs.

The Earth said :

How can you kill a woman, O king? O excellent king, though you are wise, how will you sustain these subjects without me?

Pṛthu said :

O Earth, there will be no fault if many gain by the destruction of one. I shall sustain the subjects by the power of my penance.

I do not see any fault here. Nor do I speak in vain. If one is killed to make others happy thereby, sages say that his slaughter is superior to a hundred horse sacrifices.

Brahmā said :

23. Then Devas and sages pacified the excellent king. Devas spoke to the Earth, the divine mother.

Devas said :

24. O Earth, assume the form of a cow and give great medicinal herbs in the form of milk to king Pṛthu. Then the king shall become delighted. This will result in the protection of the subjects and it will do good to all.

Brahmā said :

25. The Kapilā (tawny coloured cow) assumed the form of a cow (and stood) near Kapila. The king born of the arm of Vena milked the great medicinal herbs from the cow.

26-27. (This was at the place) where Devas along with Gandharvas, sage Kapila and others were present. O great sage, the king Pṛthu milked a lot of milk from the Earth that had assumed the form of a cow into Narmadā, Bhāgīrathī, Sarasvatī, Godāvarī in particular and in all great rivers.

28. On being milked by Pṛthu it became a river of meritorious waters. It joined Gautamī. It was as though a miracle had happened.

29-30. Thenceforth, they know that holy centre to be Kapila-saṅgama, O highly intelligent one. The sages say that there are eighty-eight thousand holy centres worthy of worship. Merely by being remembered, O Nārada, they sanctify this world in their proper order.

CHAPTER SEVENTYTWO

Devasthāna and other Holy Centres

Brahmā said :

1. The holy centre well known as Devasthāna is reputed in all the three worlds. I shall describe its efficacy. Listen attentively, O Nārada.

2-4. Formerly in the beginning of the Kṛta Age a battle between Devas and Dānavas ensued. There was a Daitya beauty well known as Siṁhikā. The extremely powerful Daitya named Rāhu was her son. At the time of churning the milk ocean and the production of Nectar Saiṁhikeya (i.e. Rāhu) was cut into two. His son was a great Daitya well known as Meghahāsa. On hearing about the murderous attack on his father he became extremely dejected and he performed a penance.

5. As the son of Rāhu was performing penance after

resorting to the banks of Gautamī, Devas and sages spoke to him as though they were afraid.

Devas and sages said :

6. O mighty-armed one, cut short your penance. Let everything that is within your mind be realized by the grace of Śiva and Gaṅgā. What is it that cannot be obtained by the grace of Śiva and Gaṅgā ?

Meghahāsa said :

7-8. My father who is worthy of worship, who is my deity, has been insulted and harassed by you. If he and I are adequately propitiated by you, I shall refrain from this penance and (my) enmity (towards you). Taking proper revenge on behalf of father is the duty of a son. If you all grant my request my desires are fulfilled.

Brahmā said:

9. Then all Devas made Rāhu a follower of planets. They made Meghahāsa honoured and worshipped by the Rākṣasas.

10-11. The son of Rāhu became the chief and lord of Rākṣasas.

Again the Daitya spoke to Devas :

"It is my opinion that the efficacy inherent in this holy place should be granted to me so that I can earn some reputation."

Saying "So be it" Devas offered him everything that he had desired.

12-14. O divine sage, the holy centre is called by the name of that leading Daitya. Since, O highly intelligent one, Devas were present in that spot, that holy centre is called Devasthānam also. It is difficult of access even to Devas. The place where the Lord of the Devas stayed is remembered as Devatīrtha.

There are eighteen holy centres, O Nārada, that are worthy of being worshipped by the Daityas. Taking bath and distributing charitable gifts there destroys great sins.

CHAPTER SEVENTYTHREE

Siddhatīrtha and other Holy Centres

Brahmā said :

1. The holy centre well known as Siddhatīrtha is conducive to the achievement of all spiritual powers by men. The lord there is Hara (called) Siddheśvara. I shall describe its efficacy.

2. Rāvaṇa who was born in the family of Pulastya and who made the world cry aloud conquered all the quarters and then went to the world of Soma.

3. As the ten-headed demon was about to fight with Soma I spoke to him. "O ten-headed one, desist from the fight with Soma. I shall grant you a Mantra."

4. After saying this, O Nārada, I granted to the great Rākṣasa the Mantra comprising one hundred and eight names of Śiva. I granted that Mantra for the purpose of peace.

5. In this world Śiva alone is the refuge of men who are devoid of splendour, who are subjected to adversity and who experience different kinds of stress and strain. No one else can be so.

6. Thereafter, he desisted (from the fight). The demon attained victory in the world of Soma. Accompanied by his ministers, the proud ten-headed demon hurriedly went through all the worlds seated in his (aerial chariot) Puṣpaka.

7. Visiting heaven, firmament, earth, serpents, elephants and brahmins he espied the great mountain Kailāsa that was the abode of lord Śiva.

8-9. On seeing these, the courageous Rāvaṇa whose mind had become pride-puffed approached them and said.

Rāvaṇa said :

Who is that noble soul who dwells on this mountain? I shall uproot this from the ground and take this mountain (to Laṅkā). After reaching Laṅkā this mountain will become really splendid. Laṅkā too shall attain glory.

Brahmā said:

10-11. On hearing these words and having understood the feelings of the lord of Rākṣasas the ministers of the demon said,

"This is not proper". The great demon did not agree to the suggestion. Stopping the aerial chariot Puṣpaka, the demon leapt on to the root of the mountain Kailāsa. The ten-headed one shook the mountain.

12-17. Since he had defeated the lords of the quarters the ten-headed demon Rāvaṇa had become proud. He began to shake the Kailāsa to and fro. Therefore the lord pressed it with his thumb (big toe). As a result of that the ten-headed one was pressed down into the nether worlds. His body was bruised. He lamented loudly. On hearing it the lord laughed along with the goddess. What Rāvaṇa desired for was granted. Although he was infuriated, Śambhu became pleased with him. There is no doubt about this that Śambhu bestows boons even on the undeserving people.

After obtaining excellent boons the heroic (Rāvaṇa) went away happily by the grace of Bhava. On his way to Laṅkā he went to Gaṅgā born of Śambhu's matted hair, for the purpose of worshipping the lord.

After worshipping Śambhu by the waters of Gaṅgā and repeating various kinds of Mantras, Rāvaṇa whose inherent strength was not of an inferior quality obtained a sword from Śiva whose crest jewel is the crescent moon. He obtained Siddhis (miraculous powers) and all types of desired prosperity.

I had granted him a Mantra for the pupose of saving the Moon. He worshipped Bhava and practised that Mantra. When the (efficacy of the) Mantra was achieved, the lord of the demons went to Laṅka again, contented.

Thenceforth this holy centre is extremely efficacious. It bestows great Siddhis and cherished desires. It destroys all sins. It is frequented by all Siddhas.

CHAPTER SEVENTYFOUR

Paruṣṇīsaṅgama and other Holy Centres

Brahmā said :

1. The holy centre named Paruṣṇīsaṅgama is well-known in the three worlds. I shall recount its characteristic features. It destroys all sins.

2-4. Atri propitiated Brahmā, Viṣṇu and Maheśvara. When they were pleased, he said : "You (three) shall be my sons. O Devas, a beautiful daughter also shall be born to me".

So Brahmā, Viṣṇu and Maheśvara were born as his sons. Atri begot a daughter named Śubhātreyī. The three sons of that noble sage were Datta, Soma and Durvāsas.

5-8. The sage Aṅgiras was born of Agni (Fire-god) along with Aṅgāras (sparks of fire). Therefore, he is called Aṅgiras. Atri gave Ātreyī of supreme splendour to that Aṅgiras.

On account of the power of Agni he always spoke harsh words to Ātreyī. Ātreyī went on serving him regularly.

Sons of great strength and valour were born of her to Aṅgiras. This sage Aṅgiras always spoke harsh words to Ātreyī. The Āṅgirasas, the sons, used to quieten their father always.

Once she was excessively dejected on account of the harsh words of her husband. The distressed lady joined her palms in reverence and spoke to her elderly father-in-law (the Fire-god).

Ātreyi said :

9-10. O carrier of Havyas, I am daughter of Atri and the wife of your son. I am always engaged in serving my husband and sons. My husband always speaks harsh words to me. For no reason he looks at me angrily. Instruct me, O eldest one among Devas, and restrain my husband.

The Fire-god said :

11-12. Your husband, sage Aṅgiras, is born of sparks of flame. O gentle lady, let some means be employed so that he becomes quiet.

Being fiery your husband has approached fire (?) O lady with excellent face. Then, at my behest you flow in the form of water.

Ātreyi said :

13. I would rather endure the harsh words. Let not my husband leap into the fire. Of what avail is life for women who are against their husbands ?

14. I wish for peaceful words. So also I must have my husband too.

Fire-god said :

15-16. Agni is present in waters, in bodies, in mobile as well as immobile beings. I am the perpetual abode of your husband. I am considered his father. Realizing that I am what I am, do not worry too much. Moreover, "Waters are divine mothers and Agni is (your) father-in-law"—keeping this firmly in mind do not be too much disheartened, dear daughter-in-law.

Ātreyī said :

17. You yourself say that waters are mothers. I am the wife of your son, O Agni. Being his wife how can I be his mother as well in the form of waters, O lord ?

Fire-god said :

18. At first you were (wife as a religious partner). Then you were (wife as the sustainer). Then you are (wife from whom the son is born). You are (wife as one who seeks the welfare of her husband). O gentle lady, you have assumed all these roles. (Hence) do as I ask you to do.

19. He who is born of her is her son. She is his mother definitely. There is no doubt about it. Hence those who are conversant with the principles of the Vedas say that she is no longer his wife when a son is born.

Brahmā said :

20. On hearing the words of her father-in-law Ātreyī flooded with water her husband who had assumed the form of fire.

21-22. The couple got mingled with the water of Gaṅgā, O brahmin. Both of them attained quiet forms and features.

The couple were on a par with Viṣṇu in the company of Lakṣmī, Śaṅkara accompanied by Umā and the Moon united with Rohiṇī.

23. Sweeping her husband by means of flood she assumed aquatic body. She became the famous river Paruṣṇī and joined the river Gaṅgā.

24-27. One shall obtain the merit of bestowing a hundred cows by taking holy plunge in Paruṣṇī. The sons of Aṅgiras performed Yajñas with plenty of monetary gifts.

Those who are well versed in the Purāṇas mention that there are three thousand holy centres there on either side of the river, dear one. They know that they severally yield the benefit of performing yajñas. The holy plunge and offering charitable gifts there, especially at the confluence of Paruṣṇī and Gaṅgā yield more benefit than a hundred Vājapeyas. It is not possible to mention adequately the benefit that accrues from the holy plunge and offerings of charitable gifts there.

CHAPTER SEVENTYFIVE

Mārkaṇḍeyatīrtha and other Holy Centres

Brahmā said :

1. The holy centre well-known as Mārkaṇḍeya is capable of ridding one of all sins. It is meritorious. It yields the benefit of all Yajñas. It dispels lots of sins.

2-4. I shall recount its efficacy. Listen to it attentively, O Nārada.

Mārkaṇḍeya, Bharadvāja, Vasiṣṭha, Atri, Gautama, Yājñavalkya, Jābāla—these and other sages, O Nārada, are the composers of scriptures. They have mastered the Vedas and the Vedāṅgas. They are conversant with the Purāṇas and the topics of discourse in Nyāya (Logic) and Mīmāṁsā. These scholars talked to one another about liberation, as much as they could as far as their intellect allowed.

5. Some of them praised knowledge, some praised Karman (holy rites) and some praised both. After discussing among themselves they asked me for my opinion.

6-7. Having known my opinion they went to the lord bearing discus and iron club. After knowing his opinion also, those sages of great power discussed once again. They attempted to ask Śaṅkara. After worshipping Bhava in Gaṅgā they mentioned to him the same topic.

8. The destroyer of the three cities (Śiva) mentioned the importance of Karman in the form of holy rites. Holy rite itself is called so (knowledge), he said.

9. Hence, all living beings shall obtain (spiritual) achievement only through Karman. Karman alone is one that pervades the whole universe. Without it nothing can be obtained.

10. The performance of Yajñas, the practice of learning, the worship of Śiva, the practice of Yoga—everything is Karman. Nowhere does a living being exist without Karman.

11-12. Karman alone is the cause (of salvation). Everything other than it is the doing of a lunatic.

Where the sages discussed (everything), where Lord Maheśvara decided that everything is acquired by men through Karman is called Mārkaṇḍa(i.e. Mārkaṇḍeya) because he was the chief (of those sages).

13-14. This holy centre is occupied by the sages on the northern bank of Gaṅgā. It purifies the Manes. It is holy always. It yields benefit even on being remembered.

The lord identical with the universe says that there are ninety-eight holy centres there. The same has been mentioned by the Vedas too. The sages have accepted it.

CHAPTER SEVENTYSIX

Yāyātatīrtha and other Holy Centres

Brahmā said:

1. The next holy centre is Yāyāta where lord Śiva is called Kālañjara. It is the dispeller of all sins. Its glory is being recounted now.

2. King Yayāti, son of Nahuṣa was like another Indra. He had two wives embellished by nobility of birth and good characteristics.

3. The senior queen was the splendid daughter of Śukra, Devayānī by name. The second one was Śarmiṣṭhā the daughter of Vṛṣaparvan.

4. Although she was a brahmin lady, the beautiful lady of slender waist, the highly intelligent Devayānī became the wife of Yayāti by the grace of Śukra.

5-8. Śarmiṣṭhā the daughter of Vṛṣaparvan too, was his wife. Devayānī the daughter of Śukra gave birth to two sons viz. Yadu and Turvasu. They were like the sons of gods.

Śarmiṣṭhā gave birth to three sons resembling Devas viz. Druhyu, Anu and Puru.

The sons of Devayānī, O brahmin, were like Śukra in form and features.

Śarmiṣṭhā's sons had the lustre of Indra, Agni and Varuṇa. Once the distressed Devayānī spoke to her father.

Devayānī said:

9. O father, scion of the family of Bhṛgu, I am unfortunate. I have only two sons. My servant woman is fotunate. She has three sons.

10. Thinking about this I have become very sad, O preceptor of Dānavas. I will die as a result of the insult committed by Yayāti. Death is far better than injury to the honour of an intelligent person.

Brahmā said:

11. On hearing these words of his beloved daughter Śukra of great valour became angry. He came to Yayāti hurriedly and spoke thus.

Śukra said:

12-14. O great king, you are proud of your handsome features. That was why this unpleasant treatment has been accorded to my daughter. Hence, you will become old.

You will be overwhelmed by sensual objects which you will be incompetent to enjoy. Nor will it be possible for you to cast them off. You will be heaving sighs and gasping for breath; your intellect will be confounded. You will be mentally longing for sensual pleasures.

Old age alone is death to the embodied beings though they be (physically) alive. Hence, O king, quickly attain the extremely unbearable old age.

Brahmā said:

15. On hearing this curse of the intelligent Śukra, king Yayāti spoke to him with palms joined in reverence.

Yayāti said :

16-18. I have committed no offence. I am not angry. I do not commit any sin. Indeed the sinners alone who commit evil should be admonished by the noble.

How is it that you have cursed me although I continue to perform pious rites, C excellent brahmin ? Devayānī has said something about me without any basis. Hence, O great brahmin, it does not behove you to curse me thus.

If even learned men, out of delusion, were to be angry with blameless persons, what fault is there in fools whose minds are scorched by the fire of hatred ?

Brahmā said :

19-20. On hearing the words of Yayāti, Śukra remembered what had been committed by his daughter, how she had become fierce and committed things unpleasant to him many times by day and night. After saying "My anger has gone" Śukra spoke to the king.

Śukra said :

21-22. I never tell lies knowingly or unknowingly. I never utter falsehood intentionally. Listen, O king, I shall convert this curse into a blessing. I grant you this boon, O bestower of honour, that you can transfer this old age to anyone of your sons as you wish.

Brahmā said :

23-25. Once again Yayāti spoke humbly to Śukra, his father-in-law, thus.

Yayāti said :

Let this be permitted, O preceptor of Daityas. Only that son shall be the king, who devoutly receives the old age transferred by me.

I shall curse that son, O preceptor of Daityas, who does not approve of my suggestion. O preceptor, permission should be granted by you in this regard.

Brahmā said :

26. The son o f Bhṛgu said to the king, "Let it be so". Thereupon, Yayāti called his son and spoke these words.

Yayāti said:

27. O Yadu, you are my son. Receive the old age that has befallen me due to the curse. You are my eldest son. You are mature and conversant with all affairs. You are the seniormost of my sons. A father can be said to be blessed with a son only when that son is obedient to his father.

Brahmā said:

28-33. Yadu said "No" to his father, Yayāti who used to distribute much by way of gifts. Yayāti then cursed Yadu and spoke to Turvasu about his desire.

Turvasu also did not like to receive the old age of his father. After cursing him he spoke to Druhyu, "Receive this old age of mine".

Druhyu also did not like to receive the old age transferred by his father, the old age that destroys the beauty of form.

The king said to Anu also, "Receive this old age of mine." Then Anu said "No". After cursing him, he spoke to Puru. Then Puru approved the suggestion of his father and accepted his old age for a thousand and one years. Then his father became glad. Contented with the youthful age of his son, Yayāti happily enjoyed the different pleasures that could be enjoyed in the course of youth. Then the king, the son of Nahuṣa, was satisfied with regard to all worldly pleasures. Then out of delight he called his son Puru and said:

Yayāti said:

34. O sinless one, I am fully satiated in regard to all worldly pleasures due to your youth. Dear son, receive your youthful age; give me back my old age that is foul and ignominious.

Brahmā said:

35-37. "No", said Puru then. "Dear father, the inevitable aberrations of the emotions of all embodied beings are being gradually destroyed by one through this old age. Old age that befalls one forcibly at the due period can be well endured by all embodied beings. If that has been accepted to help one's elderly (father), how can it be forsaken? To the embodied beings, death is preferable to the sin of casting away what is accepted. Or, O king, I shall destroy the old age by means of penance."

Brahmā said :

38. After saying this to his father he went to Gaṅgā and performed a penance on the southern bank of that sacred river.

39. After a great deal of time lord Śiva became pleased. The most excellent Deva said, "What shall I give you ?" to Puru who was bedecked in excellent jewels of magnificent qualities, far superior to what are seen ordinarily in the world.

Puru said :

40-45. O lord, O chief of Devas, O lord of Devas, be pleased to destroy old age acquired by my father due to the curse. Please rid my brothers of their curses. They have been cursed by my father due to anger. O lord, worshipped by Devas, release them from their curses.

Brahmā said:

Saying "So be it" the lord of the universe destroyed old age that was caused by the curse. The lord of the worlds made his brothers free from their curses.

Thenceforth that holy centre destroys old age and sickness. Merely by being remembered it dispels premature old age.

It is well known by his name. It is cited as Kālañjara. It is also known as Yāyāta, Nāhuṣa, Paura, Śaukra and Śārmiṣṭha.

There are onehundred and eight holy centres like this there. O highly intelligent one, it should be known as conducive to the achievement of all spiritual powers.

Holy bath in them, offering of charitable gifts there, listening and reading the text describing it suppresses all sins. They yield worldly pleasures and salvation.

CHAPTER SEVENTYSEVEN

Apsaroyugasaṅgama Tīrtha and other Holy Centres

Brahmā said :

1-4. The next holy centre to be recounted is Apsaroyuga or Apsarā saṅgama. This holy centre is on the southern bank. By remembering it one becomes highly glorious and fortunate.

By holy dip etc. performed there a man shall undoubtedly become liberated. If a chaste lady takes her menstrual bath there at the confluence, O Nārada, she shall give birth to a son. Even a barren woman shall give birth to a son if she stays there for three months along with her husband and performs holy dip. My words cannot become otherwise.

Listen attentively, O Nārada. I shall tell the reason why this holy centre is called Apsaroyuga.

5-7. O brahmin, there was a great rivalry between Viśvāmitra and Vasiṣṭha. Thereafter, the son of Gādhi (Viśvāmitra) began to perform penance and holy rites with great self-control seated at Gaṅgādvāra. Then Indra induced Menakā, "At my behest, O gentle lady, go and make him a dafaulter in his penance." On being told so by Indra, Menā forced Viśvāmitra to commit a breach of his penance, gave birth to a daughter unto him and went back to Indra's city.

8-11. When she had gone back the son of Gādhi recalled (regretfully) everything that had been committed by him. He abandoned that place and went to southern Gaṅgā, the holy centre which Devas loved and where Śiva is (called) Lord Kālañjara. Then the thousand-eyed lord Indra asked Urvaśī, Menā, Rambhā and Tilottamā to spoil his penance. Being extremely frightened they said "No". Thereupon the consort of Śacī asked Gambhīrā and Atigambhīrā who were excessively proud (of their ability in this regard). Both of them said to the thousand-eyed Indra.

Gambhīrā and Atigambhīrā said :

12-13. We shall go and by means of our dances, songs, beauty of form and youthful charms cause the downfall of the highly lustrous son of Gādhi who is performing a penance, who is not defeated by those women in whose side-long glance, laughter, speech and rich asset of graceful charms, Cupid lives for ever.

Brahmā said :

14-16. When the thousand-eyed lord said "So be it" they came to the great river and saw the great sage Viśvāmitra performing the penance. They were unable even to look at him for a thousand and one years because he was unassailable even to the god of death and seemed like Dhūrjaṭi (Śiva) stationed on the Earth. They remained far off and engaged themselves in dances, songs and coaxing speeches. On seeing them the great among the sages became extremely annoyed.

17-20. Who does not become angry on seeing an adverse act ? Although the mighty-armed (Viśvāmitra) was free from desires he appeared to say laughingly to Indra, "The thousand-eyed lord has been abandoned by these two celestial damsels". Then the son of Gādhi cursed them : "You will attain the form of liquid. That is because you had attempted to liquefy me immediately." He was then propitiated by them. Therefore, he granted them deliverance from the curse : "If you two are joined to Gaṅgā you will regain your divine forms."

As a result of the curse, they assumed the forms of rivers at that very time.

21-23. The two rivers were called 'Pairs of celestial damsels'. Their mutual confluence as well as the confluence with Gaṅgā is well known in all the worlds. Lord Śiva who yields worldly pleasures and salvation stays there. As soon as he is seen he bestows all spiritual achievements.

By taking holy plunge there and by visiting the lord, one is released from all bondage.

CHAPTER SEVENTYEIGHT

Koṭitīrtha and other Holy Centres

1. The holy centre well known as Koṭitīrtha is on the southern bank of Gaṅgā. Merely by remembering it one is rid of all sins.

2. Everything will have a crore of (merits) where the lord is Koṭīśvara. There are in all two crores of holy centres that bestow auspiciousness.

3. I shall describe its magnificence. Listen, O Nārada, with concentration. The eldest son of Kaṇva is well known as Bāhlīka.

4-7. He is honoured and praised by the people with (the name of) Kāṇva. He was a master of Vedas and Vedāṅgas. Residing on the banks of Gautamī and worshipped by all the worlds he, a master of the Vedic texts, used to perform such sacrifices as Pārvāyaṇānī, in the company of his wife. Always in the morning (everyday) he used to perform Homas in the holy fire, with great concentration and mental purity. Once he made preparations for the (Homa). He poured one ladleful of ghee in the well kindled sacred fire. In order to offer another Āhuti he took up the Havis material in his hand. In the meantime the fire had become calm.

8. Thereupon, Kāṇva became worried as to what he should do then. Becoming extremely sad he thought within himself (over the matter).

9. "In the middle of two Āhutis, the sacred fire has become calm. The other fire that should be taken up—shall it be a Vedic one or a secular one ?

10. Where should the other Āhuti, the second one be offered ?"

While he was meditating over this a divine voice spoke:

11-12. "O great brahmin, no extra fire need be fetched by you in this matter. There may be little bits of (of sparks) here and there nearby. You can very well perform Homa in the half-burnt wooden twigs".

Kāṇva said "No" then. The same voice spoke again:

13-16. "Bold is the son of Agni. The father and son are the same. What is given to the son for his pleasure shall be for the pleasure of the father. One shall give the son what should be given to the father. It will have a crore times more merit and pleasure." The divine speech spoke so. Thereupon the great sages came to a decision about the be-all and end-all of Virtue and did as was said. On realizing that what is given to the son shall be for the father in this world (the following can be justified). With none else can there be such a satisfaction as a father derives when his children are benefited.

17-19. This is well known in this world. This is well honoured in all worlds. When it is given there shall be merit. O son, everything shall increase a crore times. There shall be the cessation of mental anguish; great happiness will result.

Again that voice spoke :

"In this excellent holy spot named after Kāṇva a great holy centre cropped up by the power of the merit of Kāṇva. It yields greater benefit than any other holy centre in the three worlds.

20. If one performs holy plunge, offering of charitable gifts etc., devoutly, even if they be very little, he shall obtain all benefits increased by a crore times, O sage. He must perform these rites with concentration and mental purity."

21. Whatever is performed here by men such as holy plunge, offering of charitable gifts etc., everything should be known as (yielding) crore times the (usual benefit). Therefore they know this as the Koṭitīrtha holy centre.

22. Where this happened—the holy centre is called Āgneya, Kāṇva, Pautra, Hiraṇyaka and Vāṇīsaṁjña. It is Koṭitīrtha because it yields benefits increased by a crore times.

23-27. The greatness of Koṭitīrtha cannot be recounted even by Vācaspati and other Devas. Whatever rite is performed here, howsoever be it performed, everything shall have a crore times more benefit due to the grace of Godāvarī. If anyone gives a single cow to an excellent brahmin in the holy centre Koṭitīrtha he shall reap the benefit of gifting a crore cows, by the greatness of that holy centre. Being pure, one shall offer land gifts with a faithful mind. That shall have a benefit increased a crore times. Everywhere on the banks of Gautamī the offerings to the Pitṛs are excellent. Especially in the Koṭitīrtha it has endless benefit. Sages know that there are fortynine holy centres here.

CHAPTER SEVENTYNINE

Narasiṁhatīrtha and other Holy Centres

Brahmā said :

1. The holy centre well known as Narsiṁha is on the northern bank of Gaṅgā. I shall recount its magnificence that is capable of according all-round protection.

2. There was (a demon) formerly who was the most excellent of all strong men. His name was Hiraṇyakaśipu[1]. In the power of penance and in exploit he was indefatigable to the gods.

3-6. His mind was disturbed due to his hatred for his own son who was a devotee of Hari.

The lord manifested himself from the Pillar in the hall, thereby demonstrating his immanence in the universe. After killing Hiraṇyakaśipu, the Man-Lion routed his army. In the battle the Man-Lion killed all great Daityas gradually. After conquering the enemies stationed in the nether world, he went to the heavenly world. After conquering it he went to the Earth and killed Daityas staying on the mountains. The lord in the form of an animal killed Daityas with various forms staying in rivers, villages and forests.

7-9. He killed Daityas staying in the firmament and air as well as those who had gone to the world of Luminaries. (The Man-lion) had claws more powerful than thunderbolt. His great mane grew up. His roar was capable of causing abortion to Daitya women. He had conquered all Rākṣasas. He smashed Asuras by means of blows with his paws along with loud roars and fierce glances resembling fire at the final dissolu-

1. A great demon who propitiated Brahmā by his penance and secured rulership of all the three worlds and other boons. He became too arrogant and a hater of Viṣṇu. He tortured his own son Prahlāda for his devotion to Viṣṇu and was finally killed by Viṣṇu in his Man-Lion incarnation.

tion. He scattered their intestines. After killing many Daityas Hari went to Gautamī.

10-12. (He went to Gautamī Gaṅgā) born of his own lotus-like feet and pleasing to the mind and eyes.

There was a demon there well known as Āmbarya. He was the enemy of king of Daṇḍaka. He was a warrior invincible to Devas. He had a vast army. A terrible fight ensued between Hari and the son of the Daitya. It was extremely terrific, causing hairs to stand on end. Weapons and miraculous missiles were showered on each other. The glorious lord Hari killed that enemy on the northern bank.

13. The holy centre Nārasiṁha on Gaṅgā is well known in the three worlds. Taking holy bath and offering charitable gifts there is the destroyer of all evil planets.

14-15. It accords all-round protection. It prevents old age and death. Just as no one is on a par with Hari among all Devas, so also that holy centre is the most excellent among all holy centres. A man shall take his holy bath in that holy centre and perform the worship of Man-Lion.

16-19. To him nothing is difficult of access, whether in heaven or in the mortal world or in the nether worlds. O sage Nārada, there are eight such great holy centres there. Learned men say that they are severally the bestowers of the benefit of crores of holy centres. Even when its name is remembered irreverently there is the destruction of all sins. By whom can the benefit be described—the benefit of resorting to that holy centre where the lord Man-Lion is always present ? Just as there is no lord superior to the Man-Lion anywhere, so also there is no holy centre on a par with Nārasiṁhatīrtha anywhere.

CHAPTER EIGHTY

Paiśācatīrtha and other Holy Centres

Brahmā said :

1. The holy centre Paiśāca is said to be on the northern bank of Gaṅgā. O highly intelligent one, formerly a brahmin got rid of the state of Piśāca (vampire) there.

2-5. There was a brahmin well known in the world as Ajīgarti. He was the son of Suyava. He was extremely distressed due to the burden of sustaining the family. He was overwhelmed by famine and privation. For a great deal of money he sold his middle son Śunaḥśepa who was the most excellent among the knowers of Brahman. He sold him to a Kṣatriya for being sacrificed in a Yajña. What sin does not a person in distress commit even though he may be a learned man? The sage took much by way of monetary remuneration for performing the duty of slaughtering him also. The base brahmin accepted money for cutting him. Thereupon he was afflicted by an irremediable disease.

6. After due efflux of time he died and was thrown into hell. There is no means of dispelling previous sins except endurance and suffering.

7. At the behest of Yama he was transferred to various wombs by the servants of Yama. He took various births. Then he became a terrible vampire of terrifying shape.

8. He was dragged along and cast into lonely forests, dry woods and waterless expanses enveloped by summer forest fires during the summer season by the servants of Yama.

9. Those who sell their daughters, sons, plots of lands, horses and cows do not return from hell till all living beings are annihilated.

10. As a result of the fruition of sins committed by himself the terrible servants of Yama began to cook and roast his physical body. Thereupon, he cried aloud recollecting what had been committed by himself.

11-14. Once while he was going along the path the middle son of Jīgarti heard the voice of the ghost lamenting again and again. He heard the voice of his father who had sold him to be offered in the sacrifice. Then Śunaḥśepa said : "You are extremely distressed ! Who are you ?" Jīgarti said sadly : "I am the father of Śunaḥśepa. After committing a sinful deed I have attained a terrible state of life. I have been cooked and roasted in hells. Again I have reached a stage of suspense. This is the goal of all those who commit evil deeds."

15. Jīgarti's son told him sadly : "O father, I am your

son. Due to my fault you sold me and hence you have attained hells. Now I shall make you go to heaven."

16. After vowing thus, the excellent sage attained the state of (the adopted) son of Viśvāmitra and meditated on Gaṅgā. Desiring excellent worlds for his father he went out.

17. In the three worlds there is no other support except Gaṅgā flowing from the feet of Viṣṇu, for those persons who sink within the great ocean of delusion, for the embodied beings fumigated by the fire of all miseries.

18-19. After deciding thus, the noble-souled sage, desirous of redeeming his father from misfortune, went immediately to Gautamī and took his holy bath there. With purity (in mind and body) he remembered Śambhu and Viṣṇu and offered libation to his dead father who was highly distressed and who had assumed the form of a ghost. Merely by that offering Ajīgarti became sanctified and he obtained a highly meritorious body.

20-23. By virtue of the power of his son and the power of Gaṅgā, Śambhu, Hari and Vidhātṛ, he became one possessing the refulgence of ten thousand suns. Seated in an aerial chariot he attained Viṣṇu's foot resorted to by the groups of Devas.

Thenceforth, this holy centre became very famous as destroyer of ghostly vampires. It is extremely curative. Merely by remembering it great sins vanish.

The greatness of the holy centre has been described to you. There are three hundred such holy centres, yielding worldly pleasures and salvation.

These three hundred holy centres have been mentioned as the bestowers of all (spiritual) achievements. They have been frequented by the sages. Even by being remembered they bestow cherished desires.

CHAPTER EIGHTYONE

Nimnabheda and other Holy Centres

Brahmā said :

1. The holy centre well known as Nimnabheda is the destroyer of all sins. It is on the northern bank of Gaṅgā. It is well reputed in the three worlds.

2. Merely by remembering it, sins are dispelled. By visiting the Vedadvīpa there, one shall become conversant with the Vedas.

3. King Purūravas who was highly virtuous loved Urvaśī. Who is not fascinated and enchanted on seeing a beautiful woman ?

4-6. She came to the place where the king was present. While she was with him she would take in only a small quantity of ghee. The king accepted this and agreed to her time limit of remaining with him only as long as she espied him naked. With this condition he accepted that maiden who was charming to young men and who appeared fresh always. Once when she was lying asleep on the bed, Purūravas got up. On seeing him without a cloth she left the place at the very same time. Where is stability in women whose minds are as fickle as lightning ?.

7-10. That great king was surprised at something during the night. He looked out. At that time he had no apparel on. In the meantime the king went for a battle with his enemies. After conquering them he again went to the well-honoured world of Devas. The great king then returned. From his priest Vasiṣṭha he heard of the departure of Urvaśī. Thereupon, he became extremely distressed. He did not perform Homa. He did not take food. He did not see or hear anything.

In the meantime, with statements full of reasonable arguments the priest enlightened the excellent king who was in the state of death.

Vasiṣṭha said :

11-12. O great king, she is dead now. Do not grieve over this, O extremely intelligent one. Let not the inauspicious arrows of Cupid touch you who are in this condition. You do not know the hearts of womenfolk, O highly intelligent one. They are like those of wolves. Hence O king, do not grieve.

13-16. Who is there in the world, O great king, who has not been deceived by lovely damsels ? The following are the nutural characteristics of women : fraudulence, ruthlessness, fickleness and bad habits. How can they be the cause of happiness to man ?

Who has not been struck dead by Kāla (god of Death)? Which suppliant has been honourably treated ? Who has not been set awhirling by glory and splendour ? Who has not been betrayed by women ?

Women are comparable to (things seen in) dreams and illusions, O king. They are those whose minds are overwhelmed by haughtiness. How can they be conducive to happiness. Be steady after realizing this. Excepting Śaṅkara, Viṣṇu or Gautamī, O extremely intelligent one, there is no other refuge in the three worlds for miserable persons.

Brahmā said :

17-18. On hearing this the king strenuously annihilated his sorrow. He stood in the middle of Gautamī. The extremely virtuous Aila propitiated Śiva, Viṣṇu, Brahmā, Bhāskara (Sun-god), Gaṅgā and Devas strenuously.

19-24. What a plight does a creature find itself in, the creature that is subject to the control of Kāla (god of Death) and that is in adversity but does not resort to either holy centres or deities !

Therefore, the king considered Īśvara as his sole refuge. He was eager to serve Gautamī. He had great faith. He was averse to worldly pleasures. With the help of Ṛtviks he performed many Yajñas with plenty of monetary gifts. Therefore, that island came to be called Vedadvīpa and Yajñadvīpa. On all full-moon nights Urvaśī comes there always. If a man circumambulates that island it is as though the ocean-girt Earth had been circumambulated by him. If a meritorious person remembers the Vedas or performs Yajñas in that holy centre he shall obtain the fruit of great Vedic sacrifices.

That holy centre should be known as Ailatīrtha, Purūrava Tīrtha, Vāsiṣṭha and Nimnabheda.

25-29. When Aila ruled as a king there could be no sub-standard thing in any holy rite. What was base with respect to Urvaśī, viz. too much of passionate feelings for her—that also had been cleared away by Vasiṣṭha and Gaṅgā.

Therefore, it is called Nimnabheda. It yields the fulfilment of all desires for things seen and unseen. They say that there are seven hundred meritorious holy centres there. Taking holy bath and offering charitable gifts there yields the benefit of all sacrifices.

If anyone takes holy bath in Nimnabheda and visits these Devas he will never have anything low or base here or hereafter. Attaining height above all he rejoices in heaven like Indra.

CHAPTER EIGHTYTWO

Nanditaṭa and other Holy Centres

Brahmā said :

1. Those who are conversant with the Vedas know the holy centre well known as Nandītaṭa. I shall recount its efficacy, O Nārada, listen attentively.

2-3. The extremely energatic son of Atri is well known as the Moon god. He learnt Vedas and the Science of archery from Bṛhaspati. He learned all other arts and sciences too, O extremely intelligent one. Moon then said to Bṛhaspati, "I shall perform the worship of the preceptor". Then the delighted Bṛhaspati said to his disciple Moon.

Bṛhaspati said :

4-10. My wife Tārā who has a lustre similar to that of Rati knows it.

Brahmā said :

Then Moon went into the inner apartment to ask her. On seeing Tārā with a stellar face he caught her by the hand and forcibly dragged her to his own abode out of covetousness.

As long as one is not bound by the snares of lovely woman, one remains full of courage, a perfectly wise man, a man of intelligent behaviour and one who has subdued all sense-organs.

Whose mind does not fall a victim to the arrows of Kāma on seeing a lovely woman of wide eyes especially in a secret lonely place?

That is why a lady of noble birth should never see a man other than her husband in a secret place. She should be afraid of violation to her chastity.

The noble-minded Bṛhaspati came to know of it through the servants and stood up suddenly and hastened to the place. On seeing that indecent behaviour he angrily cursed Moon after rebuking him with unpleasant words.

11. Who will be able to endure it if he sees his beloved wife molested by another ? Therefore, Jīva fought with Moon angrily with the assistance of Devas.

12. The Moon god was not injured or harmed by the curses or weapons inspired with Mantras by Devas. Moon was not afflicted by the invocations of Bṛhaspati.

13. Without fear from anywhere Moon abducted Tārā to his abode, placed here there and enjoyed her as well as Rohiṇī for many years.

14-15. He could not be defeated by Devas either by angry outbursts or by curses or by Mantras. When Bṛhaspati could not get back his wife through the good offices of kings or sages, either by peaceful means or by threats and punishments, when he failed to redeem his wife in spite of his efforts, when all expedients had been exhausted, Bṛhaspati remembered his own Nīti (Policy).

16-18. "An intelligent man keeps insult in front and prestige behind. Thereby he pushes up his self-interest. Allowing the self-interest to drop off is foolishness. Results must be achieved by any means whatsoever by wise men. Deluded persons with false prestige fall a prey to misfortune". After deciding thus the intelligent Bṛhaspati went to Śukra and informed him. On seeing him arrive Śukra received him with honour.

19. After he had sat down and taken rest he was duly worshipped. Then the preceptor of Daityas asked him the reason for his arrival.

20. Those who are adverse to persons visiting their houses are not good men. Bṛhaspati related to Śukra the case of abduction of his wife from the beginning.

21. On hearing the words of Bṛhaspati Śukra became angry. O Nārada, he admitted that the disciple Moon was guilty. On hearing about his misbehaviour Śukra said angrily :

Śukra said :

22-23. O lord of planets, listen. Dear brother, only when I bring back your beloved wife molested by another person will I take food and drink. Only then will I sleep (or even) speak. O mighty-armed one, after worshipping Śiva and cursing the Moon who had betrayed his preceptor I shall fetch her and take my food.

Brahmā said :

24. After saying this, the preceptor of Daityas went out in the company of Bṛhspati. With great effort he propitiated Śiva and acquired superior power.

25. From Śaṅkara who was worshipped with great devotion he obtained different boons. What is difficult of access to embodied beings if the lord is favourable?

26-27. Śukra accompanied by Bṛhaspati went to the place where the Moon-god was sporting with Tārā.

With great anger Śukra cursed Moon thus : "Listen to my words, O Candra. Since a sinful act has been committed by you due to your arrogance you shall become afflicted by leprosy."

28. At once Moon became scorched by the curse of Śukra. Which of those persons who betray preceptor, master or friend have not attained destruction?

29-30. Moon gave up Tārā and Śukra took her away. He invited Devas, sages, Pitṛs, rivers of diverse kinds, medicinal herbs and chaste ladies. He then began to ask them the means of expiation in the context of Tārā episode.

31. Then Vedas said to Devas, "Let her take a holy bath in Gautamī with great devotion along with Bṛhaspati. Then Tārā will become pure.

32. This is a great secret. It should not be disclosed to

anyone and everyone. In all (adverse) situations Gautamī is the sole refuge of men.

33. Tārā performed duly the holy rite of bath along with her husband. There was a shower of flowers. Cries of "victory" rose up.

34. "Again Devas gave. Again men gave. Kings performing truthful activities gave the wife of brahmin."

35-36. After giving again the wife of the brahmin who had been rendered free from sins and impurities by Devas everything was conducive to welfare. Hence that holy centre became the destroyer of sins, O great sage. It yields all cherished desires. There was joy and welfare among Devas who were the enemies of Asuras.

37. The delight was all the more in regard to Bṛhaspati, Śukra and Tārā. Bṛhaspati who had attained the supreme pleasure spoke to Gaṅgā.

Bṛhaspati said:

38-39. O Gautamī, you are worthy of being worshipped by all. You bestow salvation on all. Especially when I am in zodiac Leo you will become the sanctifier of the three worlds. O most excellent river, you will be accompanied by all holy waters. O mother, when I am zodiac Leo the holy rivers, lakes, ponds, etc. in heaven, the mortal world and the nether worlds will go to you for taking their holy dip.

Brahmā said :

40-42. The holy centre named Ānanda is conducive to wealth, fame and longevity. It increases health and prosperity. It produces good fortune and great wealth. Gautama says that there are five thousand holy centres there. By remembering and reciting (this Purāṇa) one will attain what one wishes for. Nandin of Śiva who is installed here, performs pious rites directly on the banks of Gaṅgā always. Hence it is remembered as Nandītaṭa. This holy centre is Ānanda because it increases the joy of everyone.

CHAPTER EIGHTYTHREE

Bhāvatirtha and other Holy Centres

Brahmā said :

1. The holy centre where Bhava himself is present is called Bhāvatīrtha. He is the immanent soul of the entire Universe. He is the soul of all living beings. He is of the form of existence and knowledge.

2-3. In this context, I shall recount a splendid and holy story. Listen. There was a glorious king, the upholder of the burden of Kṣatriyas (i.e. chief among them), the cause of the perpetuation of the Solar dynasty. He was called Prācīnabarhiṣ. He was the master of all holy rites. He ruled over his kingdom for three and a half crores of years.

4-7 He had taken this vow—"When I cease to be young, when I get separted from my beloved wife, dear sons and other loveable objects, I will abandon my kingdom." This alone is proper on the part of discriminating persons of noble birth. Those who become disinterested (in worldly affairs) when riches dwindle down remain somewhere in a lonely place. When he was ruling over his kingdom there was no separation from beloved persons anywhere. There was neither mental anguish nor physical ailment, neither famine, nor mutual quarrel among relatives. While he was ruling over his kingdom noone was separated (from his near and dear ones).

8. Then, for the sake of a son the highly intelligent king performed a sacrifice. Thereupon the delighted lord granted him boons as he desired.

9. To the king who was staying on the banks of Gautamī lord Maheśvara granted boons as he desired. The king accompanied by his wife said to Bhava, "Give me a son."

10-11 Bhava said to the king lovingly, "See my third eye". When the king looked at the eye of Bhava, O (Nārada), the bestower of honour, a son was born due to the dazzling splendour of the eye. He is well known by the name Mahimā (Mahiman). It was by him that the well known sacred prayer Mahimnaḥ (i. e. Śivamahimnaḥ Stotram) was composed.

12. What is it that cannot be obtained when the destroyer

of the three cities (i. e. Śiva) is delighted. Hari, Brahmā and other Devas follow him always.

13-14. The king who had obtained a son requested for an excellent holy centre which by its power could grant fulfilment of cherished desires to men who are distressed on account of different kinds of adversities and who are overwhelmed by great sins, great ailments and vicious indulgence. Bhava (accordingly) imparted superiority to the centre which is called Bhāvatīrtha.

15-16. By taking holy plunge and offering charitable gifts there one shall obtain all desirable things. It is due to the grace of Bhava that a son (named) Mahiman was born to Prācīnabarhiṣ on the banks of Gautamī. It is called Bhāvatīrtha. There are seventy holy centres there. They are sacred. They bestow everything.

CHAPTER EIGHTYFOUR

Sahasrakuṇḍa and other Holy Centres

Brahmā said:

1. Those who are conversant with the Vedas know the holy centre well known as Sahasrakuṇḍa. Merely by remembering it a man becomes happy.

2-4. Formerly, Rāma son of Daśaratha caused a bridge to be built over the great sea. Thereafter he burnt Laṅkā and killed Rāvaṇa and other enemies with arrows. After obtaining Vaidehī (Sītā) Rāma spoke these words even as the guardians of the quarters were watching and while his preceptor was standing in front. In the presence of Lakṣmaṇa Rāma spoke these words to Sītā who had been purified in the fire : "Come on Vaidehī, you have become pure. You deserve to sit on my lap."

5-9. "No" said the glorious Aṅgada and Hanumān. "O Vaidehī we shall go to Ayodhyā along with our friends. There you must become purified even as the brothers, mothers and the general public stand watching. Then, O princess, after being purified, it behoves you to sit on the lap (of Rāma) on an auspicious day at Ayodhyā." Who can have any suspicion about the character of this lady? Still, adverse public comment and rumour should be warded off amongst one's own kinsmen. Disregarding the suggestion of these two, Lakṣmaṇa, Vibhīṣaṇa, Rāma and Jāmbavān called that daughter of the king. She was told "Svasti" (Hail) by Devas and she sat on the lap of the king.

10-12. They were delighted and hurriedly started in the shining aerial chariot Puṣpaka. They reached the city of Ayodhyā, the capital of Ikṣvāku kingdom. They were joyful and they always obeyed Rāma. After a few days he heard unbecoming slander from ignoble persons. As a result thereof he abandoned his pregnant wife Sītā who was not born of any womb. Persons of noble birth do not brook even false accusation and slander.

13. Shedding tears himself, Lakṣmaṇa abandoned the weeping Sītā who was undefiled, near the hermitage of Vālmīki, a great sage.

14-22. It was out of fear that he did so, because the command of elders should not be transgressed.

Thereafter, after few days Rāma, the son of a great king (Daśaratha), got himself initiated along with Lakṣmaṇa for a horse-sacrifice.

Both the glorious sons of Rāma, Lava and Kuśa came there. They were good musicians like Nārada. Like Gandharvas they possessed melodious voice. They came to the sacrificial chamber singing the whole of Rāmāyaṇa, the complete story of Rāma. Then they were presumed to be royel princes by obvious signs and recognized as the heroic sons of Vaidehī, i.e. Rāma's own sons.

Bringing them (into the palace) he crowned his sons one after the other. He placed them on his lap and embraced them again and again.

To all the embodied beings who are distressed due to worldly sorrows and who have no other go, the embrace of their sons alone can be the cause of peace and rest.

He embraced his sons again and again. He kissed and caressed them frequently. Meditating upon something he began to heave sighs and gasp for breath frequently.

In the meantime, Rākṣasas, the residents of Laṅkā, came there.

Sugrīva, Hanumān, Aṅgada, Jāmbavān and other monkeys came there. All of them came there with Vibhīṣaṇa as their leader.

23-26. They approached the king who was seated on the throne. Not being able to see Sītā, Hanumān and Aṅgada who had golden bracelets asked, "Where has mother (Sītā), not born of any womb, gone? Rāma is seen here alone."

The gatekeepers said, "She has been abandoned by Rāma."

They said: "Even as the guardians of the quarters were watching, when Rāma was speaking eloquently Sītā had been sanctified in fire, but the king is unchecked. Rāma has abandoned that beloved wife because of some public utterances. Let us die". After saying thus they went to Gautamī.

27. Rāma followed them closely behind along with the residents of Ayodhyā. After coming to Gautamī they performed penance there.

28. Remembering Sītā, the mother of the worlds, they heaved sighs of distress. They were devoid of any attachment to the worldly pleasures. They were eager to serve Gautamī.

29-30. Rāma himself, who was the lord of three worlds came there accompanied by his younger brother. After taking holy bath in Gautamī he became eagerly engaged in propitiating Śiva. He got rid of all distress. He was surrounded by a thousand persons there.

The place where this event happened is called Sahasrakuṇḍa.

31-34. There are ten other holy centres there which bestow all wealth and objects. Taking a holy dip and offering charitable gifts there, bestows the benefit thousand times increased. On the banks of holy Gautamī, with the help of Vasiṣṭha and other leading sages he performed Homa that redeems one from all adversities and destroys sins. He performed the same in a thousand sacrificial pits by means of uninterrupted flow of gold. He obtained all cherished desires by the grace of Gautamī, the mother of rivers. Performing great penances the slayer of Rākṣasas became famous. That place became the holy centre named Sahasrakuṇḍa. It yields great benefits.

CHAPTER EIGHTYFIVE

Kapilātirtha and other Holy Centres

Brahmā said:

1. The holy cenrte Kapilātīrtha is mentioned by various names. It is remembered as Āṅgirasa; it is called Āditya and Saiṁhikeya.

2-3. On the southern bank of Gautamī, O excellent sage, the Āṅgirasas performed sacrifice on behalf of Ādityas. Ādityas gave Earth as Dakṣiṇā (monetary gift) to Āṅgirasas. The Āṅgirasas went to perform penance. The Earth became Saiṁhikī (Lioness in form) and devoured the people.

4-5. All the people were afraid. They intimated it to Āṇgirasas. Due to their wisdom they understood that the lioness was the Earth.

Approaching Ādityas, Aṅgirasas spoke to them : "Please take back this Earth given by you." Then the Ādityas said "No".

6-10. Wise men never take back what has already been offered as Dakṣiṇā. If anyone takes back the Earth gifted away by him or by others, he is born as a worm in the faeces and remains like that for sixty thousand years.

There is no greater sin than taking back the Earth offered by oneself to others. It is an extremely terrible sin. "We will not take her back. If what is given by oneself is not taken back, what should be done? We shall take back the Earth offered as Dakṣiṇā, as a thing bought."

When they agreed saying "So be it", Devas gave a Kapilā (tawny-coloured cow) of auspicious traits instead in exchange of the Earth on the southern bank of Gaṅgā.

At that place Viṣṇu stands himself in personal form. He is the bestower of worldly pleasures and salvation.

11-14. The Kapilā Saṅgama (Confluence of Kapilā) is the destroyer of all sins. From the holy waters of the charitable gift a river Kapilā flowed.

The charitable offering of a cow is better than that of the Earth even if it is an agricultural land full of plants. The sage saved the world after making this exchange. The holy centre where this took place is cited as Gotīrtha. It has been mentioned by the wise that there are a hundred holy centres there that bestow sanctity and merit. By taking bath and offering charitable gifts there one shall obtain the benefit of gifting a plot of land. The place where Kapilā joined Gaṅgā is known as Kapilāsaṅgama.

CHAPTER EIGHTYSIX

Śaṅkhahrada and other Holy Centres

Brahmā said:

1. The holy centre where Śaṅkhagadādhara (the lord who holds conch and iron club) is the deity, is called Śaṅkhahrada. By taking a holy bath and by visiting the deity one is released from worldly bondage.

2-3. I shall describe the event that happened there. It yields worldly pleasures and salvation.

Formerly in the beginning of Kṛtayuga Brahmā was singing the Sāman songs. Rākṣasas who were born of the abode of Cosmic Egg and could assume many forms came to him in order to devour Brahmā. They were too proud of their strength and they held weapons too.

4. Then I spoke to Viṣṇu, preceptor of the universe, (pleading) for protection. Viṣṇu prepared himself for killing Rākṣasas with his discus.

5-6. After chopping off the heads of Rākṣasas with his discus he blew the conch. After making the surface (of the Earth) free of troublesome creatures and the heaven free of enemies, Hari filled his conch with great delight. Thereupon the Rākṣasas completely perished.

7. The place where this happened by the power of the conch of Viṣṇu is called Śaṅkhatīrtha. It gives peace, security and happiness to men.

8-11. It is holy and it yields all cherished desires. By being remembered it bestows auspiciousness. It produces longevity and health. It increases the quality and quantity of wealth and progeny. By remembering or by (regular) reading (of the Purāṇa), one shall achieve all cherished desires.

O sage, there are ten thousand holy centres there. They dispel all sins. These holy centres numbering ten thousand are destroyers of sins. Even Maheśvara does not know how to describe adequately their efficacy. There is no substitute for this annihilator of sins.

CHAPTER EIGHTYSEVEN

Kiṣkindhā—A Holy Centre

Brahmā said:

1. The holy centre Kiṣkindhātīrtha is said to be the bestower of all cherished desires of men. It is the place where the deity Bhava dwells. It dispels all sins.

2-4 I shall describe its form and features. Listen attentively, O Nārada.

Formerly, Rāma, son of Daśaratha, with the help of the residents of Kiṣkindhā killed in battle Rāvaṇa who caused worlds to cry. After killing him along with his sons and his army, the king, the slayer of the enemies returned taking Sītā with him. He was accompanied by his brother Lakṣmaṇa, the powerful monkeys, the mighty Vibhīṣaṇa and Devas.

5-6. The auspicious rite of *Svastyayana* (wishing him happy and prosperous journey) was performed. The glorious king flew by the aerial chariot Puṣpaka that (formerly) belonged to the lord of wealth and that could go speedily wherever one desired to go. All of them went to Ayodhyā. On his way Rāma, the slayer of enemies, who was worthy of being sought refuge in by the people in need of refuge saw Gaṅgā.

7-8. He saw Gautamī, the sanctifier of the universe, the bestower of cherished desires, the ultimate goal for the removal of mental distress and pleasant to the eyes. On seeing it the glorious king entered the banks of Gautamī and addressed the monkeys beginning with Hanumān in a voice faltering due to excessive delight.

Rāma said :

9. O monkeys, it was due to the power of this (holy river) that my lordly father became free from all sins and thereafter went to heaven.

10. She is the mother of all creatures. She is the bestower of worldly pleasures. She shall even bestow salvation. She shall destroy even terrible sins. Which other river is equal to this?

11. All the sins have been permanently destroyed. By the power of this river even enemies have become friends. Vibhīṣaṇa has become my permanent ally. Sītā has been redeemed. Hanumān has become a kinsman.

12. It is through the worship of this river that Laṅkā has been destroyed and Rāvaṇa has been killed along with his group. Gautama worshipped the excellent lord Śiva having matted hair, worthy of being resorted to, and attained the river.

13. She is the producer of all desired objects. She is the destroyer of all inauspicious things. She is the only sanctifier of the Universe. Today the mother of rivers is seen directly.

14. By body, by speech and by mind I seek refuge in Gaṅgā who is worthy of being resorted to. With all feelings (of reverence) I salute the mother of good ones, who has taken up her dwelling in the matted hair of Śiva.

Brahmā said :

15. On hearing these words of the king, the monkeys plunged into it and swam there. They duly performed worship with various flowers and objects worthy of being offered as present.

16. After worshipping Śiva duly, the king eulogized him with words endowed with feelings. The monkeys rejoiced. They danced and sang.

17. Accompanied by his beloved wife, the great soul stayed there happily for that night. He was surrounded by persons full of love. He cast off all misery that was caused by enemies. What is it that is not obtained by resorting of Gautamī ?

18. With wonder and amazement he looked at his servants. Delighted, he eulogized Godāvarī. Honouring the entire group of servants he attained a very special pleasure. Again when it

dawned and the sun became free from impurities Vibhīṣaṇa spoke to Rāma, the son of Daśaratha.

Vibhīṣaṇa said:

19. We are not at all satiated by the holy centre till now. We shall live here for some time. We shall stay here for four more nights and thereafter we shall go to Ayodhyā in a body.

Brahmā said:

20. The monkeys agreed to his suggestion. They worshipped the lord of all, Īśvara, for the next four nights. Then they went to the holy centre, the favourite of his brother (i.e. Rāvaṇa).

21. That holy centre is famous throughout the world by the name Siddheśvara. It is through his grace that Rāvaṇa became very powerful. Thus they spent five days and worshipped Liṅgas installed by themselves.

22. The son of Vāyu, Hanumān, the follower of the king, began to serve there. On his way the great king said to Hanumān—"Ceremoniously cast off all Liṅgas.

23. These liṅgas are installed by me as well as by others who are excellent knowers of Mantras. They have been installed by Śaṅkara's servants also. Without the rite of (ceremonious dischage) no external (Liṅga) of Bhava should be joined to the Great Śaṅkara.

24-25. If anyone were to remain intact in spite of slighting him, the deity or Liṅga, he would be standing steadily on the edge or blade of a sword or other similar things.

Those who have no faith, those who are indifferent and those who do not perform their duty after the worship of Liṅga, are deservedly cooked and roasted in all sorts of miserable hells by the servants of Yama."

At the behest of Rāma, the son of Vāyu, Hanumān, went there but could not uproot it with his hands.

26. Then he wished to take it out with his tail. He encircled the Liṅga with his tail. But he abandoned his effort. He was unable to uproot it. It was surprising to the great monkeys as well as the king.

27. Who is that intelligent man strong enough to shake the Liṅga of Maheśa that has attained stability and grandeur ? On seeing it steadfast the excellent king of great magnificence suddenly went out.

28. He invited Brahmins. After circumambulating and performing worship with extremely pure heart Rāmacandra bowed down to Liṅgas along with all those brahmins.

29-31. Therefore, this holy centre was resorted to by the eminent residents of Kiṣkindhā. There is no doubt that the great sins are destroyed by taking a plunge (into the waters) here.

Saying "O Mother Gautamī, be pleased" he devoutly bowed down to her once again. He blurted out these words often. He was overwhelmed by surprise. He looked at and bowed down to Gautamī.

Thenceforth, Devas say that this Kiṣkindhā is extremely sacred. He who reads, remembers or listens to this narrative devoutly gets rid of his sins. What to speak of holy plunge and offering charitable gifts !

CHAPTER EIGHTYEIGHT

Vyāsatīrtha—a Holy Centre

Brahmā said:

1. The holy centre well known as Vyāsatīrtha is called Pracetasa also. There is no other holier centre than this. It bestows all spiritual achievements.

2. The ten mind-born sons[1] of mine are the creators of the worlds too. Due to their (inordinate) power they went ahead desirous of knowing the end of the Earth.

3. Again some were created. Again they went in search of others. Neither they nor those who had gone before, returned. Those who had gone ahead had gone for ever.

---

1. The *Mahābhārata* (1.65.10) mentions the following six as the mind-born sons of Brahmā: Marīci, Aṅgiras, Atri, Pulastya, Pulaha and Kratu, who became great sages. The remaining four are: Vasiṣṭha, Dakṣa, Bhṛgu and Nārada.

4. Then O sage, the highly intelligent divine Āṅgirasas were born. They were conversant with the principles of Vedas and the Vedāṅgas. They were experts in all scriptural texts.

5. They were permitted by Aṅgiras to perform penance. those ascetics bowed down to their preceptor. They decided to perform penance without asking their mother.

6. In venerability mother is superior to all preceptors and elders. Then, O Nārada, she cursed her own sons out of anger.

The Mother said :

7. Those sons who have slighted me and begun to perform penance will never really attain spiritual achievement in any respect.

Brahmā said :

8. In their quest for success in penance they went to different countries but they did not attain Siddhi. Obstacles followed them wherever they went.

9. In some places they were hindered by Rākṣasas, in some the obstacle was created by men, in some it was created by youthful maidens and in others it was due to defects of the physical body.

10. Wandering thus, they went to sage Agastya, who was born of a pot,[1] who was the most excellent among those who perform penance and who was the preceptor of worlds.

11. The Āṅgirasas born in the race of the Fire-god bowed down to calm the lord of southern quarter, i.e., sage Agastya. Humbly they began to ask him.

Āṅgirasas said:

12-15. O saintly lord, what is the fault due to which our penance does not fructify? Though we have employed different means, and we perform penance again and again (why does it not become fruitful ?)

1. The son of Mitra and Varuṇa whose semen fell out at the sight of Urvaśī and was collected in a water pot from which he was eventually born along with Vasiṣṭha.

What shall we do? What is the (proper) method of penance? Shall we become (successful)? O great brahmin, tell us the means. Certainly you are the seniormost by virtue of your penance.

You are the best speaker. You are the most excellent speaker. You are the wisest of all wise men. O brahmin, you are the calmest among all those who have self-control. You are ever merciful and you do what is pleasing to others.

You are never angry. You do not hate. Hence, tell us what is desired to be told. Those who are arrogant, those who are devoid of sympathy, those who have abandoned service to elders, those who speak untruth, and those who are cruel do not know reality.

Brahmā said :

16. Agastrya meditated for a moment and said to all of them slowly.

Agastya said:

17. All of you are of tranquil souls. You were made creators by Brahmā. Your penance was not adequate. Remember the cause of your arrogance (?)

18. Those who had been previously created by Brahmā and those who went away are increasingly happy. Those who went later in quest of them became Āṅgirasas.

19. They are you. You went in quest of them at the proper time and you went slowly. There is no doubt that you will become superior to Prajāpati (Brahmā).

20. All of you go from here to Gaṅgā, the sanctifier of the three worlds, in order to perform penance. Excepting Gaṅgā, the beloved of Śiva, there is no other refuge in this world.

21. There worship 'the bestower of knowledge' in the holy spot in the hermitage. He is extremely intelligent. He will dispel your doubts. Without a good preceptor no one will attain Siddhi at any place.

Brahmā said :

22-23. They said to that excellent sage : "Who is called 'the bestower of knowledge?' Is it Brahmā, Viṣṇu, Maheśa,

Sun-god, Moon-god, Fire-god or Varuṇa ? O excellent sage, who will be the bestower of knowledge ?"

Agastya said again, "Let it be heard who the bestower of knowledge is.

24-25. That which is water is fire, that which is fire is sun. He who is sun is Viṣṇu. He who is Viṣṇu is (Sun-god). He who is Brahmā is Rudra and he who is Rudra is everything. It is he who has the entire and perfect knowledge. He is glorified as the bestower of knowledge.

26. There are many preceptors, viz. (1) teacher; (2) One who induces us to do something; (3) one who explains; (4) priest; (5) the progenitor. Among them the bestower of knowledge is superior.

27. That alone is called knowledge, whereby difference is dispelled. One and secondless Śambhu is called by brahmins by the different names of Indra, Mitra (Sun-god) and Agni for helping those who are deluded."

Brahmā said :

28. On hearing these words of the sage five of them went to the northern Gaṅgā and five to the southern Gaṅgā. They sang songs of praise while going.

29. In accordance with the injunctions they performed the worship of Devas mentioned by Agastya. They were seated in their special seats and they began to ponder over Reality.

30-36. Devas became pleased with them, O sage. Their (state of being creators) had already been ordained by the creator of the universe in the beginning of the Yuga.

It is for dispelling evil, for preserving the Vedas, for helping the worlds and for the attainment of righteousness, enjoyment and wealth (that they are ordained as creators).

The creatorship of the worlds was liked (by them) in order to interpret correctly the meaning of the Purāṇas, Smṛtis, Vedas and Dharmaśāstras (Ethical and Legal Codes). "You will assume such a form" (they were told).

They will have the status of Prajāpati (the state of being the lords of subjects) slowly and in due order whenever evil spreads in the world and the Vedas are slighted. If there is any danger to the Vedas they are born as Vyāsas.

Whenever there is decrease of righteousness and danger to Veda, Vyāsas are born to revive them. It is the excellent banks of Gaṅgā, that become the place of their penance.

There all of us are present always viz., Śiva, Viṣṇu, myself Brahmā, Āditya (Sun-god), Agni (fire) and Āpaḥ (waters).

37-40. There is nothing holier than these. There is nothing superior to this anywhere. They are the Brahman alone which assumes different forms.

Śiva who is the soul of everything (who is identical with all) is all-pervasive. He assumes the forms of all living beings. Especially in this holy centre he is present due to the mercy towards all livings beings. He is surrounded by all Devas. He is the cause of blessing to them. They are to be known as Dharma-Vyāsas and Veda-Vyāsas. Their holy centre is called after their names in the three worlds. The Vyāsatīrtha holy centre has waters that wash off the mud of sins. It dispels the darkness of delusion and arrogance. It is excellent and it yields all Siddhis unto men.

CHAPTER EIGHTYNINE

Vañjarāsaṅgama and other Holy Centres

Brahmā said:

1. The holy centre named Vañjarāsaṅgama is well known throughout the three worlds. It is always frequented by sages, Siddhas and royal sages.

2. Formerly, the bird Garuḍa had become a slave to the serpents. Due to the slavery of his mother his mind was extremely distressed and he felt miserable. Once he found himself in a secluded spot and thought thus heaving sighs of grief.

Garuḍa said :

3-4. Only they are blessed in this world, only they are the meritorious persons, who are free from servility to others and miseries.

They are happy, they sing and sleep and laugh. They are blessed ones, lords of their own bodies. Fie, fie upon those who remain under the control of others!

Brahmā said:

5. After being worried by these thoughts the miserable Garuḍa approached his mother. Vainateya of unmeasured soul asked his mother.

Garuḍa said:

6. O mother, by whose fault have you obtained the state of a slave? Is it that of the father, that of mine or of anyone else? Tell me the reason even as I ask you.

Brahmā said:

7-10. She[1] spoke to her own beloved son, Aruṇa's younger brother.

Vinatā said:

It is not anyone else's fault. It is my own fault. It was said by me—"She whose word is proved false shall become the slave of the other."

Kadrū and I (argued). She went (there) along with me. My dispute was with Kadrū; I was defeated by her deceitfully.

Dear boy, fate is all-powerful. What acts does it not do? It was thus that I became the slave of Kadrū. When I became a slave you too became a slave, O son of a brahmin.

Brahmā said:

11. Then Garuḍa remained silent because he was extremely distressed. He did not say anything to his mother. He began to think of the inevitability of events.

12. Desiring the welfare of her own sons and her own prosperity Kadrū once said to Vinatā, the mother of birds:

Kadrū said:

13. Your son goes to bow down to the sun without being obstructed. Oh, even though you are a slave you are highly blessed in the three worlds.

---

1. Kadrū and Vinatā, two of several daughters of Dakṣa, all married to Kaśyapa, gave birth to serpents and Aruṇa and Garuḍa respectively. Aruṇa became the charioteer of Sur-god and Garuḍa became the vehicle of Lord Viṣṇu.

Brahmā said :

14-17. She was extremely surprised and concealing her sorrow, she said to Kadrū :

Vinatā said :

Why don't your sons go to see the Sun-god ?

Kadrū said :

O excessively fortunate lady, take my sons to the Nāgaland. That cool lake is near the sea.

Brahmā said :

Suparṇa (Garuḍa) carried serpents and Vinatā carried Kadrū. Thereupon she was delighted and spoke to the mother of Vainateya:

18. "Let Garuḍa take my sons to the abode of Devas." The mother of serpents then spoke to Garuḍa who was endowed with humility.

The mother of serpents said :

19. My sons wish to see Haṁsa (the Sun-god here), the preceptor of the the three worlds. After bowing down to the Sun they will come back to my abode. O Vinatā, take my sons to the solar zone everyday.

Brahmā said :

20-21. Trembling and distressed, Vinatā said thus to Kadrū.

Vinatā said :

O mother of serpents, I am not capable of it. My son will carry your sons (there). After seeing the Sun-god let them return.

Brahmā said :

22-24. Vinatā said to her son, the lord of birds : "The mother of serpents has emphatically told me that the serpents that have attained overlordship wish to see the Sun-god."

After saying "So be it" Garuḍa said, "Let the serpents mount me."

Thereupon the host of serpents rode on Garuḍa, the lord of birds, and slowly approached the spot where the Sun was. Being scorched by the fierce heat of the sun they became distressed.

The Serpents said :

25. Return, O highly intelligent one. Obeisance to the Sun. Enough of our desire to go to the abode of the Sun. We are burned by the splendour of the Sun, O Garuḍa : We shall go along with you or leave you alone.

Brahmā said :

26. On being requested thus by the serpents Garuḍa said : "I shall show Sun-god to you all." After saying thus he hastened through the sky towards the Sun.

27. Hundreds and thousands of those serpents fell down on the island Vīrana with their bodies burned. They were afflicted and their bodies were scorched.

28. On hearing the cry of anguish of her sons who fell down on the surface of Earth, the extremely excited Kadrū came there to console them.

Kadrū said to Vinatā :

29-32. Your son has committed a grave misdeed. He is extremely evil-minded. There is no means of calming it down. The lord of serpents does not come to alter the words of the master (?). If Kaśyapa of great brilliance had been here we would have been free from ailments. As it is, O beautiful lady, how can there be peace for my sons ?

On hearing those words of Kadrū, Vinatā became terrified. She said to her noble-souled son, Garuḍa, the lord of birds.

Vinatā said :

33-35. This is not befitting you, O son. This is not proper. It is said (by elders) that it is proper to behave humbly. Otherwise it is not proper. Treachery should never be committed by good men even with regard to enemies. The moon shines impartially over the learned brahmin as well as the basest born.

My son, only those base men who are incapable of doing anything directly and forcibly, cause harm to others by fraudulent means.

Brahmā said :

36-37. Then Vinatā asked the mother of serpents as to how the remedy should be effected.

Vinatā said :

How can peace return to your sons ? I shall do what should be done for the same. They are seized by old age. Tell me the means of calming it down. I shall do so.

Brahmā said :

38. Kadrū said to Vinatā—"There is water (Gaṅgā) in the nether worlds. If my sons are sprinkled with it they will have peace."

39. On hearing those words of Kadrū, Garuḍa brought water from the nether worlds in a moment and sprinkled it on the serpents. Then Garuḍa spoke to lord Indra who had performed a hundred sacrifices.

Garuḍa said :

40-42. Let clouds shower here. They are the helpers of three worlds.

Brahmā said :

Accordingly the clouds showered and the serpents became happy. The Gangetic water was brought by Garuḍa from nether worlds. It revived the serpents. It had been brought by Garuḍa for removing sorrow due to old age. Where the serpents had been showered with it, is the land of Nāgas.

43. The place from where the water was brought by Garuḍa is nether worlds. That water of Gaṅgā is the destroyer of all sins of the people.

44. Because it prevented old age, the serpents became happy. The water from the nether worlds revived the serpents because it was (the water) of Gaṅgā.

45. For destroying the grief of old age it became the river Vañjarā that had Amṛta directly flowing along with it on the southern bank of Gaṅgā.

46-49. It dispels old age, poverty and mental distress. It prevents physical pain.

If there is a confluence of Gaṅgā of the nether worlds with that of the mortal world, how can it be (adequately) described ? Merely by remembering it all sins disappear. Who is competent to recount the benefit accruing from the holy plunge and charitable gifts performed there? Learned men say that there are one hundred and twenty five thousand holy centres there. They bestow all riches, they dispel all sins. There is no holy centre anywhere else equal to Vañjarā Saṅgama. Merely by remembering it all adversities are destroyed.

CHAPTER NINETY

The Holy Centre Devāgamatīrtha

Brahmā said :

1. The holy centre Devāgama is auspicious and it fulfils all cherished desires. It yields worldly pleasures and liberation to all men. It causes gratification of the manes.

2. I shall describe in detail what happened there, to you, O Nārada. Once there was great rivalry between Devas and Asuras for the sake of wealth.

3-4. Heaven belonged to Devas and the Earth to Asuras. Having support of the Karmabhūmi (the Earth where one can perform holy rites and enjoy their fruits) the Asuras scattered themselves everywhere. Then the Asuras began to kill those who offered shares in Yajñas to Devas. Thereupon the groups of Devas were deprived of their shares in Yajñas.

5-6. They were distressed. They came to me and said, "What should be done?" Devas were advised by me thus : "Defeat Asuras with your might. You will reach Earth and receive holy rites and great renown."

Saying "So be it" Devas who had decided upon a war went to Earth.

7. Daityas, Dānavas, Rākṣasas proud of their strength joined together and marched. They also wanted to be victorious and sought war.

8. There were the great warriors on the side of Asuras—Ahi, Vṛtra, Bali, son of Tvaṣṭṛ (i.e. Triśiras), Namuci, Śambara, Maya and many other warriors proud of their strength.

9. (The leaders of Devas were) Agni, Indra, Varuṇa,

Tvaṣṭṛ, Pūṣan, Aśvins, Maruts and the guardians of quarters. All of them were experts in different martial strategies.

10. All those demons made great efforts in fighting in the southern quarter. They stationed themselves in the southern ocean.

11. Formerly the excellent mountain Trikūṭa belonged to Rākṣasas. All of them went to the southern ocean through the forests therein along with those (Dānavas etc.).

12. All of them assembled on the mountain Malaya. This Malaya region also belonged to the enemies of Devas.

13. The assembly of Devas took place on the banks of Gautamī because lord Śiva is present there.

14. Seated in their respective chariots Devas of pure thoughts came to the banks of Gautamī, the mother of rivers.

15. She was pleased with all. She was the bestower of cherished desires of the Pitṛs. After eulogizing lord Maheśvara Devas mutually discussed as to how to attain freedom from fear.

Devas said :

16. What shall be our means, should we be defeated by the enemies ? Only one of these two shall be conducive to our welfare, victory or death. Fie upon the life of those who are overcome by the enemies (especially if) they are intelligent and noble-minded !

Brahmā said :

17-19. In the meantime, O son, an unembodied voice spoke :

The Ethereal Voice said :

Enough of your stress and strain, O Devas. Hasten to Gautamī. There propitiate lords Hari and Hara devoutly. What is impossible to do if Godāvarī and those two lords were to favour you.

Brahmā said :

20-22. From Hari and Īśa who were pleased the heaven-dwellers obtained the desired victory. They went all round protecting the lands.

The place where Devas arrived and gathered together became well known as Devāgama. Sages, the knowers of truth, praise Devāgama.

There are eighty thousand Śivaliṅgas there, O Nārada.

The mountain Devāgama is also called Priya. Thenceforth that holy centre is known as Devapriya.

CHAPTER NINETYONE

The Description of Kuśatarpaṇa and other Holy Centres

Brahmā said:

1. The holy centre well known in the worlds as Kuśatarpaṇa and Praṇitasaṅgama yields worldly pleasures and liberation.

2. I shall mention its characteristic features. Listen. It is auspicious and it dispels sins. On the southern side of the Vindhya there is the great mountain Sahya.

3-6. It is from its feet that the rivers Godāvarī, Bhīmarathī and others arose. The place where the Ekavīrā arose is Virajā (free from sins). Its greatness cannot be described by anyone. Listen attentively (to what happened) in the holy spot on that mountain, O Nārada. I shall tell the secret of secrets. It is auspicious and directly mentioned by the Vedas. Even sages, Devas, Pitṛs and Asuras do not know. I shall recount for your pleasure. It gives all cherished things on being listened to.

That supreme Puruṣa should be known as Unmainfest and Imperishable.

7. The inferior one (Apara) is Kṣara (Perishable). Hence it is accompanied by Prakṛti. The Puruṣa with limbs was born from the Nirākāra (that which has no form or shape).

8-9. The waters were born of him and the Puruṣa was born of waters (?) From both of them a lotus was born and I was born there, O sage.

The elements Earth, Wind, Ether, Waters, and Fire are anterior to me. They were evolved simultaneously, O sage.

10. I saw only these and no other beings whether mobile

or immobile. Nor were the Vedas present then. I could not see anything.

11. I could not see even that (lotus) from which I was born. When I remained silent I heard this excellent speech.

The Ethereal Voice said :

12-14. O Brahmā, perform the rite of creation of the Universe, of the mobile and immobile beings.

Brahmā said :

Thereupon I spoke to that voice of the Divine Puruṣa there, O Nārada :

"How shall I create this Universe ? With what shall I create it ?"

The same divine voice said : "It is the mother (of the Universe) that is called Prakṛti and works under the guidance of Viṣṇu."

The Ethereal Voice said :

15-16. Perform Yajña. Undoubtedly you will have the power therefrom. O Brahmā, the eternal Śruti says, "Verily Yajña is Viṣṇu". What is it that cannot be achieved by performers of Yajña in this world and the next one ?

Brahmā said :

17. Again I spoke to that goddess, "O highly fortunate lady, where should Yajña be performed ? By what should it be performed ? Tell me."

Thereupon she said to me.

The Ethereal Voice said :

18-20. The goddess who was Oṁkāra, who was identical with the universe and who was like a mother (unto all, said) : "Here in the Karmabhūmi (the land of holy rites) perform the worship of the lord of Yajñas, the Puruṣa of Yajñas.

He alone shall be your means and instrument, O lord of holy rites. Worship him with that. Hari alone is all these viz., Yajña, Svāhā, Svadhā, Mantras, brahmins, Havis etc. Hence everything is derived from Viṣṇu.

Brahmā said :

21-22. Again I said to that goddess, "Where is the Land of

holy rites, laid out?" At that time, O Nārada, there was neither Bhāgīrathī nor Narmadā. There was no Yamunā, no Tāpī, neither Sarasvatī nor Gautamī. There was neither sea nor river, no lake, no pool free of dirt. That divine power said to me again and again.

The Divine Voice said :

23. To the southern side of Sumeru as well as of Himavān, to the south of Vindhya, to the south of the Sahya is Karmabhūmi (land of holy rites) with the auspicious rise for everyone at all times.

Brahmā said.:

24. On hearing those words I left the great mountain Meru. After coming to that place I thought "Where should I stay?" Thereupon the same Unembodied Voice, spoke to me.

The Ethereal Voice said :

25-26. Go this way. Stay this side. Sit here alone. Determine to perform Yajña. That Yajña will be concluded.

After Saṁkalpa has been performed for the sake of Yajña, O Brahmā, O most excellent Deva, perform those things which those Vedas say.

Brahmā said :

27. The Itihāsas, Purāṇas and other verbal texts came out of their own accord to my mouth and they came to my recollection.

28. At the very same moment, the meaning of Vedas was understood by me. Thereupon I remembered the Puruṣa Sūkta (Hymn of Creation) that is world-renowned.

29. I prepared the necessary constituents of the Yajña mentioned therein. I made vessels of Yajñas as mentioned in it.

30. Where I stayed after being purified and having controlled myself and where I got initiated was a land of brahmins. It is glorified after my name.

31-36. The holy place of my Yajña is remembered by the name Brahmagiri. O great sage, the holy place of my Yajña extended for twenty-four Yojanas to the east of Brahmagiri. There in the middle of the Altar I prepared three sacrificial fires viz. Gārhapatya[1], Dakṣiṇa[2] and Āhavanīya.[3]

A Yajña cannot be successfully completed without the wife—so says the Veda. (Hence) O sage, I split my body into two. The former half became my wife for the fulfilment of the Yajña. The latter half was I myself. "Half of oneself is one's wife", says the Śruti.

O Nārada, I fashioned the excellent season Vasanta (spring) in the form of ghee offering. Grīṣma (summer) was considered Idhma (sacred twigs). Śarat (autumn) was the Havis offering. I fashioned the season of rains as Barhis (Kuśa grass).

37. The Vedas were the seven Paridhis. Kalā (moments), Kāṣṭhā and Nimeṣa (units of time) are remembered as sacred twig, Vessel and Kuśa.

38-39. O divine sage, Time which is beginningless and endless assumed the form of Yūpa. The three Guṇas beginning with Sattva became the post for tying the sacrificial animal, but there was no sacrificial animal. Thereupon, I spoke to the unembodied speech of Viṣṇu:

40. "Without a sacrificial animal this Yajña cannot be concluded." Thereupon, that very same eternal unembodied voice spoke to me.

The Ethereal Voice said :

41-44. Eulogize that supreme Puruṣa by means of the hymn called Puruṣa Sūkta.

Brahmā said :

Saying "So, be it" I began to eulogize Janārdana, the lord of Devas and my progenitor, devoutly by means of the Puruṣa-sūkta. That goddess then said to me, "O Brahmā, make me your Paśu." Then I realised the unchanging Puruṣa as my progenitor. I placed him at the side of Kālayūpa and tied him

1. The family fire that the householder receives from his father and passes on to his descendents.

2. The fire placed at the sonthern corner of the altar.

3. Fire prepared from the family fire and placed at the eastern corner of the altar to receive oblations.

up with Guṇapāśas (the three Guṇas as the halter). The Puruṣa stood in front of me.

45. In the meantime this entire universe cropped up from him, the brahmins from his face and the Kṣatriyas from his arms.

46. Then Indra and Agni were born of his mouth, the wind was born of his vital air, the quarters were born of his ear and the heaven was born of his head.

47. The moon was born of his mind, the sun was born of his eye, the atmosphere was born of his navel and the Vaiśyas were born of his thighs.

48. The Śūdra was born of his feet. So also the Earth was born, sages were born of the pores of hairs and the medicinal herbs were born of his hair.

49. The domestic and wild animals were born all round from his nails, the worms and insects etc. were born of his anus and genitals.

50. Some of the mobile and immobile beings and some of the visible and invisible beings of the world were born of him. Devas were born of me. In the meantime, the Ethereal Voice spoke to me :

The Ethereal Voice said :

51-53. Everything has been concluded. The desired creation has taken place. Now consign all utensils to the fire. Ceremoniously cast off the Yūpa, Praṇītā vessel and Kuśa grasses. Cast off the form of the Ṛtviks and Yajña, that which is intended and that which is to be meditated upon. Sruva (sacrificial ladle), Puruṣa, halters—cast off all these, O Brahmā.

Brahmā said :

54-58. Simultaneous with these words I began to perform sacrifice in the three sacrificial fires viz. Gārhapatya, Dakṣiṇa and Āhavanīya after meditating upon the cause of the Universe, the Puruṣa sanctified by the Mantras.

Thereupon the pure lord of Yajña, the lord of the worlds identical with the Universe, the maker of the cosmos appeared near the sacrificial pits. Viṣṇu assumed white form in the Āhavanīya fire. Viṣṇu was dark in colour in the Dakṣiṇa fire and yellow in the Gārhapatya fire. Viṣṇu was present everywhere at all times. There was nothing without Viṣṇu, the cause of the Universe.

59. Repeating the Mantras I performed the rite of Praṇaya (taking forward) of the Praṇītā vessel. The water from the Praṇītā vessel became the splendid river Praṇītā.

60-61. I ceremoniously discharged Praṇītā after scrubbing it with Kuśa grass. When the scrubbing was performed, drops of water from Praṇītā fell in various places and all those places became holy centres of great merit. O chief among sages, the river became the bestower of benefits of sacrifices when holy bath was taken therein.

62. It is for ever bedecked and embellished by Śārṅga (bow)-bearing lord of Devas. It is the flight of steps for everyone to ascend to Vaikuṇṭha.

63. The spot on the holy ground where the scrubbed Kuśa grasses fell down is called Kuśatarpaṇa. It yields much of merit and benefit.

64-65. All these were propitiated by means of the Kuśa grass. Therefore the place is called Kuśatarpaṇam. Afterwards for another reason the Gautamī joined the Praṇītā, O highly intelligent one. That became the Praṇītāsaṅgama (the confluence of the Praṇītā). The holy centre at the spot where Kuśa grass was used for propitiation is Kuśatarpaṇam.

66. The sacrificial post fashioned by me there itself to the north of Vindhya was ceremoniously cast off. It became the resort of Viṣṇu. It is worthy of worship by the worlds.

67. The glorious one became free from decay. Hence the holy fig free became Akṣaya Vaṭa. In the form of Time it is eternal. On being remembered it yields the merit of sacrifices.

68. The place of my divine Yajña is called Daṇḍaka forest. When the Yajña was concluded Viṣṇu was propitiated by me.

69-70. After bowing down I ceremoniously cast off the lord of the chief of Devas who is called Virāṭ in the Vedas, from whom the various acts of piety were born, from whom I was born and whose creation is this universe.

The splendid holy spot where I performed the divine sacrifice extended to twenty-four Yojanas.

71. There are three sacrificial pits there even today, O Nārada. They are of the form of Yajñeśvara, the discus-bearing Viṣṇu.

72. Thenceforth that holy spot of my sacrifice is well-known. Even the worms and insects there attain liberation after death.

73. The Daṇḍaka forest is called the seed of virtue and the seed of salvation. Especially the place in contact with the Gautamī is extremely meritorious.

74. He who performs the holy bath and distributes charitable gifts etc., at the confluence of the Praṇītā or in the Kuśatarpaṇa shall go to the supreme region.

75. Know that by remembering, reading or listening to this narrative with devotion all cherished desires are fulfilled. It bestows worldly pleasures and salvation.

76. Learned men say that there are eightysix thousand holy centres on both the banks. The meritoriousness of the places has been already described.

77-78. O sage, the holy centre Kuśatarpaṇa is more excellent than even Vārāṇasī. There is no other holy centre equal to this in the world consisting of mobile and immobile beings.

Merely by being remembered it destroys the sin accruing from brahmin slaughter and other sins. This holy centre, O sage, is said to be the gate unto heaven on the surface of the Earth.

CHAPTER NINETYTWO

The Holy Centre Manyu

Brahmā said :

1. The holy centre well known as Manyutīrtha destroys all sins. It yields all cherished desires unto men. It destroys sins on being remembered.

2. I shall recount its efficacy, O sage. Listen attentively. Formerly, there was a war between Devas and Dānavas.

3-4. Therein Dānavas became victorious. Devas retreated from the battle with dejected minds. They approached me and said, "Grant us freedom from fear."

I replied to them, "All of you go to Gaṅgā.

5-6. There on the banks of Gautamī eulogize lord Maheśvara who is beautiful and who confers natural bliss without any stress or strain, natural bliss that comes freely. Then you will get the means, O Devas, of victory from Maheśvara."

Saying "So be it" Devas eulogized Maheśvara.

7-8. Some of them performed penances. Others danced. Some of them bathed (the Liṅga of the lord) and others worshipped.

Then the trident-bearing lord Maheśvara became delighted. Becoming pleased he spoke to Devas—"What is desired may be asked for."

9-12. Devas spoke to the lord, "For our victory, give unto us a man who is extremely praiseworthy and who will take up command of our army in the battle. May we be happy by resorting to the strength of his arms."

Lord Maheśvara said to Devas "So be it." A certain (deity) was created by the supreme lord by his own brilliance. He was an extremely terrible fellow named Manyu. He was (to be) the leader of the army of Devas. After obtaining him, Devas bowed to Śiva and returned to their abodes accompanied by Manyu. They then stood ready for battle once again.

13. Standing ready to fight with the extremely powerful Danujas and Daityas the well-prepared Devas stood in front of Manyu and said.

Devas said :

14. Let us see your efficiency. Afterwards we shall fight with the enemies. Hence, O Manyu, show your inherent strength to us who are desirous of fighting the Asuras.

Brahmā said :

15-17. On hearing those words of Devas Manyu said smilingly.

Manyu said :

My progenitor is the omniscient lord of Devas. He is the

lord who sees everything. He knows everything. He knows the name and abode of everyone and what is in their mind. No one knows him. He knows everyone at everytime. The maker of the universe, identical with the universe knows everything with or without forms.

18. He is the greatest lord. He passes through heaven and the firmament. Who is he who knows his form. The lord identical with the universe is the maker of the Creator.

19. I am born of such (a deity). How do you deserve to know me? Or if you are still desirous of seeing, see me.

Brahmā said :

20-23. After saying thus Manyu revealed his form that had been produced from the third eye of Lord Śiva. It was that form which had been gathered together by means of brilliance. It was the same as was called Pauruṣa (manliness) in men, Ahaṁkāra (Ego) in all creatures, anger in all which is terrible and which causes annihilation.

On seeing that representative of Śaṅkara, who was resplendent on account of his own refulgence and who was holding aloft all types of weapons, Devas bowed to him. Daityas and Danujas became afraid. Devas joined their palms in reverence.

24-27. Having joined their palms in reverence they said to Manyu—"O lord, be our commander-in-chief. O Manyu, we shall enjoy kingdom won by you. Hence in every activity you are victorious. You are the person who will increase our victory.

You are Indra and Varuṇa. You alone are the guardians of quarters. Enter us, enter for the sake of our victory."

Manyu spoke to them all—"There is nothing without me. I entered everyone. I am present in everyone,. No one knows me."

Manyu was the lord himself born from him in separate forms.

28. He shall be in the form of Rudra. Rudra became Manyu and Śiva. Everything, the mobile and immobile is pervaded by Manyu (Anger).

29. After obtaining him, Devas obtained victory in battle. Victory, anger and heroism all these originated from the splendour of the lord.

30. After fighting with Daityas and attaining victory on account of Manyu, Devas protected by Manyu went the way they had come.

31. The place where Devas propitiated Śiva on the banks of Gautamī, obtained Manyu as well as victory in battle, is called Manyutīrtha.

32-33. The man who remains pure and remembers the origin of Manyu it never harassed by anyone. Victory is his.

There is no holy centre like Manyutīrtha, O great sage. It is the place where Śaṅkara is directly present always in the form of Manyu.

Taking holy bath, offering of charitable gifts and remembrance (of the lord) fulfil all cherished desires.

CHAPTER NINETYTHREE

Sārasvata and other Holy Centres

Brahmā said:

1. The holy centre named Sārasvata bestows all cherished desires and benefits. It yields worldly pleasures and salvation to men. It destroys all sins.

2. It subdues all ailments. It bestows all (spiritual) achievements. There listen to this narrative in detail, O Nārada.

3. To the east of Puṣpotkaṭa is the mountain well known in all worlds. It is the most excellent mountain named Śubhra on the southern bank of Gautamī.

4. There was a sage excessively disciplined with self-control, well reputed as Śākalya. He performed an excellent penance on the holy mountain Śubhra.

5. All living beings used to bow down to and eulogize that excellent brahmin who performed penance after resorting to the banks of Gautamī.

6. He was devoted to the service of sacred fire and the study of the Vedas on that mountain resorted to by sages, Gandharvas and Devas.

7. On that extremely meritorious mountain there was a Rākṣasa named Paraśu. He was a terrifier of Devas and brahmins. He was a hater of Yajñas and the slayer of brahmins.

8-11. He could assume any form he wished. Assuming different forms he used to wander in the forest. In a trice, he would wander in the form of a brahmin. Sometimes he would assume the form of a tiger. Sometimes he would wander in the form of a Deva and sometimes he would assume the form of an animal. Sometimes he would have the form of a young maiden. Sometimes he would wander in the form of a deer. Sometimes he would wander in the form of a boy. Thus he wandered about committing sin after sin.

Where the scholarly brahmin sage Śākalya stayed, the great sinner Paraśu, the base Rākṣasa, used to come everyday. Although Paraśu attempted to abduct and kill the brahmin of great purity, he could not do it.

12-13. One day, after scrupulously worshipping Devas, that excellent brahmin came (to the dining chamber) desirous of taking food. At that time, O sage, Paraśu too came there assum- the form of a brahmin. He was enfeebled, grey-haired and weak. There was a certain girl also with him. He spoke to Śākalya.

Paraśu said:

14-15. O brahmin, know me and this girl desirous of food. We have come at the proper time when guests should be fed. O bestower of honour, you can be contented. They alone are blessed from whose houses, guests come out with all their desires fulfilled. Others are dead though they may be physically alive.

16. After sitting down for taking food, if anyone gives away to the guest what has been prepared for himself it is as though the Earth has been gifted away by him.

Brahmā said:

17. On hearing these words Śākalya made Paraśu sit on a seat taking him to be a brahmin out of ignorance and said. "I shall give"

18. After duly worshipping him Śākalya served the food. Taking the water for ceremonious gulping down in his hand Paraśu spoke these words :

Paraśu said :

19. The deities follow the weary guest from a great distance. If he is satiated they too will be satiated. It will be otherwise if he is dissatisfied.

20. The guest and the slander-monger—these two are the real kinsmen of the whole universe. The slander-monger dispels sins and the guest bestows heaven.

21. If anyone looks at a guest weary on his way with disgust, his virtue, fame and prosperity perish immediately.

22. Hence O excellent brahmin, I, a weary guest, earnestly beg of you. If you grant me what I desire I shall take my food. Not otherwise.

Brahmā said :

23-25. Śākalya said to the Rākṣasa : "It is already given. Take your food". Then he said, "I am Paraśu the excellent Rākṣasa. I am your enemy. I am not an old brahmin, lean and grey-haired. Many years have passed by since I have been observing you. My limbs are becoming dry like a small drop of water in the summer. Hence, O excellent brahmin, I shall take you away along with your followers and shall eat you up."

Brahmā said :

26-28. On hearing the words of Paraśu Śākalya said:

Śākalya said :

Those who are born of a noble family, those who have understood all the scriptural texts strictly adhere to what is promised by them, never otherwise. O friend, you do as you please. Still listen to me. Excellent words conducive to welfare should be spoken even to those persons who are attempting to kill one.

29. I am a brahmin of adamantine body. Lord Hari is my all-round protector. Let Viṣṇu protect my feet. Let Lord protect my head.

30. Let Boar protect my arms. Let Dharmarāja protect my back. Let Kṛṣṇa protect my heart. Let Man-Lion protect my fingers.

31. Let lord of speech protect my mouth. Let lord who moves about on a bird protect my eyes. Let lord of wealth.

Kubera, protect my ears. Let Bhava protect from all round. Lord Nārāyaṇa himself is the sole refuge in different adversities.

Brahmā said :

32. After saying thus, Śākalya continued—"Take me or devour me happily, O great Rākṣasa, Paraśu, without any hesitation."

33. At his words the Rākṣasa got ready to devour him. Certainly there is not the least bit of mercy in the heart of sinners.

34. With a mouth terrible due to the curved fangs he went near him (but) immediately after looking at the brahmin Paraśu said.

Paraśu said :

35-39. O excellent brahmin, I see you as one who has conch, discus and iron-club in his hands, one who has a thousand feet and heads, one who has a thousand eyes and hands, as a lord who is the sole abode of all living beings, whose form is that of Vedas. O brahmin, I see you today as one identical with the universe. This is not your previous body. Hence, I propitiate you, O brahmin, you alone be the refuge. Grant me knowledge, O brahmin of great intelligence. Tell me the holy centre for the atonement of my sins. O brahmin, visiting great men is never futile even if it be accidental or due to hatred or out of ignorance or by mistake. The contact of a piece of iron with the jewel is conducive to its turning into gold.

Brahmā said :

40-42. On hearing these words uttered by the Rākṣasa, Śākalya sympathetically said thus—"O lord of Daityas, ere long Sarasvatī will be the bestower of boons unto you. Hence, eulogize Viṣṇu. For the attainment of desired benefit there is no other means than the prayer unto Nārāyaṇa.

There is some other cause too in this world. Listen, O Rākṣasa. That goddess will be pleased with you due to my request.

Brahmā said:

43-45. Saying "So be it", Paraśu took bath in Gaṅgā, the sanctifier of three worlds. With purity and well controlled mind he stood facing Gaṅgā. There he saw Sarasvatī who had divine form, who had smeared over herself divine scents and unguents, who is the mother of the universe, who stood by the words of Śākalya, who is the dispeller of the sluggishness of the universe, who gave birth to the universe and who is the goddess of the universe. Paraśu who was rid of his sins spoke to her humbly.

Paraśu said :

46. My preceptor Śākalya said thus to me—"Eulogize the consort of Lakṣmī, the bird-bannered lord. Let me have that power by your grace. Kindly do so."

Brahmā said :

47-48. "Let it be so", said the divine Sarasvatī to Paraśu. Due to the grace of Sarasvatī, Paraśu eulogized Viṣṇu. Then Viṣṇu was pleased. Viṣṇu, the ocean of mercy, granted boons to the Rākṣasa.

Viṣṇu said:

49-51. O Rākṣasa, whatever is in your mind, everything that you desire will take place.

Brahmā said :

Even though he was a great sinner, the Rākṣasa Paraśu went to heaven by the grace of Śākalya, the grace of Gautamī, the grace of Sarasvatī, the grace of Narasiṁha and the grace of the lord with the Śārṅga bow, whose lotus-like foot constitutes a holy centre to all.

52-53. Thenceforth, that holy centre is well known as "Sārasvata". By taking holy dip there and by offering charitable gifts one is honoured in the world of Viṣṇu.

On that Śveta Mountain there are many holy centres born of the grace of Sarasvatī, Viṣṇu, Śākalya and Paraśu.

CHAPTER NINETYFOUR

Ciñcikātīrtha and other Holy Centres

Brahmā said :

1. The holy centre called Ciñcikātīrtha destroys all ailments. It dispels all worries of men and it is conducive to universal peace.

2-3. I shall recount its characterisic features. On that excellent white mountain on the northern bank of Gaṅgā, where the deity Lord Gadādhara dwells there was the lord of birds of the species called Bheruṇḍa (named) Ciñcika. He used to live there on the white mountain eating meat.

4. The mountain was full of trees laden with different flowers and fruits, flowers blossoming in every season. It was frequented by chiefs among brahmins. It was embellished by Gautamī.

5-8. It was tumultuously occupied by Siddhas, Cāraṇas, Gandharvas, Kinnaras and Devas. Near it was another mountain wherein the bipeds and quadrupeds never suffered from ailments, hunger, thirst, anxieties and death. On the mountain endowed with qualities like these and surrounded by different sages there was a certain king of eastern land known as Pavamāna. He was prosperous. He was devotedly engaged in duties of a Kṣatriya. He was the protector of Devas and brahmins. (Once) accompanied by a great army and his own priest he went to the forest. There he sported with enchanting women indulging in pleasures of dance and musical instruments.

9-11. He had the bow in his hand. He was surrounded by habitual hunters. Wandering thus once he became weary and came to a tree growing on the banks of Gautamī and occupied by different kinds of birds. It was like a householder conversant with virtue and resorted to by the people of all stages of life. The excellent king Pavamāna resorted to that excellent tree and took rest. Surrounded by the people he looked at the excellent tree.

12. There he saw a stout bird of two beaks splendid in shape and features. He was tired and appeared worried by thoughts. The excellent king asked him.

The king said :

13. Who are you, Sir? You, a bird with two beaks, appear to be worried by thoughts. Here no one is distressed. Whence has misery befallen you ?

Brahmā said :

14. Thereupon the bird Ciñcika who was consoled in his mind frequently sighed and said to king Pavamāna slowly :

Ciñcika said :

15-16. Others have no fear from me nor do I have any fear from others. This mountain is full of trees laden with flowers and fruits. It is resorted to by sages. Yet I see it as a void. Hence I bewail myself. I do not get happiness. I am never satisfied. I do not get any sleep anywhere. I have no rest. I have no peace.

Brahmā said:

17-20. On hearing the utterance of the bird with two beaks the king was too surprised.

The king said :

Who are you, Sir ? What is the sin commited by you ? Wherefore is the mountain a void ? On the excellent mountain the living beings are satisfied with one mouth. Why then are you not satisfied even with two beaks? What is your sin ? Is it acquired in this birth or in the former ones ? Mention all these truthfully to me. I shall save you from your fear.

Brahmā said:

21-24. The bird Ciñcika said sighingly to the king.

Ciñcika said:

I shall recount what has happened before, O Pavamāna, listen to it.

I was an excellent brahmin who had mastered the Vedas and Vedāṅgas. I was of noble birth and known well as an intelligent man. But I was fond of quarrels. I was always opposed to others' interests. I used to speak one thing before and another after. I always felt miserable at the prosperity of others. I used to cheat the whole world by fraudulent means. I was ungrateful. I was devoid of truth. I was expert in speaking ill of others.

25. I was treacherous to friends, masters and preceptors. I was a hypocrite in my conduct. I was extremely ruthless. I used to give distress and pain to many people by my thoughts, acts, and speech.

26-27. Infliction of violent injuries on others was my pastime. Without thinking I used to commit sins of separating couples, annihilating groups and transgressing bounds of good behaviour. I was uninterested in serving scholars. In the three worlds there was no sinner like me.

28. Therefore I was born with two beaks. Since I used to make others distressed, I am miserable now. This mountain is a void to me.

29. Listen to what I say further, O king. My words are endowed with wisdom about virtue and wealth. (Sometimes) sins equal to brahmin-slaughter are incurred without actual slaughter.

30-31. If during battle or out of it a Kṣatriya were to kill a fleeing adversary, one who has put down weapons, one who has turned his face away, one who is seated without being aware (of enemies) and one who says "I am afraid"—If a Kṣatriya were to kill any of these he shall be (considered) a brahmin-slayer.

32. He who forgets the Vedic text that he has learnt, he who addresses superior persons disrespectfully by "theeing and thouing" them and he who insults elderly persons and preceptors they call these "a Brahmaghātaka" (brahmin-slayer).

33-34. He who speaks pleasing words in the presence of someone but harsh words in his absence, he who always thinks something, speaks something else and does something else, he who swears by his preceptors, he who hates them, he who censures brahmins, he who pretends to be humble, he who is evil-minded—all these shall be brahmin-slayers.

35. He who out of hatred censures Devas, Vedas, spiritual learning and the assemblage of virtuous brahmins shall be a brahmin-slayer.

36-37. Although, O king, I was like this, I behaved like a

man of good conduct for the sake of false prestige and arrogance and due to shyness. Hence, O king I became a bird.

Although I was like this I might have done some good deed somewhere. On account of that, O king, I myself remember what has been done before.

Brahmā said :

38. On hearing these words of Ciñcika, Pavamāna became extremely surprised. Then the king said to the bird—"By what holy rite can you be liberated?"

39-42. On hearing these words of the king, the lord of birds said to him.

Ciñcika said :

There is a holy centre named Gadādhara on this very same excellent mountain, on the northern bank of Gautamī. It is destroyer of all sins. Indeed that holy centre is extremely meritorious. O king of holy rites, take me there. That it bestows all cherished desires has been heard from great sages. There is none other than Gautamī and Viṣṇu, which destroys pain. It is my opinion that I should see that holy Tīrtha with mind full of noble feelings.

43. This is never possible by an effort solely put forth by me. How can men of evil actions attain desired objects ?

44. Although I had attempted I could not see that unattainable deity. Hence, I should see Gadādhara by your grace.

45-46. He (Gadādhara) is well aware of my misery though it has not been intimated to him. He is the ocean of mercy. If he is seen, pains of worldly existence are never observed again by men. O king of holy rites, I shall definitely go to heaven after seeing him by your grace.

Brahmā said :

47-48. On being requested thus by Ciñcika, the bird, the king showed that lord and that holy Gaṅgā to the bird. Thereupon Ciñcika said to Gaṅgā, the sanctifier of the three worlds :

Ciñcika said :

49. O Gaṅgā, O Gautamī, a person who is a sinner is called so only as long as he does not see you the sanctifier of the three worlds.

50. Hence, O excellent river, uplift me although I have committed all sins. Excepting you, O river born of the lotus-like feet of Viṣṇu, there is no other goal anywhere unto the embodied beings in this world.

Brahmā said :

51. Thus that bird whose soul was purified on account of steadfast faith, and whose sole refuge was Gaṅgā performed the rite of holy bath in it praying silently "O Gaṅgā save me".

52. Thereafter, he bowed down to Gadādhara. Even as the other dwellers on the mountain were watching, he went to heaven immediately after being permitted by Pavamāna.

53-54. Thereafter, Pavamāna went to his city accompanied by his followers. Thenceforth, those who are conversant with the Vedas know that holy centre as Pavamāna, Ciñcika, Gadādhara and Koṭitīrtha. Holy rite performed there by men shall have crores and crores of times the usual benefit in return.

CHAPTER NINETYFIVE

Bhadratirtha

Brahmā said :

1. The holy centre called Bhadratīrtha prevents all ill omens, destroys all sins and is conducive to great tranquility.

2-3. Uṣā the chaste daughter of Tvaṣṭṛ was the (first) beloved wife of Āditya (Sun). Chāya too was the wife of Sun-god and Śanaiścara (Saturn) was her son. His sister known as Viṣṭi was terrible and evil in appearance. "To whom shall I give her ?" was the worry of the Sun-god about that girl.

4-5. To whomsoever the Sun-god, the preceptor of the worlds, desired to give her he used to say on hearing about it, "What shall we do with this wife ? She is terrible."

In these circumstances the dejected girl said to her father :

Viṣṭi said :

6. A father who gives his daughter to a handsome person

even while she is still a child shall become blessed in the world. If not, the father is a sinner.

7. After the fourth year and before the completion of the tenth year the marriage of his daughter must be performed scrupulously by the father.

8. The girl should be given to a bridegroom who is rich and prosperous, learned, youthful, born of a noble family, famous, liberal-minded, and one whose father is alive.

9-10. If the father does not do accordingly he shall fall into hell. O Sun, just as a daughter is an instrument of virtue to the learned so also she is the cause of downfall into hell, of fools with minds impaired by lust.

The entire Earth along with mountains, forests and parks shall be on one side and a good girl well bedecked and free from blemishes on the other. Both are then well balanced.

11-17. If anyone sells his daughter, horse, cow or sesamum seeds, no atonement can ever save him from Raurava and other (hells). Postponement of the marrige of a daughter should never be done. If that is done, who can describe the sin accruing therefrom adequately? Before the daughter grows into a bashful girl, even while she continues to play with sand and dust, she should be given away in marriage. Otherwise the parents will have downfall. The son should be the very image of the father. He who is the father is the son as well. In this world who does not make himself happy? Charity, worship, supervision that a father performs for the sake of his daughter should be known as effectively made. What is given on behalf of them is of everlasting merit. What is given to those daughters is capable of having infinite fruit. O Sun, who does not make his sons and grandsons happy? He who makes his daughters happy shall possess riches.

Brahmā said :

18-20. When his daughter Viṣṭi said thus Sun-god said to her.

The Sun-god said :

What shall I do? No one accepts you because of your hideous features. In negotiating mutual relationship such as marriage people look into the lineage, beauty, age, wealth, learning, conduct and good habits in both women and men. We have everything, O auspicious girl, except good qualities (beauty) in you. What shall I do ? Where can I give you ? Why do you blame me in vain ?

Brahmā said:

21-22. After saying thus the Sun said to Viṣṭi once again.

The Sun said :

If you consider that you should be given to anyone, to whomsoever I may deem fit to give you, if you agree you shall be given away by me even today, O Viṣṭi, permit me.

Brahmā said :

23-26. Viṣṭi then said to her father, "Husband, sons, wealth, happiness, long life, beauty and joy—one gets these in accordance with the previous merit. Whatever action has been committed by a living being, whether good or evil, the result is derived in accordance with the same even in another birth. Only his own fault should be avoided carefully by the father. The benefit that one gets shall be only what corresponds to the previous performance of the person. Hence the giving away in marriage and the contract of alliance of his daughter shall be done by the father in accordance with the practice in his family. The rest is in the hands of fate. What should occur does occur.

Brahmā said :

27. On hearing those words of his daughter he gave terrible daughter Viṣṭi who frightened the worlds, to Viśvarūpa, the son of Tvaṣṭṛ.

28-31. Viśvarūpa too was equally terrible with hideous features. Thus the couple matched with each other in regard to conduct and physical features. They wandered here and there in secret. Sometimes they had excessive mutual love. Sometimes they had mutual quarrel. They had seven sons, viz. Gaṇḍa, Atigaṇḍa, Raktākṣa, Krodhana, Vyaya, Durmukha and the youngest son named Harṣaṇa. This son was meritorious, well behaved, calm, fortunate, pure-minded and pure. Once he went to the abode of Yama to see his uncle.

32-33. He saw many creatures, those who were in heaven

and those who were miserable. He bowed down to his uncle and asked him for instruction regarding Eternal Virtue.

Harṣaṇa said :

Sir, who are those who enjoy happiness? Who are those who rot in hell?

Brahmā said :

34. On being asked thus, Dharmarāja told everything accurately. He described to him the course of Karman in full.

Yama said:

35-37. Those men who never transgress injunctions never see hell.

Those who do not honour scripture, good conduct and persons with vast learning and those who transgress injunctions dwell in hell.

Brahmā said:

On hearing the words of Dharma, Harṣaṇa spoke again.

Harṣaṇa said:

38-40. O excellent one among Devas, tell me that holy rite whereby my terrible father, the son of Tvaṣṭr, Viṣṭi, my terrible mother and my brothers shall become noble-souled, calm-minded, handsome in features, bestowers of auspiciousness and free from blemishes. I shall perform it. Otherwise I will not go back to them.

On being requested thus Dharmarāja said to Harṣaṇa of pure mind:

"There is no doubt about about this. You are Harṣaṇa (one who delights).

41-44. There may be many sons but all of them do not perpetuate the line. There may be a single son but the entire family is sustained by him.

He alone is the true son—he who is the support of the family, he who does what is pleasing to the parents and he who redeems his ancestors. He who is not so is an ailment.

Since what is befitting me, what is pleasing to your maternal grandfather has been mentioned by you, go to Gautamī. After taking bath there eulogize Viṣṇu, the benign lord who is the origin of the universe, with a delighted and restrained mind. If he becomes pleased he will grant you everything you desire."

Brahmā said:

45-48. On hearing these words of Dharma, Harṣaṇa went to Gautamī. After taking bath, he eulogized Hari. Then lord of Devas, Hari became pleased.

He granted the welfare of all the members of the family to Harṣaṇa saying "Let there be welfare unto you and the prevention of all harms and injuries."

Hence, Viṣṭi is called Bhadrā. As the father was Bhadra, so also the sons. Thenceforth, that holy centre is called Bhadratīrtha.

It bestows auspiciousness on men. Hari there is 'Bhadrapati' (Lord of Welfare). The Tīrtha yields all Siddhis to the persons who resort to that holy centre. Viṣṇu, the lord of Devas himself is the sole storehouse of auspiciousness.

CHAPTER NINETYSIX

Patatri-Tīrtha

1. The holy centre Patatri-Tīrtha is reputed to be the destroyer of ailments and sins. A man shall derive contentment merely by listening to its name.

2. Kaśyapa had two sons Aruṇa and Garuḍa. In that family were born Sampāti and Jaṭāyu.

3-7. Aruṇa and Garuḍa were the sons of Tārkṣya Prajāpati. In his family was born the excellent bird Sampāti. His younger brother was well known as Jaṭāyu. They vied with each other because they were madly proud of their own strength. They went (far) into the sky to bow down to the sun. When they came near the sun the wings of those two excellent birds were burnt. Wearied they fell down on the top of a mountain. On seeing the two kinsmen fallen unconscious and motionless, Aruṇa was overwhelmed with sorrow and said to Sun-god—"Two birds born of our own family have fallen on the ground with their wings burned. O hot-rayed one, console them lest they should die.

Brahmā said :

8-9. Saying "So be it" the sun resuscitated those two birds. On hearing about their (miserable) plight Garuḍa came there along with Viṣṇu, consoled and cheered them up. O Nārada, then they all went to Gaṅgā for dispelling distress.

10-13. Jaṭāyu and Aruṇa, Sampāti and Garuḍa went there. Sūrya and Viṣṇu went there for their pleasure. That holy centre yields much merit. Patatri-Tīrtha is well reputed as the destroyer of poison. It yields all cherished desires. Viṣṇu and the Sun are seated there along with Garuḍa and Aruṇa on the banks of Gautamī. So also the bull-bannered lord. That holy centre is excellent because the three Devas (lords) are stationed there. One shall take bath, be pure and bow down to these gods. He shall be rid of mental anguish and physical ailments. He shall attain great happiness.

CHAPTER NINETYSEVEN

Vipratīrtha also known as Nārāyaṇatīrtha

Brahmā said:

1. There is a holy centre well known as Vipratīrtha. They know it as Nārāyaṇa Tīrtha also. I shall recount its story that causes wonder. Listen.

2. In Antarvedī i.e. the tract of land between Gaṅgā and Yamunā there was a certain brahmin who had mastered the Vedas. His sons were highly intelligent and endowed with good qualities, handsome features and kind temperament.

3. The youngest brother was quiet and endowed with a number of good qualities. He was well known as Āsandiva. He was highly intelligent and had perfect knowledge of everything.

4-7. The father made all efforts for the marriage of Āsandiva. In the meantime that son of a brahmin went to sleep at night without remembering Viṣṇu and without mental purity and concentration. He had kept his head in the direction of north. So a demoness of ruthless features with ability to assume any form as she pleased, kidnapped Āsandiva and hastily took him to a town on the southern bank of Gautamī, to the northern side of Śrīgiri. That town was frequented by many brahmins. It was an abode of virtue and prosperity.

The king there was Bṛhatkīrti who was endowed with the good qualities of a Kṣatriya.

8. At the end of the night that demoness, accompanied by the son of the brahmin reached his city endowed with unlimited and flourishing prosperity. She used to assume enchanting forms everyday.

9. She used to wander over the entire Earth accompanied by that brahmin. She used to assume any form she pleased. (Once) she assumed the form of an old lady and came to the southern bank of Godāvarī. There the terrible demoness said to the brahmin.

Rākṣasī said:

10-12. O superior brahmin, here is Gaṅgā. Let the Sandhyā be meditated upon after joining the leading brahmins. If the leading brahmins do not perform Sandhyā prayers scrupulously at the proper time, they are called by leading sages leaders of the low-caste people. You tell them that I am your mother. If not you will come to ruin now. O leading brahmin, if you carry out my suggestions I shall make you happy and do what is pleasing to you. I shall take you back again to your own abode and people.

Brahmā said:

13-14. That leading brahmin said to her, "Who are you?" That demoness who could assume any form she pleased, said after creating confidence in that son of the leading sage whose mind had been confounded : "I am famous throughout the world by the name Kaṅkālinī". The brahmin too said to her : "I shall do what has been mentioned by you. I shall speak and do what is pleasing to you."

Brahmā said:

15-16. On hearing those words of the brahmin the demoness

who could assume any form she pleased became an old lady. Still she was fascinating in her limbs. She had divine embellishments and ornaments.

Taking the brahmin with her she used to wander everywhere saying "He is my son. He is a man of good qualities."

17. (People saw) that brahmin embellished by handsome features, good fortune, youthful age and learning and that old lady endowed with good qualities. They considered her his mother.

18. A certain excellent brahmin gave his daughter bedecked in ornaments to that brahmin after honouring the demoness.

19. On obtaining him as her husband, that girl thought that she was extremely blessed and contented but that brahmin became extremely miserable when he noticed his wife endowed with good qualities.

The brahmin said :

20-21. This demoness of sinful features may swallow me. What shall I do? Where shall I go? To whom shall I say this? A great adversity has beset me. Who will save me? This wife of mine is endowed with good qualities, beauty and youth. She is lovely and agreeable. This inauspicious demoness may devour her also at any time.

Brahmā said :

22-23. In the meantime the extremely aggressive old lady had gone somewhere. Then the virtuous wife, the chaste lady came to her husband on knowing that he was sad and miserable. She then spoke to him humbly and slowly in secret.

The wife said :

24. O my lord, how has sadness beset you? Tell me.

Brahmā said :

25-26. Slowly he recounted to his wife the previous details precisely. "What is there which should not be mentioned to a dear friend or to a wife of noble birth !"

On hearing her husband's words that intelligent lady said.

The wife said :

27-28. To a man who is silly and who has not restrained

himself, there is fear from everywhere even in his own house. Whence can self-possessed persons fear? More so on the banks of Gautamī. What fear can there be to the devotees of Viṣṇu who stay on the banks of Gautamī, who are devoid of attachment and who are endowed with discrimination? Take your bath here. Be pure and eulogize the lord free from ailments.

Brahmā said:

29. On hearing this the brahmin took bath in Gaṅgā and rid himself of all sins. He eulogized Nārāyaṇa on the banks of Gautamī river.

The brahmin said:

30-33. O lord, you are immanent soul of the universe. O Mukunda, you are its maker, annihilator and protector. O Narasiṁha, the friend of parentless ones, wherefore do you not protect me, a wretched one ?

On hearing this request of his, Nārāyaṇa, the dispeller of the sorrow of the universe slew that sinful demoness with his refulgent discus Sudarśana which has a thousand spikes. The lord granted him all desired boons and took him back to his father.

Thenceforth, they know that holy centre Vipra or Nārāyaṇa. It is a spot where desired things are achieved by holy dip, charitable offerings, worships, etc.

CHAPTER NINETYEIGHT

Bhānu-Tīrtha and other Holy Centres

Brahmā said:

1. The holy centres well known as Bhānutīrtha, Tvāṣṭra, Māheśvara, Aindra, Yāmya and Āgneya are destroyers of all sins.

2. There was a king of very pleasing appearance well known as Abhiṣṭuta. He began to worship Devas by performing a holy horse-sacrifice.

3-6. There were sixteen Ṛtviks there the leaders whereof were Vasiṣṭha and Atri. A doubt arose among them.

"When a Kṣatriya is the sponsor of a sacrifice, how shall the altar of sacrifice be made ready? When a brahmin gets himself initiated it is the king who has to arrange for the sacrificial ground. But when a king gets himself initiated who is the person to make an altar. If a Brahmin were to do that, it would be sinful. It could cause all unhappiness. Therefore, the Kṣatriya king should not employ Brahmins for that job."

When the brahmins were discussing this among themselves the highly intelligent Vasiṣṭha, the most excellent among the knowers of Dharma, spoke :

Vasiṣṭha said :

7-9. When the king gets himself initiated the sun should be requested for the job.

The sun should be requested by the king thus—"O lord Savitṛ, prepare on my behalf the sacrificial ground befitting the deities. You are the divine Kṣatriya, O (supreme) lord of living beings. Obeisance be to you."

Savitṛ thus requested by the king will certainly grant the splendid sacrificial ground for Devas. Hence, O king, pray to Sun-god.

Brahmā said:

10. Saying "So be it" Abhiṣṭuta faithfully prayed to Sun-god, lord of Devas, Ravi who is identical with Hari, Śiva and Brahmā.

The king said :

11-14. O Savitṛ, obeisance be to you. Grant us the sacrificial ground of Devas.

Brahmā said :

Since the sun is a divine Kṣatriya the ground was given to the lord of the Earth. Savitṛ, the lord of the chiefs of Devas, spoke—"I shall give".

He who performs a sacrifice thus will never have misfortune. When the holy Satra, the horse-sacrifice was begun by brahmins, the masters of the Vedas, the sun was eulogized by the king.

The placs where the Sun-god came to grant the divine sacrificial ground is called Bhānutīrtha.

15-18. The Daityas, Danujas and other destroyers of sacrifice assumed the guise of brahmins and came to that divine sacrifice, the excellent horse sacrifice presided over by Devas. Since they were reciting hymns like the highly intelligent Sāman-singers they could enter without being stopped (at the entrance). Some of the Asuras (in disguise) began to ridicule the sacrificial ladle and other vessels, the wooden ring on the top of the sacrificial post, Sāman, the drinking of Soma juice, Havis offerings, the priests and the king. Others began to throw sacrificial articles helter-skelter. Still others began to laugh. Excepting Viśvarūpa none else knew about these activities of theirs.

19. Viśvarūpa said to his father—"These are the Daityas". On hearing his son's words Tvaṣṭṛ said thus to Devas.

Tvaṣṭṛ said:

20-21. Take water and Kuśa grass and sprinkle all round. Saying "All those who censure the holy sacrifice, the ladle, vessel and the Soma juice have been removed by me" you sprinkle water.

Brahmā said:

22-24. Devas did so. Tvaṣṭṛ also did the same. The demons were reduced to ashes. Then they fled.

Saying "The sinners have been killed by me" he sprinkled the water. Thereupon Daityas whose lives had been crippled became angry and started from that place. The place where Tvaṣṭṛ, the Prajāpati of worlds sprinkled water is reputed as Tvāṣṭra Tīrtha. It is the destroyer of all sins.

25-28. Then Yama killed Daityas who had fallen as a result of the (rebuking) words of Tvaṣṭṛ. Angrily he killed them with Kāladaṇḍa (Black Staff), Kāla Pāśa (Black Noose) and discus. The holy centre where Daityas were killed is called Yāmya.

The place where the sacrifice was completed after offering Amṛta into the fire, the place where the Fire-god became satisfied with the incessant flow (of ghee) in the manner of a flight of arrows in that great sacrifice and became pleased with

Abhiṣṭuta is known as Agnitīrtha. It yields the same benefit as the horse sacrifice.

Indra accompanied by Maruts said auspicious words to the king.

29. "O king, you will become the Emperor of both worlds. You will undoubtedly become my perpetual dear friend."

30. He who performs the holy rite of water libation in the Indratīrtha is the most blessed in the mortal world. For the propitiation of manes he must perform Tarpana particularly in the Yamatīrtha.

31. That holy centre where Śiva was eulogized and worshipped with devout mind by the brahmins who were experts in all holy rites is called Māheśvaratīrtha.

32-35. The king worshipped with a concentrated mind Maheśvara who is worthy of worship. He worshipped him in various ways such as by Vedic Mantras and non-Vedic prayers, dances and songs, musical intruments, Pañcāmṛtas (the five sweet articles—honey, ghee, jaggery, curd, milk), prostrations, circumambulations, incenses, lights, flowers scents and Naivedyas (food offerings). Thereupon, the delighted lords of Devas granted him boons along with great power. They granted the great king Abhiṣṭuta both worldly pleasures and liberation. Similarly, they granted the holy centre excellent efficacy.

36-38. Thereafter, that holy centre is called Śaiva and Vaiṣṇava (pertaining to Śiva and Viṣṇu). They know that a holy plunge and monetary gifts performed there are the bestowers of all cherished desires. He who remembers or reads about all these holy centres shall be rid of all sins and shall go to the cities of Śiva and Viṣṇu. Especially having a holy bath in the Bhānutīrtha bestows all riches. In this holy spot there are a hundred holy centres.

CHAPTER NINETYNINE

The Holy Centre Bhilla

Brahmā said :

1. The holy centre well known as Bhilla destroys sins and ailments. It bestows devotion to the lotus-like feet of Mahādeva.

2-3. Listen to a holy story about this, O highly intelligent one.

On the southern bank of Gaṅgā, on the northern region of Śrīgiri, Mahādeva the bestower of all cherished desires, is always present in the form of Liṅga. The lord is well known as Ādikeśa and worshipped devotedly by the sages.

4. There was an extremely virtuous sage known as Sindhudvīpa. His brother was well known as Veda. He too was a great sage.

5-6. Everyday he used to worship Lord Ādikeśa, the three-eyed enemy of the three cities, with great devotion. When the sun reached midday, the intelligent Veda used to go to the village for receiving alms. Whenever that noble brahmin had gone to the village, a highly virtuous hunter used to come for hunting over that holy excellent mountain.

7-13. After wandering in various places and killing animals as he pleased he used to place the meat at the tip of the bow. The tired hunter then came to the place where Lord Śiva, Ādikeśa had his Liṅga. He used to keep the meat outside. Then he went to Gaṅgā and taking water in his mouth and some leaves in his hand, he returned to the lord with great devotion. He took the meat in the other hand for offering Naivedya with great devotion. He then came to Lord Ādikeśa who had already been worshipped elaborately by Veda (the sage of that name). He then removed flowers left by Veda after his worship by means of his foot. After bathing lord Śiva with the water brought by him in his mouth and after offering those leaves by way of worship he used to place the meat there as Naivedya saying "May lord Śiva be pleased with me."

Excepting devotion of a splendid nature unto Śiva he did not know anything else. Thereafter he used to go back to his own abode in the manner he had come, taking the rest of the meat with him.

14. Everyday he used to come there and do this by himself. However, Īśa was pleased with him. Indeed, wonderful are the ways of the lord.

15. As long as the Bhilla did not come to Him, Lord Śiva was not happy. Who knows the (magnitude of) Śiva's compassion towards his devotees ? It is beyond all measure.

16-17. Thus a great deal of time passed by when both Veda and Bhilla continued to worship Ādikeśa Śiva everyday along with Umā. Then Veda said angrily—"Who is the sinner who spoils my worship which is performed with devotion to Śiva, and with Mantras ? He shall die at my hands.

18. One who maliciously betrays preceptors, Devas, brahmins or his master is worthy of being killed even by a sage. A man who is treacherously perfidious to Śiva deserves to be killed by everyone."

19-23. After saying so decisively that intelligent Veda, the younger brother of Sindhu, thought thus—"Whose evil action can this be ? He is wicked and the most sinful. He has spoiled my worship performed with divine flowers of the forest, splendid roots, fruits and bulbous roots and has performed another sort of worship with flesh and leaves of trees. He deserves to be killed by me. I shall hide myself and see that sinful worshipper of the lord."

In the meantime the hunter came to the lord as before. When he worshipped as usual Ādikeśa spoke to him.

Ādikeśa said :

24. O hunter of excessive intelligence, you are tired. You are coming after a long time. Why is it so? I am miserable without you. I do no get any happiness. Be pacified, dear son.

Brahmā said :

25-26. On hearing the lord say thus and on seeing (these activities) Veda became surprised as well as angry. He did not say anything.

As usual the hunter performed his daily worship and returned to his abode. Veda became angry. He approached the lord and said :

Veda said:

27. This hunter is engaged in sinful activities. He is devoid of sacred rites and perfect knowledge. He is ruthlessly engaged in injuring living beings violently. He is without mercy for any creature.

28. He is of a low caste. He does not know anything. He is devoid of the knowledge of due order of preceptors. He is a perpetual perpetrator of improper actions. He has not conquered his sense-organs.

29-31. You have revealed yourself to him but you do not speak anything to me. O lord, I have controlled my sense-organs. I perform holy rites. I perform worship with necessary Mantras and in accordance with pious injunctions. I have you as my sole refuge for ever. I have no wife and sons. This hunter performs your worship with defiled flesh. But you, O lord, have become pleased with him. This is highly surprising. I shall chastise this Bhilla who performs misdeeds.

32. Some are pleased with the soft-hearted people. Some are pleased with the evil-minded ones. Hence, I shall undoubtedly let fall a boulder on your (Śiva's) head.

Brahmā said:

33-39. When Veda spoke thus the lord laughed and said thus.

Ādikeśa said:

Wait till tomerrow. Then you can drop the boulder on my head.

Brahmā said:

Saying "So be it" Veda cast aside the boulder with his hand. He controlled his anger. "I shall do it tomorrow," he said.

He returned next day in the morning and performed the holy dip and other rites. After performing worship as usual he looked at the the head of the Liṅga. Veda saw a terrible wound on the Liṅga covered with blood. Veda was surprised at it. "What is this on the head of the Liṅga? A great calamity may befall us. What does this indicate?" After thinking thus he applied clay and cowdung over it. He scrubbed it with Kuśa grass and washed it with the waters of Gaṅgā. Then he performed the worship as usual.

In the meantime the hunter, devoid of all sins, came there.

40. Entering (the sanctum sanctorum) he saw the head of the Liṅga of Śaṅkara Ādikeśa with a bleeding wound.

41. Immediately after seeing this he said, "What is this? It is mysterious." After saying so he split himself into hundred and thousand pieces with sharp arrows.

42. No man of noble ideas can brook it if he sees that his master is wounded. He censured himself saying frequently—"This has occurred even when I am alive."

43. What a painful thing has befallen us due to the perversity of fate ! On seeing this activity of his, Mahādeva was exceedingly surprised. Then the lord spoke to Veda, the most excellent among those conversant with the Vedas.

Ādikeśa said:

44-45. O highly intelligent one, see this hunter who is a devotee endowed with noble feelings. But you touched my head with clay, Kuśa grass and water.

But, O brahmin, this hunter has dedicated his life to me suddenly. Devotion, love and power are there where is intense thought. Hence, O excellent brahmin, I shall grant him boons first and then to you.

Brahmā said:

46-47. Lord Maheśvara asked the hunter to choose a boon as he pleased. The hunter said to the lord of Devas, "O lord, let your Nirmālya be given to us. Let this holy centre be called, after my name. Let this holy centre yield the benefit of all sacrifices merely by being remembered."

Brahmā said:

48-49. The lord of Devas said, "So be it" Thenceforth that excellent holy centre is called Bhillatīrtha. It destroys all sins. It generates devotion towards the feet of Mahādeva. By a holy dip here and offerings of charitable gifts etc., it yields worldly pleasures and salvation. Lord Śiva granted Veda also many kinds of boons.

CHAPTER ONE HUNDRED

Cakṣustīrtha and other Holy Centres

Brahmā said:

1. The holy centre well known as Cakṣustīrtha on the southern bank of Gautamī is one that bestows beauty and conjugal felicity. The lord here is Yogeśvara.

2. There is a well known city named Bhauvana on the top of a mountain wherc there was a king named Bhauvana. He was devoted to the duties of a Kṣatriya.

3. In the excellent city there was a brahmin named Vṛddhakauśika. His son was known as Gautama. He was the most excellent of all those who were conversant with the Vedas.

4. Due to defect in the mind of his mother this brahmin had opposite (qualities). He had a merchant friend named Maṇikuṇḍala.

5. The brahmin had friendship with that merchant though that was odd for a poor brahmin and a rich and flourishing Vaiśya. They wished for mutual welfare.

6. Once Gautama said these words to Maṇikuṇḍala the Vaiśya who was a lord of riches. He repeatedly mentioned this in secret.

Gautama said :

7. We shall go to the mountains and seas in order to seek wealth. Youthful age should be known as futile if it lacks facilities for pleasure. How can that be without wealth? O, fie upon a men devoid of riches !

Brahmā said :

8. Kuṇḍala said this to the brahmin: "There is a vast amount of wealth earned by my father but, O excellent brahmin, what shall I do now with the wealth?"

Again the brahmin said this emphatically to Maṇikuṇḍala.

Gautama said :

9. Who is praised if he is content with his righteousness, wealth, knowledge and amorous sports? Dear friend, the attainment of the highest degree in these things by the embodied beings should be worthy of praise.

10. Creatures that are blessed live (in the real sense) by their own efforts. Those who are satisfied with the wealth given by others live a miserable existence.

11. If the son does not desire his father's money, if he does not even mention it in so many words, that son is praised in the world and he is applauded by his parents.

12. The son who earns wealth solely depending on the might of his own arms shall be blessed in the world. He shall not touch his father's wealth.

13. He who earns wealth himself and gives it to his father and other kinsmen is the real son. Know him alone as the real son. Others are mere worms in their mother's womb.

Brahmā said:

14-18. On hearing these words of the covetous brahmin the Vaiśya thought his words to be true. He hurriedly gathered together his wealth and jewels and handed them over to Gautama saying, "With this wealth we shall daily wander over all lands and return home with (more) wealth."

The Vaiśya said so in all sincerity but that brahmin was an evil-minded cheat. The Vaiśya did not know that the brahmin was evil-minded. The two, viz. the brahmin and the Vaiśya started without the knowledge of their parents and went from place to place. The brahmin wished to take away the money that the Vaiśya had with him.

The Brahmin thought:

19-22. I shall take away that wealth by some means. Oh! there are thousands of beautiful cities in the world. Women are as though the goddesses of love. They bestow what is desired. These charming ladies are in different places. What shall be done by me? After gathering together some wealth with great effort, if it is given to the women they can be enjoyed for ever. That life then is fruitful. I shall always enjoy dance and music. I shall be accompanied by harlots. I shall enjoy everything. But how can that wealth come to my hands from the Vaiśya?

Brahmā said:

23-25. After thinking thus, Gautama laughingly said to

Maṇikuṇḍala thus: "There is no doubt about this that creatures attain prosperity, happiness and everything they desire only through evil. Virtuous petsons are seen to be miserable in the world. Therefore, of what avail is virtue which results only in one thing, namely, misery?

Brahmā said:

26. "No" said the Vaiśya thereupon. "It is in Dharma (virtue, piety) that happiness is based. There is misery, fear, grief, poverty and pain in evil and sin. Where there is virtue there is liberation too. How can (the benefit of) the performance of one's own duty be lost?"

Brahmā said:

27-31. Even as they were arguing thus a quarrel ensued between them. They said—"He whose opinion proves superior (i.e. held by the majority of the people) shall get the wealth of the other. Let us ask (the people): who is more powerful, the virtuous or the non-virtuous?" "The worldly things are superior to the Vedas." "It is in the world that happiness results from virtue." Arguing thus they asked the people—"Of these two which has the greater power in the world, dharma or adharma? Please say the truth."

Some of the people said thus—"Pain and misery is experienced by those who follow dharma (virtue). Sinful persons are happy." Since he was thus defeated in the quarrel (the Vaiśya) handed over his wealth to the brahmin.

32. Maṇimān (the Vaiśya Maṇikuṇḍala) who was the most excellent one among those conversant with Dharma, began to praise Dharma once again. The brahmin said to Maṇimān, "Why? Do you still praise Dharma?"

Brahmā said:

"That is so" said the Vaiśya.

Thereupon, the brahmin said again.

The brahmin said:

33. O Vaiśya, all the wealth has been won by me. Why do you prattle shamelessly? Dharma which consists in doing what one pleases has been won by me.

Brahmā said:

34-36. On hearing those words of the brahmin, the Vaiśya said smilingly.

The Vaiśya said:

Dear friend, I consider those persons who do not possess virtue like the shrivelled ones among the grains or like the small bees among winged ones. Dharma is mentioned first among the four aims of a man's life. Artha (wealth) and Kāma (love) are mentioned only thereafter. That Dharma is present in me. How can you then say, O excellent brahmin, that you have won?

Brahmā said:

37-38. The brahmin then said to the Vaiśya again—"Let the wager be the pair of hands." The Vaiśya agreed to the proposal saying "So be it". As before they went to the general public and said the same thing. Then the brahmin said that (the bet) was won (by him). He cut off his hands and said "How do you consider Dharma now?" Provoked thus by the brahmin the Vaiśya spoke these words.

The Vaiśya said:

39. I consider Dharma as the supreme thing to the very last breath of my life (even when the vital airs have come to the throat). Dharma alone is the mother, father, friend and kinsman of all embodied beings.

Brahmā said:

40-41. Thus they argued between themselves. (As a result thereof) the brahmin became wealthy and the Vaiśya became bereft of his arms as well as riches.

Wandering thus they reached Gaṅgā and Hari the lord of Yogas, by chance. Then they talked to each other.

42. The Vaiśya began to praise Gaṅgā, the Lord of the Yogas and virtue alone. The brahmin angrily rebuked the Vaiśya and spoke again.

The brahmin said:

43. Your wealth is gone. The hands have been cut off. You

are now left with the barest of your vital breaths. If you speak otherwise I will cut off your head with a sword.

Brahmā said:

44-46. The Vaiśya laughted and said this suddenly to Gautama.

The Vaiśya said :

I think that Dharma (Virtue) is the greatest thing. You can do whatever you please. The sinner who censures brahmins, preceptors, Devas, Vedas, Dharma and Viṣṇu should not be touched. The evil-minded sinner, doer of wicked actions and base conduct, who blasphemes Dharma should be cast off and neglected.

Brahmā said :

47-49. Then he said angrily—"If you praise Dharma we shall have our respective lives as wager." When this was said, O sage, by Gautama, the merchant said "So be it". Again they addressed the general public and the public too said as before.

In front of Yogeśvara on the southern bank of Gautamī the brahmin felled the Vaiśya, plucked out his eye and said :

The brahmin said :

50. You have come to this plight, O Vaiśya, because you have been praising Dharma everyday. Your wealth is gone. Your eyes are gone and your sprout-like hands have been cut off. I am asking you for leave, my friend. I am going. Do not speak thus in another (similar) discussion.

Brahmā said :

51-54. After he had gone the Vaiśya thought thus, in his mind: "O lord, what a pity ! What has happened to me in spite of the fact that my mind is solely devoted to virtuous acts."

That excellent Vaiśya, Kuṇḍala who had become poor and bereft of his hands and eyes attained great sorrow although he was always thinking of Dharma alone. Thinking in diverse ways as mentioned above he sat on the ground dejected and motionless. He had fallen into the ocean of grief.

On the eleventh day in the bright half of every lunar month

Vibhīṣaṇa came there at the end of the day during the night after the rise of the moon.

55. Vibhīṣaṇa was accompanied by his son and surrounded by the Rākṣasas. He took his bath in Gautamī Gaṅgā and worshipped Lord Yogeśvara duly.

56. The son of Vibhīṣaṇa was like another Vibhīṣaṇa. He was well known as Vaibhīṣaṇi. He saw the Vaiśya and talked to him.

57. On hearing the words of the Vaiśya narrating everything in the manner it happened that (Rākṣasa) who was conversant with virtue intimated the same to his father the noble-souled lord of Laṅkā.

The lord of Laṅkā lovingly spoke to his son who was the mine of good qualities.

Vibhiṣaṇa said :

58-63. The glorious Rāma was my honourable preceptor. His friend who was well known as Hanumān is worthy of my respect and reverence. A great mountain was brought by him formerly when an occasion for the same arose. That mountain was a receptacle of all medicinal herbs. When the purpose was served he took the same back to the Hamālayan range. The names of the main medicinal herbs were (i) Viśalyakaraṇī (that which rids one of pain) and (ii) Mṛtasañjīvanī (that which resuscitates the dead). The Highly intelligent (Hanumān) brought it and handed it over to Rāma of unimpaired activities. He informed Rāma what could be achieved by the same. When the purpose was served he took the mountain back to the divine mountain range (Himavān). While he was going rapidly the medicinal herb Viśalyakaraṇī fell on the banks of Gautamī where the lord is Hari, the lord of Yogas. Bring that medicinal herb and remembering Hari place it over the heart of this (Vaiśya). Thereby this (Vaiśya) of liberal minded nature will obtain everything necessary.

Vaibhiṣaṇi said :

64. Show me that medicinal herb quickly, dear father. Do not delay. There is nothing else in the three worlds more conducive to welfare than the eradication of other people's anguish.

Brahmā said :

65. Vibhīṣaṇa said "So be it" and showed that medicinal herb to his son. Out of love for the Vaiśya, his son (i.e. Vaibhīṣaṇi) repeated the Vedic Mantra "Iṣe tvā" etc. and cut off the branch of the tree. Good men are (always) engaged in the welfare of others.

Vibhīṣaṇa said :

66. The tree on the mountain where it (i.e. the medicinal herb) fell has become powerful. Take a branch of it and place it on the heart of this (Vaiśya). Immediately after the contact with the same he shall obtain his (former normal) features.

Brahmā said :

67-68. On hearing these words of his father the liberal-minded Vaibhīṣaṇi did so. He placed the piece of wood precisely on the heart. The Vaiśya (regained his original form) with hands and eyes. No one can (adequately) understand the efficacy of jewels, Mantras and the medicinal herbs.

69-74. The Vaiśya took the twig of the tree with him. He took his bath in the Gautamī Gaṅgā and bowed down to Hari, the lord of Yogas. Again he took the twig and wandered over (many lands). There was the city of a king well-known as Mahāpura. The extremely powerful king there was well known as Mahārāja. He had no son. His only daughter was a blind girl. The king considered his daughter his son. He took a vow like this—"He who revives the eyesight of this (princess) shall be given my daughter (in marriage) whether he be a Deva or Dānava, a brahmin or a Kṣatriya, a Vaiśya or a Śūdra and whether he has any merit or not." The king proclaimed that she would be given along with the kingdom. The Vaiśya heard this announcement day and night. He said :

The Vaiśya said :

75-77. Undoubtedly I shall revive the eyesight of the princess.

Brahmā said :

The (officers) immediately took the Vaiśya to the presence of the great king. Merely due to the contact of that twig the princess regained her eyesight. The wonder-struck king said—"Who are you Sir ?" The Vaiśya intimated everything to the king in the manner it had taken place.

The Vaiśya said :

78. I possess this sort of power due to the favour of the brahmins, virtue, austerity and different kinds of sacrifices performed by me with plenty of monetary gifts. It is by virtue of charitable gifts and the divine medicinal herbs that I have this power.

Brahmā said :

79-80. On hearing these words of the Vaiśya the king was surprised much.

The king said :

Oh this (gentleman) is highly glorious and exalted. Most probably he is a Deva. Otherwise how can he have such a power as this. No one else has this sort of power. Hence I shall give my daughter to this (Vaiśya) along with the kingdom.

Brahmā said :

81-83. After mentally deciding thus he gave him his daughter and the kingdom.

(One day) (this Vaiśya who had become king) went on an outing but he was highly distressed. (He thought) "The kingdom without my friend (is no good). There is no happiness without my friend". The Vaiśya began to think of that selfsame brahmin. This alone is the characteristic sign of embodied beings of noble birth that their minds always melt with pity even in regard to those of inimical views.

84-85. The great king went to the forest. Maṇikuṇḍala had become king. While he was reigning he saw the brahmin Gautama once. All his riches and assets had been taken away by sinful gamblers. Taking the brahmin with him the Vaiśya conversant with virtue, honoured him duly.

86. He intimated to him the efficacy of pious activities entirely. He made him bathe in Gaṅgā for the removal of his sins.

87-89. Surrounded by his kinsmen that brahmin and the

Vaiśya accompanied by his kinsmen, the chief of whom was Vṛddhakauśika, performed Yajñas near the lord of Yogas. They worshipped Devas and went to heaven.

Thenceforth, they know that holy centre as "Mṛtasañjīvana", "Cakṣustīrtha" and "Yogeśa". It bestows merit even on being remembered. It causes delight and pleasure unto the mind. It destroys all miseries.

CHAPTER ONE HUNDRED AND ONE

Urvaśī and other Holy Centres

Brahmā said :

1. The holy centre Urvaśītīrtha is mentioned as the bestower of the benefit of a horse-sacrifice by means of holy bath, charitable gifts and the worship of Mahādeva and Vāsudeva.

2. Here the lord is Maheśvara and Viṣṇu is the wielder of Śārṅga.

There was a powerful Emperor named Pramati.

3. After conquering his enemies he went immediately to the world of Indra inhabited by Devas. There, O Nārada, he saw the lord of Devas along with the Maruts.

4. Pramati, the bull among Kṣatriyas, laughed at Indra who had dice in his hands. On seeing, Pramati laughing Indra spoke to him.

Indra said :

5. O highly intelligent one, enough of your play with the Maruts in the abode of Devas. You have attained heaven after conquering the quarters. Play with me.

Brahmā said :

6. On hearing the astringent words of Indra, king Pramati said to Devendra, "So be it. But what is it that you offer as requital?"

On hearing these words of Pramati the king of Devas spoke to him.

Indra said :

7. Urvaśī alone is the stake offered by us. It is only through all sorts of sacrifices that she can be obtained. I consider Urvaśī as the proper requital. O king, what is it that you offer ?

Brahmā said :

8. On hearing these words of Indra, Pramati said arrogantly : "O lord of Devas, I think of offering whatever you say."

9. Indra said to Pramati : "In the same manner, give as requital your virtuous right hand along with its protecting cover as well as arrows. We shall gamble."

Brahmā said :

10. After entering into an agreement like this both of them began to play at dice. Pramati won the stake, viz., Urvaśi, the divine damsel. After winning her Pramati said to Indra audaciously.

Pramati said :

11. (Offer) something else as requital. I shall then, O lord, play at dice with you.

Indra said :

12. O king, (I offer as stake) the thunderbolt worthy of Devas and the excellent chariot famous for having been used in victorious campaigns. Without minding it much I shall play against your stake of your arm.

Brahmā said :

13. Then Pramati laughingly took other dice decorated with jewels and said to Indra, "It is won by me."

14. In the meantime, O Nārada, the leading chieftain of the Gandharvas who was well conversant with the game of dice and who was well known as Viśvāvasu came there.

Viśvāvasu said:

15. O king, we shall gamble with you by means of Gandharva lore. The king then said : "So be it", and continued, "It is won by me."

16-17. After conquering both of them the king foolishly spoke to Devendra in disgraceful words.

Pramati said :

You will not at all be victorious either in battle or in the game of dice, O Mahendra. Hence be a worshipper of mine. Tell me by what means was the status of Devendra attained by you ?

Brahmā said :

18. Then he arrogantly said to Urvaśī, "Go, be (our) servant maid."

Urvaśī said : "I shall behave towards you in the same manner as towards Devas. I shall have noble feelings towards you. It does not behove you to despise and disregard me."

19-20. Thereupon Pramati said to her, "I have servant maids like you. O noble lady, why are you ashamed ? Go, be (our) servant maid."

On hearing these words uttered by the king, the lord of Gandharvas, the powerful son of Viśvāvasu well-known as Citrasena said thus :

Citrasena said :

21. O king, O lord of the Earth, I shall play at dice with you with all these as stake—the kingdom, my life as well as your life.

Brahmā said :

22. Saying "So be it," Citrasena and the excellent king gambled with great excitement. This time Citrasena won.

23-24. With strong nooses of the Gandharvas he bound the king. Citrasena won everything that Pramati possessed from the beginning such as his kingdom, treasury, army and other wealth the chief of which was Urvaśī herself.

25. (In the meantime) Pramati's son who was a mere boy spoke to his Priest Madhucchandas emphatically. He asked his highly intelligent priest who belonged to the family of Viśvāmitra :

Pramati's son said :

26. What sin has been committed by my father ? Where

has that highly intelligent (king) been imprisoned ? How will he come back to his own abode ? How will he get rid of the nooses ?

Brahmā said :

27. On hearing the words of Sumati (son of Pramati) the excellent sage Madhucchandas meditated (for a short while) and spoke about the whereabouts of Pramati.

Madhucchandas said :

28-31. O highly intelligent one, your father is kept imprisoned in the world of Devas. He has been ousted from his kingdom by the cunning gamblers.

Even he who walks into the assembly of gamblers becomes victim of pain and sorrow. O Prince, gambling, liquor, meat and other similar things are the vices of sinners. They are sinful by nature. Even severally everyone of these causes downfall into hell and great sin.

With various likes (and dislikes) for vehicles, seats etc. influenced by gamblers and cheats even men of noble birth begin to indulge in quarrels. What then about persons who are confirmed gamblers and cheats ?

32-35. The wife of a gambler is perpetually dejected. The sinful gambler too looks at his wife and feels dejected.

On seeing her, he does not experience any pleasure. The sinner says (to himself thus): "Alas, in the whole of this global world there is no sinner like me. I don't have even the slightest sensual pleasure in the world."

No gambler is seen happy in either of the two worlds.

He is clearly seen as a person with scorched mind perpetually due to shame. He has lost his virtue. He is devoid of joy. He wanders with all his possessions forfeited (by others).

36. In regard to brahmins, any avocation other than that of cheating and gambling is praiseworthy. He can even take to agriculture, breeding of cattle or trading. But he shall never take to gambling.

37-39. This is an activity, which has been forbidden in the Vedas because it is faulty. But it has been eagerly taken up by your father. Therefore what shall we do ? Dear boy, whatever you say shall be carried out. Which learned man transgresses the path laid down by the Creator ?

Brahmā said :

40-43. On hearing the words of the priest Sumati said :

Sumati said :

What must my father Pramati do to attain the kingdom once again ?

Brahmā said :

Meditating once again Madhucchandas spoke thus to Sumati: "Dear boy go to Gautamī. There you worship Śaṅkara, Aditi, Varuṇa and Viṣṇu. Thereby he will get rid of his nooses.

Brahmā said :

44-48. Saying "So be it" he hastened to Gaṅgā. After bowing down to Viṣṇu he worshipped Śiva. Maintaining all observances he performed penance.

He released his father from Devas after he had been kept imprisoned there for a thousand (and one) years. He regained his kingdom.

Through the grace of Śiva and Viṣṇu and through the endeavour of his own son he got rid of nooses and regained his kingdom. Since he had acquired the Gandharva lore he became a favourite of Indra.

Thenceforth that holy centre is called Śāmbhava, Vaiṣṇava, Urvaśītīrtha and Kaitava.

What cannot be acquired through the grace of Śiva, Viṣṇu and Mother of all rivers, Gautamī ? A holy bath and charity performed there bestow the benefit of a number of virtuous actions. It releases one from sinful nooses. It dispels all miseries.

CHAPTER ONE HUNDRED AND TWO

Meeting of Godāvari and the Sea in Seven Branches

Brahmā said :

1. The holy centre Samudratīrtha is the bestower of benefits of all holy centres. I shall mention its characteristic features. Listen attentively, O Nārada.

2. Discharged by Gautama, this Gaṅgā, the destroyer of sins, flowed towards the Eastern ocean for the good of the worlds.

3. While it was coming down, the divine river was held in the Kamaṇḍalu by me. The goddess was held in matted hair of Śambhu, the supreme soul.

4-7. The Ocean saw Gaṅgā that was born of Viṣṇu's feet, that was brought over to the mortal world by a noble-souled brahmin, that destroyed sins merely on being remembered and that which was worthier than the worthiest. On seeing her, the Ocean thought about his duty. "She is worthy of being saluted by the Universe. She is the goddess of worlds, she is bowed down to by Brahmā, Śiva and others. If I do not receive her duly, Dharma would be defiled. If anyone, out of delusion, does not honour duly a visiting noble-souled person there can be no saviour unto that sinner in both the worlds."

After thinking thus, the lord of rivers, the lord of jewels, assumed a physical form endowed with humility. With palms joined in reverence he spoke thus to Gaṅgā.

Sindhu said :

8. The water that is present in the nether worlds, in the Earth and in the firmament—may it enter me. I will not say anything.

9. There are jewels, Nectar, Rākṣasas, Devas, and mountains in me. I am bearing all these and other terrible things as well.

10. Accompanied by Goddess Lakṣmī, Viṣṇu sleeps in me perpetually. In the whole world consisting of the mobile and immobile, there is nothing that is impossible for me.

11. He, who, out of pride, does not duly honour a great

person coming as guest shall fall off from Dharma and fall into the hell.

12-14. I have no pain or sorrow in holding these, except the discomfiture I had sustained from Agastya. But in regard to dignity you are extremely distinguished from them. Therefore I am saying this, O goddess Gaṅgā. You join me on a footing of equality. If you come in your whole form (i.e. in a single stream) I will be unable to join you. O goddess, if you join me in many different streams I shall join you and not otherwise. O Gaṅgā, if you (are willing) to join in several streams I shall consider it.

Brahmā said:

15. That Gautamī Gaṅgā said thus to the lord of waters, Ocean who had spoken thus : "Do as I suggest.

16-18. You, bring here Arundhatī and others, the wives of the seven sages along with their husbands. Then I shall become smaller in size. Thereafter I shall join you."

Saying "So be it" the Ocean brought the wives of the seven sages along with those sages. He brought them to the goddess. She divided herself into seven streams. The Gautamī Gaṅgā went to the Ocean in seven channels.

19-20. These seven Gaṅgās (channels) came to be known by the names of seven sages.

Taking holy bath, offering charitable gifts, listening to, reading and remembring this narrative devoutly is auspicious and it yields all cherished desires.

In the three worlds there is no other greater holy centre than the Ocean for one who wishes the destruction of sins, the attainment of worldly pleasures and liberation and mental satisfaction.

CHAPTER ONE HUNDRED AND THREE

Ṛṣisatra and Bhimeśvaratīrtha

Brahmā said :

1. Ṛṣisatra is well known, O Nārada. The seven sages sat in order to perform penance in the place where Lord Śiva is called Bhīmeśvara.

2. In that connection I shall narrate this story which has grown in importance due to Devas, sages and Pitṛs. Listen attentively. I shall tell the auspicious story that bestows all cherished things.

3-7. The seven sages, O Nārada, divided Gaṅgā into seven streams. The Vāsiṣṭhī was to the extreme right. The Vaiśvāmitrī flows next. Vāmadevī should be known as another (stream). The splendid Gautamī is in the middle. Another stream is the Bhāradvājī. Ātreyī comes next and the Jāmadagnī is the last. Thus the seven streams have been named.

A great sacrifice was performed by those noble-souled sages who wished to perform sacrifice and who were seers with great vision.

In the meantime a powerful enemy of Devas, well known as Viśvarūpa, came to the Satra of the sages. After propitiating all those sages by means of celibacy and penance in accordance with the injunction he humbly asked them in the proper way.

Viśvarūpa said :

8. O sages, it behoves you to speak out how I can beget a powerful son who will be invincible even to Devas. All of you do certainly endeavour for the sake of my health. Kindly tell me whether it shall be through sacrifice or penance.

Brahmā said:

9-12. Thereupon the highly intelligent, noble-minded Viśvāmitra said :

Viśvāmitra said:

Dear one, different kinds of benefits accrue from the performance of pious rites and benevolent activities. There are three types of causes. Of them Karman is the primary cause. Next is the doer himself. Then there is the material cause.

Learned men know that the seed is Karman. How can we say that Karman is a cause? When all possible causes are present sometimes there the fruit appears and sometimes, not. Therefore (we say) that the fruit is dependent upon Karman.

13-17. Karman should be known to be of two types; 1) that which is being done; 2) that which has been done. (The idea of) that which ought to be done is the means of that which is being done. The respective bhāvas (feelings / ideas) are the cause of Karman in both the cases. The attainment of fruits is in accordance with the feelings/ideas with which the creature performs Karman. If anyone performs a Karman duly but without having any feeling the fruit shall be adverse. Everything shall be in conformity with the respective feelings. Hence, austerities, vows, charitable offerings, Japas, Yajñas and other holy rites will be yielding benefits in accordance with the feelings/ideas that the performer has. Hence a Karman will yield fruit in accordance with the agent's feelings/ideas.

18-19. Feelings/ideas should be known to be of three types, viz. Sāttvika, Rājasa and Tāmasa. The benefit is in accordance with the Karmans and the accompanying feelings. Thus the course of Karman is mysterious. Hence, a clever person shall have bhāvas (feelings/ideas) in accordance with his wish.

20-22. Afterwards he must perform Karman too. The donor of fruits grants fruit in a befitting manner. If the person who performs Karman directs his activity towards the fruit of the fruitful the benefit does not accrue. One shall perform Karman in a natural way. The material cause etc. begins to function as befitting the different bhāvas (feelings/ideas) such as Sattva, etc. They function through Bhāvas and the fruit is derived by means of Bhāvas. Karman alone is the cause of virtue, wealth, love and liberation.

23-25. The Karman sustained by bhāva (feeling) is the cause of bondage as well as salvation. One's own Karman shall conform to one's own nature. It yields different kinds of benefit here and in the other world in accordance with equality(?). The selfsame thing appears different on account of feelings. Karman is performed and the fruit is enjoyed in accordance with the feeling. Hence, feeling is especially important. Perform Karman in accordance with the feeling. You will attain whatever you desire.

Brahmā said :

26-29. On hearing the words of the intelligent sage Viśvāmitra, Viśvarūpa assumed a Tāmasa attitude and performed penance for a long time. He performed a terrible rite that terrified Devas even as the chief sages were watching and even as he was being prevented for ever. In accordance with his own fury he performed the terrible rite. He meditated upon the Ātman lying within the cavity of the heart as a terrifying terrible person present within a terrible fire blazing in a terrible pit that had been dug. On seeing him blazing (performing the penance) the unembodied divine voice spoke.

30-33. "(Consign into the fire) yourself without the matted hair. You will beget a son. O Viśvarūpa, he who consigns himself into the fire shall become Indra, Varuṇa, (nay) he shall become everything. Abandoning himself, (that demon) born of sin consigned into the fire leaving the matted hair alone. He is called Vṛtra in the Veda. He too became wicked. Who knows the grandeur and greatness of the terrible lord of the worlds. He creates everything but he is not smeared with (the sin of) the contact."

O leading sages, after expressing this that voice ceased.

34-35. The leading sages bowed down to Bhīmeśvara and went to their respective hermitages.

Viśvarūpa who was extremely terrible, whose activities were terrible, whose shape and size were terrible and whose feeling was terrible meditated on the supreme being in the form of a terrible one and consigned himself into the fire. Hence the lord is mentioned in the Purāṇa as Bhīmeśvara. Holy plunge and charity performed there are undoubtedly the bestowers of liberation (mukti).

36. He who devoutly reads and listens to this, he who bows down to Śiva who is the lord of Devas, whose from is terrible, whose feet are the refuge, whose memory dispels all sins and who yields salvation (that devotee prospers).

37. Godāvarī is the destroyer of all sins; she is the bestower of supreme wealth—always and everywhere but especially so where she joins the ocean.

38-39. The embodied soul who takes holy plunge there, in the confluence of Godāvarī and the sea, is meritorious. He redeems his ancestors from the terrible hell and goes to the city of Śiva.

Bhīmanātha is the Brahman itself which is to be understood through the Vedas and which should be prayed to, bowed to, and meditated upon. When he is seen the embodied beings never enter again the worldly scene of terrible misery.

CHAPTER ONE HUNDRED AND FOUR

The Confluence of Gaṅgā with Sea

Brahmā said:

1-5. That Gaṅgā who is worthy of being respected and honoured even by the gods joined the eastern sea, followed by all the Devas and eulogized by the sages and Maruts and Vasiṣṭha, Jābāli, Yājñavalkya, Kratu, Aṅgiras, Dakṣa, Marīci, Vaiṣṇavas (devotees of Viṣṇu).

Śātātapa, Śaunaka, Devarāta, Bhṛgu, Agniveśya, Atri, Marīci, Dakṣa, Manu, Gautama and others along with Kauśika, Tumbaru, Parvata and so on had their sins destroyed completely.

Agastya, Mārkaṇḍa etc. devoted to yogic practices, along with Gālava, Pippala and others, including Vāmadeva, descendants of Aṅgīras and Bhṛgu who were proficient in Smṛtis and agreeable due to their knowledge of the Vedas went to the divine river Gautamī. All of them were fully conversant with the subjects treated of in the Purāṇas. Indeed they knew many things. They began to pray by reciting Mantras and many Vedic passages of lovely nature. They were contented and pleased in their minds.

On seeing the river in confluence Śiva and Hari revealed themselves to the sages.

6. The immortal ones began the eulogy of the two lords, the dispellers of the distress of everyone, while they were being (respectfully) watched by the Manes.

7. The Ādityas, Vasus, Rudras, Maruts, the Guardians of the

Quarters—all these joined their palms in reverence and prayed to Hari and Śaṅkara.

8. O Nārada, these two lords are ever established in the seven well known confluences as well as the meeting place of the ocean and the Gaṅgā.

9. It is the place where lord Maheśvara is called Gautameśvara. There Mādhava is ever present along with Ramā (Lakṣmī).

10. Śiva well known by the name Brahmeśvara has been installed by me for helping all people and for my own reasons.

11. The lord well known as Cakrapāṇi was eulogized by me in the company of the Devas. Viṣṇu is present there along with the Devas and the groups of Maruts.

12-13. A certain Tīrtha is well known as Aindratīrtha. The Tīrtha is otherwise called Hayamūrdhaka. Viṣṇu is (installed) there as Hayamūrdhan (Horse-headed). The Devas too are on the top thereof. There is (another) Tīrtha well known as Somatīrtha, where Śiva is called Someśvara. For the sake of Indra whose reṅown was on a par with that of Soma, Soma (Soma juice, Moon) was formerly prayed to by the Devas and the sages with the Ṛk Mantras ending with *Indrāyendo Parisrava* (O Indu—Soma juice, moon—flow out everywhere for the sake of Indra).

14. (3rd Mantra, 114th Sūkta of the IX Maṇḍala) (Tr. According to Sāyaṇa) "O Soma, protect us with all these, viz. the seven Diks (quarters) (excluding that of which Soma is the lord, i.e. north) presided over by different suns, the seven Hotṛs (Vaṣaṭkartṛs), the seven Ṛtviks, the seven dazzling sons of Aditi (excepting Mārtāṇḍa who was thrown up, according to RV X. 72-8). O Indu, flow out everywhere for the sake of Indra."

15. (4th Mantra, 114th Sūkta, IX Maṇḍala) "O Rājan (Lord as the person making them work) Soma, protect us by means of the Havis cooked for your sake. Let not the inimical assailant kill us nor destroy anything (wealth etc.) belonging to us. O Indu, flow out everywhere for the sake of Indra."

16. (2nd Mantra, IX-114) "O Sage (self-address by the seer of the Mantra) Kaśyapa, adore the king Soma making your eulogies come up flourishing, thanks to the Sūktas of the seers of the Mantras. That Soma has become the lord, protector of

the creepers. O Soma, Indu, flow out everywhere for the sake of Indra."

17. (3rd Mantra, IX-112) "I am the composer of the Sūktas. Hence I am the father and son. I am the physician, Brahmā of the Yajña. This lady who makes the groats, gruel etc. is the mother or daughter. All of us of diverse mental predilections and activities are desirous of wealth and like cows we serve the world. O Indu, flow out everywhere for the sake of Indra."

18. By saying thus (i.e. by eulogizing Soma thus) the Soma was obtained for the Vajra-wielding Indra. By giving (the same Soma) to them Indra got his hundred sacrifices complete.

19-21. Hence that Tīrtha is called Somatīrtha. Āgneyatīrtha is in front. Agni performed great Yajñas and having pleased me thereby obtained what he desired by my favour. I am stationed there for ever for the sake of helping the world. Similarly Viṣṇu and Śiva too are stationed there. Hence the Tīrtha is called Āgneya. Beyond that is the Āditya Tīrtha where the Sun full of the Vedic Mantras, comes everyday for adoration.

22. He comes in some other guise at midday in order to see me, Śaṅkara and Hari. There, at midday, all people should be bowed to always.

23. That is because it is not certain in what guise Savitṛ (Sun) comes there. Hence it is called Āditya Tīrtha. Thereafter comes the Bārhaspatya Tīrtha.

24. It is said that Bṛhaspati was worshipped by the gods in that Tīrtha. He also performed different Yajñas there. Hence they know this Tīrtha as Bārhaspatya.

25. Merely by remembering that Tīrtha, propitiation of (malignant) planets can be achieved. Another Tīrtha is on the excellent mountain Indragopa.

26. For some reason the great Liṅga was installed there by Himālaya. Hence it is called Adritīriha.

27-28. Ablution therein and offering gifts yield auspicious results fulfilling cherished desires.

Thus that Gautamī Gaṅgā originated from Brahmādri and proceeds towards the ocean. A few of the Tīrthas there have been mentioned by me. These are auspicious and holy secrets.

29. O Nārada, who has the power to narrate in full that

highly powerful Gautamī that is famous in the Vedas and Purāṇas and revered by the sages and all the people.

30. There can be no offence if the description by one prompted by devotion is inadequate. There is no doubt about it. For the sake of the benefit of the world certain features of that river have been indicated with very great difficulty.

31-33. Who is competent to describe Gautamī's power in every Tīrtha? Perhaps Viṣṇu, lord of Lakṣmī, and Śiva Someśvara may be. Only in due course of time, do some Tīrthas somewhere become meritorious, O highly intelligent one. But Gautamī is always so unto men. It is meritorious everywhere and always. Who can fully narrate her good qualities? Hence it is but proper to offer obeisance to her.

CHAPTER ONE HUNDRED AND FIVE

The Benefits of listenings to the Purāṇa

Nārada said :

1-2. O lord of Suras, O master of the Suras, you say that the holy Gaṅgā has three presiding deities. She had been brought down by a Brahmin and she is a splendid river sanctifying the Universe. On both of her banks at the beginning, middle and end she is pervaded by Viṣṇu, Īśa (Śiva) and you, O most excellent one among the Suras. Narrate once again succinctly. I have not been fully satisfied.

Brahmā said :

3-4. At the outset she was stationed in a Kamaṇḍalu (waterpot). Then she flowcd from the feet of Viṣṇu. Thereafter she was stationed within the mess of the matted hair of Maheśvara. It is bowed to by all. Thanks to the Brahminical power, it was brought to the holy mountain after propitiating Śiva assiduously. Thereafter she proceeded towards the eastern sea.

5. Proceeding thus the divine river joined the sea. She has all the Tīrthas (on her banks) and fulfils all the desires of men. Her power is unique.

6. I do not think that there is any Tīrtha superior to it in

all the three worlds. Whatever thing one cherishes in one's heart can be realized by her own power.

7-8. Till today her greatness has not been adequately described by anyone. Whatever little is mentioned is out of devotion. This is my opinion that there will not be any Tīrtha greater than this river which is virtually Brahman (Supreme Absolute) itself. There cannot be any propriety in comparing her with another Tīrtha.

9. Wherefore has the intellect of everyone not been rendered completely calm even after hearing the eulogy of the Gaṅgā through the nectar-like statements of mine? O sage, this appears to be the most mysterious thing in all the three worlds.

Nārada said :

10-12. You are fully conversant with piety, wealth, love and salvation and hence competent to advise thereon. The Vedas with their secrets, the Purāṇas and the Smṛtis and whatever there is besides—all these are rooted in your utterance. O lord, kindly mention which is the best and foremost among the Tīrthas, Dānas, Yajñas, Tapas', services to the deities and practising of the Mantras. O lord, whatever you say with devotion should necessarily be so and not otherwise.

13. O Brahman, it behoves you to dispel this doubt of mine.

On hearing from him what had been lurking within his mind Brahmā was surprised and he said :

Brahmā said :

14. Listen, O Nārada. I shall tell you the secret of the excellent Dharma.

The Tīrthas are of four kinds. The Yugas also are as many.

15. The Guṇas are three, the Puruṣas are three and the eternal deities are three. The Vedas in combination with the Smṛtis are enumereted as four.

16. The aims of human life are four; speech is of four kinds. The Guṇas too are four along with Samatva (equilibrium), O Nārada.

17. Dharma (piety, righteousness) is universal everywhere because virtue is eternal. That too is considered to be of

various kinds inasmuch as the Sãdhya (what is to be attained) and Sãdhana (means of attaining) are different.

18. Its basis always is of two kinds—place and time. Dharma with the time as the basis waxes and wanes for ever.

19. In accordance with the Yugas it wanes quarter by quarter, O highly intelligent one. Dharma stands in need of Deśa (Place) in both respects.

20. Dharma based on time is ever firmly established in Deśa. When the Yugas wane Dharma does not wane in the Deśas.

21. If it were to be wanting in both Dharma would have been totally non-existent. Hence Dharma based on Deśa has the full complement of the four quarters.

22. That Dharma abides in the Deśas in the form of Tīrthas. In the Kṛta Yuga Dharma leans on the prop of Deśa and Kāla and settles down.

23. In the Tretā Yuga Dharma is deficient in one Pāda but has the full complement of the four quaters in respect to Deśa. In Dvāpara the deficiency is half in respect to Time but in Deśa it is fully present.

24. In the Kaliyuga Dharma moves about unsteadily on one leg (having only a quater of itself). But it does not wane for one who comprehends Dharma in this way.

25. The differences in castes are maintained in accordance with the power of the Yugas. Dharma is of diverse nature as it follows Guṇas and those who work according to Guṇas.

26. It is in accordance with the Guṇas that the Tīrthas, Varṇas, Vedas, heaven and salvation take their origin or lose their power.

27. By virtue of such a form and activity Dharma becomes unique. Kāla is said to be Abhivyañjaka (that which makes something manifest) and Deśa is said to be Abhivyaṅgya (that which is manifested).

28. Whenever Kāla assumes Abhivyakti (manifestation) that itself, O Brahman, is its token. Hence there is no doubt in this respect.

29. The form of the Devas and the Vedas shall be in accordance with the Yugas. Those of Karmans (rites), Tīrthas, castes and stages of life too (are in accordance with the Yugas).

30. A Tīrtha having three presiding deities is adored in all the worlds in the Satyayuga; in the other Yuga (i.e. Tretā) that with two presiding deities; and in the Dvāpara Yuga one with a single presiding deity.

31. It should be known that there is no such thing in Kaliyuga. Now listen to another thing. In the Kṛtayuga a Tīrtha is Daiva (of divine significance). They know that the same in Tretā is Āsura (of Asura significance).

32. It is said to be Ārṣa (of the saintly significance) in Dvāpara and Mānuṣa (of human significance) in Kaliyuga. I shall henceforth mention another reason. Listen, O Nārada.

33-35. What you have asked in respect to Gautamī, I shall explain to you in detail. O great sage, ever since the Gaṅgā came to the matted hair of Hara's head she had become the great favourite of Śambhu. Umā, the goddess of the three worlds, the mother and benefactress of the universe, well known as the quiescent Śruti, the bestower of enjoyment of pleasures and salvation, knew this mental proclivity of the lord and said so to the elephant-faced one (Gajānana).

Brahmā said :

36. On hearing those words of his mother the elephant-faced one spoke :

Gajavaktra said :

37. What is to be done ? Tell me my mother. Undoubtedly I shall do so.

Brahmā said :

38. Umā said this to her son, "Gaṅgā is stationed in the matted hair of Maheśvara and as such has truly become the favourite of Īśa. Just make her come down.

39. Further this is surprising that Īśa occupies that place always, O son. Where Śiva stays, the Suras and the eternal Vedas too stay.

40. The sages too stay there itself, so also all the men and the Manes. Hence make Īśāna, Maheśvara the lord of the Devas, leave the place.

41. When the lord is turned away from Gaṅgā, they too

are turned away. Listen to these words of mine. Turn Śaṅkara away from her in every respect."

Brahmā said :

42. On hearing those words of his mother, Gaṇeśvara said once again :

43-46. "Lord Śiva cannot be turned away from her by me. In case Śiva is not turned away from her the Devas too cannot be turned away, O mother of the Universe. There is another reason too. Formerly Gaṅgā was made to come down by Gautama, the noble-hearted sage, worthy of being worshipped by the entire world and the benefactor of all the three worlds. It was through the means suggested by me and adopted at your instance that the venerable Brahminical splendour propitiated the lord of the Devas, Bhava by means of austerities and prayers. At that time, that Gautama was told thus by the delighted Śaṅkara."

Śaṅkara said :

47. O highly intelligent one, choose as boons all good and pleasing things that you cherish in your heart. I shall grant you everything that you may desire.

Brahmā said :

48. When Gautama was told thus by Śiva, he said thus, even as I was listening: "O Śaṅkara, to me who beg of you give the meritorious Gaṅgā enmeshed in the matted hair. Of what avail to me is another boon ?"

Brahmā said :

49. Śambhu, the benefactor of all the worlds, said to him once again :

Śambhu said :

50. Something that is to your own benefit has not been mentioned. Hence request for something very difficult.

Brahmā said :

51. With palms joined in reverence Gautama said to Bhava with his spirit undepressed :

Gautama said :

52. This itself is the most difficult thing that I have been able to see you. O Śaṅkara, by your grace, that has been achieved by me today.

53. Noble-minded persons become blessed and contented merely by remembering thy feet. What to speak when, Thou, the great Lord, have been seen directly ?

Brahmā said :

54-56. When this was spoken by Gautama, Bhava said to the Brahmin with great delight: "Request has been made by you for helping the three worlds. O highly intelligent one, not for yourself. (Now) ask something for your own self".

On being told thus the Brahmin thought it over and begged Śiva with great humility and devotion with undepressed spirit. He made the request once again for rendering help unto all the worlds. Even as the guardians of the quarters were listening Gautama said thus :

Gautama said :

57. Inasmuch as the divine river extending up to the ocean has been released from Brahmā's mountain, O bull-bannered one, it is incumbent upon thee to stay thereon everywhere and always.

58. O lord of the worlds, thou alone art the giver of the fruit unto those who desire benefits. O lord of the Devas, other Tīrthas are auspicious only in certain places.

59. They know that place alone to be the yielder of auspiciousness where thy presence is constant. It is the place where Gaṅgā stationed in the crown of thy matted hair has been handed ever. O Śaṅkara, thou being present everywhere there are Tīrthas (everywhere).

Brahmā said :

60. On hearing those words of Gautama, Śiva said again with delight :

Śiva said :

61-64. A devotee may give away anything anywhere but

that should be given with excessive devotion. He may offer libation unto the (departed) ancestors, he may listen to sacred stories, he may recite or remember them, O Gautama. Whatever the man does on the Gadāvarī with due observances of vows bears ample fruit. Merely by remembering Gautamī one acquires that piety and virtue that one obtains by gifting away the entire beautiful earth adorned with Dharma and consisting of mountains, forests and parks and decorated with gems and handed over with all medicinal herbs and the oceans too. O brahmin, the earth near the river Godāvarī is mentioned to be of this sort.

65-67. O excellent brahmin, by performing holy ablution, Dāna etc. devotedly in the great river Gautamī, worthy of the veneration of the entire universe, a man obtains more merit than what is acquired by a wise devotee when he observes all the vows in my presence at the time of the solar of lunar eclipse and gifts away beautiful cows adorned with everything unto Viṣṇu or a king along with their calves at a confluence famous all over the world.

68. Hence the Gaṅgā Godāvarī led by you shall become the destroyer of all sins and the bestower of everything desired.

Gaṇeśvara said :

69. O mother, this has been heard by me directly from Śiva who was speaking to Gautama. For this reason Śambhu is invariably present in the Gaṅgā.

70-72. O mother, who can make that ocean of mercy leave the place ? Still, Mother, this can be done. Fettered by the nooses of hindrances (i.e. due to unexpected obstructions,) men may not go to the Godāvarī though it is nearby. They may not bow down to Śiva nor remember the lord and eulogize him. However, Mother, I will do something for your satisfaction, for there is distress in disobeying what you say. Forgive me.

Brahmā said :

73-74. Ever since then, Vighneśa creates some obstacles in regard to men. He who devoutly goes to Gautamī ignoring the obstacles gets his purpose fulfilled. No further duty remains for him.

75. To the base man many obstacles do occur even as he desires to set off from his house. If he goes to the Gaṅgā after setting his foot firmly over it does he not obtain any benefit from it ?

76. Who can describe its power (completely) should he be even Sadāśiva himself? Everything has been succinctly narrated by me closely following the tradition and mythology.

77. In the extensive mythological legends there is everything conducive to the attainment of piety, wealth, love and liberation in the entire world consisting of mobile and immobile beings.

78. The Purāṇa has been narrated for the benefit of all the worlds. It consists of many pious rites. If perused carefully it contributes to the good of the worlds. It contains everything mentioned in the Vedas. It consists of all the secret doctrines of the Śrutis. The very name (Purāṇa) indicates that it is the cause of everything excellent.

79. If anyone devoutly listens to or recites one verse or one word out of this or utters 'Gaṅgā', 'Gaṅgā', he shall obtain the spiritual benefit thereby.

80. The word Gaṅgā uttered or the water of the Gaṅgā imbibed becomes excellent. It is cabable of destroying the stigma of Kali age. It is auspicious. It gives splendour and all Siddhis (super-natural powers). It is worthy of veneration in the world. It grants desired things.

81. Well done, O Gautama ! Welfare unto you. Who else is equal to you ? It is you who eagerly brought this Gaṅgā to the Daṇḍaka forest.

82. He who utters 'Gaṅgā Gaṅgā' even from hundreds of Yojanas away becomes rid of all sins : He goes to the world of Viṣṇu.

83. In all the three worlds there are thirtyfive millions of Tīrthas. When Jupiter is in the sign of Leo, all these Tīrthas come to the Gaṅgā for a bath.

84. Holy ablution in the Bhāgīrathī for sixty-thousand years is equal to a single bath in the Godāvarī when Bṛhaspati (Jupiter) is in Siṁha (Leo).

85. O son, this Gautamī grants salvation unto all men who bathe therein anywhere at any time. That is due to Śiva's bidding.

86. Merely by listening to it one gets that benefit which is obtained by performing thousands of Aśvamedhas (Horse-sacrifices) or hundred of Vājapeya sacrifices.

87. O Nārada, if this Purāṇa narrated by Brahmā is kept in the house by anyone he need not be afraid of the Kali age.

88-90. This excellent Purāṇa should not be narrated to anyone and everyone. This should be recited only to a noble-hearted devotee of Viṣṇu who is calm and has great faith. This accords worldly pleasures and salvation. It destroys sins. Merely by listening to it a man becomes contented and his desires are fulfilled. If one copies this and gives the book to a Brahmin he gets rid of all sins. He never enters a womb thereafter.

INDEX

L

M

T